STUDIES IN GREEK CULTURE
AND ROMAN POLICY

STUDIES IN GREEK CULTURE AND ROMAN POLICY

BY

ERICH S. GRUEN

UNIVERSITY OF CALIFORNIA PRESS

Berkeley   Los Angeles   London

University of California Press
Berkeley and Los Angeles, California

University of California Press, Ltd.
London, England

First paperback printing by the University of California Press 1996

© 1990 by E. J. Brill, Leiden, The Netherlands

Cataloging-in-Publication data on file with the Library of Congress

ISBN 0-520-20483-2 (pbk.)

Printed in the United States of America

9 8 7 6 5 4 3 2 1

Filiae filiisque meis

CONTENTS

PREFACE

This work had its origin in a set of lectures delivered in May, 1985. The Classics Department at the University of Cincinnati provided the occasion: a gracious invitation to deliver the Louise Taft Semple lectures. I am deeply grateful not only for that invitation but for many kindnesses shown me by members of the department and, most especially, by its chair, Professor Getzel M. Cohen.

Two most welcome awards made time available for research and preparation of the lectures: a Humanities Research Fellowship from the University of California, Berkeley and a National Endowment for the Humanities Fellowship for Independent Study and Research. Those generous grants enabled me to arrive in Cincinnati with at least the rudiments of a manuscript.

The manuscript has undergone notable changes since that time. Improvements owe much to comments, criticisms, and suggestions freely offered by friends and colleagues. Every chapter benefited from the scrutiny and valuable advice of two or more scholars, most of whom may still dissent from the conclusions but each of whom has left an imprint on the product. The registering of their names is small repayment for their contributions: W.S. Anderson, A.M. Eckstein, E. Fantham, S.M. Goldberg, T. Habinek, P.B. Harvey, Jr., R.C. Knapp, J.C.B. Lowe, M.G. Morgan, J.A. North, R.E.A. Palmer, L. Roller, N. Rosenstein, G. Ryan, N.W. Slater, and J. Zetzel. Special gratitude is due to Professor Sander Goldberg whose wise and cogent disagreement with a critical portion of the manuscript persuaded me to reverse my position and to produce a much more plausible case.

Some of the propositions advanced here were first floated in two graduate seminars at Berkeley. Students, as ever, raised objections and exposed weaknesses, much to my benefit. I note in particular the insightful remarks of A. Futrell, C. Hallett, M. Ierardi, R. Kallet-Marx, J. McInerney, R. Talman, and P. Vaughn. Confidence in certain conclusions was bolstered when they were reached independently by Michael Ierardi and Pamela Vaughn.

My research assistant Jeremy McInerney contributed significantly to the final product by his capable assemblage of relevant scholarly literature, as did Peter Wyetzner by sharp-eyed proofreading and the compilation of an index.

Finally and most pleasantly, my warmest thanks and love go to my children, to Bonnie for help in preparing parts of the manuscript at an important time, to Keith for introducing me to the mysteries of the computer, and to Jason Philip for composition of the bibliography,—and to my wife Joan whose presence sustained the work from beginning to end.

May, 1988

INTRODUCTION

Moribus antiquis res stat Romana virisque sang the poet Ennius. The line is a *locus classicus* for Roman pride in national character and values. That self-assured trust in native traditions took precedence throughout Roman history. An equally familiar but very different refrain issued from the pen of Horace: *Graecia capta ferum victorem cepit.* The contrast is sharp, yet both writers express basic truths. Rome yielded to the allure of Greek culture, while retaining a profound sense of closeness to her roots. Indeed it was precisely the confrontation with Hellenism that stimulated Roman intellectuals to formulate and articulate the principles that they associated with (or imposed upon) their past. The challenge of Greek culture prompted the drive to delineate the special quality of Rome's own values.

Romans receive high praise for adaptability, their openness and receptiveness to foreign influence. Justly so. But the course of adaptation did not run smooth. Assimilation and resistance went hand in hand. Romans incorporated alien religious practices but persecuted the Bacchic cult. They imported Greeks to educate their children but expelled philosophers and rhetoricians. They borrowed intellectual traditions but frowned on intellectuals.

Paradox and inconsistency recur with regularity. They give a peculiar character to the pivotal and formative period of interaction between Hellenic culture and Roman values, the era of the 3rd and 2nd centuries B.C., a time that witnessed the identification of a national character and the maturation of a national culture. Growing pains are everywhere evident. Yet the Romans were by no means boorish rustics, awestruck and intimidated by Hellenism, gripped by an inferiority complex that produced a mix of clandestine acceptance and ostensible rejection. The success of Greek culture in Rome came in part because it could serve certain public purposes—whether in a positive or a negative fashion. Roman leaders were attuned to the possibilities. They engaged in adaptation, modification, and manipulation—not merely reaction. Posturing and symbolic activity held a more central place in Roman civic life than has generally been recognized. And the serviceability of Hellenism in that context merits special attention.

The essays presented here do not pretend to exhaust this large and intricate subject. They constitute a beginning, with hope of continuation at a later time. Nor do they form a tight, consolidated entity. They explore a series of particular episodes and developments, each a separate and discrete topic, but each in its own way touching the broader subject of Greek culture and the Roman public scene.

Two chapters examine striking instances of the interaction of Hellenic traditions with Roman religion. The first concerns the arrival of the Great Mother of the Gods from Asia Minor and the installation of her worship in Rome in the last years of the Hannibalic War. A variety of circumstances and objectives converge to explain that extraordinary event. Most importantly, it needs to be set in the context of Rome's expropriation of the Trojan legend (a step toward defining her own self-image) and cultivation of Hellenic sentiment on the eve of the great invasion of Africa. The second study addresses the notorious and dramatic persecution of the Bacchic cult in the early 2nd century. That nearly unique episode, so puzzling and opaque, is scrutinized from an unusual angle. The analysis seeks to establish that the inquisition aimed less at rooting out any real or perceived evil than at asserting the collective ascendancy of the Roman senate and at disassociating state policy from the more insidious effects of Hellenism. Both essays stress the importance of symbolic gestures in Roman public behavior and the relationship with Greek culture that helped to shape that behavior.

Two other chapters grapple with the issues of patronage and politics in the earliest age of Latin literature. The first explores the interests of state in calling upon poets imbued with Greek learning, encouraging literary productivity, and prodding intellectuals to advance the national image. Emphasis rests upon public support for the guild of writers and dramatic artists, and upon the atmosphere in the late 3rd and early 2nd century that fostered the talents of the first great Latin poets, Livius Andronicus, Naevius, and Ennius. The emergence of Latin letters owed less to the aspirations of individual *nobiles* and *gentes* than to the communal aim of articulating Roman national goals and accomplishments. The subject receives further elaboration in another chapter concentrating upon the comic dramatist Plautus. It steers a course between conventional treatments of Plautus that find numerous veiled references to contemporary political figures and events and those that deny any concrete contemporaneity to the plays. The study highlights those Plautine themes that reflect on the larger and continuing issues of his day—and most particularly on the central cultural issue: Roman attitudes toward and engagement with Hellenism.

The fifth essay treats still a different aspect of Roman-Greek relations and their repercussions on the public scene. It confronts a peculiarly puzzling tension: the increasing attraction of Hellenic philosophy and rhetoric for Roman intellectuals in the 2nd century on the one hand and the periodic banishment of Greek philosophers, orators, and professors from Rome on the other. The study emphasizes again the symbolic character of official acts and pronouncements. Expulsion of Greek intellectuals in the early 2nd century proclaimed the autonomy of native values, an index of cultural immaturity that demanded ostensible removal of the alien presence. The token gestures tended to concentrate in the aftermath of Rome's eastern wars, when the number of learned Greeks in Italy noticeably increased and when a reaction would have conspicuous value. Circumstances, however, evidently changed by the early 1st century. Hellenism had gained an established and acknowledged place in the education of Roman intellectuals. An edict of the censors in 92 even equated the *mos maiorum* with rhetorical training steeped in Greek tradition. That measure, examined *in extenso* here, signals arrival at a cultural plateau, and points the way to a resolution of the long-standing tension between the cultures.

The book will generate more dissent than consent. It takes a number of unorthodox and unconventional positions. It should not (and certainly will not) be the last word on the subject. The issues addressed are ambiguous, complicated, and difficult—but also of high importance in understanding the place of Greek culture in Roman public life and in the articulation of national values. These essays offer a contribution to continuing debate.

t, the basic facts. Unusual prodigies in the year 205 prompted con-
ion of the Sibylline Books. A prophecy was discovered therein of the
: of Hannibal if the Great Mother should be brought to Rome. Con-
tion came from Delphi. A Roman delegation of distinguished
crats secured the assistance of Attalus I, king of Pergamum, in
ning the sacred stone or meteorite in which the goddess was wor-
ed, and then delivered it to Italy. Its reception in Rome occurred
t, and the official recipient, as the Delphic Oracle had directed, would
e *optimus vir* of the state. The senate had named young P. Scipio
a to that honor, joined by the chaste matron Claudia Quinta. A
s throng welcomed the arrival of the goddess, and accompanied her
emporary home in the Palatine Temple of Victory. The Megalen-
Games were decreed as annual celebration to commemorate the
ion.[3]

hat generated this sequence of events? The matter is complex and
i-faceted. But a negative conclusion must first be asserted to clear
ath. A number of texts state or imply that the dire circumstances of
Iannibalic war stimulated a search for divine assistance against the
idable Carthaginian foe.[4] In fact, however, Rome turned to the
t Mother not after Trasimene or Cannae, when fear or desperation
it have supplied the motive and when military fortunes sank to
tening depths, but when the tide had been reversed and the
iblic was on its way to inevitable victory. The great achievement at
Metaurus had come in 207. A major Carthaginian relief army had
wiped out, and Hannibal was isolated again in Italy.
recedented joy and relief greeted the news in Rome, where its
lications were fully understood.[5] Roman victories in Spain during the
e year seemed to assure that no additional troops could reinforce
nibal from that region.[6] Restoration of farmers to their property in
underscored the confidence that Rome was once more in control of
. Far from calling upon the gods to rescue the Republic, Rome's

---

The principal testimony resides in Livy, 29.10.4-29.11.8, 29.14.5-14, and Ovid,
. 4.247-348. Some troubling discrepancies exist between these texts, but do not
ire discussion here. They concur on the main outlines. The tale is alluded to by
erous other authors, but none adds any substantial information. The evidence is
nbled, recapitulated and categorized by E. Schmidt, *Kultübertragungen* (Giessen,
), 1-18. Schmidt's skepticism about the entire tradition, however, is extreme and
stified; *op. cit.* 27-30. On the *Ludi Megalenses*, see Habel, *RE*, Suppl. 5, 626-630.
Cic. *De Har. Resp.* 27; Sil. Ital. 17.1-43; *Vir. Ill.* 46.1; Julian, *Or.* 5.159-161. This
anation has unfortunately been adopted and elaborated by H. Graillot in his classic
k on the Magna Mater, *Le cult de Cybèle, mère des dieux, a Rome et dans l'empire romain*
is, 1912), 30-32.
Polyb. 11.3.4-6; Livy, 27.50.2-27.51.10.
Cf. Livy, 28.2.13.

CHAPTER ONE

THE ADVENT OF THE MAGNA I

A remarkable event occurred late in Rome's great w
Consultation of the Sibylline Books revealed an
removal of Hannibal from Italy's shores if Magn
Idaean Mother of the Gods, should be transported
Rome. The Romans took that prophecy seriously,
sacred stone, symbol of the goddess, installed it on th
established the Megalensian festival in her honor. '
Hannibalic war came to an end.

The decision to fetch a foreign deity from distant pz
in a position of signal esteem in Rome demands atten
did not come lightly. Moreover the Romans, it seen
than they bargained for. The cult of Cybele brougł
eunuch priests, flamboyant in their colored robes, be
panied by shrill flute-players, tambourines, drums,
bals, occasionally engaging in frenzied dances and ev
The spectacle offended Roman sensibilities, obliging
exclude citizens from the alien priesthood and to se
celebration from the Phrygian ceremonies.[2] Yet the M
were in place, an annual festival, and a temple for C
204, completed and dedicated thirteen years later,
honored cult on the Palatine.

The event itself is arresting and baffling. Though oft
discussed, it has never received satisfactory explanatior
beyond the event. Implications and ramifications demz
advent of Magna Mater, the revered mother earth
raises issues of magnitude, depth, and complexity:
ideas, the politics of the Hannibalic war, foreign poli
Mediterranean, cultural associations with the Helleni
Roman sense of self-identity. With such far-reaching si
sider, a fresh investigation is amply justified.

---

[1] See, e.g., Catullus, 63.1-38; Lucretius, 2.598-643; Dion. Hal.
4.179-190, 4.207-214; Sil. Ital. 17.18-22. Further references and dis
RE, 11, 2259-2261; M.J. Vermaseren, *Cybele and Attis* (London, 19
G. Thomas, *ANRW*, II.17.3 (1984), 1525-1528.
[2] Dion. Hal. 2.19.4-5.

leaders proclaimed that divine favor had already lifted the war from Rome and Latium.[7] All of Lucania returned to Roman allegiance. Hannibal faced the prospect of no succor from Carthage or Spain.[8] The issue that confronted Rome in 205 was not how to save herself from the Punic menace, but whether to finish off Hannibal in Italy or to crush the enemy in Carthage. This sets the matter in a very different context—and a much more revealing one. Magna Mater arrived when Rome was on the brink of victory, not in the throes of defeat.[9] The background to this episode belongs in a broader setting.

Roman religious practices need to be taken into account. Adoption and incorporation of foreign deities held a long and honored place in those practices.[10] Hellenic influence permeated the religious scene, and the 3rd century B.C. witnessed some of the most prominent instances of alien cults welcomed in Rome.

The Sibylline Books supply a significant link in the chain. As sacred verses that contained Greek oracles, they were consulted regularly by a priestly college of *decemviri* to obtain elucidation of prodigies. Legend had it that Tarquinius Superbus bought the *libri Sibyllini* from an elderly foreign woman, the Sibyl from Cumae, thus attesting an early and Hellenic origin. Consultation of the Books occurred on several occasions during the early Republic, if tradition is to be believed. But one need not insist on credulity. By the beginning of the 3rd century, at least, the Sibylline Books acted as a resource, examined through Greek rituals but interpreted by Roman priests.[11] The acceptance of Hellenic rites as mediated through the Roman officialdom became in the 3rd century a

---

[7] Livy, 28.11.8-11: *deum benignitate summotum bellum ab urbe Romana et Latio esse.*

[8] Livy, 28.11.15, 28.12.6-9.

[9] Livy, 29.10.6-7. Cf. Ovid, *Fasti*, 4.255-256: *ut Roma....edomito sustulit orbe caput*; Herodian, 1.11.3: ἐπεὶ δὲ Ῥωμαίων ηὔξετο τὰ πράγματα. See also P. Lambrechts, *BullSocBelge d'anthropologie et de prehistoire*, 62 (1951), 45-48.

[10] See W. Warde Fowler, *The Religious Experience of the Roman People* (London, 1911), 223-269; K. Latte, *Römische Religionsgeschichte* (Munich, 1960), 148-194, 213-263; G. Dumézil, *Archaic Roman Religion* (Chicago, 1970), II, 407-431, 446-456; J. Bayet, *Histoire politique et psychologique de la religion romaine*² (Paris, 1969), 120-127.

[11] Tradition on the origins is recorded in Aulus Gellius, 1.19.1; Dion. Hal. 4.62; Lactantius, *Div. Inst.* 1.6.10-11; Zonaras, 7.11.1; Servius, *Ad Aen.* 6.72; Tzetzes, on Lycophron, 1279. For an acute critique of the tradition, see W. Hoffmann, *Wandel und Herkunft der Sibyllinische Bücher in Rom* (Diss. Leipzig, 1933), 6-36. Some have argued that Etruscan rather than Greek influence lies behind the introduction of the Sibylline Books; e.g. Dumézil, *Archaic Roman Religion*, 601-602. Or else that the Romans reached for Greek practises as a reaction to Etruscan cultural influences; Latte, *Römische Religionsgeschichte*, 160-161. A more complex religious heritage is suggested by J. Gagé, *Apollon romaine* (Paris, 1955), 27-38, 196-204. The speculation can here be bypassed. The Cumaean Sibyl is attested as early as Lycophron, perhaps drawing on Timaeus; Lycophron, 1278-1279. The college of *decemviri* dates from 367, replacing an earlier one

characteristic means of meeting emergencies and serving state interests. Foreign ceremonies provided outside legitimation—especially as they were controlled by Roman authorities.[12]

In 293, after a widespread epidemic devastated the Italian countryside, the Sibylline Books recommended that Rome seek assistance from the healing god Aesculapius. A delegation of dignitaries then sought out Aesculapius in his sanctuary at Epidaurus, bringing back the snake sacred to the god, whose arrival on the Tiber island prompted construction of a temple dedicated to him in 291. Story-tellers embellished the facts liberally, having the serpent glide spontaneously and miraculously onto the Roman vessel in Greece and off again later toward the designated spot on the Tiber island, thus terminating the epidemic. But the readiness to import Hellenic deities in the service of Roman needs is here plain and incontrovertible.[13]

Menacing portents also provoked the Romans to consult the *libri Sibyllini* at a critical time in the First Punic War, in 249. The Books authorized celebration of the Secular Games, to be held for three nights with sacrificial victims and ceremonies for the Greek deities Dis Pater and Proserpina who preside over the Underworld.[14] Propitiation of the infernal gods combined with a festival to commemorate renewal of the *saeculum*.

The cataclysmic events of the Second Punic War intensified recourse to divine assistance. The disaster at Trasimene was laid to neglect of proper rituals and auspices. Q. Fabius Maximus, as dictator in 217, prevailed upon the senate to seek guidance from the Sibylline Books. Among other pronouncements, the Books once again advised, through the intermediacy of the decemvirs, that a foreign deity be imported. This time the oracular advice called for the building of a temple on the Capitol to Venus Erycina. The goddess, who owed her characteristics to a blend

of *duumviri*; Livy, 6.37.12, 6.42.2. And Varro affirms the usage of Greek rites; *LL*, 7.88: *et nos dicimus xv viros Graeco ritu sacra non Romano facere.* On the Sibylline Books generally, see H. Diels, *Sibyllinische Blätter* (Berlin, 1890), *passim*; cf. G. Radke, *Gymnasium*, 66 (1959), 217-246. On Apollo in early Rome, see E. Simon, *JDAI*, 93 (1978), 202-215, with bibliography.

[12] Cf. J.A. North, *PBSR*, 31 (1976), 9.

[13] Livy, 10.47.6-7; *Per.* 11; Val. Max. 1.8.2; *Vir. Ill.* 22.1. According to Ovid, *Met.* 15.626-744, the advice came from Delphi, rather than from the *libri Sibyllini*. Other sources in Latte, *Römische Religionsgeschichte*, 225-226. On Aesculapius and Rome generally, see now P. Roesch, in G. Sabbah, *Médicins et médecine dans l'antiquité* (Saint-Etienne, 1982), 171-179.

[14] Varro, in Censorinus, 17.8-10; cf. Val. Max. 2.4.5; Livy, *Per.* 49. Discussion and additional references in Latte, *Römische Religionsgeschichte*, 246-248. Testimony on the Secular Games is set out in full by G.B. Pighi, *De Ludis Saecularibus populi romani quiritium* (Amsterdam, 1965), 33-72.

of Punic and Hellenic elements, had been worshipped at Eryx in north-western Sicily. Rome's successes on the island during the First Punic War had brought the cult within her sphere of influence and she used it to win Greek sympathies against the Carthaginians. Now the favor of Venus Erycina would be transferred directly to the Capitol.[15] Political considerations entered into this development as well. Fabius Maximus utilized the occasion to deliver a vow personally for the erection of the temple—for the *libri Sibyllini* had specified that the man with greatest *imperium* in the state should have the job.[16] Two years later Fabius received senatorial authorization to dedicate the new temple on the Capitoline.[17] The Sicilian-Greek goddess was then installed in a place of conspicuous honor.

In a closely parallel development during these same years, Rome established connections with the great oracle of Apollo at Delphi.[18] C. Marcellus' magnificent and memorable victory over the Gauls at Clastidium in 222 stimulated the joyous Romans to dispatch a golden bowl in commemoration of victory and the conclusion of the war.[19] The event is particularly notable for it stands outside the context of crisis and desperation wrought by the Hannibalic war. Associations with Delphi arose not from an intensification of religious emotion but from conscious decision to reach out to the Hellenic world.[20]

---

[15] Livy, 22.9.7-10. On the cult during the First Punic War, see R. Schilling, *La religion romaine de Vénus* (Paris, 1954), 233-242; D. Kienast, *Hermes*, 93 (1965), 478-489. Whether the worship of Mens, also called for by the Sibylline Books, had Hellenic elements as well cannot be established. Cf. Schilling, *op. cit.*, 248-254; M. Mello, *Mens Bona* (Naples, 1968), *passim*.

[16] Livy, 22.10.10: *ita ex fatalibus libris editum erat, ut is voveret cuius maximum imperium in civitate esset.*

[17] Livy, 23.30.13-14, 23.31.9. A combination of religious, political, and military considerations were involved; I. Bitto, *ArchStorMessinese*, 28 (1977), 121-133.

[18] Tradition records consultations of Delphi that date to the times of Tarquin the Proud, the siege of Veii, and the Samnite Wars. For Tarquin, see Livy, 1.56.4-13; Ovid, *Fasti*, 2.711-720; Val. Max. 7.3.2; Dion. Hal. 4.64; Zonaras, 7.11. On Veii, see Livy, 5.15, 5.16.8-5.17, 5.28.1-5; Dion. Hal. 12.11-17; Zonaras, 7.20; Plut. *Cam.* 4.4-5, 7.5; Appian, *Ital.* 8; Val. Max. 1.6.3; Diod. 14.93. On the Samnite War, see Pliny, *NH*, 34.26; Plut. *Num.* 8.10. But it is doubtful that any of those events is historical. See, especially, W. Hoffmann, *Rom und die griechische Welt im 4. Jahrhundert* (Leipzig, 1934), 129-131; H.W. Parke and D.E.W. Wormell, *The Delphic Oracle* (Oxford, 1956), 265-271; R.M. Ogilvie, *A Commentary on Livy, Books 1-5* (Oxford, 1965), 216-218, 660-661; Gagé, *Apollon romaine*, 130-146, 255; J. Fontenrose, *The Delphic Oracle* (Berkeley and Los Angeles, 1978), 65, 314, 334, 342-343.

[19] Plut. *Marc.* 8.6. Marcellus himself dedicated spoils in the temple of the gods at Samothrace and the temple of Athena at Lindos after the conquest of Syracuse; Plut. *Marc.* 30.4.

[20] The point is missed by those who date the first Roman contact with Delphi to 216, thus ignoring the gesture in 222; e.g., Latte, *Römische Religionsgeschichte*, 223-224; Dumézil, *Archaic Roman Religion*, II, 479-480.

The Hannibalic war did, of course, heighten motivation to consult Delphi. The disaster at Cannae in 216 naturally generated frightening portents that provoked a number of measures to propitiate the gods. Prominent among them was the appointment of Q. Fabius Pictor, Roman aristocrat and cultured Hellenist, as emissary to Delphi to discover what prayers and entreaties might appease the wrath of the gods. The legate returned with good tidings and detailed prescriptions. Pictor translated the Greek oracular verses into Latin: they specified the offerings to be provided for particular deities, promised success in war, and stipulated a return from the spoils for Delphic Apollo. The emissary performed all ceremonies as directed. And, on the instructions—or so he claimed—of the oracle, he wore the laurel crown, with which he had come to the priest at Delphi, all the way back to Rome, thus to lay it upon the altar of Apollo.[21] The gestures carried weighty symbolic significance. Terrors stemming from the Carthaginians in Italy do not fully explain them. Romans here practiced rites on the directive of a Greek oracle. Pictor's laurel crown, worn at Delphi and deposited in Rome, signified the identification of Delphic Apollo and the divinity worshipped at Rome.[22] And the association was to be sealed with the fruits of victory promised to Delphi, thereby taking it out of the realm of mere *ad hoc* and temporary contact. The relationship would be an enduring one. Rome redeemed the promise in 205, sending a lavish gift to Delphi, constructed from the spoils and in celebration of the saving triumph at the Metaurus. The embassy which carried that donation to Apollo also offered sacrifice and received in return the welcome forecast that additional and still greater triumph was in store.[23] Rome had now embraced the most sacred of Hellenic shrines and could advertise Hellenic sanction for her mission against Carthage.

This sequence of adoptions and adaptations of Greek rituals, divinities, and oracular authority supplies the proper setting for the acquisition of the Magna Mater. It is not incidental that both the Sibylline Books and Pythian Apollo at Delphi play a role in empowering Roman officials to fetch her from Asia and institute her cult at home. The event had its precedents and its parallels. It belongs in a growing series of thrusts by the Roman political and religious elite to expand and exploit connections with the cultural world of the Greek East.

---

[21] Livy, 22.57.4-5, 23.11.1-6; Plut. *Fab.* 18.3; Appian, *Hann.* 27.

[22] Cf. Bayet, *Histoire politique*, 150. Observe also the decision in 212 to make the *ludi Apollinares* an annual festival, celebrated *Graeco ritu*; Livy, 25.12.10; cf. Gagé, *Apollon romaine*, 270-279.

[23] Livy, 28.45.12, 29.10.6.

That aspect, though of central importance, tells only part of the story. The Romans reached for Hellenic culture, but resisted absorption by it. Roman intellectuals had already endorsed the tale that the origins of Rome stemmed from Troy. And Troy had been the foe of Greece. Trojan legends too had their part in the complex patterns that lurk behind the adoption of the Magna Mater.

The idea that Rome's origins had some connection with Troy and the wanderings of heroes after the Trojan War is a creation of Greek intellectuals. A form of it was known already to the 5th century writer Hellanicus of Lesbos who has Aeneas arrive in Italy together with Odysseus to found the city. That version gained acceptance in some authors.[24] A multitude of variations turns up in later works, with no obvious pattern or structure. Greek writers had only the haziest knowledge of Rome before the end of the 4th century, but they were endlessly inventive in fabricating or embellishing the tales with which they worked. Trojan founders of Rome or of its mother cities appear in some but not all of the versions. Other forms of the story link Rome's beginnings with Achaean migrations and Hellenic settlements. Heraclides Ponticus characterized Rome simply as a "Greek city."[25] More serious investigations were undertaken by Timaeus who accepted and argued for Trojan ancestry.[26] But his analysis did not sweep away all competitors. The Hellenic character of Rome, whether stemming from Odysseus' wanderings or on some other basis, continued to attract certain writers.[27] What is important, however, is the fact that the

---

[24] Dion. Hal. 1.72.2. N. Horsfall, *CQ*, 29 (1979), 376-383, expresses doubts. But see now F. Solmsen, *HSCP*, 90 (1986), 93-110. The connections of Odysseus and Italy are exhaustively discussed by E.D. Phillips, *JHS*, 73 (1953), 53-67.

[25] Plut. *Cam.* 22.2. The development of a tradition is nearly impossible to trace, in view of our ignorance of the dates of most of the writers whose names alone are known—not to mention a substantial number of anonymous versions. See, e.g., Dion. Hal. 1.72-73; Plut. *Rom.* 2; Festus, 326, 329, L.; Servius, *Ad Aen.* 1.273. Scholarly discussions are numerous. The extensive treatment by J. Perret, *Les origines de la légende troyenne de Rome (281-31)* (Paris, 1942), *passim*, is ingenious but controversial; cf. the criticisms of P. Boyancé, *REA*, 45 (1943), 275-290 = *Etudes sur la religion romaine* (Rome, 1972), 153-170, and A. Momigliano, *JRS*, 35 (1945), 99-104. See also Hoffmann, *Rom und die griechische Welt*, 108-115. More recent examinations by E. Bickermann, *CP*, 47 (1952), 65-68; H. Strasburger, *Zur Sage von der Gründung Roms* (Heidelberg, 1968); T. J. Cornell, *PCPS*, 201 (1975), 16-27; Momigliano, *Settimo contributo alla storia degli studi classici e del mondo antico* (Rome, 1984), 437-462; J. Poucet, *Les origines de Rome; tradition et histoire* (Brussels, 1985), 184-192, with valuable bibliography.

[26] On Timaeus, see Momigliano, *RivStorItal*, 71 (1959), 529-556 = *Terzo contributo alla storia degli studi classici e del mondo antico* (Rome, 1966), I, 23-53, with bibliography.

[27] Note, e.g., the story that Alexander the Great and, subsequently, Demetrius Poliorcetes requested that Rome halt her piratical activities, on the ground of a common kinship between Romans and Greeks; Strabo, 5.3.5 = c232. The argument by G.K. Galinsky, *Aeneas, Sicily, and Rome* (Princeton, 1969), 157-158, that the kinship actually

Romans themselves eventually adopted the concept of Trojan origins, already combined by Greek researchers with the indigenous tales of Romulus and Remus. The combination is attested by Naevius in the late 3rd century.[28] And the canonical version, with Aeneas' descendants as rulers of Alba, whence came the founders of Rome, found voice in Fabius Pictor's history, here largely based on the reconstruction of a Greek writer, Diocles of Peparethus.[29] By the end of the 3rd century, therefore, learned Romans had embraced Hellenic formulations of their past, but elected to identify their ancestors with Trojans rather than with Greeks.

Just when this concept took hold in Rome is impossible to pinpoint. Testimony is fragmentary. But the fragments, when pieced together, suggest that the idea of Trojan origins was familiar to Romans through much of the 3rd century.

In a celebrated episode, king Pyrrhus of Epirus made reference to the legend when he planned an invasion of Italy in 281. The king took heart from the tale of Troy captured by Greeks: he would duplicate the success as descendant of Achilles by bringing a Hellenic war upon the Romans, colonists of the Trojans.[30] Pyrrhus' posture as incarnation of Achilles gains further confirmation from the coins he issued in Magna Graecia and Sicily, with representations of Thetis and Achilles.[31] The propaganda campaign shows plainly enough that the idea of Roman descent from Troy was familiar to Pyrrhus and that he anticipated its resonance in Italy.[32] This does not, of course, prove that Romans themselves had adopted the story. But it indicates that, at least from Pyrrhus' perspective, it had already made its way to Italian shores.

The First Punic War supplies a more telling instance. The people of Segesta in 263 threw off their Carthaginian allegiance and attached themselves to the Roman cause, announcing as their reason a common descent from Aeneas. One may well wonder whether other considerations, strategic or political, entered into the calculation. And the notice

---

alludes to Trojan ancestry is unconvincing. For other versions later than and different from Timaeus, see E. Gabba, *RivStorItal*, 86 (1974), 625-642; Cornell, *PCPS*, 201 (1975), 25-27.

[28] Servius, *Ad. Aen.* 1.273. See Perret, *Les origines*, 478-488.

[29] Plut. *Rom.* 3-4. The synthesis of the Trojan and Romulus-Remus legends is confirmed by a recently published inscription with reference to Fabius' work; G. Manganaro, *PP*, 29 (1974), 394-397. Divergent and confused traditions persisted thereafter as well; cf. G. D'Anna, *Problemi di letteratura latina arcaica* (Rome, 1976), 43-113; *Cultura e scuola*, 17 (1978), 22-31.

[30] Paus. 1.12.1: στρατεύειν γὰρ ἐπὶ Τρώων ἀποίχους ᾿Αχιλλέως ὢν ἀπόγονος.

[31] *BMC* Thessaly, 111, #7-8; 112, #9-19.

[32] Nothing in the evidence warrants Perret's extraordinary conclusion that the legend was created at this time; *Les origines*, 409-434. By contrast, E. Weber, *WS*, 85 (1972), 214-215, goes too far in stating that this demonstrates widespread knowledge of the legend.

of this event occurs only in Zonaras. Yet there is no good reason to cast doubt upon it—and some evidence in support.[33] Segesta may well have had her own reasons for joining the Roman side. What matters, however, is the explanation she offered. Segestans rather than Romans took the initiative here in exploiting the Trojan tale. But they would hardly have done it without expecting a sympathetic hearing.[34]

A tale preserved by Justin points in the same direction—though its authenticity is questionable. The narrative reports that Acarnania, ca. 237, called upon the Romans for assistance in a conflict against Aetolia. The senate sent legates who demanded that Aetolian garrisons be removed and the Acarnanians be left free, for they were the only Greek peoples who had not contributed contingents against Troy, ancestress of the Romans. Aetolian spokesmen treated the request with disdain, and the Roman legation departed with nothing to show for its efforts.[35] Dubious elements predominate in this story. And little weight can be placed upon it. But one may note, at least, that reference to the Trojan connection is incidental, not an item around which the tale is built. It thus lends support, however slight, to the idea that that connection had been acknowledged by Rome before the mid-3rd century.[36]

At about this same time, if we can believe our one source, the Romans held communication with King Seleucus of Syria, evidently Seleucus II. The king had requested an *amicitia* with Rome. And the reply was cordial: the Romans promised *amicitia* if Seleucus relieved the Ilians, their *consanguinei*, of all tribute. That information was contained in a letter,

---

[33] Zonaras, 8.9.12. Cicero attests to the consanguinity of Segestans and Romans; Cic. *Verr.* 2.4.72, 2.5.83, 2.5.125; cf. Plut. *Nic.* 1.3. The coins of Segesta show Aeneas with father Anchises on his shoulder; *BMC*, Sicily, 59ff. It is possible that the Segestans referred only to Trojan antecedents; the specific allusion to Aeneas may be due to a later source; cf. Perret, *Les origines*, 452-453—who, however, remains unsure of the story's authenticity.

[34] So, rightly, Galinsky, *Aeneas, Sicily, and Rome*, 173. The lengthy discussion of F. P. Rizzo, *Studi ellenistico-romani* (Palermo, 1974), 15-43, adds little of substance. Kienast's conjecture, *Hermes*, 93 (1965), 478-489, that Rome utilized the legend to organize support against Carthage, around the cult of Venus Erycina, is attractive but speculative.

[35] Justin, 28.1.5-28.2.14; esp. 28.1.6: *qui soli quondam adversus Troianos, auctores originis suae, auxilia Graecis non miserint.* Cf. Strabo, 10.2.23 = c460; 10.2.25 = c462.

[36] A heavy assault on the episode's genuineness was made by M. Holleaux, *Rome, la Grèce, et les monarchies hellénistiques au III͏ᵉ siècle avant J.-C. (273-205)* (Paris, 1935), 5-22; followed, among others, by Perret, *Les origines*, 64-66. That Rome sent a mission to Acarnania seems contradicted by Polyb. 2.12.7, a point rightly stressed by Holleaux. But his view that the story stemmed from confusion with the events arising out of the Antiochene war in 192-189, is implausible. Not very convincing defenses of the tradition may be found in E. Manni, *PP*, 11 (1956), 179-190, and Rizzo, *Studi*, 65-82. Cf. also D. Golan, *RivStorAnt*, 1 (1971), 93-98. Weber, *WS*, 85 (1972), 218-219, accepts the narrative without question.

composed in Greek and read out to the senate three centuries later by the emperor Claudius.[37] Its authenticity too has been assailed, with some justice. The evidence is thin and unsubstantiated. Yet no compelling argument discredits the idea of diplomatic relations between Rome and Syria in the mid 3rd century—especially as such relations are firmly attested between Rome and Egypt.[38] Whether Rome enforced her conditions or carried out her promise is unknown and immaterial. Reference to the association with Ilium enhances the impression that Roman leadership had already adopted the legend of Trojan origins.

In 217 the senate, on advice of the Sibylline Books, summoned the goddess Venus Erycina from Sicilian Eryx to the Capitoline in Rome, where a temple was constructed for her two years later.[39] The resonances felt in her wake can hardly be missed. Eryx had been visited and honored by Aeneas, the shrine dedicated to his mother, acknowledged as ancestress of Rome.[40] The overtones of the Trojan legend gave special import to the transferral of that cult.

An oracular pronouncement discovered in 212 reinforces the interpretation. It was included in books purportedly composed by the seer Marcius who had correctly predicted the defeat at Cannae and now advised institution of the *ludi Apollinares*. The first of these began with the words *"amnem, Troiugenam fuge Cannam.*[41] As is obvious, designation of Romans as descendants of Trojans could by then be taken for granted.[42]

After the Hannibalic war, allusion to the Trojan origins and to the consanguinity of Rome and Ilium became almost a commonplace in diplomatic dealings. The city of Lampsacus, located in the Troad, pleaded for inclusion in the treaty between Rome and Philip V that terminated the Second Macedonian War in 196. In order to make their case, the Lampsacenes placed special stress upon their "kinship" with the Romans.[43] Principal victor in that war, T. Quinctius Flamininus,

---

[37] Suet. *Claud.* 25.3: *recitata vetere epistula Graeca senatus populique R. Seleuco regi amicitiam et societatem ita demum pollicentis, si consanguineos suos Ilienses ab omni onere immunes praestitisset.*

[38] Dio, fr. 41 = Zonaras, 8.6.11; Dion. Hal. 20.14.1-2; Val. Max. 4.3.9; Appian, *Sic.* 1; Justin, 18.2.9; Livy, *Per.* 14; Eutrop. 2.15. Holleaux's attack on the authenticity of the notice succeeds only in refuting the idea of a "treaty" of *amicitia*; *Rome, la Grèce*, 46-58. But Suetonius' text does not imply a treaty anyway. More recent skeptics add nothing new; Weber, *WS*, 85 (1972), 217-218; M.R. Cimma, *Reges socii et amici populi romani* (Milan, 1976), 69-70. The story's genuineness is accepted by Rizzo, *Studi*, 83-88, and W. Orth, *Königlicher Machtanspruch und städtische Freiheit* (Munich, 1977), 72-73.

[39] Livy, 22.9.7-10, 22.10.10, 23.30.13-14, 23.31.9. See above, notes 15-17.

[40] Diod. 4.83.4-7; Vergil, *Aen.* 5.759-760; Galinsky, *Aeneas, Sicily, and Rome*, 63-65, 173-177; Bitto, *ArchStorMessinese*, 28 (1977), 121-125.

[41] Livy, 25.12.1-10.

[42] On this passage, cf. Perret, *Les origines*, 454-457; Galinsky, *Aeneas, Sicily, and Rome*, 177-178.

[43] *Syll³* 591, lines 18-19, 21-22, 24-25, 30-31, 54-56, 60-61.

made dedications at Delphi in 194, including inscribed verses of his own composition in Greek, which presented himself both as descendant of Aeneas and as the man who had brought freedom to the Greeks.[44] Conflict with Antiochus III of Syria engaged Roman troops for the first time in Asia. A naval contingent under C. Livius Salinator undertook initial preparations for the crossing of the army in 190. And Salinator made it a point at the outset to offer sacrifice to Athena at Ilium.[45] When the army arrived, headed by the consul L. Scipio, the ceremony was repeated and the symbolic significance doubly dramatized. The consul paid homage to Athena in the citadel of Ilium, while Romans and Ilians mutually proclaimed their kinship as heirs of ancient Troy.[46] In the peace settlement of 188 that followed the Antiochene war Ilium received her reward: freedom from taxation, and the assignment of two towns to her authority. As Livy puts it, the benefits came not so much for recent services as in commemoration of the Trojan origins.[47] The Ilians capitalized on their connections shortly thereafter. They interceded with Rome on behalf of the Lycians in their quarrel with Rhodes. The Ilians successfully played upon their kinship and gained concessions for Lycia.[48] The legendary association had produced concrete consequences in the diplomacy of the 3rd and early 2nd centuries. It permitted Rome to strike an effective international posture, while encouraging Greeks to exploit it for their own purposes.

What relevance does all this have to the summoning of the Magna Mater to Rome? The testimony is ambiguous and inconsistent, but intriguing. A relationship between Rome and a Hellenic state in Asia Minor, involving both diplomacy and religion, immediately suggests the presence of the Trojan myth. The suspicion grows when one realizes that the state in question is the kingdom of Pergamum which exercised dominion in the Troad and whose influence extended both over Ilium itself and over Mt. Ida, home of the Magna Mater.

The text of Ovid offers the most beguiling testimony. The poet directly connected the Mother Goddess, Mt. Ida, and the legend of Aeneas bear-

---

[44] Plut. *Flam.* 12.6-7: Αἰνεάδας Τίτος ὕμμιν ὑπέρτατον ὤπασε δῶρον/ Ἑλλήνων τεῦξας παισὶν ἐλευθερίαν. Note also the oracle which circulated about this time, alluding to a forthcoming clash of Rome and Macedon and ascribing victory over Carthage to descendants of the Trojans; Plut. *Mor.* 399c: ἀλλ᾽ ὁπότε Τρώων γενεὰ καθύπερθε γένηται Φοινίκων ἐν ἀγῶνι.

[45] Livy, 37.9.7.

[46] Livy, 37.37.1-3; Justin, 31.8.1-4. The hypothesis of M. Sordi, in M. Sordi (ed.), *Politica e religione nel primo scontro tra Roma e l'Oriente* (Milan, 1982), 136-149, that Athena Iliaca and Cybele were exploited by the Scipios and Manlius Vulso respectively in political struggles against one another, is imaginative speculation.

[47] Livy, 38.39.10: *non tam ob recentia ulla merita quam originum memoria.*

[48] Polyb. 22.5.1-6.

ing the legacy of Troy to Italy. In his version, Rome's acquisition of the Magna Mater from Mt. Ida is set squarely in the context of reaffirming her Trojan heritage.[49] The association is repeated in a much later source, the historian Herodian, who has Roman envoys secure the image of the goddess by proclaiming their descent from Aeneas.[50]

But no other ancient writer makes the connection. A puzzling fact. Livy's extended narrative has no hint of it. Indeed, he locates Cybele in Pessinus, whence she was procured for the Romans by Attalus of Pergamum, thus implicitly severing any geographic ties with the Troad.[51] That site finds favor in the large majority of our sources: the Magna Mater came from Pessinus in Galatia.[52] And still a third possibility gains support. The assiduous researcher Varro places the Mother Goddess in a temple in Pergamum itself, where Attalus handed her over to the Romans.[53]

A choice among alternatives confronts various hazards. The temple state of Pessinus was situated near the border between Galatia and Greater Phrygia—a very long distance from Pergamum. For Attalus to have obtained the stone from that locale required Pergamene influence in the region. Did the king's reach extend so far?[54] Our knowledge of Pergamene holdings during these years is woefully inadequate.[55] Three items deserve mention. In 208 Attalus hastily withdrew his forces from Greece and returned home to face an invasion of his territory by Prusias I of Bithynia.[56] The outcome of that conflict escapes record. A few years later, ca. 204, as an inscription happens to reveal, the city of Teos had come under Seleucid authority, a further erosion of Attalid influence.[57] And, by the time of Attalus' death in 197, his successor Eumenes II

---

[49] Ovid, *Fasti*, 4.247-272; *in Phrygios Roma refertur avos*. A link between Troy and the Sibylline oracle is alluded to also by Tac. *Ann.* 6.12. Ovid's account has recently been treated, with different purposes, by R.J. Littlewood, *CQ*, 31 (1981), 381-395, and J. Jope, *EMC*, 32 (1988), 13-22.

[50] Herodian, 1.11.3: καὶ τὴν ἀπ' Αἰνείου τοῦ Φρυγὸς ἐς αὐτοὺς διαδοχὴν καταλέγοντες.

[51] Livy, 29.10.5, 29.11.7.

[52] E.g., Cic. *De Har. Resp.* 27-28; Diod. 34/35.33.2; Strabo, 12.5.3 = c567; Val. Max. 8.15.3; Appian, *Hann.* 56; Dio, fr. 57.61; *Vir. Ill.* 46; Amm. Marc. 22.9.5.

[53] Varro, *LL*, 6.15.

[54] The possibility was discountenanced long ago and frequently; e.g., K. Kuiper, *Mnemosyne*, 30 (1902), 283-285; Schmidt, *Kultübertragungen*, 23-26; Graillot, *Le culte de Cybèle*, 46-49. But none offered a thorough argument.

[55] The view of E.V. Hansen, *The Attalids of Pergamum*[2] (Ithaca, 1971), 51-52, that Attalus had Galatian connections and even an alliance with Pessinus lacks any evidence.

[56] Livy, 28.7.10; Dio, 17.58.

[57] P. Herrmann, *Anatolia*, 9 (1965), 29-159. The argument of A. Giovannini, *MH*, 40 (1983), 178-184, that Antiochus III was an ally of Attalus when he promised to liberate Teos of tribute paid to Attalus, is ingenious but implausible.

inherited a shrunken realm with insignificant holdings.[58] The combined testimony carries some weight: Attalus, it appears, was in no position to exert pressure on Pessinus in 205.[59] A subsequent event confirms the conclusion that Magna Mater did not come to Rome from Pessinus. When Roman forces under Cn. Manlius Vulso marched into the interior of Anatolia fifteen years later, the goddess still had her seat in Pessinus. Her priests hastened to greet Manlius and informed him that Cybele had forecast a great victory. The texts offer no suggestion that there had been a prior association with Rome.[60] The Romans had made connection with a different shrine.

The voice of Varro is more authoritative. He located the goddess in Pergamum and had Roman envoys receive her directly from Attalus. The testimony is too often reckoned as reflecting a third tale, at variance with all other traditions.[61] An unlikely conclusion. The character of this evidence needs to be taken into account. The notice does not have place in a historical narrative; it represents an etymological conjecture. Varro traces the term *Megalesia* to the temple Megalesion in Pergamum, whence

---

[58] Polyb. 23.11.7, 32.8.3; cf. 21.22.15; Livy, 40.8.14; Strabo, 13.4.2 = c624. The Peace of Apamea in 188 restored to Pergamum the territory of Mysia and both Phrygias which had been taken from her by Prusias; Livy, 38.39.15; Polyb. 21.46.10. Control of Greater Phrygia might give Pergamum access to Pessinus. When did she acquire the territory initially and when did Prusias deprive her of it? The first came probably through agreement between Attalus and Antiochus III in 216; Polyb. 5.107.4; cf. C. Habicht, *Hermes*, 84 (1956), 93, with earlier literature. The second is far more problematical. Habicht, *op. cit.*, 94-95, puts it in 196, shortly after Attalus' death, an opportunity for Prusias to take advantage of the change in regime. So also F.W. Walbank, *A Historical Commentary on Polybius*, III (Oxford, 1979), 172. But testimony is unanimous that the kingdom had already dwindled to insignificant proportions before Eumenes took over. H.H. Schmitt, *Untersuchungen zur Geschichte Antiochos' des Grossen und seiner Zeit* (Wiesbaden, 1964), 276-277, dates it to 198 as a corollary to Antiochus' encroachments on Pergamene territory. But there is no evidence for any move by Prusias. The one occasion in this period when evidence attests a clash between Bithynia and Pergamum and advancement by Prusias is 208; Livy, 28.7.10; Dio, 17.58. Attalus' losses most plausibly come in that year or shortly thereafter. By 205 Pessinus would be out of reach. R.E. Allen, *The Attalid Kingdom: A Constitutional History* (Oxford, 1983), 63-64, doubts that Attalus ever held much sway in Greater Phrygia.

[59] B. Virgilio, *Il tempio stato di Pessinunte fra Pergamo e Roma nel II-I secolo a.C.* (Pisa, 1981), 37-47, entertains the possibility that the first letter in the dossier of correspondence between Pergamum and Pessinus was sent by Attalus I in 208, soliciting cooperation against Bithynia; *OGIS*, 315 A1 = C.B. Welles, *Royal Correspondence in the Hellenistic World* (London, 1934), #55. But that letter was convincingly dated to the reign of Eumenes II by Dittenberger, *OGIS, loc. cit.*, a conclusion ultimately embraced by Virgilio as well, *op. cit.* 46-47.

[60] Polyb. 21.37.4-7; Livy, 38.18.9-10—in 189.

[61] E.g. Schwann, *RE*, 11, 2267; Habel, *RE*, Suppl. 5, 626. For G. Wissowa, *Religion und Kultus der Römer²* (Munich, 1912), 318, Attalus purloined the stone from Pessinus and installed it in Pergamum where he eventually yielded it to the Romans.

the goddess came to Rome.[62] But the statement is entirely consistent with the stone's origin at Mt. Ida. Attalus transferred it to Pergamum, there to present it to the legates of Rome. Nothing in Varro's testimony undermines the narrative of Ovid. His researches may even lie behind that narrative.

The location of Mt. Ida takes on greater plausibility—and with it the link to the Trojan legend.[63] Mt. Ida was not the only cult center of Cybele. Nor even the only one in Asia Minor.[64] But it held special significance for the Roman tradition. By the era of Augustus, Mt. Ida and the Great Mother had been incorporated into the tale of Aeneas and the matrix of legends surrounding the origins of Rome. Hellenic myth associated the mountain with the ancestors of the Trojans themselves, who selected the site to inaugurate the cult of the Great Mother.[65] Mt. Ida became the refuge for Aeneas and his supporters when Troy fell— and the place of assemblage before they sailed to Europe.[66] The Magna Mater interceded for the Trojans with Zeus and pleaded with him for their safety.[67] She nearly accompanied them herself, but held back, for her appointed time in Latium still lay in the future—an allusion to the transferral in 204.[68] But the goddess remained a protective deity for the Trojan exiles, prayed to by Aeneas, and a symbol of their divine tutelage.[69] There is nothing to prove that these conceptions of the Augustan age had been fully formed two centuries earlier when Roman legates brought home the sacred stone of Cybele. But the choice of this

---

[62] Varro, *LL*, 6.15: *Megalesia dicta a Graecis, quod ex libris Sibyllinis arcessita ab Attalo rege Pergama; ibi prope murum Megalesion templum eius deae, unde advecta Romam.* See the acute analysis of F. Bömer, *P. Ovidius Naso. Die Fasten*, II (Heidelberg, 1958), 229-230.

[63] The importance of the Trojan legend in this connection was recognized by S. Aurigemma, *BullCommArchRoma*, 37 (1909), 32-33; Lambrechts, *BullSocBelge d'anthropologie et de prehistoire*, 62 (1951), 44-60. The conclusion of Schmidt, *Kultübertragungen*, 27, that discrepancies in the evidence imply that the whole story can be discarded as a fabrication is a counsel of despair.

[64] See the survey by Vermaseren, *Cybele and Attis*, 24-32.

[65] Dion. Hal. 1.61.4; Vergil, *Aen.* 3.102-113.

[66] Dion. Hal. 1.46-48. Mt. Ida as the birthplace of Aeneas is attested already in Homer, *Iliad*, 2.820-821; cf. Hesiod, *Theog.* 1010.

[67] Vergil, *Aen.* 9.80-92.

[68] Ovid, *Fasti*, 4.251-254.

[69] Vergil, *Aen.* 6.784-787, 7.135-140, 9.617-620, 10.156-158, 10.228-235, 10.250-255; cf. 2.788; Paus. 10.26.1. The view of Latte, *Römische Religionsgeschichte*, 260, n.3, that Vergil was the first to tie the Magna Mater to the Trojan legend, is unlikely. Rightly criticized by S. Weinstock, *JRS*, 51 (1961), 213, who stresses the importance of the temple on the Palatine. Bömer, *MdI*, 71 (1964), 140-143, goes further and gives principal credit for the story to Ovid. See also Thomas, *ANRW*, II.17.3 (1984), 1504. Perret, *Les origines*, 453-454, seems oddly unaware of any testimony earlier than Herodian. On Vergil's allusions to Cybele, see now T.P. Wiseman, in T. Woodman and D. West, *Poetry and Politics in the Age of Augustus* (Cambridge, 1984), 117-128.

particular deity, the elaborate ceremonial, the elevation to a place of such honor and distinction on the Palatine itself receive readiest explanation as Rome's reassertion of her Trojan origins. Even Livy, who does not place the episode in that context, lets slip the true meaning that Cybele held for the Romans by her designation itself: she was Mater Idaea. The designation was official and unambiguous. Cybele in Rome carried the cult title *mater deum magna Idaea*.[70]

Why then did Livy and the bulk of the tradition ignore the Trojan connection and refer the events to Pessinus? A solution lies to hand. For Romans of the later Republic, the cult of Cybele at Pessinus was the principal functioning shrine of the goddess in Asia Minor. Galli from that shrine greeted Cn. Manlius Vulso in 189 and predicted victory over the Galatians. An extant correspondence between the king of Pergamum and the priest of Pessinus in the 160s and 150s attests to the stature of the latter. And, a half century later, another priest from Pessinus actually reached Rome, addressing magistrates and senate in official capacity.[71] It was easy enough for an annalistic writer of the late 2nd or early 1st century to assume that the symbol of Magna Mater must have been sought at Pessinus. That assumption need not bind us. Different circumstances prevailed in 204. The initial proposition can still hold: that the legend of Troy hovered over the political, diplomatic, and religious negotiations between Rome and Attalus of Pergamum. The king was an especially suitable collaborator: *amicus* of Rome and overlord of the Troad. Installation of the deity on the Palatine, a site linked to Rome's earliest tradition, underscored the symbolism of antiquity.

The episode thus takes its place among the series of allusions to Rome's Trojan heritage in the international diplomacy of the later 3rd century. But more needs to be said on this matter. As we have seen, Greek writers had evolved a large group of complex and inconsistent tales about Roman origins, including several that named Odysseus as ancestor or made of Rome a Greek city. The Romans themselves, however, some time in the 3rd century, accepted and propagated the version that traced their history from Troy. In short, the same era which saw Roman intellectuals become increasingly engaged with Hellenic culture also saw

---

[70] *Inscr. Ital.* 13.2, 127; Livy, 29.10.5, 29.14.5. Cf. Cic. *De Sen.* 45. It is noteworthy that when Livius Salinator sacrificed at Ilium in 190, he did so to Athena; Livy, 37.9.7. The same was true for L. Scipio later in the year; Livy, 37.37.1-3; Justin, 31.8.1-4. An implied acknowledgement that the Mater Idaea had settled in Rome? The Galli who made appeal to Salinator came from Sestus, not Ilium; Polyb. 21.6.7; Livy, 37.9.9.

[71] Galli and Manlius: Polyb. 21.37.4-7; Livy, 38.18.9-10; diplomatic correspondence: *OGIS*, 315 = Welles, *RC*, #55-61; visit of the priest in 102: Plut. *Mar.* 17.5-6; Diod. 36.13. Cicero refers to Pessinus as seat of the goddess in the 50s B.C.; Cic. *De Har. Resp.* 28; *Pro Sest.* 56; cf. Strabo, 12.5.3 = c567-568.

them embrace the association with Troy and reject the idea of the city's Hellenic character. On the face of it, the attitude seems inconsistent and baffling.[72] In fact, it makes eminently good sense.

Pyrrhus had used the Trojan myth to rally Greek support against the western power. The Romans, however, viewed the matter very differently. They did not take up their Trojan posture as antagonists of Greece. Nor were they so judged by the Greeks. Segesta's transferral of allegiance to Rome in the First Punic War through appeal to their common Roman heritage was hardly an anti-Greek move. The negotiation with Seleucus II of Syria assumed that Romans could be champions of Ilium at the same time as they entered into *amicitia* with a Hellenic power. The Greek city of Lampsacus found no contradiction between its Hellenic character and its claim on Roman kinship through Troy. Most striking of all, Flamininus broadcast his descent from Aeneas, while simultaneously taking credit for liberating the Greek world. The same implications emerge unmistakably from the sacrifices at Ilium by Roman generals who carried the banner of Hellenic freedom against Antiochus III. The fable of Troy served Rome in two fundamental ways: it gave her a place in the cultural milieu of the Greek world—and, by the same token, it announced her distinctiveness in that world. Roman intellectuals welcomed incorporation into the cultural legacy of Hellas, but utilized it to sharpen a sense of their own identity.[73] Relocation of the Magna Mater from Mt. Ida to the Palatine advanced that purpose with dramatic display.[74]

---

[72] Bömer, *Rom und Troia* (Baden-Baden, 1951), 39-49, sets the problem too narrowly: why did Rome choose Aeneas rather than Odysseus as her ancestor? And the answer, that Aeneas' *pietas* better suited the Roman temperament, is equally narrow. Bömer fudges the main issue by stressing that certain Hellenic traditions made Greeks of the Trojans themselves. Cf. also Galinsky, *Aeneas, Sicily, and Rome*, 93-102; P. Toohey, *Arethusa*, 17 (1984), 11.

[73] A similar view, reached independently, in Momigliano, *Settimo contributo*, 447, 458-459.

[74] Bömer, *MdI*, 71 (1964), 130-146, argues that Romans generally neglected Cybele after the transferral until the cult received new impetus in the Augustan age, ascribing this to horror at the ecstatic rituals of the cult and its threat to traditional Roman religion. The theory is flawed and unnecessary. In fact, official worship of Cybele persisted in Rome throughout the Republic, the Megalensian Games were an annual event, and the anniversary of her reception an annual celebration; cf. Latte, *Römische Religionsgeschichte*, 261. The Romans even included Cybele's consort Attis in the cult; Th. Köves, *Historia*, 12 (1963), 321-322. Note also Caesar's lavish celebration of the Megalensian games in 65; Dio, 37.8.1. Perhaps an allusion to his supposed descent from Venus and the Trojan forebears of Rome? Cf. Suet. *Iul.* 6; Boyancé, *Latomus*, 13 (1954), 337-342 = *Études*, 195-200. Insofar as the ritual seemed alien to Roman tradition, this was dealt with by excluding citizens from the priesthood itself: praetors later supervised the sacrifices and the games, foreigners performed the unsavory ceremonies; Dion. Hal. 2.19.4-5. That Romans paid little homage to the cult in Asia is understandable enough. The goddess had her shrine on the Palatine. A critique of Bömer, with different arguments, now by Thomas, *ANRW*, II.17.3 (1984), 1508-1512.

The advent of Cybele in Rome, as is plain, carries significant import, well beyond the event itself. It reflects certain key patterns of development: Roman eagerness to become associated with and benefit from the Hellenic religious experience, an articulation of Rome's origin and heritage, and a heightened interest in the international implications of those legendary roots. This helps to place the Magna Mater's arrival in its proper intellectual setting.[75] But it still provides only a portion of the answer. The background is essential, but the timing needs explanation. Why did the summoning of Cybele come in 205, and not earlier or later? Specific circumstances add an indispensable dimension. Two major events in 205 call for special attention: the vigorous debate over carrying the Hannibalic conflict to Africa, and the termination of the First Macedonian War. Their connection with the arrival of Cybele has usually escaped notice. But they serve, upon scrutiny, to place this event in relation to the critical realms of domestic politics, military strategy, foreign policy, and the diplomatic posturing of the Roman state.

First, politics and strategy. The combination, ever present during the Hannibalic war, urged itself upon public attention in an especially forceful way in 205. Young P. Cornelius Scipio, barely thirty years old, arrived in Rome after five spectacularly successful years in Spain. Accomplishments in the Iberian peninsula had demoralized Carthage and eliminated her principal recruiting ground. Scipio's achievement was received with acclaim, and a grateful electorate voted him into the consulship by unanimous choice of all the centuries. An unusually large number crowded to the elections, not only to register their votes for Scipio but to catch a glimpse of the great man.[76] The zeal of the voters, however, surged for reasons beyond just gratitude for past successes. Control of Spain, combined with the critical victory at the Metaurus in 207, brought Rome to the brink of a new phase of the war. One could now contemplate the previously unthinkable: an invasion of Africa. Scipio's record, spirit, and promise made him logical leader of such a venture. The electorate anticipated it—and Scipio broadcast it.[77]

The wishes of the majority were clear. Scipio had been elected to the consulship together with P. Licinius Crassus. That Crassus acted as political ally is generally assumed but an unnecessary and questionable

---

[75] Romans may well have come to know the cult of Cybele in Italy. An archaic inscription indicates that she was worshipped at Locri as early as the 6th century B.C.; M. Guarducci, *Klio*, 52 (1970), 133-138. But importation of the cult from southern Italy, of course, would not serve the diplomatic, political, and propagandistic purposes that loomed so large in 205.

[76] Livy, 28.38.5-8.

[77] Livy, 28.38.9-10, 28.40.1-2; Plut. *Fab.* 25.1-2; Appian, *Pun.* 6.

conjecture.[78] Crassus had a strong following of his own: *pontifex maximus,*
magister equitum, and censor, all before he held the consulship, a man of
wealth and distinction, striking in appearance, eloquent, and scholarly.[79]
What matters is Crassus' current post as *pontifex maximus*. The office prohibited service outside Italy, a fact well known to the electorate. In the
assignment of consular provinces, Sicily went to Scipio, Bruttium to
Crassus, without recourse to the lot. Since Crassus could not go abroad,
the result was foreordained and expected.[80] And Sicily would be jumping-
off point for an invasion of Africa, a prospect also readily anticipated and
then confirmed by the elections.[81]

The stunning rise of Scipio, however, produced repercussions. Success
bred envy and dissent, as ever in Roman aristocratic politics.[82] Scipio's
formidable accomplishments at so tender an age worried his peers—
especially as he had received fanatical adulation in Spain.[83] But larger
issues too were at stake. Debate swirled about the feasibility and
desirability of embarking upon a wholly new phase of the war while Hannibal was still on Italian soil. Q. Fabius Maximus Cunctator, most eminent of Roman senior statesmen and architect of the strategy that had
kept Hannibal at bay, spoke forcefully against a commission for Scipio
to carry the fight to Africa. Fabius produced a raft of arguments, both
strong and weak. He claimed that Hannibal's presence obliged both consular armies to be in Italy and that Roman resources were inadequate to
maintain two widely separated armies—and fleets besides—and he added
some disparaging remarks about Scipio's achievements and ambitions.[84]

---

[78] The hypothesis of political cooperation between Scipio and Crassus predominates
in the scholarship; cf. F. Münzer, *Römische Adelsparteien und Adelsfamilien* (Stuttgart, 1920),
183-190; W. Schur, *Scipio Africanus und die Begründung der römischen Weltherrschaft* (Leipzig,
1927), 118-120; R.M. Haywood, *Studies on Scipio Africanus* (Baltimore, 1933), 53-54;
H.H. Scullard, *Roman Politics, 220-150 BC*² (Oxford, 1973), 75-77; F. Cassola, *I gruppi
politici romani nel III secolo a. C.* (Trieste, 1962), 410.

[79] Livy, 25.5.3-4, 27.5.19, 27.6.17, 30.1.5-6. The fact that Fabius Maximus hoped to
gain his cooperation against Scipio surely implies the absence of any Scipionic-Crassan
alliance; Plut. *Fab.* 25.4-5.

[80] Livy, 28.38.12; Plut. *Fab.* 25.5.

[81] Livy, 28.40.1, 28.40.3-5.

[82] Note that Scipio's request for a triumph for his Spanish victories was declined, on
the grounds that he had held no previous magistracy; Livy, 28.38.2-4; Dio, 17.57.5-6;
Val. Max. 2.8.5. Political opposition doubtless entered into this rejection—though there
may well have been general sentiment against violating the precedent. Scipio, in any
case, did not press the matter. Sources that do report a triumph are plainly erroneous;
Polyb. 11.33.7; Appian, *Iber.* 38; cf. J.S. Richardson, *JRS*, 65 (1975), 52. Scullard,
Roman Politics, 75, needlessly postulates the private celebration of a triumph.

[83] Cf. Polyb. 10.40.2-5; Livy, 27.19.3-6.

[84] The need for both consuls in Italy: Livy, 28.41.2-3, 28.41.7-13, 28.42.12-19;
Appian, *Pun.* 7. Resources: Livy, 28.41.12. Disparagement of Scipio: Livy, 28.42.1-11,
28.42.14-15, 28.42.20-22; Plut. *Fab.* 25.2. The problem of resources, at least, had some
substance to it; Livy, 28.46.4. The speech of Fabius is, of course, Livy's composition,
but there is no reason to doubt its general aptness to the debate.

The essence of the case, however, amounted to a single proposition: Hannibal must be expelled from Italy before Romans give thought to an invasion of Africa.[85] Scipio's strategic plan was equally simple, employing different means to obtain the same ends. The assault on Africa would pull Hannibal out of Italy, relieve the land of Carthaginian presence, and compel the enemy to fight on their own soil.[86]

Battle lines were drawn and the senate sharply divided. A majority in the *curia*, and especially the older among them, inclined toward Fabius.[87] Scipio intended, so report had it, to bring the matter before the people, a prospect which elicited severe rebuke from the eminent Q. Fulvius Flaccus, four times consul and ex-censor.[88] The intention, if such it was, never materialized. The tribunician college intervened to prevent the matter from reaching the assembly: the senate's decision would be final.[89] Discussion ended in a compromise. Scipio received the province of Sicily with an option of crossing to Africa, if he felt it in the interests of state.[90] But his opponents served notice that the task would be no easy one. Scipio was denied permission to recruit forces in Italy.[91] Not that this slowed him down. The consul, in fact, had means of enlisting volunteers.[92] But the issue of taking the war to Africa remained technically unsettled, enmeshed in politics, and of heightened intensity in public discussion.[93]

The issue was unresolved still when the Sibylline Books advised the transfer of the Great Mother to Rome. Is there a connection? Scholarship

---

[85] Livy, 28.41.3-10: *pax ante in Italia quam bellum in Africa sit.* Cf. Appian, *Pun.* 7.

[86] Livy, 28.41.8, 28.42.16, 28.44.9-10; Appian, *Pun.* 7; Zonaras, 9.11.

[87] Livy, 28.43.1; Plut. *Fab.* 25.3.

[88] Livy, 28.45.1-5; cf. 28.40.2.

[89] Livy, 28.45.6-7.

[90] Livy, 28.45.8. Granting the option of going to Africa did not guarantee exercise of that option. Others had been awarded that prerogative in the past, but did not go to Africa; Livy, 27.7.16, 27.22.9.

[91] Livy, 28.45.13; Plut. *Fab.* 25.5-26.2; Appian, *Pun.* 7; Zonaras, 9.11.

[92] Livy, 28.45.13-20; Plut. *Fab.* 25.5; Appian, *Pun.* 7; Zonaras, 9.11. Prohibition on the normal raising of a levy may have been motivated in part by recent difficulties in recruitment; Livy, 25.5.5, 26.35-36, 27.9, 27.38.1-5, 27.38.9.

[93] The contest between Fabius and Scipio was bitter, both personal and political, involving sharp differences on the appropriate strategy for terminating the Hannibalic conflict—as well as on who should receive credit for it. But it is unwarranted to see this as a fundamental ideological clash, Fabius as champion of rural interests with attention confined to Italy, Scipio as advocate of imperialist and commercial expansion in the Mediterranean; as, e.g., Scullard, *Scipio Africanus: Soldier and Politician* (London, 1970), 168-169; Cassola, *I gruppi politici*, 281, 393. A corrective in R. Develin, *The Practice of Politics at Rome, 366-167 B.C.* (Brussels, 1985), 231-237. Observe, for example, that Fabius was willing to encourage Crassus to undertake the African invasions; Plut. *Fab.* 25.4. Dispute over the accuracy of particulars in Livy's narrative continues, but does not affect the points at issue here. See Cassola, *op. cit.*, 282-283, and Develin, *op. cit.*, 233-235, with bibliography.

has largely neglected it. Yet the language in Livy's presentation strikes familiar chords. The Books produced an oracle which promised that if the *mater Idaea* were conveyed to Rome, the alien foe who brought war to Italian shores would be driven from Italy and conquered.[94] That cheering prognostication carries echoes of the heated controversy over how best to remove Hannibal from the land of Italy. One will not conclude that the oracle spoke for one of Rome's political factions or leaders. The board of *decemviri*, through whose interpretation the Books gave their message, had no obvious association with a particular bloc.[95] Nor does the commission of five which was directed to seek out the Magna Mater possess any clear political coloration, none of them an attested ally of Fabius or Scipio.[96] Consultation of the *libri Sibyllini* themselves, however, must be seen in conjunction with an atmosphere both of heady excitement and of anxiety about the prospect of invading enemy shores.[97]

The message of the oracle may not have had partisan bias—but it was subject to partisan interpretation. Its statement, as reported by Livy, that the arrival of Cybele would permit expulsion of Hannibal from Italy, could lend support to the Fabian position. Fabius's speech, in Livy's formulation, had employed the same terminology: *expellere*.[98] And advocates of his strategy doubtless urged the interpretation that Hannibal first be driven out before mounting an expedition against Africa. Yet Scipio's proponents could turn it to their own advantage as well. The Sibylline Books' announcement arrived at about the same time as news brought by Roman envoys who had just returned from Delphi. The latter reported a response forecasting an even greater victory than the Metaurus. Champions of the Scipionic strategy immediately seized upon the combination of pronouncements and interpreted its meaning as

---

[94] Livy, 29.10.5: *quandoque hostis alienigena terrae Italiae bellum intulisset, eum pelli Italia vincique posse, si mater Idaea a Pessinunte Romam advecta foret.*

[95] See the cautious discussion by R. Develin, *Journal of Religious History*, 10 (1978), 17-19, who rightly finds that the evidence on the personnel of *decemviri* does not permit a political interpretation.

[96] For the names, see Livy, 29.11.3. Köves, *Historia*, 12 (1963), 339-340, sees the commission as representing the "Claudian faction" with a decidedly anti-Scipionic flavor. But none of the delegation's activities hampered Scipio's purposes—and the results advanced those purposes. It is tempting to assume that appointment to the commission implied familiarity with or interest in the Greek East; so G. Clemente, *Athenaeum*, 54 (1976), 326-327. Its leader, M. Valerius Laevinus, had commanded Roman forces in the early years of the First Macedonian War. But eastern service is not attested for any of the other legates. And even Laevinus' campaigns may be irrelevant. The embassy's chief task was cooperation with Attalus I. The Pergamene king had engaged in the First Macedonian War, but well after the conclusion of Laevinus' command; Livy, 26.26.4, 26.27.10, 27.29.10. The notice in Jerome, *Chron.* Olymp. 143.1, is erroneous.

[97] Cf. Livy, 29.14.1-4.

[98] Livy, 28.41.3, 28.41.5, 29.10.5.

presaging a triumph for Scipio in Africa and a swift end to the war. They could now with confidence regard the messages from both Delphi and the *libri Sibyllini* as sanctioning Scipio's request for Africa as his *provincia*.[99]

To what extent politics entered into the later stages of the affair is difficult to discern. The five-man delegation to Asia, as we have seen, does not appear to have been the instrument of any party—perhaps, indeed, a deliberate attempt to avoid partisanship. Their stopover in Delphi, however, injected a new element into the reckoning. The oracle advised that when the goddess reached Rome she should be received by the "best man in Rome."[100] The criteria applied for such a designation remain obscure. Livy found nothing in his sources to elucidate the matter and he declined to offer his own conjecture.[101] Other writers understood it in an ethical sense: the man of greatest piety, rectitude, integrity.[102] That was a logical assumption by later authors, but only an assumption, for they had no evidence to go on.[103] The senate, in any case, debated the choice of *vir optimus* and eventually selected young P. Scipio Nasica, cousin of Africanus, a man without public office and not even of quaestorian age.[104] The choice is baffling, but perhaps not inexplicable. A political dimension can hardly be denied. Twelve years earlier, when a vow was made to dedicate a temple to Venus Erycina, the Sibylline Books had assigned the task to the man "of greatest *imperium* in the state." That signal honor went to Q. Fabius Maximus Cunctator, supplying still further prestige and influence.[105] In 204, the nomination as *optimus vir* was ardently coveted as sign of the highest esteem.[106] The naming of Scipio Nasica, Africanus' cousin, certainly kept the Scipionic family in the limelight and gave a further boost to Africanus' ambitions.

Yet politics does not suffice as explanation. Nasica's youth and inexperience proved to be a recommendation rather than a liability. He was

---

[99] Livy, 29.10.4-8: *in eiusdem spei summam conferebant P. Scipionis velut praesagientem animum de fine belli, quod depoposcisset provinciam Africam.*

[100] Livy, 29.11.6-8: *vir optimus Romae*; Val. Max. 8.15.3; Sil. Ital. 17.1-7; Appian, *Hann.* 56; Dio, 57.61; Cic. *De Har. Resp.* 27; Diod. 34/5.33.2.

[101] Livy, 29.14.9.

[102] Val. Max. 7.5.2, 8.15.3: *sanctissimo viro*; Diod. 34/5.33.2-3; Dio, 57.61: εὐσεβὴς καὶ δίκαιος; Juvenal, 3.137-138.

[103] So, rightly, Köves, *Historia*, 12 (1963), 324-325. The inference is taken seriously by J.Vogt, *Hermes*, 68 (1933), 84-92, who believes that the pronouncement at Delphi injected this basically Greek notion of ἄριστος ἀνήρ, otherwise unknown at Rome. But a similar designation is applied in the *elogium* of L. Cornelius Scipio, consul 259; *ILLRP*, 310: *optumo viro*. Vogt, *op. cit.*, 89-90, sets the inscription after 204 and sees it as motivated by the events of that year—a questionable hypothesis. Note the earlier epitaph of A. Atilius Caiatinus; Cic. *De Sen.* 61: *populi primarium fuisse virum.*

[104] Livy, 29.14.8.

[105] Livy, 22.10.10.

[106] Livy, 29.14.7.

in no position to exercise political authority, to challenge or to threaten rivals. That very fact rendered his appointment as *vir optimus* acceptable. The appointment had greater symbolic value than political meaning.[107] The naming of Nasica came in 204, shortly before arrival of the Magna Mater herself. By that time, Africanus' strategic plans had matured and the invasion of Africa was imminent. The issue was no longer whether to go to Africa, but how successful the expedition would be—a source of considerable anxiety.[108] Nasica, as honored welcomer of the goddess whose arrival promised victory and as cousin of Africanus, virtually represented a portent himself. His designation suggested that divine favor stood behind the new direction of the war. The appointment came less on partisan grounds than as a means to alleviate fears, bolster confidence, and imply the backing of the gods. Insofar as political rivals of the Scipios might take it amiss, a woman was named to greet and accompany the goddess, together with Nasica: Claudia Quinta, of a family without connection to and often at odds with the Scipios. Her nomination too was couched in terms of purity and piety, emblematic of the gods' benefaction. The dual appointment took this development beyond the realm of partisan politics.[109] It exemplified closing of the ranks, a show of unity in the leadership.

---

[107] Köves, *Historia* 12 (1963), 322-335, recognizes that Nasica's youth and lack of magisterial experience actually recommended him for the nomination. But he sees the young man as wholly Africanus' creature, a symbolic figurehead for the Scipionic party's emphasis on youth, and even as stand-in for Cybele's consort Attis. The speculation is far-fetched. But political interpretations remain popular; see, most recently, Thomas, *ANRW*, II.17.3 (1984), 1504-1508.

[108] Livy, 29.14.1-4.

[109] Cic. *Pro Cael.* 34; *De Har. Resp.* 27; Diod. 34/5.33.2-3 (who gives the name as Valeria); Livy, 29.14.12. The story of Claudia Quinta became elaborated and romanticized in later accounts, culminating in her miraculous, single-handed tow of the ship which carried the emblem of the Magna Mater, thereby to establish her chastity against popular rumor; Propertius, 4.11.51-52; Ovid, *Fasti*, 4.291-344; Seneca, fr. 80 (Haase); Sil. Ital. 17.23-47; Appian, *Hann.* 56; Herodian, 1.11.3-5. For the development of the tradition, see Graillot, *Le culte de Cybèle*, 60-64; T.P. Wiseman, *Clio's Cosmetics: Three Studies in Greco-Roman Literature* (Leicester, 1979), 94-99; and especially, J. Gérard, *REL*, 58 (1980), 153-175. On Ovid's treatment, see now Jope, *EMC*, 32 (1988), 13-22. For parallels in other legends, with some anthropological speculations, see J. Bremmer, in M.J. Vermaseren, *Studies in Hellenistic Religions* (Leiden, 1979), 9-22. A precedent exists for Claudia Quinta in the person of Sulpicia, *pudicissima matronarum*, named to dedicate the image of Venus Verticordia, by authorization of the Sibylline Books, in 216; Val. Max. 8.15.12; Pliny, *NH*, 7.120; Solinus, 1.126. Rightly noted by Köves, *Historia*, 12 (1963), 340-347, who, however, sees the affair almost exclusively in terms of factional politics. Vogt, *Hermes*, 68 (1933), 86, on no good grounds, rejects the tale of Claudia Quinta altogether; properly refuted by Köves, *op. cit.*, 346, n. 88. On the identity of Claudia Quinta, see Bömer, *MdI*, 71 (1964), 146-151. Her statue was later set up in the temple of the Magna Mater and, as traditions reported, twice miraculously escaped damage in fires; Val. Max. 1.8.11; Tac. *Ann.* 4.64. The view of D. Porte, *Klio*, 66 (1984), 96-97, that the choice of Nasica and Claudia aimed to embarrass the Scipiones and the Claudii is unreasonable.

Magna Mater arrived at Ostia in 204, to be greeted in grand ceremony by Scipio Nasica and by Claudia Quinta, at the head of the state's most esteemed matrons. The trip to Rome brought out the crowds to welcome the image of Cybele with gifts and to pray for her beneficence.[110] It was a carefully orchestrated scene. And it culminated in the delivery of the goddess' image to the temple of Victory on the Palatine.[111] The symbolic significance stands out plainly. The installation of Cybele in the temple of Victory came at a time very close to the embarkation of Scipio Africanus for the Carthaginian homeland. Divine favor, endorsed both by the Sibylline Books and by Delphi, would now smile upon that momentous expedition that promised to terminate at last the protracted struggle with Carthage. What had begun as a partisan conflict over strategy and leadership ended as overwhelming sentiment for the Scipionic invasion. The Great Mother played her part in that evolution. The prospect of bringing her to Rome found its way into the debate on transforming the war, a spiritual support on both sides. And her arrival coincided with a display of national solidarity, symbolized in her joint reception by Scipio Nasica and Claudia Quinta.

The year 205 also marked an event of magnitude across the Adriatic: the conclusion of the First Macedonian War. That contest had engaged the participation or attention of a large part of the Greek world. A coalition developed against Philip of Macedon, promoted and encouraged by Rome. Philip had framed alliance with Carthage in 215, and his encroachment upon Greek cities near the straits of Otranto brought Roman resistance. The western power cast about for allies in Hellas, induced the Aetolian League into cooperation in 212 or 211, and through that medium brought a number of states into action against Macedon. Rome's purpose was simple enough: to mobilize Hellenic resources which could keep Philip at a distance while she concentrated her energies against Hannibal. Six years of erratic, sometimes ruthless, but generally inconclusive fighting followed. The Romans, preoccupied with a Carthaginian war in Italy, paid only limited attention to the eastern front. After the first full year of campaigning, Rome reduced her contingents and by 207 her military engagement had nearly ceased altogether. For the Roman senate this was a war fought mainly by proxy. So long as her allies stayed in the fight, occupying Philip, Rome's purposes were served.[112]

---

[110] Livy, 29.14.10-14; Ovid, *Fasti*, 4.343-347.
[111] Livy, 29.14.14.
[112] Cf. Appian, *Mac.* 3.1: ὅτι Ῥωμαίοις συμφέρει πολεμεῖν Αἰτωλοὺς Φιλίππῳ.

The Aetolians bore the main burden against Macedon, with increasing pleas for Roman aid and increasing irritation at failing to get it. Aetolian patience snapped in spring, 205, and the League concluded its own peace treaty with Philip. Only then did the Romans swing into action with some vigor. The senate dispatched a new army across the Adriatic, 11,000 men and 35 ships. Not that commitment to the war effort had expanded. Rome made a show of force in hopes of sabotaging peace negotiations and inducing Aetolia back into the fray. But it was too late. The Aetolians held to their agreement with Philip. No other Greek states were both capable of and willing to carry on the contest, and Rome could not afford the resources to continue it. In 205 she concluded the Peace of Phoenice that ended the First Macedonian War.[113] The whole experience had been unsatisfactory, frustrating — and generally ignominious.

The Peace of Phoenice ended the stalemate, though hardly in Rome's favor. The warring parties were brought together through the mediation of the Epirotes. Philip and Rome made mutual concessions, but Rome's were the larger in terms of reputation and image. The king yielded up one Illyrian tribe and three towns; the Romans conceded Macedonian control over Atintania and other territory in Illyria for whose security they had earlier claimed responsibility.[114] Release from this irritating and distracting contest was no doubt welcome, but the costs in prestige proved to be high. Rome's armies had gained notoriety for ruthlessness, giving rise to Greek charges of barbarism.[115] Worse still, the Romans had not lived up to expectations, their involvement had been erratic and fruitless, they had encouraged others into the fight, then abandoned them to take their losses. Criticism could be anticipated, and it came. Rome was perceived—not without reason—as having used her allies as cannon fodder and having betrayed their trust.[116] The image had been tarnished.

Rome would, of course, have preferred a different outcome. None was possible. The debate over a crossing to Africa and the conviction that Hannibal had to be dealt with decisively made it quite unthinkable to go

---

[113] Full discussions of the war may be found in Holleaux, *Rome, la Grèce*, 213-257; F.W. Walbank, *Philip V of Macedon* (Cambridge, 1940), 84-107. A summary of Roman involvement and intentions, with references, in E.S. Gruen, *The Hellenistic World and the Coming of Rome* (Berkeley and Los Angeles, 1984), II, 377-381. A different view now in J.W. Rich, *PCPS*, 30 (1984), 126-180.

[114] Livy, 29.12.8-13; cf. Gruen, *Hellenistic World*, II, 381.

[115] Cf. Polyb. 9.37.5-8, 9.39.1-3, 11.5.4-8; Livy, 31.29.12-15, 32.22.10; Appian, *Mac.* 7.

[116] Livy, 29.12.1: *Aetolos desertos ab Romanis, cui uni fidebant auxilio*; 31.29.3: *inutili societate Romana*; 31.31.19, 32.21.17. Cf. Polyb. 10.25.3; but see Rich, *PCPS*, 30 (1984), 134-135.

on fighting Philip without allies. But Romans were sensitive to their loss of face in Hellas, especially at a time when leaders and intellectuals were expanding cultural connections. It may, therefore, not be too bold to suggest that the quest for the Magna Mater, coming near the time of the Peace of Phoenice, had the Roman image abroad very much in view. The goddess would give external sanction to Rome's crusade against Carthage and the final push to eliminate Hannibal, thus indirectly justifying a withdrawal from the eastern front. An embrace of the widespread and influential cult might help to advertise Roman sensitivity to foreign traditions and to restore a sagging reputation.[117] Such aims could also be best implemented through conspicuous cooperation with a Greek state of high repute and a professed champion of Hellenic causes—namely Pergamum and her ruler Attalus I.

Attalus had his own reasons for cooperation. He too had been a participant in the First Macedonian War, but not a very vigorous or effective one. And he was a man who jealously guarded his reputation. The fact is amply demonstrated by the epigraphic and artistic monuments erected to commemorate his earlier victories over the Gauls.[118] The Roman alliance with Aetolia against Philip permitted participation on equal footing of *amicitia* with the friends of both partners. Among those specifically envisioned as a potential combatant was Attalus. The Pergamene king's connection was with Aetolia, not Rome, a connection that stretched back to some time before 219 when Attalus helped finance Aetolian fortifications.[119] His entrance into the war came on Aetolian invitation, but he kept his own interests to the forefront. The League presented him with the highest token of its esteem by electing him as *strategos* in 210, and then gave him further inducement by selling him the island of Aegina for a mere 30 talents. Attalus finally brought his fleet into Aegean waters in 209, basing his ships on Aegina, but active engagement in the war confined itself to part of the campaigning season of 208. When he learned of attacks on Pergamene territory by Prusias I of Bithynia, Attalus promptly pulled out his forces to protect his own

---

[117] On the widespread extent of the cult in the east, see Vermaseren, *Cybele and Attis*, 13-37. Roman concern for the religious sensibilities of western Greeks as well is indicated by the severe senatorial response to Q. Pleminius' plundering of the temple of Proserpina at Locri at about this very time; Livy, 29.8.9-11, 29.18.2-9, 29.19.5-8, 29.21.4, 29.21.12, 29.22.7-9; Appian, *Hann.* 55.

[118] Discussions in D. Magie, *Roman Rule in Asia Minor* (Princeton, 1950), II, 737-739, n. 20; Hansen, *Attalids*, 26-38; R.B. McShane, *The Foreign Policy of the Attalids of Pergamum* (Urbana, 1964), 58-65; Allen, *Attalid Kingdom*, 28-35, 195-199.

[119] Polyb. 4.65.6-7; cf. McShane, *Foreign Policy*, 101, n. 29.

kingdom.[120] The king's ambitions in the west have often been debated. He certainly welcomed the acquisition of Aegina and the spoils of war. But larger schemes of territorial expansion or a maritime empire remain speculative. Attalus enjoyed the acclaim afforded by election as Aetolia's *strategos* and as protector of Greeks against Macedon.[121] Reputation mattered. Involvement in the war itself, however, was brief and tangential. Prusias' invasion preempted his options, and Attalus played no further part in the contest against Philip. His reputation had not been matched by his accomplishments.

At conclusion of the First Macedonian War, Attalus, like Rome, had reason to rebuild connections and reestablish credentials. He gained inclusion as an *adscriptus* to the Peace of Phoenice in 205, on the side of Rome.[122] Drawing closer to Rome might have potential benefits. The outcome of Attalus' war with Bithynia remains uncertain. And the king had other rivals in western Asia Minor as well, including the formidable Antiochus III of Syria who, as we now know, replaced Attalus' influence with his own on Teos in this year or the next.[123] It was an appropriate time to reconfirm prestige in Greece. The affair of the Great Mother provided an ideal vehicle for collaboration.

The interests of Rome and Attalus converged on Delphi. The Pergamene's association with that sacred shrine was of long standing. His treasury financed the building of a terrace, with a small portico, adjoining the temple of Apollo and dedicated to the god.[124] Quite apart from funds, Attalus sent skilled workers to help implement the building projects.[125] In the First Macedonian War itself Pergamene troops garrisoned the Phocian town of Lilaea near Delphi and afforded it protection, for which they were subsequently rewarded through a series of honorary decrees set up in the sacred city.[126] And Rome, as we have seen, cultivated Delphi in this same period, dedicating a golden bowl to commemorate defeat of the Gauls in 222, sending the mission of Fabius

---

[120] Livy, 28.7.10; Dio, 17.58. On Attalus in the First Macedonian War generally, see Hansen, *Attalids*, 47-50; McShane, *Foreign Policy*, 105-110; Gruen, *Hellenistic World*, II, 530.

[121] Holleaux, *Rome, la Grèce*, 204-208, sees insatiable territorial ambition on Attalus' part. More restrained and generous views in McShane, *Foreign Policy*, 100-109; Allen, *Attalid Kingdom*, 66-69.

[122] Livy, 29.12.14.

[123] P. Herrmann, *Anatolia*, 9 (1965), 29-159. The rivalry is unduly minimized by Allen, *Attalid Kingdom*, 47-55. The critical lines of the document are I, 17-20, 32-34, 47-48.

[124] *Syll*³ 523; see R. Flacelière, *Les Aitoliens à Delphes* (Paris, 1937), 407, #38b; G. Roux, *BCH*, 76 (1952), 141-196; Allen, *Attalid Kingdom*, 70-71.

[125] *SGDI*, 2001.

[126] FDelphes, II, 4, 132-135; *ISE*, 81.

Pictor after Cannae, and depositing some of the spoils of war that derived from victory at the Metaurus.[127] Delphi played a central role in the Magna Mater episode, a role quite probably arranged in concert by Rome and Attalus. Roman envoys who had delivered the spoils of battle to Delphi returned with the most promising prognostications from Apollo about victories to come. Their arrival coincided conveniently with the consultation of the Sibylline Books which advised the transfer of the Great Mother—a coincidence that was hardly accidental.[128] When the senate took steps to bring about that transfer, an intermediary seemed appropriate. The suggestion of a contact with Attalus, Rome's *amicus* in the war on Philip, naturally arose. Delphi confirmed the proposal. Rome's delegation to the East stopped at the holy city, there receiving assurance that their task would be accomplished through the assistance of the Pergamene monarch—as indeed it was. Such is the account in Livy.[129]

A variant occurs in Ovid's *Fasti*. In that narrative, the *libri Sibyllini* gave an ambiguous and obscure pronouncement requiring recourse to Delphi for clarification. The oracle made matters explicit: the Great Mother was to be summoned from Mt. Ida. Romans then sought the aid of Attalus who controlled the region, but the king held back. Divine intervention broke the deadlock. The earth rumbled and the goddess insisted that transfer to Rome was meet and proper. Attalus, duly terrified, yielded and released the Magna Mater for her voyage to the west.[130] The tale is romanticized, perhaps altogether fictitious. But perhaps not. Attalus saw the value of collaboration with Rome. Delphic proclamations sanctioned and legitimized it. Yet the king, ever sensitive to his own image among Greeks, would not wish to be perceived as accepting dictates from Rome. The scene described by Ovid may well be a staged routine. Attalus deferred not to the western power but only to the goddess. In any event, prior orchestration by Pergamum and Rome seems an inescapable conclusion. Delphi provided the divine authorization for a prearranged plan which would advertise Attalus' patronage and elevate Roman prestige in Hellas.[131]

Association between Rome and Pergamum was asserted still again at the Peace of Phoenice. Attalus figures prominently among the signatories

---

[127] See above pp. 9-10.
[128] Livy, 29.10.4-6.
[129] Livy, 29.11.1-7. Cf. Val. Max. 8.15.3; Dio, 57.61.
[130] Ovid, *Fasti*, 4.255-272.
[131] Scholarly efforts to manipulate the texts have been largely misguided. Kuiper, *Mnemosyne*, 30 (1902), 280-281, finds Livy's report of a decision to seek Attalus' help inconsistent with his notice that Delphi made the suggestion, thus discrediting the whole narrative—an extreme and needless conclusion. Delphi, well primed, gave divine confir-

to the treaty on the side of Rome. His name, in fact, stood second on the list, behind one people only: the citizens of Ilium.[132] This inclusion is telling and significant—but also controversial. Scholarship for the most part has impugned the appearance of the Ilians as false, a creation of later annalistic propaganda: Ilium had not fought in the war, hence has no place in the peace.[133] That approach, however, misses the point. In fact, Greek practice allowed interested parties who had been neutrals or noncombatants to affix their signatures as *adscripti* to a peace treaty and thus receive its protection.[134] The authenticity of Ilium's inclusion in the pact can be asserted with some confidence in light of this investigation. The city took pride of place among Rome's *amici*, juxtaposed to Attalus I of Pergamum. The symbolic value of the juxtaposition should now be clear enough. Ilium's appearance in the Peace of Phoenice made conspicuous Rome's assertion of her Trojan origins, her ties to Hellenic traditions, as well as her distinctiveness within those traditions. Attalus, suzerain of the Troad and instrumental figure in transmitting the Great Mother of Mt. Ida to Rome, thus holds his appropriate spot adjacent to Ilium in the Peace of Phoenice. That document reinforces and underscores the interrelationship of Rome, Troy, and Pergamum, an interrelationship announced in the same year through the transplantation of the cult of Cybele.[135] The rather sorry conclusion of the First Macedonian War was

---

mation to the idea already circulated in Rome. For Schmidt, *Kultübertragungen*, 20-21, the narratives of Livy and Ovid are mutually contradictory and one or the other must be chosen—though he declined to choose. But his notion that the advice to seek out the goddess must have come from either the Sibylline Books or Delphi, but not both, has no force. In fact, the accounts of Livy and Ovid bring both of these elements into play in each narrative, though in somewhat different ways. The fact that Diod. 34/5.33.2, Appian, *Hann.* 56, and Sil. Ital. 17.1-7 mention only the Books in their abbreviated versions hardly counts as evidence against Delphic involvement; *pace* Graillot, *Le culte de Cybèle*, 51-52. Graillot does, however, recognize the collaborative enterprise of Pergamum and Rome, though he does not probe the matter very far; *op. cit.*, 50-51.

[132] Livy, 29.12.14. The others were the Illyrian prince Pleuratus, Nabis of Sparta, the Eleans, Messenians, and Athenians.

[133] Bibliography on this subject is immense. A valuable summary of scholarly opinions may be found in W. Dahlheim, *Struktur und Entwicklung der römischen Völkerrechts im 3. und 2. Jahrhundert v. Chr.* (Munich, 1968), 210-211, n. 75, and see now C. Habicht, *Studien zur Geschichte Athens in hellenistischer Zeit* (Göttingen, 1982), 138-141.

[134] The thesis was argued vigorously and convincingly long ago by E. Bickermann, *RevPhil*, 61 (1935), 59-68—a thesis that holds independently of his misguided attempt to characterize the Peace of Phoenice as a κοινὴ εἰρήνη. Dahlheim, *Struktur und Entwicklung*, 209-220, fails to establish the proposition that signatories must have been combatants.

[135] Even those scholars who accept the genuineness of Ilium's appearance among the *adscripti* have failed to explore the implications. So, McShane, *Foreign Policy*, 111-115, sees Ilium essentially as a dependent of Attalus and her inclusion in the treaty as Attalus' doing—a one-sided (and wrong-sided) analysis. Ilium, first and foremost, represented the Roman heritage. Habicht, *Studien*, 140, rather surprisingly, asserts that Ilium's insignificance makes it unthinkable that Rome would have wished to include her. Such an approach cuts away the whole cultural dimension of this affair.

here counterbalanced by a proud expression of the links that connected Rome to Hellenic legends and that associated her with a champion of Hellenic traditions.

The coming of the Magna Mater illuminates a number of central themes in Roman cultural and political history of the 3rd century BC. It offers a focal point for long-term developments in Rome's religious attitudes, for the evolution of the Trojan fables, for the intellectual associations and diplomatic connections with the Greek world, for the molding of public opinion and the building of morale through recourse to the divine, and for the refurbishing of a national image that had sustained damage in the international community. The affair provides good illustration of Rome's willingness to reach out to alien conventions to help shape her own: the consultation of the Sibylline Books, the summoning of foreign deities, the resort to Delphi. It represents adaptations to Hellenic intellectual traditions through embrace of and elaboration on the myth of Trojan origins. And it gives insight into the cultivation of relationships with Hellenic communities, most notably the concerting of efforts with Attalus of Pergamum.

Yet Roman receptivity to the culture of Hellas had its limits. This was no mere enthusiasm for or eager absorption of an eastern heritage. Rome stopped short of absorption. Her own interests took precedence. Implications arising out of the transfer of Cybele's cult punctuate that central point most revealingly. Romans adopted the myth of Trojan origins rather than other reconstructions of their past, for through that myth they could do more than link themselves to Hellas—they could differentiate themselves from her. Cybele's attraction, at least in part, lay in the fact that, besides offering a means of collaborating with Pergamum, she represented the protectress of Aeneas and the eastern heritage of Rome.

Military and political elements played their role as well. The affair served to focus more clearly the alternatives faced when contemplating a dramatic new turn in the Hannibalic war and to give spiritual reassurance, the fortifying of a united will, once that turn had been chosen. Similarly, the arrival of the Great Mother, coming at the time of Rome's chagrined conclusion of war with Macedon, supplied a means to resuscitate reputation and enhance image in the international community. Pergamum benefited, as did Ilium and Delphi, and indeed the prestige of Cybele herself. But Rome pursued those associations less for their advantage than for her own. Acquisition of the Magna Mater exemplifies Rome's solicitation of Hellenic culture to advance her own political, diplomatic, and military purposes, to elevate her international prestige, and to sharpen her sense of national identity.

CHAPTER TWO

THE BACCHANALIAN AFFAIR

The revels of Dionysus had captured the fancy of worshippers through much of the Mediterranean world by the 2nd century B.C. Adherents of the god could be found not only in Greece, Macedon, Thrace, and Asia Minor, but in the west as well. The cult spread to Sicily, Magna Graecia, Etruria, and even to Rome herself. In the form of Liber or Bacchus, Dionysus gained popularity and notoriety, his rites celebrated in numerous communities and regions of Italy. The government had accepted Liber in Rome and tolerated him in Italy.

But only up to a point. In the year 186 B.C. scandal erupted and everything changed. Roman officialdom reversed itself with suddenness and without warning. The full power of the state was directed against the Bacchanalian worship, dissolving its gatherings, persecuting its leaders, hunting down its adherents, and meting out severe punishments to suppress its rites. The action came like a thunderbolt, scattering the faithful and terrifying sympathizers. Devotees of the cult can only have felt shock and horror at a policy that seemed incomprehensible.

The "Bacchanalian affair" has generated countless discussions and abundant speculation. Yet understanding remains limited and explanations inadequate. The event resists conventional categorization. The extraordinary character of the episode, the unexpected and unprecedented behavior of the Roman establishment, demands special attention. The affair, spectacular and notorious, also bears in its train larger implications—political, institutional, religious, and cultural. It merits a new assessment.

First, the ancient testimony. Almost all of it resides in Livy's narrative—a riveting and fascinating tale. The rites of Bacchus, he avers, had reached Rome via Etruria, having been brought to that region by an obscure Greek who professed expertise in sacrifice and prophecy and who conducted secret nocturnal rituals. The religion spread in alarming fashion, an excuse for clandestine meetings with private initiations, combining men and women, promoting sexual license, and providing the organization for a variety of illicit activities ranging from forgery to murder. Cries of the victims were drowned out by the drums, cymbals, and wailings of the devotees. The cult permeated Rome like a foul disease.[1]

---

[1] Livy, 39.8.3-39.9.1.

Yet the authorities remained unaware of it, so Livy asserts. The city's size and tolerance permitted the contagion to expand undetected.[2] A fortuitous combination of events was required to capture the attention of the government. That premise shapes the romantic story retailed by Livy—replete with innocent and mistreated youth, wicked stepfather, noble prostitute, and patriotic Roman consul. The narrative may be briefly recapitulated. The mother and stepfather of young P. Aebutius sought to cheat him of his inheritance by cajoling him into the initiation rites of the Bacchic worship. The youth naively concurred, but confided his intentions to his devoted mistress, the courtesan Hispala Faecenia, who dissuaded him by lurid tales of Bacchic felonies. Harsh recriminations followed at home, driving Aebutius to seek the counsel of his elderly aunt Aebutia who referred him to no less a figure than the consul of 186, Sp. Postumius Albinus. The cast of characters in the drama grows apace. Postumius resorted to his own mother-in-law Sulpicia to check on Aebutius' story through his aunt. Two successive consular audiences followed. Aebutia appeared, at Sulpicia's request, and confirmed her nephew's plight. And then the freedwoman Hispala obeyed Sulpicia's summons, faced the stern demands of Postumius for full revelation, broke down under questioning, and finally poured out details about the sinister activities of the Bacchanals. She ascribed to them every form of wickedness and crime, nocturnal orgies, homosexual excesses, frenzied rituals, the initiation of young boys, and the murder and sacrifice of objectors. Having unburdened herself, the freedwoman and her lover were both held in safe custody on orders of the consul.[3]

Postumius now had the testimony he needed to expose the Bacchanalian menace to the senate. The revelations, so Livy reports, sent the *patres* into panic. They promptly mandated a *quaestio extra ordinem*, authorizing the consuls to seek out Bacchic priests not only in Rome but in the *fora* and *conciliabula* and to place them in custody, to send instructions throughout Italy prohibiting Bacchic assemblages, and to institute proceedings against all initiates who combined or conspired to perpetrate crimes. The consuls implemented the directives immediately. Subordinates were ordered to arrest the priests and to distribute guards around the city. Postumius then addressed a *contio* in which he emphasized the threat posed by an alien religion, with members in the thousands, given to fanaticism and debauchery, seducing innocent youths into villainy, and conspiring both to undermine traditional worship and to seize power

---

[2] Livy, 39.9.1.
[3] Livy, 39.9.2-39.14.3.

in the state.[4] Senatorial decrees were published which detailed procedures for arrests and hearings, encouraged informers, and prohibited the concealment of fugitives. Word of the senate's decisions and consular orders reached much of Italy, provoking panicked flights, numerous arrests, summary judicial proceedings, and even suicide. More than seven thousand men and women, it was announced, had some involvement in Bacchanalian activities. Known leaders were placed in custody, initiates who had pledged themselves to the cult but refrained from criminal acts were held in chains, those who had actually engaged in felonies suffered the capital penalty. The latter constituted a majority.[5]

The methods employed had been brutal and devastating. But there were limits. The consuls had orders to root out all forms of Bacchic worship, and a *senatus consultum* banned the religion forever in Rome and Italy. Exceptions, however, were allowed. Ancient altars or religious images of venerable age gained exemption from destruction. And an individual worshipper too could secure permission to continue his devotions, so long as he pleaded his case to the urban praetor, received approval in a senatorial meeting with at least one hundred members present, and participated in a rite with no more than five persons and without a priest or overseer of sacrifices.[6] The *patres* thus showed leniency—but only to assert control. Proceedings concluded with rewards conspicuously voted by senate and assembly and bestowed upon P. Aebutius and Hispala Faecenia whose information had led to the unmasking of the Bacchanalian *coniuratio*.[7]

Persecution continued beyond the year 186. L. Postumius as propraetor in 184 exercised sway in Tarentum and carried through the *quaestio* on the Bacchanals in that region. He summoned those who had fled to the area, condemned some, and sent others to Rome under arrest.[8] Further investigations took place in Apulia in 182 and 181 to control Bacchanalian activities and to maintain Roman authority over them.[9] The cult now seemed stilled.

Such is the evidence of Livy. Certain salient points recur in an official document. A bronze tablet found at Tiriolo in Bruttium records a letter of the consuls of 186 conveying the substance of the *senatus consultum de Bacchanalibus*.[10] The text coincides in welcome fashion with Livy's report

[4] Livy, 39.14.3-39.16.13.
[5] Livy, 39.17.1-39.18.6.
[6] Livy, 39.18.7-9.
[7] Livy, 39.19.1-7.
[8] Livy, 39.41.6-7; cf. 39.29.8-9.
[9] Livy, 40.19.9-10.
[10] *ILLRP*, 511.

of steps taken by the *patres* to curb Bacchanalian activities. It is addressed to the *foederati*, in fulfillment of the senatorial directive that edicts be sent throughout the Italian peninsula.[11] The initial clauses ban Bacchic shrines and forbid participation in Bacchic rites, except under application to the urban praetor and consent by the senate in a meeting with at least one hundred members present. Those provisions parallel Livy's account and reinforce it.[12] The document then offers a more precise formulation than is provided by the historian: no man is permitted to serve as priest of the cult and neither man nor woman may act as administrative overseer or official; a common fund is prohibited; and devotees are forbidden to exchange oaths, vows, pledges, or promises.[13] The inscription further bars any secret ceremonies, and requires public or private rites to obtain permission of the *praetor urbanus* and the senate with a quorum of one hundred or more.[14] Livy conveys the information that, even when such permission is granted, the worshippers can be no more than five in number. Greater detail comes from the bronze tablet which specifies a maximum of two men and three women.[15]

The remainder of the edict offers a conjunction of directives. It orders public proclamation of the contents for a *trinum nundinum*, it reports the senatorial decision that violations of the edict will bring capital penalty, it provides for publication on a bronze tablet, and it commands immediate dismantling of Bacchic establishments.[16] Those clauses, oddly

---

[11] *ILLRP*, 511, lines 2-3: *quei foideratei esent*; cf. Livy, 39.14.7: *per totam Italiam edicta mitti*. The term *foideratei* here has been interpreted not as "allies" but as "those who belong to the Bacchanalian cult" or "those who are engaged in conspiracy against the state"; H. Rudolph, *Stadt und Staat im römischen Italien* (Leipzig, 1935), 162, n. 1; L. Fronza, *Annali Triestini*, 17 (1947), 214-215; H. Galsterer, *Herrschaft und Verwaltung im republikanischen Italien* (Munich, 1976), 169. Cf. the remarks of M. Gelzer, *Hermes*, 7 (1936), 278, n. 4. The hypothesis is unjustified. The latter part of the document is unmistakably addressed to local officials who are to proclaim and post the senate's orders in public and to dissolve the Bacchic meetings; lines 22-30. And there is no reason to doubt that the same holds of the earlier portion. Restrictions imposed by the decree applied to Latins and *socii*, as well as to citizens; lines 7-8.

[12] *ILLRP*, 511, lines 3-9; cf. Livy, 39.18.7-9. On the meaning of *Bacanal habuise*, see E. Fraenkel, *Hermes*, 67 (1932), 369-372; a less plausible interpretation by Fronza, *Annali Triestini*, 17 (1947), 218-219.

[13] *ILLRP*, 511, lines 10-14. An abbreviated and imprecise report of these provisions appears in Livy, 39.18.9: *neu qua pecunia communis neu quis magister sacrorum aut sacerdos esset.*

[14] *ILLRP*, 511, lines 15-18. The exceptions allowed here apply to participation in the ceremonies, not to the preceding clauses regarding sacred officials, the common fund, and exchange of vows; so, rightly, J.J. Tierney, *Proceedings of the Royal Irish Academy*, 51 (1947), 92.

[15] Livy, 39.18.9; *ILLRP*, 511, lines 19-22. The inscription allows for exceptions here as well, under the same procedures. This may refer only to the proportion of men and women rather than any flexibility in the total number; cf. Tierney, *Proceedings of the Royal Irish Academy*, 51 (1947), 92.

[16] *ILLRP*, 511, lines 22-30.

juxtaposed, with syntactical peculiarities and a surprising termination, have given rise to scholarly dispute and unsettled controversy. Various hypotheses see a deliberate shifting of the provisions by a Bruttian official responsible for the last part of the inscription, a combination of clauses deriving from two or three separate senatorial meetings, and ascription of the capital penalty to offenses committed in the past rather than to future infractions—to mention but a few.[17] The debates do not, however, affect our investigation. That there should be some discrepancies between the document and Livy's narrative is unsurprising. The difference in genres alone assures it. Livy omitted or abbreviated certain resolutions, the bronze tablet perhaps combined decisions made at more than one senatorial session. But discrepancies, in fact, are minor. The two sources buttress one another.[18] Official policy, proclaimed throughout the peninsula, had mounted an assault on the disciples of Dionysus.

No other source provides information of any substance. But persecution of the Bacchants left its mark on the tradition. Later writers ignore

---

[17] The fullest and most provocative philological analysis was provided by Fraenkel, *Hermes* 67 (1932), 369-396. Fraenkel's idea that a local official in Bruttium revised the consular letter to direct it more pointedly toward his fellow Bruttians was endorsed by W. Krause, *Hermes*, 71 (1936), 216-218, but has found little favor. Rightly so. Local leaders were not likely to tamper with the Roman wording or redistribute clauses to their taste. No parallels can be found, and there are good examples of drafters adhering to Roman formulations. See J. Keil, *Hermes*, 68 (1933), 309-312; Gelzer, *Hermes*, 71 (1936), 278-280; Fronza, *Annali Triestini*, 17 (1947), 210-213. Livy records two separate senatorial sessions which passed resolutions regarding the Bacchants; 39.14.3-9, 39.18.7-9. Provisions on the inscription reflect both those meetings. Gelzer, *op. cit.*, 280-283, concluded that there was but one sitting, wrongly divided into two by Livy. By contrast, Krause, *op. cit.*, 215-218, postulated three separate sittings, arbitrarily distributing the clauses of the inscription among them. It is best not to meddle with the Livian text here. A *quaestio* was authorized in the first meeting, more detailed directives on sanctions and control of the Bacchants in the second. Cf. S. Accame, *RivFilol*, 66 (1938), 226; Tierney, *Proceedings of the Royal Irish Academy*, 51 (1947), 99-104; A. Dihle, *Hermes*, 90 (1962), 376-379. The sentence in the midst of the inscription's last portion regarding a *sententia* of the senate and referring to the imposition of capital punishment upon offenders is awkwardly placed and puzzling; *ILLRP*, 511, lines 23-25: *eorum sententia ita fuit: sei ques esent, quei arvorsum ead fecisent, quam suprad scriptum est, eeis rem caputalem faciendam censuere.* Fraenkel, *op. cit.*, 373-376, 389-395, argued that this clause must originally have stood near the head of the *s.c.* and that it applied to past offenses rather than to future ones. That position was effectively challenged by Keil, *op. cit.*, 310-311; A.H. McDonald, *JRS*, 34 (1944), 30, n. 146; Fronza, *op. cit.*, 221-222. The consuls' task was to root out present offenders and discourage future ones. Both groups were encompassed by the sanctions. When the consuls imposed the death penalty, in fact, they did so on the basis of the type of crime, not the time of commission; Livy, 39.18.3-4.

[18] Cf. Accame, *RivFilol*, 66 (1938), 225-234; McDonald, *JRS*, 34 (1944), 28-31; P.V. Cova, *Athenaeum*, 52 (1974), 84-85, n. 6. To be sure, the document, or the substance thereof, may have been reported by Livy's source, in which case it cannot strictly be regarded as altogether independent testimony. But Livy does not reproduce the text, and has much else besides. The combination of sources takes on enhanced value.

the details but recall the episode as a prime example of Roman severity, a determined campaign to rid Italy of the alien, subversive cult.[19] With announcements of its intentions and its demands posted throughout the land, the government had ostensibly declared a crusade.

What provoked it? An intriguing and puzzling question which has yet to receive a satisfactory answer. The matter is more difficult and complicated than most have been willing to acknowledge. What needs to be stressed is just how extraordinary and exceptional are the features of this episode in Roman cultural and institutional history.

First and foremost, a Roman onslaught against a foreign religion is itself strikingly uncharacteristic. Rome had usually been hospitable to deities and cults from abroad, an attribute attested from early in her history.[20] The momentum picked up in the 3rd century as Romans both expanded their horizons and faced severe crises at home that called for divine assistance. The Sibylline Books, themselves an alien religious force embraced by Roman officialdom, provided guidance in the adoption of gods and rites from abroad. Rome imported Aesculapius, Dis Pater and Proserpina, and Venus Erycina, established ties with Apollo at Delphi, and acquired the sacred stone of the Great Mother from Asia Minor. Far from being suspicious of foreign cults, the Romans welcomed and exploited them. The process included even assimilation of certain Dionysiac characteristics by the Italian god Liber, enshrined from an early date on the Aventine in Rome.[21] The more ecstatic "Bacchic" features did not, of course, enjoy official sanction. And it can be argued that Rome made a distinction between rites admitted under public auspices and those which entered without governmental endorsement. Nevertheless, no clear precedent exists for outright assault on this or any other foreign sect.

An earlier event, to be sure, appears to provide background to the Bacchanalian affair. The frustrations and anxieties of the Hannibalic War had driven many Romans to seek new religious outlets and to cultivate alien priests and prophets. The matter came to a head in 213, when com-

---

[19] Cic. De Leg. 2.37: quo in genere severitatem maiorum senatus vetus auctoritas de Bacchanalibus et consulum exercitu adhibito quaestio animadversioque declarat; Val. Max. 6.3.7: consimili severitate senatus...mandavit ut de his, quae sacris Bacchanalium inceste usae fuerant, inquirerent; cf. 1.3.1; Tert. Apol. 6; Ad Nat. 1.10; Aug. CD, 6.9, 18.13.

[20] W. Warde Fowler, The Religious Experience of the Roman People (London, 1911), 223-269; K. Latte, Römische Religionsgeschichte (Munich, 1960), 148-194; G. Dumézil, Archaic Roman Religion (Chicago, 1970), II, 407-431; J. Bayet, Histoire politique et psychologique de la religion romaine[2] (Paris, 1969), 120-127.

[21] A. Bruhl, Liber Pater (Paris, 1953), 13-29; R. Rousselle, CJ, 82 (1987), 193-195, with bibliography.

plaints about rampant foreign superstitions and about crowds of gullible devotees in the city provoked the government into action. A senatorial decree authorized the urban praetor to call a halt to this alarming development. The praetor's edict then directed that all written works containing prophecies, prayers, or instructions on sacrifice be surrendered to him for confiscation and that no one offer sacrifice in a public or sacred place in accordance with any unknown or foreign ritual.[22] On the face of it, the action taken here supplies a parallel or serves as precursor for the suppression of Bacchants. But close inspection shows that the similarities pale before the differences. The edict of 213 addressed itself only to the city, not to the Italian municipalities and countryside. And even within that range one may question its effectiveness. How many men and women would voluntarily bring all sacred writings of foreign derivation to the praetor? No provisions are recorded for search and seizure or for enforcement. Indeed, the results go unrecorded altogether. Livy ignores the matter thereafter. Certainly there is nothing to compare with the consular investigations, judicial hearings, armed intervention, arrests and executions that accompanied the Bacchanalian episode. By that measure, the senate's actions in 213 were mild, probably designed to alleviate public pressure and to reestablish order in the city.[23] We hear of no further repercussions. The assault on the Bacchants came more than a quarter century later. Rome was not at that time in the grip of a terrifying war but brilliantly successful in military contests all over the Mediterranean. The events of 213 fail to furnish an antecedent. Roman attitudes toward external religions had been generally tolerant and frequently adaptive.[24] The decision to strike against the followers of Bacchus suddenly and surprisingly broke that pattern.

No less astonishing was the establishment of a *quaestio extraordinaria*. The institution gained frequency and familiarity during the 2nd century. Hence the novelty of its occurrence in 186 has gone largely unnoticed. That novelty needs emphasis. The senate alone sanctioned the *quaestio* headed by both consuls *extra ordinem*, authorized to conduct investigations, hold hearings, pass judgment, and impose penalty—without

---

[22] Livy, 25.1.6-12: *edixit ut quicumque libros vaticinos precationesve aut artem sacrificandi conscriptam haberet, eos libros omnes litterasque ad se ante kal. Apriles deferret, neu quis in publico sacrove loco novo aut externo ritu sacrificaret.* Only one other instance of public action against foreign rites is known—much earlier (in 428), of questionable historicity, and perhaps embellished on the model of the episode in 213; Livy, 4.30.9-11.

[23] Cf. Livy, 25.1.9-11.

[24] Postumius' statement that Roman magistrates had frequently banned foreign cults, expelled their practitioners, burned oracular books, and abolished all sacrifices except the traditionally Roman ones indulges in rhetoric and offers no concrete examples; Livy 39.16.8.

appeal or reversal.[25] Nowhere in the testimony is there hint of tribunician intervention, a *lex* of the people, *provocatio*, or trial before the assembly. The senate's decree gave the consuls full power.

Previous Roman experience fails to provide a model. Examples of *quaestiones extraordinariae* from the early Republic stand on record, but few in number and ambiguous in implication. And none provides a clear instance in which the senate's decision held absolute sway. The earliest known *quaestio extraordinaria*, in 413, stemmed from a *senatus consultum* but its sanction came from an act of the people.[26] An investigation into poisoning charges in 331 produced numerous defendants and convictions; but the sources disclose neither the body which authorized trial nor that which passed judgment.[27] In 314, a dictator, appointed by the senate to conduct investigations in Capua, carried his activities to Rome and indicted some members of the nobility.[28] Legitimacy of the proceedings, however, evidently derived from the overriding *imperium* of the dictator, not from senatorial directive.[29]

Proceedings closer in time to the Bacchanalian affair give the proper perspective. A celebrated example occurred in 205: the scandal of Scipio Africanus' legate in Locri, Q. Pleminius. Pleminius' misdeeds and ruthlessness engendered sharp reaction in Rome. The senate appointed a praetor, two other officials, and a ten man commission to inquire into Pleminius' offenses against the people of Locri—and also to ascertain the degree of Scipio's responsibility. No evidence was found against Scipio, but the commissioners indicted Pleminius and sent him to Rome in chains.[30] To this point it certainly appears as if the senate had ordered a *quaestio extraordinaria* and its representatives had imposed a judicial verdict. The appearance, however, deceives. Proceedings hitherto had been

---

[25] Livy, 39.14.6: *quaestionem deinde de Bacchanalibus sacrisque nocturnis extra ordinem consulibus mandant.*

[26] Livy, 4.51.2-3. When the senate sought to act of its own accord, a tribunician intervention prevented it; Livy, 4.50.8. For differing views on the authenticity of the case, an irrelevant matter here, see T. Mommsen, *Römisches Strafrecht* (Leipzig, 1899), 172, n. 1; R.M. Ogilvie, *A Commentary on Livy, Books 1-5* (Oxford, 1965), 611-612; W. Kunkel, *Untersuchungen zur Entwicklung des römischen Kriminalverfahrens in vorsullanischer Zeit* (Munich, 1962), 57, n. 216.

[27] Livy, 8.18.4-11. Kunkel, *Untersuchungen*, 58, n. 216, takes for granted that the consuls headed a *quaestio extraordinaria* here, a possible interpretation, but not explicitly attested.

[28] Livy, 9.26.5-20; cf. Diod. 19.76.3-5.

[29] Cf. Livy, 9.26.9: *latiorque et re et personis quaestio fieri haud abnuente dictatore sine fine ulla quaestionis suae ius esse.* The dictator himself, after stepping down from office, was tried by the consuls on authority of the senate. But that hearing came on the dictator's own suggestion and of his own volition; Livy, 9.26.18-20.

[30] Livy, 29.20-21. Livy's term, *damnaverunt*, in view of what followed, is plainly nontechnical; 29.21.12: *Pleminium....damnaverunt atque in catenis Romam miserunt.*

merely preliminary. A trial before the assembly of the people awaited Pleminius. He did not live to suffer actual condemnation, escaping it only by perishing in prison. Livy's text makes clear that the *populus* remained final arbiter in criminal cases of public import.[31] That principle continued to hold even in the year prior to the Bacchanalian affair itself. L. Cornelius Scipio Asiagenus, brother of Africanus, was arraigned in a *quaestio extraordinaria*, presided over by a praetor appointed at senatorial behest. The entire proceeding, however, depended upon a *lex* issued by the assembly of the people.[32] The *patres* had not taken it upon themselves to ordain, administer, and implement special tribunals on criminal offenses.[33] The prosecution and persecution of the Bacchants, in short, seem to represent a new departure in criminal justice. The Roman senate now seized responsibility for *ad hoc* judicial procedures to suppress offenses in the city and in Italy.[34]

A significant corollary attached itself to this shift in direction. The affair of the Bacchanals entailed a noticeable jump in Roman interference in the local concerns of Italy. The senate's decree of 186 instructed the consuls to hunt down Dionysiac priests not only in Rome

---

[31] Livy, 29.22.7-9: *mortuus tamen prius in vinclis est quam iudicium de eo populi perficeretur.* Livy also mentions the variant version of Clodius Licinus who had Pleminius survive for ten years in prison, then make an unsuccessful attempt to escape, whereupon he was confined to the Tullianum and executed; Livy, 29.22.10, 34.44.6-8; cf. Appian, *Hann.* 55. That variant is plainly implausible and unacceptable. It is ignored by Livy at 31.12.2. The analysis of A.W. Lintott, *ANRW*, I.2 (1972), 241-243, unfortunately accepts Clodius Licinus' fanciful account without question, thus to argue that Pleminius had already been condemned when imprisoned. The alternative story is clearly preferable; cf. J. Briscoe, *A Commentary on Livy, Books XXXI-XXXIII* (Oxford, 1973), 87.

[32] Livy, 38.54-55. The case stands even if the trial's authenticity is itself in question; see below, Chapter IV, n. 54.

[33] The senate would hear complaints against officials abroad and act upon them—as in the case of the praetor M. Furius Crassipes, accused by the Cenomani of depriving them of arms without provocation in 187. The matter was turned over to the consul for investigation and decision, and he upheld the complaint of the Cenomani. Furius received orders to return their arms and to vacate the province; Livy, 39.3.1-3; Diod. 29.14. The *patres* here reasserted control over their magistrates. But this was no criminal proceeding. Polybius, in a famous passage, 6.13.4, maintains that the senate's authority extended to crimes in Italy that required public investigation, such as treason, conspiracy, poisoning, and assassination. But he refers to powers exercised since the time of the Bacchanalian affair. They need not extend any earlier.

[34] On the senatorial role in *quaestiones extraordinariae* generally, see P. Willems, *Le sénat de la république romaine* (Louvaine, 1883), II, 278-289; J.L. Strachan-Davidson, *Problems of the Roman Criminal Law* (Oxford, 1912), I, 225-245; H. Siber, *AbhLeipz*, 43.3 (1936), 48-53. Kunkel, *Untersuchungen*, 58, n. 216, asserts without argument that special courts must have preceded the Bacchanalian *quaestio*. But the only example he can find is the questionable case in 331; Livy, 8.18.4-11; see above, n. 27. Even if that were an instance of a special tribunal governed by a *senatus consultum*, however, it can hardly have served as a lively model a century and a half later.

but in all the *fora* and *conciliabula* and to distribute their anti-Bacchic edicts throughout Italy.[35] Those instructions were reinforced and elaborated at a subsequent meeting of the senate: the consuls should extirpate all Bacchic rites, first in Rome, then everywhere in Italy; and no further Bacchanalia should be tolerated in Rome or Italy.[36] The inscription discovered at Tiriolo carries an address to *foederati* and issues specific orders to local officials to implement the wishes of Rome.[37] Magistrates of the Roman government took charge, empowered to deal with the offending cult and its adherents wherever they surfaced. The *patres* delivered peremptory commands to Latin and Italian communities.[38] And the campaign against the Bacchants that continued or resumed in 184 and 181 carried operations into the district around Tarentum and into Apulia generally.[39] The senate had here asserted the prerogative of exercising jurisdiction and enforcing decrees in the municipalities and rural regions of Italy.

Intervention of this sort and on this scale gave a new turn to the role claimed by Rome in the peninsula. Not that she had been timid in displaying her authority in the past when circumstances called for it. The trying times of the Second Punic War called forth some devastating reprisals. Rome treated Italian defections to Hannibal as base betrayal and retaliated against the defectors.[40] Those actions, however, took place

---

[35] Livy, 39.14.7: *non Romae modo sed per omnia fora et conciliabula conquiri.... edici praeterea in urbe Roma et per totam Italiam edicta mitti.* Galsterer's view, *Herrschaft und Verwaltung*, 38, that Livy here equates *tota Italia* with *fora et conciliabula*, is special pleading.

[36] Livy, 39.18.7-8: *ut omnia Bacchanalia Romae primum, deinde per totam Italiam diruerent...ne qua Bacchanalia Romae neve in Italia essent.* There is no hint of restriction to *fora* and *conciliabula* here.

[37] *ILLRP*, 511, lines 2, 22ff. The *ager Teuranus*, where the document was set up, may, strictly speaking, have been in Roman, rather than allied, territory. The Brutii had certainly suffered expropriation after the Hannibalic war; Appian, *Hann.* 61; *Pun.* 58; Gellius, 10.3.19. See the arguments of Fronza, *Annali Triestini*, 17 (1947), 213-217. It does not follow, however, that instructions to local officials, of which the extant inscription is but one example, limited themselves exclusively to Roman settlements and the *ager Romanus*. The notion that Bacchanalian revelries would be tolerated in all other Italian (and Latin?) communities is quite inconceivable. And it is refuted decisively by Livy, 39.17.2 (with reference to prosecutions of those associated with the cult): *si quis eorum, qui tum extra terram Italiam essent, nominaretur, ei laxiorem diem daturos.* A similar conclusion, on different grounds, in A.J. Toynbee, *Hannibal's Legacy* (Oxford, 1965), II, 397, n. 2.

[38] E.g., the instructions to Ardea; Livy, 39.19.2: *Minium Cerrinium Campanum Ardeam in vincula mittendum censuerunt, magistratibusque Ardeatium praedicendum ut intentiore eum custodia adservarent.*

[39] Livy, 39.41.6-7, 40.19.9-10.

[40] A number of instances can be registered: Capua in 211 and 210: Livy, 26.14-16, 26.27, 26.33-34, 27.3.1-5, 28.46.6, 31.31.10-15; Tarentum in 209: Livy, 27.16.1-9, 27.25.2-3; twelve Latin colonies in 204: Livy, 27.9.7-14, 29.15.2-15; Etruscan towns on several occasions between 209 and 203: Livy, 27.21.6-7, 27.24, 28.10.4-5, 29.36.10-12, 30.26.12; Locri in 205: Livy, 29.8.1-3; Italian communities in Lucania and Bruttium at the end of the war: cf. Toynbee, *Hannibal's Legacy*, II, 117-121.

in the context of military emergency or the need to demonstrate the power and righteousness of the victor. Punishment of the enemy or sympathizers of the enemy motivated and legitimated the severity. This did not entail molding of Italians to the Roman will.

Nor did the immediate post-war years witness increasing encroachment by Rome upon the prerogatives of Italian communities.[41] A praetor in Bruttium in 200, with *imperium* prorogued for 199, conducted hearings on a theft of sacred funds at Locri, hearings which expanded into prosecutions for conspiracy, then arrests and punishments. The language of Livy seems to foreshadow the Bacchanalian affair: *de coniurationibus quaestiones*.[42] But the resemblance is superficial. The activities of the Roman praetor must be understood in a different context: the imposition of a settlement upon southern Italy after the Second Punic War. Bruttium was his *provincia*, and *coniurationes* evidently referred to the final rooting out of hostile elements in the region. It is noteworthy that those arrested for sacrilege and shipped to Rome were then returned to Locri for punishment and that the praetor, on senatorial insistence, saw to it that the stolen funds were restored to the Locrian shrine whence they had been taken. The episode does not qualify as arbitrary Roman interference in Italian affairs.[43]

As a rule Rome avoided such interference, a needless and potentially dangerous activity. Ostensible exceptions do not shake the rule. When servile elements rose in insurrection anywhere in Italy, Rome mobilized. The government crushed slave rebellions in Latium and Etruria respectively in 198 and 196.[44] Those were essential operations, an unquestioned obligation of the state. Authorities in Latium and Etruria raised no objections. In war time, of course, Rome expected the cooperation of *Latini* and *socii*, in accordance with mutual agreements. Enforcement of the agreements was the proper prerogative of the hegemon.[45] But Rome could acknowledge legitimate needs after the war. When Latin colonies

---

[41] Attacks on Rome for oppressing her allies put by Livy into the mouths of her foreign foes do not count as evidence; Livy, 31.29.10-11, 35.16.3. They are, in any case, simplistic and erroneous. See Briscoe, *Commentary, XXXI-XXXIII*, 132; *A Commentary on Livy, Books XXXIV-XXXVII* (Oxford, 1981), 169.

[42] Livy, 31.12.1-4, 32.1.7-8.

[43] Livy, 32.1.7-8. Cf. McDonald, *JRS*, 34 (1944), 14, n. 23. Briscoe's view, *Commentary, XXXI-XXXIII*, 87, that this was typical of "semi-judicial inquiries often set up by the senate in the early part of the second century," is unsupported.

[44] Livy, 32.26.4-18, 33.36.1-3; Zon. 9.16.6; see M. Capozza, *Movimenti servili nel mondo romano in età repubblicana* (Rome, 1966), 101-141.

[45] E.g. Livy, 34.56 (193 B.C.). Cato's speech against Q. Minucius Thermus, cos. 193, charges that he had ordered magistrates of an allied community to be flogged for failing to care for his provisions; *ORF*, fr. 58. Even if the charge is justified, however, it reflects on the personality of the individual, not on official policy.

requested additional recruits to make up depleted numbers, Rome met each request with a positive response, finding new settlers to reinforce the colonies—even when the requests came from communities which had been recalcitrant during the Hannibalic conflict.[46]

Benign relations with Latins and Italians prevailed at the beginning of the 2nd century.[47] Even those who had felt Rome's wrath in the Hannibalic war now encountered a more generous attitude. The Campanians had lost their civic identity when Rome stripped Capua of her independence. In 189, however, the senate allowed them to be registered on the censors' roll at Rome. And in the following year the *patres* honored their request to marry Roman women, retain as wives those who already had Roman citizenship, and protect the legitimacy and inheritance rights of their children.[48] Comparable generosity issued from the assembly of the people in that same year of 188. Even without explicit sanction of the senate, the *populus* elevated the cities of Fundi, Formiae, and Arpinum, formerly *civitates sine suffragio*, to the status of fully enfranchised municipalities.[49] In view of that record, Rome's reaction to the Bacchants in 186, with its usurpation of judicial procedures and widespread intrusion into the area of allies' prerogatives, comes as a surprise.

Equally notable is the severity of treatment meted out against offenders. The senate's decree, as conveyed on the Tiriolo inscription, authorized the death penalty for any violator of its provisions.[50] A

---

[46] Livy, 31.49.6 (Venusia in 200); 32.2.6-7 (Narnia in 199); 33.24.8-9 (Cosa in 197); 37.46.9-10, 37.47.2 (Placentia and Cremona in 190). Only Cosa's request was deferred, for reasons unspecified, but then granted two years later; Livy, 32.2.7, 33.24.8-9. Narnia was among the twelve Latin colonies which declined to supply troops or money in 209; Livy, 27.9.7. In that same category was Cales which received additional settlers later, in 184; *CIL*, I²,1, xxxii, p. 200. Cf. Toynbee, *Hannibal's Legacy*, II, 91-92; E.T. Salmon, *Roman Colonization under the Republic* (London, 1969), 100-103. Rome could also deny requests when they were unjustified; Livy, 34.42.5-6, on which see R.E. Smith, *JRS*, 44 (1954), 18-20; Galsterer, *Herrschaft und Verwaltung*, 161-162; D. Piper, *Historia* 36 (1987), 38-50.

[47] The measure of 193, obliging Latins and allies to follow the same regulations on debt and usury that held in Roman law, was designed to curb fraud and prevent fictitious transfer of debts from Roman to allied creditors; Livy, 35.7.2-5. It did not disturb the judicial procedures of allied states nor infringe on their autonomy. So, rightly, W.V. Harris, *Historia*, 21 (1972), 640-642; followed by Galsterer, *Herrschaft und Verwaltung*, 131-132; Briscoe, *Commentary, XXXIV-XXXVII*, 153-154. The older view of Roman infringement stemmed from Mommsen, *Römisches Staatsrecht³* (Leipzig, 1887-1888), III, 693-696. Similarly, E. Badian, *Foreign Clientelae, 264-70 BC* (Oxford, 1958), 146, n. 3; W. Dahlheim, *Struktur und Entwicklung des römischen Völkerrechts im 3. und 2. Jahrhundert v. Chr.* (Munich, 1968), 121, n. 25.

[48] Livy, 38.28.4, 38.36.5-6.

[49] Livy, 38.36.7-9.

[50] *ILLRP*, 511, lines 24-25; *sei ques esent, quei arvorsum ead fecisent, quam suprad scriptum est, eeis rem caputalem faciendam censuere.*

vigorous speech by the consul Postumius, armed by senatorial instructions to conduct the inquisition, provoked panic. Letters posted through
Italy, regarding the senate's measures and the consul's speech and edicts,
extended the alarm. Large numbers fled Rome in terror, some were
captured at the gates, others escaped only to find the *quaestiones* instituted
outside the city as well. Seven thousand persons were implicated, so
rumor had it. Some committed suicide to avoid capture. Adherents of the
cult were thrown into prison, those convicted of criminal activities
associated with the religion suffered capital punishment. As Livy reports
it, the executioner claimed more victims than the jailer.[51] The campaign
against the cult still raged two years later when the praetor assigned to
the area around Tarentum pursued the Bacchants hiding in that region,
condemned a number of them himself, and sent the rest to be judged in
Rome, where all were promptly imprisoned.[52] Nothing in earlier Roman
history provides a parallel to this witch hunt. The stringency of the
measures, the widespread character of the pursuit, the harshness of the
penalties, and the number of those penalized all exceeded previous
precedent.

Finally, one ought not to overlook the dramatic and colorful events
that led to the senate's actions against the Bacchants. Intrigue in the
household of Aebutius set that train of events in motion: the schemes of
mother and step-father to deprive Aebutius of his legacy by involving
him in the sinister cult, the visit to the mistress who by fortuitous cir-
cumstance had knowledge of that cult's wickedness and warned off her
lover, the violent quarrel at home and the son's expulsion, his appeal to
the consul, the machinations to corroborate his story, climaxed by the
hysterical revelations of the courtesan who portrayed Bacchic rites as the
vehicle for every kind of depraved and felonious activity.[53] Inquiry into
the accuracy of this elaborate tale can be postponed for the moment. But
the melodramatic character of the prelude to persecution itself removes
these events from the ordinary. Indeed, every feature of the episode pro-
claims its extraordinary character: the sensational manner of discovery,
the assault on an alien religion, the unprecedented judicial proceedings,
the interference in affairs of Latin and Italian states, and the spread and
severity of the inquisition.

How does one account for events so unexpected and so exceptional in so
many ways? Simple explanations will not do. A variety of solutions has

---

[51] Livy, 39.17.1-39.18.5: *plures necati quam in vincula coniecti sunt.*
[52] Livy, 39.41.6-7.
[53] Livy, 39.9-13.

been offered, each tempting and ostensibly plausible, but none that dispels all doubts.

The term *coniuratio* appears repeatedly in connection with the affair.[54] That appellation stigmatizes the movement immediately. The "Bacchanalian conspiracy", it can be argued, represented a political threat in religious guise to the establishment. Nocturnal meetings carry sinister and suspicious overtones. Moreover, the *lucus Stimulae* served as prominent site for the performance of Bacchic ritual, a grove bordering on the Aventine—the hill traditionally employed as rallying point for the Roman *plebs*. Did the adherents of Dionysus then utilize the cult to stir political upheaval from below against the Roman leadership? Or, whatever the truth of the matter, did the gatherings at night and secretive behavior frighten the leadership into believing in a *coniuratio* and thus taking steps to crush it?[55]

The thesis is hard to maintain. Nothing in the testimony alludes to any political tinge in the Dionysiac worship. Even the most slanderous charges with regard to criminal offenses go only so far as perjured witnesses, forged seals, wills, and documents, poisonings, and assassinations within the group.[56] However heinous the alleged crimes, they do not pertain to political objectives. The consul and senate labelled the cult's activities as *coniuratio*, thereby to assimilate it in the public mind to subversion and insurrection. The term's meaning was elastic, applicable as well to defection from Rome during war time as to a slave rebellion.[57] Its connotation was rhetorical rather than technical. *Coniuratio* had no place in Roman criminal law.[58] But use of the term would deliver a duly alarming effect upon popular opinion—and perhaps upon some senatorial opinion, ready to believe the worst of secretive cults whose reported behavior rendered them suspect. Certain *senatores* feared incrimination for themselves, a fear that may have made them more zealous persecutors.[59] Labels apart, however, the leadership had no concrete evidence on political insurgency lurking in the Bacchanalian cells. Livy's presentation admits as much. In his narrative the senate springs

---

[54] Livy, 39.8.1, 39.8.3, 39.13.13, 39.14.4, 39.14.8, 39.15.10, 39.16.3, 39.16.5, 39.17.6; cf. *ILLRP*, 511, line 13: *neve posthac inter sed conioura[se]*.

[55] So Y. Béquignon, *RevArch*, 17 (1941), 187-189; Bruhl, *Liber Pater*, 88-89, 99-100, 107, 116; R. Turcan, *RevHistRel*, 181 (1972), 21-27; J.-L. Voisin, *MEFRA*, 96 (1984), 640-653. Reference to the *lucus Stimulae* in Livy, 39.12.4. Cf. C. Gallini, *Protesta e integrazione nella Roma antica* (Bari, 1970), 16-17. The text itself is uncertain; mss. read *Simile*. Hence, political conjectures are doubly hazardous.

[56] Livy, 39.8.7-8, 39.13.10-13.

[57] E.g., Livy, 30.26.12, 32.26.10.

[58] Mommsen, *Römisches Strafrecht*, 564, n. 1.

[59] Livy, 39.14.4.

to action out of fear that the gatherings *might* introduce secret treachery or danger to the public.[60] He has the consul Postumius concede in his speech that, although the Bacchants seek supreme power in the state, they have not as yet gone beyond private offenses.[61] Plainly, none of their activities represented an active challenge to the political order. And it is difficult to believe that many in the leadership seriously thought that they might.[62]

A different proposition can be considered. Did the worship of Bacchus threaten traditional religious practice, thus presenting a menace to the *pax deorum*? That proposition has been held in various forms by various scholars.[63] The speech set by Livy into the mouth of Sp. Postumius lays heavy stress upon this element. The consul appeals to ancestral religion, the gods worshipped by forefathers of the present generation, against depraved foreign sects leading their devotees into every form of wantonness and criminality.[64] The Bacchanalia undermine morality and corrupt the character and patriotism of Roman youth.[65] The whole Roman religious structure is jeopardized when alien rites replace native ones and perverse superstition employs religion as a screen for criminal activity.[66] Postumius' hyperbole does not command implicit faith. Is it, however, mere embellishment upon an authentic Roman anxiety regarding the infiltration of unfamiliar and outlandish ritual?

The question of the cult's roots in Italy has long exercised scholarly imagination and ingenuity. Livy ascribes it to an unknown Greek, a self-styled expert in sacrifice and prophecy, who introduced the creed into Etruria—at an unspecified date.[67] Elsewhere, he points to the influence

---

[60] Livy, 39.14.4: *ne quid eae coniurationes coetusque nocturni fraudis occultae aut periculi importarent.*

[61] Livy, 39.16.3: *adhuc privatis noxiis...coniuratio sese impia tenet...ad summam rem publicam spectat.*

[62] The notion that the *lucus Stimulae* was a haven for plebeian activity is far-fetched and unfounded. Béquignon, *RevArch*, 17 (1941), 189, wrongly locates it on the Aventine. The grove was in the vicinity of the Aventine. Ovid, *Fasti*, 6.501-503, 6.518. And nothing associates it with plebeian traditions. The ecstatic and emotional connotations prevail, not the political; see O. de Cazanove, *MEFRA*, 95 (1983), 55-82.

[63] Among recent studies, see A. Luisi, in M. Sordi (ed.), *Politica e religione nel primo scontro tra Roma e l'Oriente* (Milan, 1982), 184-185; R.J. Rousselle, *The Roman Persecution of the Bacchic Cult, 186-180 B.C.* (Diss. SUNY Binghamton, 1982), 101-112. J.-M. Pailler, *Annales ESC*, 37 (1982), 936-939, postulates a complex interweaving of religious and philosophic elements that embraced Bacchus, Ceres, Orphism, and Pythagoreanism.

[64] Livy, 39.15.2-3: *hos esse deos, quos colere venerari precarique maiores vestri instituissent, non illos, qui pravis et externis religionibus captas mentes velut furialibus stimulis ad omne scelus et ad omnem libidinem agerent.*

[65] Livy, 39.15.12-14.

[66] Livy, 39.16.6-9: *nihil aeque dissolvendae religionis esse, quam ubi non patrio sed externo ritu sacrificaretur.*

[67] Livy, 39.8.3-5.

of a Campanian woman, Paculla Annia, who introduced important innovations into the ritual. One of those innovations was the admission of men to the sect, the first to be initiated being her own sons.[68] And in still another passage, Livy identifies leaders of the cult in 186 as two members of the Roman *plebs*, one Faliscan, and one—the son of Paculla Annia—a Campanian.[69] Conjectures on the provenance of the cult have consequently focused upon Etruria, Campania, and southern Italy. A favored solution sees Magna Graecia as the source: the capture of numerous Tarentine prisoners in 208 and the social dislocations wrought by Hannibal in the southern part of the peninsula created large numbers of refugees who brought their Hellenic religious baggage into central Italy and into Rome itself.[70] Others see Etruria as the place where the religion was molded before it made its way to Rome.[71] A recent suggestion reckons the Bacchanalian movement as stemming from Italian regions sympathetic to Hannibal in the Second Punic War.[72] The speculation can be suspended. Whatever the provenance of the sect in Italy, it found fertile soil there and proliferated until it provoked reaction from Roman authorities.[73] And much modern opinion interprets that reaction as generated, in part at least, by apprehensions regarding religion. The ecstatic, emotional, orgiastic character of the creed disturbed the traditional sensibilities of Rome's leadership.[74]

The various forms of the thesis share a common assumption: that the Bacchic cult won numerous adherents and spread its influence emotionally and territorially with astonishing swiftness between the end of the Hannibalic War and the suppression in 186. But the assumption violates

---

[68] Livy, 39.13.8-9.

[69] Livy, 39.17.6-7. Cf. the analysis of these passages by G. Tarditi, *PP*, 37 (1954), 266-268.

[70] See, especially, T. Frank, *CQ*, 21 (1927), 128-132, who, among many other things, rightly disposes of the idea that Dionysiac rites came to Italy in the train of Manlius Vulso's campaign in Asia Minor. Vulso's army and captives only returned in 187, a year before the Bacchanalian affair, which implies long-standing and organized cults. Frank's belief in a south Italian provenance has been shared by many; e.g. F. Altheim, *A History of Roman Religion* (London, 1938), 293-294, 311, 313-314; G. Méautis, REA, 42 (1940), 485; Béquignon, *RevArch*, 17 (1941), 192; McDonald, *JRS*, 34 (1944), 26-27; Tierney, *Proceedings of the Royal Irish Academy*, 51 (1947), 115.

[71] Warde Fowler, *Religious Experience*, 346; Turcan, *RevHistRel*, 181 (1972), 13-14.

[72] Voisin, *MEFRA*, 96 (1984), 640-653.

[73] Bruhl, *Liber Pater*, 86-87, rightly dampens speculation. Cf. also Cova, *Athenaeum*, 52 (1974), 92.

[74] Altheim, *History of Roman Religion*, 316-317; Béquignon, *RevArch*, 17 (1941), 189-190; McDonald, *JRS*, 34 (1944), 26-28; Bruhl, *Liber Pater*, 99, 115-116; Tarditi, *PP*, 37 (1954), 273-278; Gallini, *Protesta*, 20-23, 60-69, who argues—without evidence—that the orgiastic character of the cult as manifested in the early 2nd century is a revival of early, primitive Dionysiac worship. See the criticisms of Turcan, *RevHistRel*, 181 (1972), 15-18.

what little evidence we possess. Livy's own text provides contrary testimony. He has Postumius declare (perhaps with rhetorical exaggeration) that the sect has long since been known throughout Italy and, more recently, in various locations in the city itself.[75] Several thousand men and women were involved, it was alleged, panic spurred a near stampede of Bacchants who sought to escape the city, notices to dissolve the cells went throughout the peninsula, and government actions against Bacchic worship still continued five years later. This hardly resembles a recent phenomenon. The evidence of archaeology reinforces the conclusion. Terra-cotta statuettes, coins, vase paintings, tomb decorations, sarcophagi, and frescoes all attest eloquently to the popularity of Dionysus in southern Italy, Campania, and Etruria in the 4th and 3rd centuries—long before the events of 186.[76]

Furthermore, the cult was far from unfamiliar to the Romans themselves. The plays of Plautus supply welcome illumination. The comic dramatist makes frequent allusion to Bacchic rites, a strong suggestion that his audience had acquaintance with those rites. The references occur in several plays, most if not all written prior to the *quaestio* of 186, some well before, indicating clearly that the Bacchanalia were a known institution. Whatever the playwright's own attitude, or indeed that of his audience, the comedies reveal those characteristics associated in the public mind with Bacchic rituals and devotees of the sect. The image was decidedly negative, the cult an object of scorn, derision, or hostility. Plautus presents it as the very epitome of a secret society.[77] The worshippers of Bacchus conduct revels, engage in violence, and engender fear.[78] Worse yet, they are reckoned as raging, irrational, and insane.[79] How far these descriptions approximate reality is irrelevant. Stereotypes count.

---

[75] Livy, 39.15.6: *Bacchanalia tota iam pridem Italia et nunc per urbem etiam multis locis esse.*

[76] See the valuable collection of evidence in Bruhl, *Liber Pater*, 58-81. A summary, with additional bibliography, in Rousselle, *Roman Persecution*, 21-26. More briefly, S.G. Cole, *GRBS*, 21 (1980), 234-236. Note the inscription of the Etruscan *haruspex* Laris Pulenas, ca. 200 B.C., a priest of Bacchus, whose epitaph indicates that the sect was well established and publicly acknowledged in Etruria; J. Heurgon, *REL*, 35 (1975), 106-121. The fact was reconfirmed by discovery of a subterranean Bacchic place of assemblage at Volsinii, dated to the later 3rd century; Pailler, *MEFRA*, 83 (1971), 384-392; *Mélanges Heurgon* (1976), II, 739-742; *MEFRA*, 95 (1983), 7-39. On Dionysiac legends in Etruscan art, especially in southern Etruria, see now Y. Bomati, *REL*, 61 (1983), 87-107.

[77] Plautus, *Miles*, 1016: *cedo signum si harunc Baccharum es.*

[78] Plautus, *Casina*, 979: *nam ecastor nunc Bacchae nullae ludunt; Aul.* 408-413: *neque ego umquam nisi hodie ad Bacchas veni in Bacchanal coquinatum,/ita me miserum et meos discipulos fustibus male contuderunt; Bacch.* 53: *Quia, Bacchis, bacchas metuo et bacchanal tuom;* cf. *Cist.* 156-159; *Vid.* fr. 1, Lindsay.

[79] Plautus, *Bacch.* 371-372: *Bacchides non Bacchides, sed bacchae sunt acerrumae,/apage istas a me sorores, quae hominum sorbent sanguinem; Men.* 828-841; *Amph.* 702-705: *Bacchae bacchanti si velis advorsarier,/ex insana insaniorem facies, feriet saepius.*

They represent popular impressions, and they demonstrate that the dramatist could assume immediate understanding (however distorted) on the part of his audience. The Bacchanalian cult was a familiar entity well before the government elected to suppress it.[80] Fragments of Naevius' tragedy, *Lycurgus*, reinforce the conclusion: Liber and the Bacchanals play central parts in the drama.[81] Bacchic devotees had a long-standing notoriety. In the hands of the poets that notoriety features ecstatic worship, irrational behavior, violence, and lunacy. An important conclusion remains to be drawn. Not that public distaste for the Bacchants built to the point of sanctioning persecution. Rather that the negative image and dubious reputation of the cult existed for an indefinite period *without* persecution. The decision to dissolve the sect did not come from sudden revelation of its existence. The Bacchants were well known—and tolerated.

The problem of why the persecution came at all, therefore, becomes even more difficult. A slightly different approach has endeavored to get around this difficulty. Granted that the worship of Bacchus had ensconced itself on Italian soil for some time and had functioned with impunity, recent changes in the cult rendered it more suspicious and disquieting and brought it to the attention of the authorities.[82] The narrative of Livy offers apparent support. In discussing the origins of the cult and its spread from Etruria to Rome, the historian provides no chronology.[83] But the courtesan Hispala's disclosures about the Bacchic mysteries yield

---

[80] So, rightly, J.A. North, *PCPS*, 25 (1979), 88. Uncertainty continues to prevail about the dates of Plautus' plays, hence muddying the waters on the issue here at stake. The *Amphitryon* is customarily dated to 186 on the basis of the passage quoted above; lines 702-705—seen as showing that it must have been produced at a time when the Bacchants had been exposed to public attack; cf. H. Janne, *RevBelge*, 12 (1933), 527-528. The same claim is made for the *Casina*, for line 979 can be interpreted to imply suppression of the sect; see now W.T. MacCary and M.M. Willcock, *Plautus: Casina* (Cambridge, 1976), 11, 207, with bibliography. Neither inference is compelling. See below, Chapter IV, n. 145. But even if accepted, one can hardly jam the other plays which make reference to Bacchic rites into the last year or two of Plautus' life. The poet died in 184; Cic. *Brutus*, 60. See the sensible remarks of Bruhl, *Liber Pater*, 111-114. Cf. Tarditi, *PP*, 37 (1954), 273. An unsatisfactory treatment by W. Stockert, in R. Hanslik et al., *Antidosis: Festschrift für W. Kraus* (Vienna, 1972), 398-407.

[81] Naevius, 191-198, Marmorale. Cf. also Ennius on Bacchic revelry; *Scenica*, fr. 123-127, Vahlen. Rouselle, *CJ*, 82 (1987), 193-198, proposes that dramatic productions fostered negative public opinion that helped to promote the persecutions.

[82] Such a reconstruction lies behind Gallini's hypothesis of a "revival" of the passionate and ecstatic aspects of the cult by the Bacchants prior to their suppression by Rome; *Protesta*, 20-23, 60-61. For Rouselle, *Roman Persecution*, 104-112, the changes represented perversion of the traditional worship of Liber and the Aventine triad of Ceres, Liber, and Libera. A syncretism of various elements is proposed by Pailler, *Annales ESC*, 37 (1982), 936-939, 945-946.

[83] Livy, 39.8.3-39.9.1.

some intriguing information. Hispala makes reference to a Campanian priestess Paculla Annia whose reforms radically altered the practice and rituals of the sect. Since Paculla's son, Minius Cerrinius, was among the Bacchic leaders arrested in 186, the innovations presumably belong to a time not far from 200.[84] The allegations of Hispala specify three major changes. The cult originally admitted only women as initiates; Paculla introduced men, beginning with her own sons. Initiations in the past had been confined to three days a year; Paculla increased the number of ceremonies considerably, having initiations occur five times a month. And what had once been daytime rituals became nocturnal celebrations at behest of the reforming priestess.[85] The innovations readily lent themselves to hostile interpretation: the cult would rapidly multiply in numbers, the mingling of male and female worshippers encouraged sexual license and misconduct, and the secretive doings could proceed freely under cover of night.[86] Hispala revealed one further deviation from previous practice, this one within the past two years and not explicitly connected with Paculla Annia: a policy that new initiates can be no older than twenty years of age.[87] These changes, when taken in combination, might alarm authorities to the point of provoking a reaction.

So much for the Livian text. How far is it reliable? Some accept the information wholesale.[88] Yet closer scrutiny causes misgivings. That the sect was open only to women at its early stages is clear enough. Euripides' *Bacchae* suffices to establish the fact.[89] Ritual maenadism evidently continued to be restricted to women through the Hellenistic period.[90] But men had gained admittance to a wide variety of Dionysiac festivals and had become full-fledged members of Dionysiac cells by the 4th century—at least in the Greek world.[91] No evidence or reason sug-

---

[84] Livy, 39.13.9, 39.17.6, 39.19.2.

[85] Livy, 39.13.8-9.

[86] Cf. Livy, 39.13.10: *ex quo in promiscuo sacra sint et permixti viri feminis, et noctis licentia accesserit, nihil ibi facinoris, nihil flagitii praetermissum.*

[87] Livy, 39.10.6, 39.13.14.

[88] So A.-J. Festugière, *MEFRA*, 66 (1954), 89-94, who does not question Hispala's facts, only her interpretations. The information is unchallenged also by Gallini, *Protesta*, 13-14. North, *PCPS*, 25 (1979), 89, does at least argue for its authenticity, but only briefly. A fuller defense by Rousselle, *Roman Persecution*, 28-34.

[89] Cf., e.g., Euripides, *Bacchae*, 822-823.

[90] A. Henrichs, *HSCP*, 82 (1978), 133; *idem*, in B.F. Meyer and E.P. Sanders, *Jewish and Christian Self-Definition* (Philadelphia, 1982), III, 143, 147; *idem*, in H.D. Evjen, *Mnemai: Classical Studies in Honor of Karl K. Hulley* (Chico, California, 1984), 69-91.

[91] Some testimony in M.P. Nilsson, *The Dionysiac Mysteries of the Hellenistic and Roman Age* (Lund, 1957), 4-12. Cf. Bruhl, *Liber Pater*, 93, with literature cited there; R.S. Kraemer, *HTR*, 72 (1979), 69-72. See, e.g., *IG*, XII, 1, 155; *I Magn.* 215, with the discussion of Henrichs, *HSCP*, 82 (1978), 123-137. North, *PCPS*, 25 (1979), 89, 100, n. 26, seeks to skirt this fact by claiming that male and female sects were kept separate in

gests that Bacchic organizations in Italy, an outgrowth of the Hellenic worship, altogether reversed that trend and reverted to an older system. Indeed, Livy's own account, at variance here with Hispala's alleged report, affirms that the mingling of men and women existed already in the Etruscan cults, long before the religion was brought to Rome.[92] It can safely be inferred that Bacchic regulations with regard to the gender of participants varied in Italy as they did in the Hellenistic world. Nocturnal meetings were also no novelty at the time of the cult's suppression. They go back at least to the 5th century in Greece, and it is hard to believe that the Italian offshoots abandoned the practice.[93] As for increased frequency of initiation ceremonies, we lack the evidence to test that proposition. Livy's scheme, however, seems too schematic: a sudden jump from three per year to five per month. More probably, the number and frequency of such celebrations varied rather than adhering to a fixed pattern.[94] A sharp and sudden increase at a particular—and unspecified—moment in time seems implausible. Livy becomes more specific on the decision to admit no one over twenty years of age: it occurred within two years of 186.[95] The statement need not be challenged. But its implications are hardly sinister. Far from supplying a means for propagating the cult, this policy would restrict its membership largely to families who already belonged.[96] Increase in initiation ceremonies anticipated such a move. The need to keep up numbers would become more pressing. The Bacchants seem inclined toward a shoring up of their stability rather than an expansive growth.

The revolutionary character of Paculla Annia's innovations thus fades as hard historical fact. The context in which they appear is enough to provoke suspicion in itself. Hispala's accusations aimed to depict the cult

---

the Hellenistic world. So also Rousselle, *Roman Persecution*, 28-32. Most of the evidence is ambiguous. But see *OGIS*, 735—a clear instance of admission of male and female into the same group. The existence of male initiates in the cult is, in any case, indisputable.

[92] Livy 39.8.3-6. Note that, in Livy's presentation, the seer who introduced the sect into Etruria was himself a man.

[93] Sophocles, *Antigone*, 1151-1152; Euripides, *Bacchae*, 469, 485-486; *IG*, XII, 2, 499; Plutarch, *De Mul. Vir.* 15; Bruhl, *Liber Pater*, 93; Z. Stewart, *JRS*, 50 (1960), 38-39. North, *PCPS*, 25 (1979), 89, has to assume that the Italian rites deviated from Hellenistic practice, only to be brought back to cultic origins by Paculla Annia. But why should the Italian Bacchants eliminate nocturnal meetings in violation of the sect's traditions? Livy's tale of the spread of the Bacchanalia to Etruria has gatherings at night as part of the ceremonies from the start; Livy, 39.8.4-6.

[94] Bruhl, *Liber Pater*, 94—admittedly speculative. But see Pailler, *Annales ESC*, 37 (1982), 945-946.

[95] Livy, 39.13.14: *biennio proximo institutum esse*.

[96] The implication was acutely noted by North, *PCPS*, 25 (1979), 89-90. It does not, however, preclude hostile characterization of this policy by contemporaries in alarmist fashion to suggest corruption of young minds.

as burgeoning in size, promoting licentiousness, and concealing its wickedness in nocturnal orgies. She even portrayed the recent age limits imposed on new initiates as a means of leading impressionable youths into delusion and debauchery.[97] The tale hardly promotes confidence. And the idea that Bacchic routines underwent major transformation around 200 which rendered the sect suddenly more formidable and menacing to Roman state and religion is, at best, questionable. The unpleasant impression made by the Bacchants on the outside world— their orgiastic ritual, secretiveness, reputation for violence and frenzied behavior—had become a convention familiar already to the audiences of Plautus. That impression did not await any restructuring by Paculla Annia.[98]

The idea that Rome faced a religious crisis in 186 thus rests on very shaky testimony. The invented speech of Postumius and the extorted calumnies of Hispala inspire little trust. That testimony apart, the circumstances of 186 itself give no reason for religious alarm on the part of men or gods.

Did the perceived perils of the Bacchants lie in the very fact of their organization? The cultic cells appear to have developed an administrative structure of some sophistication. That much may be inferred from the regulations and restrictions imposed by the Tiriolo decree. The inscription reveals priests and priestesses, as well as male and female lay officials: *sacerdotes* and *magistri*. Indeed, both *magistratus* and *promagistratus* are attested, indicating regular terms of office and extensions beyond those terms when appropriate and necessary.[99] The cells possessed a common fund, their members swore oaths of allegiance, and the sect met at cult centers.[100] Such features most particularly drew the fire of the

---

[97] Livy, 39.13.14: *captari aetates et erroris et stupri patientes.*

[98] It is true that the god Liber, long since established in Rome and Italy, became transmuted into Bacchus, the Hellenic import and deity with orgiastic rites that did not attach to Liber. Both the Livian text and that of the Tiriolo document speak only of Bacchus. See Warde Fowler, *Religious Experience*, 344-345; Latte, *Römische Religionsgeschichte*, 271-272; Bruhl, *Liber Pater*, 87. But the testimony already discussed makes it most unlikely that this conversion took place in the years just prior to suppression of the sect. Rousselle's lengthy discussion, *Roman Persecution*, 97-112, reaches no clear conclusion on this point. See further *idem*, *CJ*, 82 (1987), 193-195.

[99] *ILLRP*, 511, lines 10-12: *sacerdos nequis vir eset; magister neque vir neque mulier quisquam eset...neve magistratum neve pro magistratu[d] neque virum [neque mul]ierem quisquam fecise velet.* North, *PCPS*, 25 (1979), 92, rightly cautions that the titles of Bacchic officials would have been in Greek, for which we have only the Latin approximations. But he is perhaps too cautious in suggesting that the *promagistratus* may have been inserted by the Roman draughtsman to close a possible loophole, rather than revealing an authentic structural pattern in the religion.

[100] *ILLRP*, 511, lines 3, 11, 13-14; Livy, 39.18.8-9.

senate. Shrines were outlawed, women but not men could serve in the priesthood, neither could become *magister* or receive appointment to *magistratus* or *promagistratus*, common funds were banned, and restrictions imposed on oaths and secret gatherings.[101]

The anxiety of Roman authorities, it has been argued, expressed itself in the drive to break down these structures. The senate traditionally exercised control over religious activities affecting the *res publica*, its ranks supplied the religious officialdom of the state, and its leaders made decisions which guided the religious behavior of the citizenry. Sects and practitioners unsanctioned by the government made the establishment nervous. Such was the burden of Postumius' speech, and the attitude prevailed among the Roman upper classes.[102] The Bacchanalian organization compounded the problem. They had as models the *collegia* of artisans, merchants, workers, or professionals familiar in Roman social life. But although the *collegia* did serve as vehicles for religious functions, they were multi-faceted in their activities and their membership depended upon a common trade or upon locality. The Bacchanalian cells employed comparable structures with hierarchical leadership and administrative organization, but they drew their recruits without regard to occupation, background, or region, they admitted them into the mysteries with elaborate initiation ceremonies and held them with solemn oaths. In short, the cult combined an intense religious commitment with a carefully designed system outside the control of the state. This movement toward the compartmentalization of religious life independent of and unregulated by public authority has been seen as prime motivation for the suppression of the Bacchants.[103]

The thesis is plausible and tempting—and it doubtless contains some truth. But by no means the whole truth. Organized structures in Dionysiac societies have a long history.[104] Such structures, in one form or another, must have accompanied their transplantation onto Italian soil. If groups organized for strictly religious purposes and outside state

---

[101] *ILLRP*, 511, lines 10-14, 28; cf. Livy, 39.18.8-9; Gallini, *Protesta*, 55-57.

[102] Livy, 39.15.2-3, 39.16.6-9; cf. Cic. *De Nat. Deor.* 1.56, 2.71; *De Div.* 1.132. The desire of the nobility to impose state control over sects that might lead the populace astray is stressed by Gallini, *Protesta*, 65-73, who contrasts the circumstances surrounding the introduction and establishment of the Magna Mater—that was an operation carefully orchestrated by the political leadership.

[103] Gallini, *Protesta*, 81-86; North, *PCPS*, 25 (1979), 92-97. On the *collegia* generally, see J.-P. Waltzing, *Étude historique sur les corporations professionelles chez les Romains* (Louvain, 1895-1900); F. De Robertis, *Il diritto associativo romano dei "collegia"* (Bari, 1938); *Storia delle corporazione e del regime associativo nel mondo romano* (Bari, 1971).

[104] Cf. Euripides, *Bacchae*, 680-682; Plato, *Phaedo*, 69C. In general, see Nilsson, *The Dionysiac Mysteries*, 45-66.

supervision made the governing classes anxious, why wait until 186 before making a move against them? The Bacchanalia, as already noted, were a familiar phenomenon to Romans well before that date. Timing of the suppression remains unexplained on this theory. Further, and equally important, it fails to account for the vigor of the reaction. To assert state authority over this religious corporation hardly required extorting information from a courtesan, suspending regular judicial procedures, reversing conventional tolerance of alien cults, encroaching widely on Italian prerogatives, and ordering a persecution that issued in large numbers of arrests and executions. The same objective could have been achieved with much less trouble and cost. Other reasons must be sought to illuminate the events of 186.[105]

Did the decision to undertake a witch-hunt of the Bacchanals betoken an outburst of anti-Hellenism? Such a conclusion would be important— and disturbing. It certainly does not cohere with other actions and propaganda produced by the state during this period. A xenophobic attitude would be difficult to square with the summoning and enshrinement of Cybele whose temple was consecrated only five years earlier. And, even more recently, the grand claims of Rome's officialdom to liberate the Greeks from the suzerainty of Antiochus III had just come to fruition in Rome's decisive triumph over Antiochus. This hardly forms the prelude to an anti-Hellenic campaign.[106] Yet the attack on the Bacchic mysteries frequently receives interpretation as a move by M. Cato and like-minded Roman conservatives against the philhellenic tendencies of the Scipionic party.[107]

Evidence for this reconstruction is altogether wanting. The Scipios, of course, held center stage in the politics of the Republic at the end of the 3rd century and the early years of the 2nd. But the story of the Bacchanalian ''conspiracy'' and its suppression contains not a whisper of Scipionic involvement. As for Cato, the mere title of a speech has borne the burden of excessive speculation. Cato delivered an oration entitled *de coniuratione*,

---

[105] The ingenious but misguided theory of C. Cichorius, *Römische Studien* (Leipzig, 1922), 21-24, that Rome adopted measures against the Bacchants in imitation of Ptolemy IV who took similar steps at the end of the 3rd century, has fortunately found few takers. See the criticisms of Bruhl, *Liber Pater*, 107-109. But cf. Pailler, *Annales ESC*, 37 (1982), 933-934.

[106] For the dedication of the temple to Cybele, see Livy, 36.36.3. On Roman propaganda and the ''freedom of the Greeks'', see E.S. Gruen, *The Hellenistic World and the Coming of Rome* (Berkeley and Los Angeles, 1984), 148-153—with references and bibliography collected there.

[107] So, e.g., G. de Sanctis, *Storia dei Romani* (Florence, 1969), IV.1, 583-584; Bruhl, *Liber Pater*, 115-116; Tarditi, *PP*, 37 (1954), 271-278; Bayet, *Histoire politique*, 152-155; Luisi, in Sordi, *Politica e religione*, 182-185.

of which precisely one word survives—and that one quite irrelevant to the point.[108] Commentators customarily date the speech to 186 and have as its subject the *Bacchanalium coniuratio*, with the further assumption that Cato led the movement to suppress it. The entire construct rests on no foundation. Romans employed the term with some regularity to label upheavals or resistance of every variety. A speech *de coniuratione* could as easily have been delivered in the context of a slave rebellion or a war against Ligurians.[109] The single fragment tells us neither the occasion nor the topic of Cato.[110]

Available testimony points in a very different direction. Among the more striking characteristics of our narrative on the Bacchanalian affair is the absence of any debate or dissent on the actions to be taken. No sooner had Postumius laid his information before the *patres* than they passed resolutions expressing their gratitude and directing the chief magistrates to root out the insidious sect all over Italy with every possible vigor.[111] And when summoned to session again, the senate issued additional decrees that provided for regulation of the cult and rewards for the informers. Concurrence in the *curia* brought swift ratification by the *plebs*. No opposing voice appears in the record.[112] To be sure, Livy (or his source) was perfectly capable of suppressing reference to disagreement or controversy within senatorial ranks. Yet his pages for these years are filled with accounts of internal political strife, including contention over repeal of the *lex Oppia*, resistance to the triumphs of Fulvius Nobilior and Manlius Vulso, the trials of the Scipios, and fierce competition for the censorship of 184. The absence of anything comparable with regard to treatment of the Bacchants stands out markedly by contrast. It does not follow that the *patres* were united and unanimous on the matter. Backstage maneuvering remains hidden from sight. The consul Postumius may have lobbied vigorously behind the scenes. And his speech labored to convince colleagues, stirring immoderate suspicions and anxieties. But to postulate an ideological debate is unwarranted, unpersuasive, and methodologically unsound.

A more serious and difficult matter needs to be confronted: the social character of the Bacchanalian movement. Did the government step in to

---

[108] Namely, "*precem*"; Cato, *ORF*, fr. 68.

[109] Cf. Livy, 33.36.2, 34.56.2. Note also Livy's version of Cato's own speech on repeal of the *lex Oppia*; Livy, 34.2.3: *coniuratione muliebri*.

[110] A properly skeptical attitude by A.E. Astin, *Cato the Censor* (Oxford, 1978), 74. Association with the Bacchanalian affair is reiterated by M.T.S. Cugusi, *M. Porci Catonis Orationum Reliquiae* (Turin, 1982), 216-217, with bibliography. See now J.-M. Pailler, *PBSR*, 54 (1986), 29-39.

[111] Livy, 39.14.3-8.

[112] Livy, 39.18.7-39.19.7.

check a growing amalgam of the underprivileged against the leadership of state and society? The argument carries weight and has attracted much scholarly opinion.

The passionate, personal, and deeply intense quality of the creed appealed to the humble and unsophisticated. Such, at least, has been common doctrine. Slaves and proletarians, the uprooted in society, victims of the Hannibalic war, migrants from south Italy, powerless rural workers or refugees from the countryside became ready converts to an orgiastic religion.[113] The analysis has troubling overtones: that mystery religions with strong personal and emotional content held special appeal to lower class mentality, providing ecstatic outlet to those with little access to political power or social status. That such a conclusion is inadequate for understanding the Bacchic cult should be clear enough from Euripides' *Bacchae* alone. Psychological motives that drew men and women to a mystery cult knew no class boundaries. More complex and perceptive analysis sees a broad range of types attracted to the sect, not social outcasts alone but "marginal" peoples. On this reconstruction, the Dionysiac adherents included members of the *plebs* who worshipped on the Aventine, immigrants into the city from rural areas who had lost their farms in the dislocation of the Hannibalic war and its aftermath, women who sought the emotional attachments of a Bacchic cell as substitute for a passionless and formalistic domestic life, restive slaves in Etruria, rebellious herdsmen in Apulia, anti-Roman elements in Campania, and ambitious men of equestrian rank on the rise who assumed leadership roles in the burgeoning Bacchanalian movement.[114] The assemblage could form a potent combination—and give strong reason for the state to react with firmness and vigor.

But was there ever such an assemblage? This proposition depends upon fragmentary information of disparate variety concerning widely different individuals and groups. The idea that they all huddled under the Bacchanalian umbrella and thus presented a real or perceived threat to the established order is inspired but largely imaginative hypothesis. Livy's narrative of the "conspiracy" and identification of particular persons at the center of it give little hint of "marginal" elements. P.

---

[113] Cf. McDonald, *JRS*, 34 (1944), 26-27, 33; R. Günther, *Klio*, 42 (1964), 246-248; Toynbee, *Hannibal's Legacy*, II, 392-393; Dumézil, *Archaic Roman Religion*, II, 516-517.

[114] The construct is built with imagination and acuity by Gallini, *Protesta*, 16-17, 28-44. Criticisms delivered by Turcan, *RevHistRel*, 181 (1972), 18-21; Cova, *Athenaeum*, 52 (1974), 82-83, n. 1; North, *PCPS*, 25 (1979), 94-95—but no systematic or thorough refutation. That the active role of women in the cult provoked official reaction is argued by A.P. Arciniega and M.E. Sanahuja Yll, in *Paganismo y Cristianismo en el Occidente del imperio romano* (Oviedo, 1983), 143-151.

Aebutius' father had been an *eques equo publico*, his mother Duronia evidently came from a senatorial family, and his step-father T. Sempronius Rufus had a brother or cousin who held the tribunate three years earlier.[115] Such families were not on the fringes of society. Livy specifies as heads of the *coniuratio* M. and C. Atinius from the Roman *plebs*, the Faliscan L. Opicernius, and the Campanian Minius Cerrinius.[116] Testimony fails on Opicernius, but a few helpful items survive on the others. The Atinii have connections in Campania, a suggestive fact. But the family, which attained some prominence in Rome, hailed from Aricia. Three Atinii reached the praetorship between 195 and 189, and members of the house sponsored important legislation during these years. Their association with the men arrested cannot be pinpointed. The linkages, however, weaken any theory of humble origins.[117] The Cerrinii show no branches in Roman politics, but the clan attained distinction in Pompeii.[118] These persons do not belong in a category of social outcasts.

One must, of course, go beyond the few named individuals. Their status may, in any case, be unrepresentative of Dionysiac worshippers generally. Yet Livy's presentation contains little to suggest a lower class movement. He had Hispala observe that the vast numbers in the sect included certain men and women of the Roman nobility.[119] *Matronae*—a term reserved for respectable upper class women—engaged in some of the more fanatical rituals.[120] When the matter came up before the senate, each of the *patres* immediately took alarm lest he be tainted by personal involvement.[121] The under classes, at best, play but a secondary role. An argument from silence is here permissible. Livy's diatribes against the excesses of Bacchic devotees and Postumius' vitriolic speech on the vices and crimes of those infected by alien creeds would not likely omit reference to the base born, the proletarian, and the slave. Yet they are omitted.

---

[115] On Aebutius' father, see Livy, 39.9.2. A certain L. Duronius reached the praetorship in 181 and, indeed, received responsibility to pursue the Bacchanalians in that year; Livy, 40.19.9-10. On the tribunate of C. Sempronius Rutilus, see Livy, 37.57.12. A useful discussion of these families by Rousselle, *Roman Persecution*, 12-15.

[116] Livy, 39.17.6.

[117] Maras Atiniis appears as aedile on a Pompeian inscription that may have come from a Bacchic sanctuary; Bruhl, *Liber Pater*, 86. On the Atinii generally, see Astin, *Hommages Renard* (1969), II, 34-39. Livy's phrase, *de plebe Romana*, refers to the origin of the family and does not imply lowly status. For their Arician provenance, see Cic. *Phil.* 3.16. Astin plausibly suggests that the arrest of the Bacchant Atinii helps explain the plummeting of the house's political fortunes for the next two generations—although he regards the fallen Atinii as mere clients, perhaps freedmen or descendants of freedmen.

[118] Cf. F. Münzer, *RE*, 3.2, 1985-1986.

[119] Livy, 39.13.14: *in his nobiles quosdam viros feminasque*.

[120] Livy, 39.13.12.

[121] Livy, 39.14.4: *patres pavor ingens cepit...privatim suorum cuiusque vicem, ne quis adfinis ei noxae esset*.

Social dislocations during and after the Hannibalic war certainly brought distress and upheaval. But the connection between uprootings, migrations, and economic unrest on the one hand and participation in Bacchic rites on the other remains pure speculation. Certain texts are cited repeatedly to establish the connection—most notably those that concern the crushing of servile insurrections in the 190s and 180s. Roman officialdom struck against slaves or herdsmen in Latin cities in 198, Etruria in 196, and Apulia in 185 and 184.[122] Closer scrutiny shows the fragility of that alleged connection. Only a single passage brings slave rebellion and the Bacchanalian movement into conjunction. The Roman praetor L. Postumius, responsible for Tarentum in 184, suppressed hostile uprisings by slave herdsmen in the area and assiduously pursued what remained of the Bacchanalian investigation. The two operations are distinct. Livy's text does not authorize amalgamation here. Nor does any other passage warrant it.[123] We know of but a solitary slave who became an initiate of the mysteries in this period: Hispala Faecenia who divulged the cult's secrets to the consul. But she gained access only as companion and servant of her mistress, while still a young girl.[124] Far from establishing active slave participation, the example shows merely that slaves might enter the cult as favored stewards of upper-class worshippers.

Two further items, unnoticed in this connection, warrant attention. First, Postumius' speech rails against the shameless and obscene debauchery to which Roman youths succumb once initiated into Bacchic rites. Among the dire consequences of that moral corruption, so Postumius affirms, is to render young men unfit to serve in the military and untrustworthy in defense of the nation.[125] The implication is clear enough: the male initiates referred to are free men and potential soldiers, not propertyless proletarians and slaves.[126] Second, the *quaestio de Bacchanalibus*, however unprecedented and arbitrary it may have been, involved indictments, hearings, legal proceedings, trials, and judicial

---

[122] Livy, 32.26.4-18, 33.36.1-3, 39.29.8-9, 39.41.6-7.

[123] Livy, 39.41.6-7: *L. Postumius praetor, cui Tarentum provincia evenerat, magnas pastorum coniurationes vindicavit, et reliquias Bacchanalium quaestionis cum cura exsecutus est.* The earlier episodes of 198, 196, and 185 include no mention of Bacchants. And continuation of the Bacchanalian *quaestio* in 181 is unconnected with any servile movement; Livy, 40.19.9-10.

[124] Livy, 39.10.5: *ancillam se ait dominae comitem id sacrarium intrasse*; 39.12.6: *puellam admodum se ancillam initiatam cum domina ait.*

[125] Livy, 39.15.12-14. One need not conclude that loss of military manpower to the Bacchanalian cells was a principal fear in the senate, as Rousselle, *Roman Persecution*, 145-151.

[126] Cf. Livy, 39.8.7: *stupra promiscua ingenuorum feminarumque erant.*

pronouncements.[127] Such technicalities would not have been observed if slaves and commons comprised most of the victims.

Women, of course, had a large part to play in Bacchic ritual and administration. And it is reasonable enough to suppose that many joined the religion out of dissatisfaction with domestic circumstances or with the restrictions placed upon them by social and political traditions.[128] But female involvement in Dionysiac worship had a long history. Indeed the cult excluded males at the outset, and for some time thereafter. Insofar as transformation had taken place, it entailed a proportionate decline rather than increase in women's influence. All the leaders singled out by Livy are male. And it is noteworthy that regulations imposed by Rome in 186 prohibited male priests but placed no ban on women in those positions.[129] As is plain, female participation in the sect did not make it more volatile or potentially revolutionary. The severity of Rome's crack-down needs explanation beyond any menace posed by women.

None of this is to deny the social and economic grievances that built up in Rome and ranged over Italy in the aftermath of the Hannibalic war.[130] Nor should one doubt that many disgruntled, unsuccessful, and frustrated individuals found welcome refuge in the cult of Bacchus. Further conclusions, however, require leaps into the dark. Nothing justifies the inference that Bacchanalian cells served as vehicles to promote class aspirations and threaten the social order—or that the government felt obliged to curb them on that score.

Analysis of proposed solutions has helped to clear the ground. But understanding of the government's behavior remains elusive. Indeed, that behavior appears, if anything, even more baffling. The senate and its representatives had no sound reason to fear that the Bacchants threatened to undermine traditional religion, to erode Roman values, to challenge state control, to promote political upheaval, or to attack the social order. Where then does this leave us?

The first step must be a return to Livy's text. Use of this evidence, however, runs into an immediate stumbling-block. How much of the information is reliable? The narrative has engendered repeated criticism and skepticism. It contains a romanticized and embellished tale,

---

[127] Livy, 39.17.1-3, 39.18.1-6, 39.41.7.

[128] See Kraemer, *HTR*, 72 (1979), 72-80.

[129] *ILLRP*, 511, line 10: *sacerdos nequis vir eset; magister neque vir neque mulier quisquam eset.*

[130] Rousselle, *Roman Persecution*, 40-50, stresses the dislocations in Campania and southern Italy as explanation for growth of the cult. Yet those areas were steeped in Bacchic worship long before the Second Punic War. And Etruria, also a haven for Bacchants, suffered no dislocations as consequence of the war.

designed more for literary effect than for historical exactitude. The interplay of Aebutius, Hispala, Duronia, Sempronius, Sulpicia, and Postumius evokes the atmosphere of a romantic novel—or, better, Hellenistic and Roman New Comedy: the innocent and victimized youth, the warm-hearted courtesan, the scheming mother and step-father, the noble matron, and the resourceful magistrate. It is tempting to dismiss most or all of it as invention.[131] The wickedness and excesses ascribed to the sect and its devotees strain belief: indulgence in drink and sex; false witnesses, forgery, and murder; wild howlings and deafening noises to conceal the vices; moral corruption of every sort; torture of the recalcitrant or faint-hearted; fanatical rituals and wild orgies. Those accusations and similar ones are placed in the mouth of Hispala who informs on the "conspirators" and of Postumius who denounces them. But Livy also presents them in his own voice as introduction to his entire account of the Bacchanalian affair. Does this inspire greater confidence?

Repetition only diminishes credibility. The charges reek of rhetoric. Patent exaggeration and hyperbole reveal the slander, a not untypical means of discrediting alien creeds whose rites are open to initiates alone.[132] The Tiriolo document takes no note of criminal offenses and private vices assigned by Livy to the Bacchants—debauchery, perjured testimony, forgery, poisoning, murder of wayward initiates. It imposes only restrictions on meetings and worship, on the officialdom of the cult, on oaths, pledges, and vows. In short, the senate's directives, as dispatched to the *foederati*, addressed themselves to the religion, not to the felonies and lurid activities that prevail in Livy's account.[133]

---

[131] Cf. Fraenkel, *Hermes*, 67 (1932), 388: "die Novellenmotive"; G. Méautis, *REA*, 42 (1940), 477-480: "roman-feuilleton"; Tarditi, *PP*, 37 (1954), 283: "la fabula di Ebuzio e di Fecenia." A general literary analysis of the Bacchanalian affair in Livy's narrative by Cova, *Athenaeum*, 52 (1974), 82-109, especially, 95-96: "l'introduzione del romanzo diventa inevitabile." By contrast, J.P.V.D. Balsdon, *Roman Women* (London, 1962), 37-43, accepts the entire story without question.

[132] Livy, 39.8.6-8, 39.10.6-7, 39.13.10-14, 39.15.6-39.16.5. A sharp and emotional challenge to the Livian portrayal by S. Reinach, *RevArch*, 11 (1908), 249-252. See also Tierney, *Proceedings of the Royal Irish Academy*, 51 (1947), 106-117; Bruhl, *Liber Pater*, 95-98, 114-115; Toynbee, *Hannibal's Legacy*, II, 294-296. For Cova, *Athenaeum*, 52 (1974), 97-104, Livy's presentation employs invention and rhetoric to transform moral transgressions into political offenses. In his view, *op. cit.*, 85, only three chapters out of twelve on the Bacchanalian affair (39.14, 39.17-18) command trust for historical purposes.

[133] Gelzer, *Hermes*, 71 (1936), 283-287, points out that neither Cicero, *De Leg.* 2.37, nor Augustine, *CD*, 6.9, drawing on Varro, makes reference to private or public offenses. In his reconstruction, they consulted older and more trustworthy annalists, whereas Livy incorporated material from questionable later sources as well. Gelzer finds only 39.14.7 and 39.18.7-9 based on sound authorities—an unduly skeptical and schematic construct. For defenses of Livy's account, though not compelling ones, see Béquignon, *RevArch*, 17 (1941), 184-198; Festugière, *MEFRA*, 66 (1954), 83-99; Rousselle, *Roman Persecution*, 4-15.

The reliability of Livy's narrative depends on that of his sources. With regard to the Bacchanalian affair, they go unspecified. Moderns have filled the gap with conjectures. Suggestions include the 2nd century historian A. Postumius Albinus, contributing to the fame of his family through celebrating Sp. Postumius, consul of 186, or a combination of the later annalists Claudius Quadrigarius and Valerius Antias, with a portion from Cato the Censor.[134] The conjectures need not be expanded or analyzed. Livy's story alone undermines credibility.

The presentation of Bacchic ritual shows clear signs of distortion and deliberate misrepresentation. So, for example, the historian alleges that the cacophony of drums, cymbals, and wailings served to drown out the screams of victims subjected to rape or murder.[135] In fact, the use of drums and cymbals to accompany choral singing is common practice in Dionysiac ritual. The ceremony alluded to by Livy evidently involved new young initiates. It may be a form of puberty ritual, or perhaps a reenactment of Dionysus' slaying at the hands of the Titans.[136] The horrors depicted by Livy reduce themselves to ceremonial rites. Similar horrors are evoked by the historian's reference to a Bacchic custom of fastening men to a machine and hiding them away in a cave, whence they were said to have been snatched away by the gods—i.e. those who had resisted conspiracy, crime, and vice.[137] Suggestions about the true meaning of the rite see it as an initiation ordeal, a dramatization of the punishment of Dionysus' enemies, a foreshadowing of the heavenly bliss of the initiate, the representation of a descent into Hades, a form of possession by the deity, or a theatrical recreation of the triumph of faith over the unbelievers.[138] However one interprets the ritual, Livy's hostile portrayal perverts it. The same holds for the ceremony of Bacchic matrons plunging fiery torches into the Tiber and pulling them out still lit. The practice plainly simulates a miracle to attest to the presence of the god. But Livy's text presents it as a fanatical and delusive act.[139]

---

[134] On Postumius, see Fronza, *Annali Triestini*, 17 (1947), 224-227; Rousselle, *Roman Persecution*, 16-19. On the combination, see Tarditi, *PP*, 37 (1954), 282-287, with further bibliography.

[135] Livy, 39.8.8, 39.10.7.

[136] Cf. Tierney, *Proceedings of the Royal Irish Academy*, 51 (1947), 108-109; Turcan, *RevHistRel*, 181 (1972), 16-17.

[137] Livy, 39.13.13.

[138] Méautis, *REA*, 42 (1940), 481; Tierney, *Proceedings of the Royal Irish Academy*, 51 (1947), 110-112; Festugière, *MEFRA*, 66 (1954), 94-95; Pailler, *Mélanges Heurgon* (1976), II, 731-742; de Cazanove, *MEFRA*, 95 (1983), 107-111; cf. Bruhl, *Liber Pater*, 98; Rousselle, *Roman Persecution*, 37-39.

[139] Livy, 39.13.12; cf. Méautis, *REA*, 42 (1940), 480-481; Bruhl, *Liber Pater*, 96-98; Gallini, *Protesta*, 58-60.

Exaggeration, distortion, and calumny dominate the Livian picture of Dionysiac ritual and its participants. By setting the cult in the worst possible light, Livy or his sources transform alleged moral turpitude into outright *coniuratio*. Private corruption thereby becomes indistinguishable from conspiracy against the public welfare. And this in turn helps to justify rigorous suppression by the state. The transition, or rather equation, is assumed and not documented. The label of *coniuratio* evokes images of rebellion and subversion of the public order. But it lacks both evidence and plausibility. Indeed the very core of Livy's tale shatters confidence. He (or persons in his narrative) asserts that Bacchic worship pervaded the city like a plague, that the hue and cry of devotees rang through the streets, that Bacchic cells were known throughout Italy, that participants numbered in the several thousands, and that even the *patres* expected to find the sect's contagion among themselves.[140] The religion, on that showing, was hardly a secret. Yet Livy, at the same time, has the consul depend upon information from a courtesan and ex-slave, information prompted by a lover's revelation and elicited through the intercession of the consul's own mother-in-law! The story, on the face of it, is senseless and ridiculous.

Strong temptation inclines to jettison the whole tale. But that would miss the point. The objective is not simply to expose inconsistency and improbability, but to explain it. One can detect flaws in the story without difficulty. But that does not settle the matter. Why these flaws and why this story? Livy would hardly have invented it, nor is there any reason for his sources to have done so. The narrative needs to be taken seriously—not as accurate characterization of the Bacchic cult, but as a campaign to justify its suppression.

The entire course of events smacks of a staged operation. Postumius and his collaborators set it up with skill. The *eques* Aebutius brought the matter to the attention of the authorities, his character vouched for by the worthy Aebutia and indirectly by the noble Sulpicia. Then Hispala Faecenia delivered the damaging information, but did so with feigned reluctance, thereby to boost confidence in its authenticity. An innocent, wronged youth and an unselfish, devoted mistress served to generate sympathy and trust. The scene duly played itself out in the consul's quarters. Hispala swooned and wept, her testimony extracted by combining intimidation and encouragement. Postumius browbeat the

---

[140] Livy, 39.9.1: *huius mali labes ex Etruria Romam veluti contagione morbi penetravit;* 39.15.6-8: *Bacchanalia tota iam pridem Italia et nunc per urbem etiam multis locis esse, non fama solum accepisse vos sed crepitibus etiam ululatibusque nocturnis, qui personant tota urbe, certum habeo;* 39.14.4: *patres pavor ingens cepit...ne quis adfinis ei noxae esset.*

panicked courtesan, and Sulpicia stepped in to reassure her, while mollifying the consul.[141] The preliminaries out of the way, Hispala proceeded to beg forgiveness and protection, and then conveyed her slanderous testimony. Postumius transmitted it to the senate and received immediate authorization to take firm steps against the cult. The principals, it appears, devised their drama to promote a predetermined end.

Livy reports no senatorial debate. Doubters may have questioned the scenario when the consul first presented it. But rhetoric and persuasion evidently prevailed. Some senators took alarm lest they themselves be implicated, a fact that doubtless hastened a closing of the ranks.[142] In the end, the *patres* determined upon a show of unity. Postumius added a final touch, placing Aebutius and Hispala in protective custody, thus to suggest that they were in danger and to exhibit his own precautions and magnanimity. The consul could now come before the public with an arresting tale, heightened by the drama of unexpected discovery, exposing the lurid secrets of an alien sect, discrediting religious ritual as excessive fanaticism and lewd orgies, and branding private mysteries as conspiracy to overturn the social and political order. By blackening the cult and magnifying its threat to society, Roman leaders obtained the support needed to suspend normal judicial processes, to cross the legal boundaries between Roman and Italian jurisdiction, and to display their authority in Italy. In short, the *coniuratio* was not that of the Bacchants, but of those who sought to make an example of them.[143]

The most difficult problems still remain. Why single out the cult of Bacchus, and why in 186? The former question has not received satisfactory answer, and the latter none at all. The issues can be approached in two separate but ultimately converging paths: a shift in emphasis in Roman foreign policy, and an assertion of collective authority by the Roman senate. The Bacchants became victims in the implementation of those developments.

Dramatic and decisive victories in the east marked the opening of the decade of the 180s. Rome had crushed her most persistent and irritating foe, the Aetolian Confederacy, and had brought the Greek mainland to

---

[141] See, especially, Livy 39.13.3: *Postumius accensus ira...et Sulpicia attollere paventem, simul illam adhortari, simul iram generi lenire.*

[142] Livy, 39.14.4.

[143] For a similar approach, largely ignored, see Méautis, *REA*, 42 (1940), 477-480, who sees the story as derived from a fabricated report made by Postumius to the senate. Only Turcan, *RevHistRel*, 181 (1972), 25-27, has cited the idea with favor, but he believes that the Bacchanalian movement was a potential threat and that the Romans had reason to be anxious.

submission in 189. More momentous still was the stunning defeat of
Antiochus III, greatest of the Seleucid kings, which extended Roman
power across the Aegean and through much of Asia Minor. Further campaigns brought the recalcitrant Galatians to heel. And Antiochus, in the
Peace of Apamea of 188, surrendered all lands, cities, and holdings
beyond the Taurus mountain range.[144] Roman ascendancy in the east
seemed established. Aetolia had to agree to a treaty in which she bound
herself to respect the empire and majesty of Rome.[145] At about the same
time, perhaps in 188, Rome also concluded a formal alliance with the
Achaean League, reigning power in the Peloponnese. The two
agreements served to signal concord and order in Greece, thus permit-
ting Rome to withdraw without need of further direct involvement. A
comparable situation was envisioned for Asia. The Peace of Apamea proclaimed an *amicitia* for all time between Rome and Antiochus the Great.
The king's realm had been diminished, but his hold on the throne was
acknowledged and his future cooperation anticipated. He would now
become an associate in the maintenance of stability in the eastern
Mediterranean. A combination of monarchs and states from Macedon to
Egypt represented the means to provide an equilibrium. The message
delivered by Roman pacts with Aetolia, Achaea, and Syria, and
arrangements with Pergamum and Rhodes, among others, was that of
enduring balance and harmony in the east through an aggregate of
Hellenic powers. For Rome, this network of agreements supplied a
rationale for withdrawal.[146]

By contrast, Roman leaders turned their attention more energetically
and intensively to the affairs of Italy. After the evacuation by Hannibal,
the Republic's forces engaged in more than a decade's warfare against
Gallic tribes for the control of Cisalpine Gaul. Submission of the fierce
Boii in 191 finally settled the matter.[147] Contests with the Ligurians of
the Cisalpina, however, stretched on, a prolonged and seemingly endless
series of battles that occupied consular armies almost annually until the
mid 2nd century.[148] The need for solidifying dominion in northern Italy

---

[144] For the course of the wars, e.g., B. Niese, *Geschichte der griechischen und makedonischen
Staaten seit der Schlacht bei Chaeronea* (Gotha, 1883-1903), II, 695-770; De Sanctis, *Storia dei
Romani*, IV.1, 144-228; E. Will, *Histoire politique du monde hellénistique* (Nancy, 1967), II,
173-193.

[145] Polyb. 21.32.2; Livy, 38.11.2: *imperium maiestatemque populi Romani gens Aetolorum
conservato sine dolo malo*.

[146] All of this is argued in detail, with full citations and bibliography, by Gruen,
Hellenistic World, 25-38, 86-88, 547-550, 640-643.

[147] See discussion by Toynbee, *Hannibal's Legacy*, II, 264-272; McDonald, *Antichthon*,
8 (1974), 44-53.

[148] Toynbee, *Hannibal's Legacy*, II, 273-285.

and guaranteeing Roman security in the penisnula held chief priority. That fact gains clear expression through Rome's settlement policy in the years immediately subsequent to the defeat of the Boii. Appeals to the senate by the Latin colonies Placentia and Cremona in 190 for additional manpower brought an immediate response: 6000 recruits moved into the two towns. In addition, the *patres* determined to establish two new foundations in territory previously occupied by the Boii.[149] As it turned out, insufficient numbers reduced the two to one: the Latin colony of Bononia, planted in 189 on a site once employed by the Boii as their capital.[150] The founding of colonies continued in the later 180s and early 170s: Potentia and Pisaurum in Picenum and the Ager Gallicus respectively in 184; Mutina, Parma, and Saturnia in 183; Gravisca on Etruscan land in 181; the great foundation of Aquileia, authorized in 183 and finally put into place in 181; Pisa in 180; and Luna on territory seized from the Ligurians in 177.[151]

The combination of settlements aimed to consolidate Rome's hold on northern Italy. Foundations on both the Adriatic (Potentia and Pisaurum) and the Tyrrhenian (Luna and Pisa) coasts, in addition to key inland sites (Bononia, Mutina, Parma) put Rome in a position to exploit the regions of Cisalpine Gaul and to press ahead with the subjugation of Liguria. Those aims were markedly facilitated by the important new roads built by the consuls of 187, the year before the Bacchanalian affair. The Via Aemilia would extend from Placentia to Ariminum and the new Via Flaminia would traverse the Appenines from Bononia to Arretium.[152] The two highways joined at Bononia, and the Aemilia gained reinforcement from colonial foundations at Mutina and Parma. Roman leaders plainly pursued a systematic policy of tightening the state's grip on northern Italy.[153]

Movement toward a stronger Roman role in Italy can be detected in other ways. The new colonies of the 180s were, in almost every case,

---

[149] Livy, 37.46.9-10, 37.47.2.

[150] Livy, 37.57.7.

[151] Potentia and Pisaurum: Livy, 39.44.10; Mutina, Parma, and Saturnia: Livy, 39.55.6-9; Gravisca: Livy, 40.29.1; Aquileia: Livy, 39.55.5, 40.34.2; Pisa: Livy, 40.43.1; Luna: Livy, 41.13.4-5; cf. 45.13.10; Vell. Pat. 1.15.2-3. With the exception of Aquileia, these were all citizen colonies. The increasing attractiveness of Roman citizenship made it difficult to staff Latin colonies. The citizen foundations were now much larger and more imposing than their earlier counterparts. The exception of Aquileia is perhaps explicable by the distance from Rome.

[152] Livy, 39.2.6, 39.2.10. An exhaustive study of the roads by G. Radke, *RE*, Suppl. 13 (1973), 1539-1595.

[153] Other roads too may have been built at or around this time; cf. Salmon, *The Making of Roman Italy* (London, 1982), 99.

Roman rather than Latin foundations. Principal motivation for this shift undoubtedly lay in the difficulty of attracting settlers to Latin colonies. But a by-product, plainly expected and not unwelcome, was an increasing number of Roman citizens in Italy. The leadership appears to have promoted and encouraged this development. Both censors of 189, we are told, enrolled onto the citizen lists any applicant who had two free-born parents.[154] In the following year, three Volscian *civitates sine suffragio*, Arpinum, Fundi, and Formiae, obtained full franchise—and they were probably not alone.[155] The Campanians, without citizen rights since 211, received the senate's sanction to be registered at Rome in 189 and then obtained important private rights, namely *conubium*, in 188.[156] The policy of encouraging an increase in Roman citizens, however, had some troublesome consequences. Large numbers of Latins had settled in Rome and gained entrance on the Roman citizen rolls, many of them through the generosity of the censors of 189. The loss of manpower put pressure on Latin governments which could no longer fulfill military quotas contracted under agreements with Rome. The senate yielded to the pleas of the Latin communities in 187 and ordered expulsion of all those who had been registered (or whose fathers had been registered) in Latin cities in or after 204. As a consequence, 12,000 Latins returned to their home communities under compulsion. Rome had complied with the wishes of the governments but overrode those of the immigrants, and perhaps went further to restrict future immigration through limiting Latin rights.[157] Justification for these moves lay in protecting the manpower quotas that balanced the contingents of Rome and her allies. At the same time, the Republic had reasserted its authority to make decisions and to establish (or remove) regulations that affected relationships among the states of Italy. That assertion too came in the year prior to the affair of the Bacchanalians.

---

[154] Plut. *Flam*. 18.1; cf. Livy, 38.28.1-2, 41.9.9.

[155] Livy, 38.37.6-9; cf. Salmon, *Making of Roman Italy*, 117-118.

[156] Livy, 38.28.4, 38.36.5-6.

[157] Livy, 39.3.4-5. The *ius migrationis* was modified to require a Latin who moved to Roman territory to leave a son behind in his home town; Livy, 41.8.9. The restriction is generally dated to 187 or shortly thereafter; McDonald, *JRS*, 34 (1944), 21-23; Toynbee, *Hannibal's Legacy*, II, 139-141; Salmon, *Roman Colonization*, 102; *contra*: E. Frézouls, *Ktema*, 6 (1981), 119-121. The problem had to be addressed again a decade later because of various and ingenious evasions by Latins determined to obtain Roman citizenship. Latin communities again complained, and the senate again responded positively: another round of expulsions took place and additional tightening of the restrictions; Livy, 41.8.6-12, 41.9.9-12. On the expulsion of Latins in 187 and 177, see the discussion of Frézouls, *op. cit.*, 115-132, who sees them as motivated in part by a conservative movement in Rome unwilling to share the benefits of empire with the Latins.

Roman policy in the early 180s now takes on discernible shape. The senate disengaged itself from commitments in the east, leaving the Greek world to a consortium of powers which could hold a measure of stability without the Republic's involvement. Rome focused her energies on Italy, completing the absorption of Cisalpine Gaul, waging intensive campaigns in Liguria, establishing a firm network of roads and colonies in the north, and playing a more conspicuous role in the affairs of the peninsula.

At the same time, the *patres* faced a need to reaffirm their own collective predominance in the affairs of state. The eastern wars had not only brought handsome victories for the nation but created resplendent reputations for certain generals. They celebrated magnificent triumphs and put on display spoils that dazzled the populace. But the more conspicuous their success, the greater the urgency for the combined leadership to hold them in check. That strain also contributed to the drive to express the aristocracy's firm control of policy and politics.

T. Flamininus' triumph in 194 paraded captured weaponry, vast sums of gold and silver, and impressive numbers of art objects, not only seized from the defeated king of Macedon but gathered from the grateful cities of Greece.[158] Greater treasures still awaited victors in the Aetolian and Antiochene wars. M.' Acilius Glabrio, who turned back Antiochus at Thermopylae and drove him out of Greece, led a splendid procession in 190 that included cash, silver vessels, and some of the royal possessions themselves, an impressive personal advertisement.[159] L. Scipio, victor at Magnesia, the decisive battle of the Antiochene war, returned to heady honors and a triumph in 189 that eclipsed all predecessors: large numbers of gold crowns, ivory tusks, and even models of towns were included among the silver and gold bullion, coins, and engraved vases.[160] M. Fulvius Nobilior brought the war in Greece to a successful conclusion and imposed a peace settlement upon the rancorous Aetolians. He obtained his triumph at last at the beginning of 187, exhibiting lavish spoil that encompassed not only the by now expected haul of silver and gold but also every variety of modern weapon and huge numbers of bronze and marble statuary. Fulvius added further to his own self-display by employing part of the booty to finance a new temple of Hercules of the Muses.[161]

---

[158] Livy, 34.52.4-8.
[159] Livy, 37.46.2-6: *magnificus et spectaculo et fama rerum triumphus fuit.*
[160] Livy, 37.59.3-6.
[161] Livy, 39.5.13-17; Pliny, *NH*, 35.66; Cic. *Pro Arch.* 27.

The triumph of Cn. Manlius Vulso at the end of the consular year
in 187 earned the greatest notoriety. Manlius laid claim to the distinction
for victories over the Galatians in Anatolia and for supervising the final
settlement with Antiochus the Great. The triumphal procession
displayed the customary plunder of wealth, with crowns, gold and silver
bullion, coined money, and captured arms. But Manlius' supporters
advanced even greater publicity for him. His veterans serenaded him in
song, and his political backers promoted a *senatus consultum* which directed
that any arrears owed by citizens to the treasury be paid out of the cash
presented in Manlius' triumph.[162] The opulent spoils procured by
Manlius Vulso became a landmark in the hindsight of later Latin writers.
The late 2nd century historian L. Calpurnius Piso had reason to comment on elaborately decorated furniture that Manlius brought to Rome.
And Livy, or his source, delivers the most damaging condemnation:
Manlius' booty ushered in the era of foreign luxury in Rome. For the
first time, so Livy maintains, Romans indulged themselves in couches
made of bronze, costly robes, tapestries and furnishing, slave girls
appeared as entertainers at banquets, cooks became prized and formal
dinner parties required elaborate preparations and great expense. From
a moralist's view, Manlius' introduction of luxury items from the
Hellenic world signalled the beginning of corruption in the Roman
citizenry.[163]

Victories in the eastern wars carried the special advantages of considerable wealth, triumphal distinction, personal popularity, and
political prestige. It is hardly surprising, therefore, that the commanders
who seized the limelight and availed themselves of these assets also
became principal targets of abuse and attack. The early years of the 180s
constituted precisely the densest period of assaults. Glabrio came under
fire in 189, when it was alleged that much of the loot captured from the
camp of Antiochus had not reappeared in his triumph and had not been
deposited in the treasury. The accusation, forcefully seconded by M.
Cato who offered himself as witness, sufficiently tainted Glabrio's
reputation to wreck his candidacy for the censorship and, in effect, to terminate his political career.[164] Fulvius ran into comparable difficulties.
Opponents challenged his right to a triumph, claiming that his assault on
Ambracia was unjustified and carried out with wanton brutality, even
producing Ambraciote witnesses to attest to Fulvius' atrocities. A pro-

---

[162] Livy, 39.7.1-5.
[163] Livy, 39.6.7-9: *luxuriae enim peregrinae origo ab exercitu Asiatico invecta in urbem est*;
Pliny, *NH*, 34.14, 37.12; Augustine, *CD*, 3.21.
[164] Livy, 37.57.12-37.58.1.

longed wrangle ensued, and, although Fulvius got his triumph in the end, the public vilification cost him dearly. He failed in his quest for the censorship of 184, and reached the office five years later only after a staged display of reconciliation with his foes. The blemish on his reputation stuck, as Cato's strictures show, even after the censorship.[165] Cn. Manlius Vulso fared no better. His request for a triumph encountered determined resistance. Critics charged that he had fought an undeclared war against the Galatians, that he had burdened the peoples of Anatolia with excessive exactions, and that his heedless ambition had caused unnecessary and inexcusable loss of life. Manlius too overbore opposition to obtain his triumph. But the sequel follows a pattern. Voters rebuffed his censorial campaign in 184, and Manlius disappears from the record thereafter.[166]

The most celebrated episodes, of course, concern the Scipio brothers. Africanus' fame had already touched the skies as consequence of the Hannibalic war. And he shared Asiagenus' exhilarating success at Magnesia in 190, the battle that shattered Antiochus' dreams. Yet even Asiagenus' triumph in 189 did not receive authorization without some back-biting and sarcasm. Adversaries claimed that the war's difficulty had been magnified, that a single battle had sufficed to finish Antiochus, that Thermopylae had been the real turning point, not Magnesia.[167] The carping failed to deny Asiagenus his triumph. But it was the opening shot in a campaign that ultimately hit its targets. The so-called "trials of the Scipios" followed in 187, perhaps one trial only, but both P. and L. Scipio came under heavy attack. Charges of embezzlement and peculation were hurled about, investigation of moneys confiscated from Antiochus III and unaccounted for, and even a whiff of treason. The outcome of these accusations remains obscured by the rhetorical coloring and inventiveness of the literary tradition. Scipionic influence persisted in Roman politics. But neither brother again attained high office. The episode tarnished the fame of the Scipios.[168]

Personal and political rivalries played a role in these contests. But the remarkable consistency with which the commanders of the Aetolian and

---

[165] The efforts to deny Fulvius a triumph: Livy, 38.43-44, 39.4-5. Failure in the censorial elections for 184: Livy, 39.40.3. Political reconciliation to obtain the censorship in 179: Livy, 40.45.6-40.46.16; Cic. *De Prov. Cons.* 20; Val. Max. 4.2.1; Gellius, 12.8.5-6; cf. M. Martina, *QuadFilClass*, 2 (1979), 21-37, with references to the scholarly literature. Cato's attacks: Cato, *ORF*, fr. 148-151.

[166] Opposition to the triumph: Livy, 38.44.9-38.50.3, 38.54.7, 38.58.11-12, 39.1.4, 39.6.3-6, 39.7.3; Florus, 1.27.3; *Vir. Ill.* 55.1. The failed censorial candidacy: Livy, 39.40.2.

[167] Livy, 39.58.7-8.

[168] Analysis of the Scipionic trials must be reserved for a separate discussion.

Antiochene wars came under assault at home and suffered career set-
backs indicates more than factional sniping. Reprimands, criticism, and
systematic opposition suggest a strong current within the Roman
aristocracy committed to checking the aspirations of men whose excessive
power might threaten the political equilibrium. Heady victories in the
East could be particularly worrying. They offered access to unusual influence, prestige, and wealth. One will not claim that attacks on the
generals derived from a concerted design by the nobility. An unspoken
consensus recognized the need to exercise restraint. At a time when Rome
boasted spectacular conquests abroad and individual leaders introduced
vast sums into the Republic, that need gave emphatic incentive to the
patres. Under the circumstances, an occasion whereby to reassert the
general authority of the senate would be welcome.[169]

The collective interests of the political class promoted a basic solidarity
weightier than and occasionally even advanced by factional and personal
strife. The targeting of the preeminent or would-be preeminent helped
to safeguard a proper sense of proportion. Attacks on the generals, like
extension of control in Italy, served as a vehicle to express the corporate
power of the aristocracy. Those attacks, concentrated upon the conquerors of the East, also signalled dissatisfaction or uneasiness with certain effects of the conquests: the ostentation and excesses that could
be associated with Hellenism, and the allure of the East that could divert
attention from Rome's first order of business, the consolidation of Italy.

All of this fills in essential background to the episode of the Bacchanalians. Rome had little reason to fear the cult as threat to religion,
society, or public order. But Bacchic sectarians supplied convenient victims for purposes that had little to do with the sect itself. The campaign
against Dionysiac worship must be seen largely as a demonstration—a
posturing by the leadership to exhibit senatorial authority, to declare
dominion in Italy, to distinguish collective interest from individual

---

[169] Notice also the *lex Orchia* of 182, an extensive piece of sumptuary legislation, placing restrictions on the number of guests to be invited for dinner, and perhaps other
restrictions as well; Macrobius, 3.17.2-3; Cato, *ORF*, fr. 139-146. The measure
announced official aversion to the display of wealth, and reduced opportunity for enter-
taining and building one's *clientelae*. On sumptuary legislation, see D. Daube, *Aspects of
Roman Law* (Edinburgh, 1969), 117-128; I. Sauerwein, *Die Leges Sumptuariae* (Hamburg,
1970); M. Bonamente, *Tra Grecia e Roma* (Rome, 1980), 67-91; G. Clemente, in *Società
romana e produzione schiavistica*, 3 (1981), 1-14, 301-304. In the same year of 182 a *senatus
consultum* restrained magistrates in the solicitation of funds to produce their lavish games;
Livy, 40.44.11-12. The measures hang together as part of a public message to discourage
the very successful from conspicuously eclipsing their peers.

excesses, and to distance itself from some of the manifestations of Hellenism.

The senate exploited the Bacchanalian affair to arrogate to itself exceptional, if not unprecedented, judicial powers. Installation of a *quaestio extraordinaria* by senatorial decree and appointment of the consuls to carry out senatorial instructions and to arrest and punish offenders without popular sanction or review entailed assumption of unusual power. Moderns have offered legalistic or semi-legalistic explanations. It can be claimed that the tribunes voluntarily yielded their right to intervene, given the special danger faced by the state, or that regular procedures generally were suspended for the occasion, or that the senate merely ordered an investigation, with a full-fledged trial still to come, or that consular *imperium* entailed power to conduct unhindered prosecutions for treason, or that senatorial authority already encompassed *quaestiones extraordinariae*, or that the nature of the crime precluded resistance to summary action.[170]

The legal approach, however, may be misleading. Criminal law in the early 2nd century was still rudimentary, procedures unsettled, and jurisdictional lines fluid. Senatorial spokesmen branded the Bacchanalians as conspirators, magnified their crimes, and exaggerated their threat to the commonwealth. The very fact that *coniuratio* did not fall under a legal category permitted the *patres* to seize the occasion and to take responsibility for the security of the state.[171] The actions set rather than followed a precedent. Magistrates in subsequent years, still under senatorial mandate, continued to hold hearings, try, and punish Bacchants.[172] In addition, *quaestiones* took place, on orders of the senate, to investigate and prosecute cases of poisoning both inside and outside the city in the years 181 to 179.[173] The *patres*' prerogatives in this area went unchallenged. By the mid 2nd century Polybius could affirm that crimes in Italy requiring public investigation, such as treason, conspiracy,

---

[170] Tribunes voluntarily yielded their right: Accame, *RivFilol*, 66 (1938), 226-227. Regular procedures suspended: Bruhl, *Liber Pater*, 100-101. Senate only ordered investigation: Mommsen, *Strafrecht*, 153, n. 1; Willems, *Le sénat*, II, 285. Consular *imperium* sufficed: Siber, *AbhLeipz*, 43.3 (1936), 8-9, 49. Senatorial authority sufficed: Kunkel, *Untersuchungen*, 25-27. Nature of crime precluded resistance: Lintott, *ANRW*, I.2 (1972), 244.

[171] Strachan-Davidson, *Problems*, I, 239, speaks of the senate's usurpation of authority. But this obscures the lack of clear authority prior to these events. Cf. Cova, *Athenaeum*, 52 (1974), 94-95. McDonald, *JRS*, 34 (1944), 16-17, sees the senate as taking emergency powers, analogous to the earlier appointments of dictators and the later *senatus consultum ultimum*.

[172] Livy, 39.41.6-7, 40.19.9-10.

[173] Livy, 39.41.5, 40.37.4-7, 40.43.2-3, 40.44.6; Val. Max. 2.5.4.

poisoning, and assassination, came under the jurisdiction of the senate.[174] The Bacchanalian affair had served as the model.[175]

The invention of the senate's new judicial responsibility went hand in hand with the extension of that responsibility to the land and communities of Italy. Checking of the Bacchants entailed senatorial directives to magistrates and officials all over the peninsula on a scale hitherto unprecedented. And the restrictions placed upon worshippers applied to citizens, Latins, and *socii*.[176] Here too lines of jurisdiction are fuzzy. None can say with certainty that the *patres'* action amounted to illegitimate intrusion or interference in allies' affairs. We hear of no objections from Latin or allied constituencies. On the other hand, there is little point in excogitating legal or moral grounds for Rome's exercise of authority here.[177] What matters is the senatorial decision to assume responsibility for policing the Bacchanalian cult throughout Italy. Instructions to local officials, inscribed on bronze plaques and set up in the most conspicuous places, gave high visibility to the senate's predominance.[178] The containment of the Bacchants came hard on the heels of Rome's establishment and reinforcement of colonies in the north, the building of great new highways to link settlements and garrisons, and the forced migration of 12,000 Latins back to their home

---

[174] Polyb. 6.13.4. Cf. Livy, 45.16.4; *Per.* 48; Cic. *Brutus*, 85.

[175] Cf. Cic. *De Leg.* 2.37: *quo in genere severitatem maiorum senatus vetus auctoritas de Bacchanalibus et consulum exercitu adhibito quaestio animadversioque declarat.*

[176] *ILLRP*, 511, lines 7-8.

[177] For a recent attempt, see M.A. Levi, *Klearchos* (1969), 15-23 = *Il tribunato della plebe* (Milan, 1978), 79-85. Levi's view that Roman interference was justified by the religious bonds inherent in *foedera* with Italian states is far-fetched. Rousselle, *Roman Persecution*, 51-65, makes much of the three men listed as witnesses to the *s.c.*, M. Claudius, L. Valerius, and Q. Minucius, arguing that they were selected as patrons of communities in southern Italy and as religious leaders, thus to soothe the anxieties of Latins and allies and to reassure Romans that the *pax deorum* required suppression of the Bacchants. The hypothesis ascribes far too great a role to men listed merely as contributors to the drafting of the decree. Insofar as they served a symbolic function, it may have been as senior ex-consuls to lend weight to the document's importance.

[178] Cf. *ILLRP*, 511, lines 25-27: *atque utei hoce in tabolam ahenam inceideretis, ita senatus aiquom censuit, uteique eam figier ioubeatis, ubei facilumed gnoscier potisit.* For McDonald, *JRS*, 34 (1944), 29-32, the consul's letter, represented on the Tiriolo tablet, deliberately emphasized senatorial instructions on certain matters, e.g. the order to set up the inscription and imposition of the death penalty, because of embarrassment regarding interference in local jurisdiction. Cf. also Accame, *RivFilol*, 66 (1938), 228-232. But the authority of the senate prevails throughout the document; lines 3, 6-7, 8-9, 17-18, 21, 23-26. McDonald finds a distinction between general orders, delivered as a common practice by Rome to her allies, and specific decrees that interfered with local prerogatives: magistrates issued the first type regularly, but were embarrassed by the second and shunted responsibility to the senate. But the distinction is not attested. And the notion that the senate customarily issued overriding orders of a general variety to allies is supported by no instances earlier than the Bacchanalian affair itself.

communities. Those events provide the proper preamble for the Bacchanalian episode. Rome tightened her hold in Italy and asserted her right to supervise Italian matters. The Bacchanalian affair underscored the fact that supervision rested with the collective eminence of the Roman senate.[179]

The *patres* employed the occasion to stake their claim on yet another prerogative: the regulation of religion. Suppression of Dionysiac worship was incomplete—indeed unintended. The terms of the *senatus consultum* laid emphasis not on elimination of the cult but on its subordination to senatorial will. Bacchants could keep their shrines, could continue to partake in ceremonies, and could hold public or private rites in groups of five or fewer—so long as they made application to the *praetor urbanus* and gained formal consent of the senate with a quorum of 100 present.[180] That procedure alone would declare overt capitulation to senatorial dictate. *Cives, Latini,* and *socii* all fell equally under the same restraints. The effectiveness of these conditions—or indeed of the entire campaign against the Bacchanalians—eludes detection. It is not easy to imagine full sessions of the senate summoned to process requests by every devotee who sought to protect a shrine, join a ceremony, or attend a meeting. The procedure itself would intimidate most would-be worshippers. At best, the praetor screened applications and moved a selection of them for consideration (and summary action) by the *patres*. The number of requests granted or denied (or heard at all) mattered less than the acknowledgment of the senate's ultimate adjudication.

The history of the cult during the remainder of the Republic is almost entirely unknown. That need not, however, demand the conclusion that Rome had successfully stamped it out—or that she had sought to do so. There is as little information on Dionysiac worship before 186 as after, which hardly implies that it sprang up *de novo* shortly before that time.[181] One Bacchic shrine, at least, survived the persecutions, a cult center near Pompeii, whether through successful application or disregard. And it was surely not alone. The god himself was still prominent at the end of the Republic, as attested by the Augustan poets.[182] The campaign in 186 net-

---

[179] Note, e.g., a senatorial decree, followed by consular edict, in 181, directing a three-day *supplicatio* and festival to be held throughout Italy; Livy, 40.19.5: *senatus censuit et consules edixerunt ut per totam Italiam triduum supplicatio et feriae essent.*

[180] *ILLRP*, 511, lines 3-22; Livy, 39.18.8-9.

[181] As is rightly observed by North, *PCPS*, 25 (1979), 97.

[182] On the shrine, see Bruhl, *Liber Pater*, 121-122. The evidence of Val. Max. 1.3.3, with regard to the cult of Sabazius, implies that Bacchic worship, or something very close to it, still had a following in the mid-2nd century. The testimony of Servius, *Ad Ecl.* 5.29, that Caesar first brought the rites of Liber Pater to Rome is transparently false, and any attempts to wring some truth out of it are pointless; see Bruhl, *op. cit.*, 124-127. On Bacchus and the Augustan poets, see Bruhl, *op. cit.*, 133-144.

ted victims in significant numbers: arrests, convictions, and incarceration. Authorities needed to follow through in order to confirm the seriousness of the threat and to prove that the senate had not raised a groundless alarm. Yet the number of 7000 is suspect, and the report that more were executed than imprisoned belongs to the realm of romance.[183] The Tiriolo document does specify the death penalty for failure to observe its provisions.[184] That may be more show than substance. Even Livy indicates that capital punishment was administered upon those convicted of specified felonies, like murder, sexual offenses, false witness, forgery, or fraud—not for membership in the sect.[185] The senate adopted dramatic measures, terrifying the Bacchants, scattering many of their cells, and making public display of their prosecutions. A symbolic significance, however, pervades this activity. The episode served to exhibit senatorial vigilance and responsibility for the security of state and to legitimize senatorial authority in the regulation of alien worship.

The symbolic character of the affair also helps to explain its place in the ongoing tension between Roman values and Hellenic assimilation. To interpret Roman actions here as an effort to stem the tide of Greek cultural influence or as the product of an anti-Hellenic faction would be naive and simplistic. The senate's leadership itself consisted of men drawn to Hellenic culture and much influenced by it—a cohort that included Cato the Censor. Roman attitudes toward that culture were ambiguous and intricate, rarely articulated and never simple. As we have seen, developments of the Trojan legend and the special emphasis placed upon it in the later 3rd century expressed, on the one hand, a wish to gain close association with the matrix of Greek tradition and, on the other, a desire to declare distinctive identity that would not be swallowed up in that tradition.[186]

The Bacchanalian affair shows some comparable tendencies. The cult evidently held strong allure for numerous Romans and Italians of various social classes who did not find its alien origins repellent. Nor did the measures of 186 propose to wipe out the Hellenic sect, let alone to challenge the Hellenic god. Yet the senate's action takes on added meaning as a gesture, especially when viewed in the historical circumstances in which it occurred. Heavy Roman involvement—by officers, diplomats, and rank and file—in the eastern wars made it the more

---

[183] Livy, 39.17.6, 39.18.5.

[184] *ILLRP*, 511, lines 24-25: *sei ques esent, quei arvorsum ead fecisent, quam suprad scriptum est, eeis rem caputalem faciendam censuere.*

[185] Livy, 39.18.3-4. For the subsequent *quaestio* of 184, we hear only of arrests and imprisonment; Livy, 39.41.6-7.

[186] See above pp. 19-20.

imperative to promote a sense of independence from the cultural world of Greece. The appeal of Hellenism ran deep in the private realm but needed restraint at the public level. Control of the Bacchanalian cult enabled Rome to turn her public face against a Hellenic creed that absorbed too much Roman energy and seduced too many Romans. Enforcement of private belief was undesirable and, in any case, quite impossible. The senate's measures did not target private beliefs. Rather, they placed the manifestations of the cult under public scrutiny and obliged it to submit to public regulation. The state had thereby reasserted its authority to govern alien religions when they impinged upon the interests of the commonwealth. Individuals might absorb the teachings of Hellas and transmit the culture of the East. But state policy concentrated on interests at home and distanced itself from Hellenism. The curbing of Bacchus' enthusiasts suited that policy.

No explanation of this baffling but fascinating affair can ever claim decisiveness. Irrational fears and narrow prejudices may have played a role concealed to us. And it will not be imagined that the Bacchants were altogether passive and meek worshippers, with innocent devotion to their creed. Adherents of the cult may indeed have made themselves offensive or suspicious, and some of its opponents may well have felt anxious or apprehensive. A rise in numbers and increasingly frequent celebrations also gave the devotees greater visibility—and made them likelier victims. But the emphasis must be placed elsewhere. Rome's assault on the Bacchants was a demonstration, not a crusade.

Roman leaders built a carefully constructed scenario in 186. Sympathetic witnesses appeared, their characters scrutinized and their stories verified, the testimony then presented to the *patres*, who sanctioned firm consular action, without apparent dissent. Denunciation of the Bacchants came in virulent terms, stressing the alien features of the cult, alleging a combination of crimes, and stigmatizing the movement as a *coniuratio*. The measures taken enhanced the drama by exaggerating the danger. The senate wrote the death penalty into its decree, aediles and *tresviri capitales* were mobilized to seal the city, numerous arrests took place, and summary judgments were delivered, even executions. Investigations pursued their course not only in Rome but in various parts of Italy to round up offenders and make examples of them. It is unlikely that the *patres*, or any significant portion of them, genuinely feared the Bacchants as purveyors of political or social upheaval, as threatening established religion, as developing organizations outside state control, or as insidious infiltrators of Hellenism. But the worshippers of Dionysus provided serviceable targets. They were both secretive and noisy, their initiatory rites mysterious and their nocturnal meetings suspicious, and they had reputations as revellers, fanatics, and madmen. The reputation had existed for some time; the senate chose to exploit it in 186. It was not the last time in history that adherents of a religion with a questionable public image were singled out as scapegoats to protect an alleged national interest. A melodramatic preliminary prepared the way. Then by magnifying supposed crimes and branding the cult as a *coniuratio*, Rome's officialdom justified unprecedented measures and a highly visible inquisition.

The outcome had less significance for the persecuted than for the persecutor. Bacchic worship survived, its constituency shaken but not eliminated. The campaign against it had a larger meaning for the senate as an institution. The Bacchanalian affair became a vehicle to assert the collective ascendancy of that institution, to claim new prerogatives in the judicial sphere, in the regulation of worship, and in the extension of authority in Italy. And, not least, the episode supplied a means to declare state policy independent of and a restraint upon individual inclinations toward Hellenism. In each aspect the gesture counted for more than the substance. The real portent for the future lay not in the impact upon the Bacchants but in the increasing tension between private assimilation of Hellenism and public distancing from it.

CHAPTER THREE

POETRY AND POLITICS:
THE BEGINNINGS OF LATIN LITERATURE

Obscurity envelops the beginnings of Latin literature. Scholarly investigation has stirred lively debate regarding the extent of Greek influence and the impact of an Italian pre-literary background.[1] Guesswork predominates in this sphere, inevitably so. The remains of early Roman writers are frustratingly fragmentary. The question of literary origins can here be left aside for a different, though no less difficult, assignment: inquiry into the political context and connotations of the oldest Latin literature. Private and personal motives in the composition of poetry and prose, of epic, drama, and history, escape documentation and elude research. But a public dimension adheres to the work of Rome's great figures in the first two generations of literary achievement: from Livius Andronicus to Ennius. Complex connections, only dimly perceivable, hold among culture, politics, and the interests of state in this early period. A definitive reconstruction lies beyond our grasp. But some tentative explorations may pay dividends. The early poets played a public role, a fact that need not have compromised their art but does set it in a larger framework.

Scholarship too often narrows the focus upon a particular phenomenon: patronage by nobles and noble *gentes* of dependent writers who promoted the prestige of their benefactors. The patron/client relationship that pervades Roman society serves as model, in most interpretations, for the nurturing of poet by potentate. The bestowal of *beneficia*, both material and non-material, and the discharge of *officia* mark the association. Reciprocal advantages follow: *otium* and support for the poet, enhanced fame for the patron. Of course, the terms *patronus* and *cliens* were generally avoided: it would be impolite to call attention to the dependency. *Amicus* had a better ring to it. The word could be used by either partner, thus obscuring distinctions in status and influence. The nature of literary patronage in Rome has provoked considerable discussion in recent years. A number of questions predominate: how wide is the social gap between patrons and poets, what differences hold

---

[1] A summary and critique of much recent scholarship by J.H. Waszink, *ANRW*, I.2 (1972), 869-927. A good brief survey by G. Williams in *The Cambridge History of Classical Literature*, II (Cambridge, 1982), 53-59, and A.S. Gratwick, *ibid*, 77-84.

between ancient and modern patronage, to what degree do literary clients resemble clients in other social contexts, and in what ways did subsidy and support shape the themes and content of creative artistry. Inquiry naturally concentrates on the late Republic and early Empire where the material is more abundant and answers seem within reach.[2] Yet writers of the 3rd and 2nd centuries command special interest. Almost all were of marginal social standing, either *peregrini* or *libertini*. Extensive backing by the powerful is an obvious inference—and the backers would expect return on their subvention. The circumstances have prompted assumptions about the emergence of Latin letters as a feature of social and political advancement by Roman aristocrats and aristocratic clans.[3]

The analysis contains truth, but only partial truth. Emphasis can be placed elsewhere. The public context of early Latin literature has a broader dimension that transcends the personal aspirations of Roman political figures and families. Pursuit of that dimension is here the principal objective.

Solid and widespread tradition places Livius Andronicus at the inception of Rome's literary history. Apart from that consensus, all else on Andronicus rests on shifting sands. Chronology of his life and career generated dispute even in antiquity. The tragic dramatist L. Accius, who was also a literary scholar, ought to have been in a position to know. Accius composed his *Didascalia* some time in the later 2nd century and may have had access to records of the poets' guild.[4] His information had Livius Andronicus taken as war captive from Tarentum in 209 and produce his first play at the Ludi Iuventutis of 197.[5] Explicit confirma-

---

[2] See now B.K. Gold, *Literary Patronage in Greece and Rome* (Chapel Hill, 1987), with selective bibliography. Professor Gold kindly made available an advance copy of her proofs. Among other recent works, raising some of these matters with particular pointedness, see P. White, *JRS*, 68 (1978), 74-92; Gold (ed.), *Literary and Artistic Patronage in Ancient Rome* (Austin, Texas, 1982), with the review article by E. Badian, *CP*, 80 (1985), 341-357; R.P. Saller, *CQ*, 33 (1983), 246-257; J. Griffin, in F. Millar and E. Segal, *Caesar Augustus: Seven Aspects* (Oxford, 1984), 189-218. Terminological definitions on a broader level are treated by Saller, *Personal Patronage under the Early Empire* (Cambridge, 1982), 6-39.

[3] In the formulation of F. Marx, *SitzSächsGes*, 63 (1911), 53, plebeian leaders were the principal benefactors of poets in order to enhance their own influence on the political scene. L. Ferrero, *Mondo Classico*, 11 (1941), 205-231, rightly questions the relevance of a patrician/plebeian distinction, but stresses the influence of individual *nobiles* and *gentes* upon the early writers. That interpretation still prevails. For particulars, see below.

[4] Accius was born in 170; Cic. *Brutus*, 229; cf. Jerome, *Chron.* Olymp. 160.2. And he lived long enough to hold conversations with the youthful Cicero; Cic. *Brutus*, 107. Accius' membership in the *collegium poetarum* is attested by Val. Max. 3.7.11.

[5] Cic. *Brutus*, 72-73.

tion of those statements is wanting, but other testimony provides general support for a *floruit* around the end of the 3rd century.[6] The thesis came under heavy fire, however, in the late Republic. Cicero's friend and confidant Atticus provided a very different chronology, based perhaps on the researches of the erudite Varro. His findings showed that Andronicus produced his first play in 240. Cicero accepted the Attican chronology, denouncing and dismissing Accius' version. For this he found independent authority in the *antiqui commentarii*, evidently early records of Roman ceremonies and public performances. Cicero then completed the refutation of Accius's dating by pointing out its incompatibility with the known sequence of Latin writers: Livius was acknowledged as Rome's first playwright; Accius' reconstruction would have him younger than Plautus and Naevius who had already created numerous plays by 197![7]

Cicero's denial is definitive. A minority of moderns still opt for Accius' late dating. But the authority of the *antiqui commentarii* stands, and the scholarship of Varro and Atticus inspires confidence. A reshuffling of the entire tradition on the sequence of early Roman poets can hardly be justified on Accius' aberrant chronology.[8] Accius himself evidently

---

[6] Jerome, in fact, locates the height of Livius' fame in 187; *Chron.* Olymp: 148.2. A verse of Porcius Licinus, the scholar-poet and contemporary of Accius, places the Muse's arrival in Rome in the time of the Second Punic War; Gellius, 17.21.45. For Horace, Roman interest in Greek drama post-dated that war; Horace, *Epist.* 2.1.161-163. On the passages, see G. D'Anna, *RendIstLomb*, 87 (1954), 120-128. A useful summary of all the evidence, eschewing undue speculation, by H.J. Mette, *Lustrum*, 9 (1964), 41-46.

[7] Cic. *Brutus*, 72-73: *minor fuit aliquanto is, qui primus fabulam dedit, quam ei, qui multas docuerant ante hos consules, et Plautus et Naevius.* The date of 240 for Livius' first play is reiterated by Cic. *De Sen.* 50, and *Tusc. Disp.* 1.3. See also Gellius, 17.21.42-43, citing Varro's *De Poetis.* The year 239 is given in Cassiodorus' *Chronicon.* Accius is, on any reckoning, wrong to associate a dramatic performance in 197 with games vowed by Livius Salinator after the battle of the Metaurus. Those games were not celebrated until 191; Livy, 36.36.5-6.

[8] H.B. Mattingly, *CQ*, 51 (1957), 159-163, seeks to make a case for Accius, questioning, among other things, the value of the *antiqui commentarii.* For Mattingly, Cicero would not have resorted to the argument on relative dates of the early poets if he felt that the *commentarii* had settled the issue. Similarly, A.E. Douglas, *M. Tulli Ciceronis Brutus* (Oxford, 1966), 63. The skepticism is indecisive. Cicero took the opportunity to score an additional point off Accius. To draw the logical conclusions from Accius' thesis and to deride their incongruities is a familiar scholarly device. Varro, to be sure, questioned the *commentarii* on another matter, the date of Naevius' death; Cic. *Brutus*, 50—here called *veteres commentarii.* But their authority carries much greater weight on an item like the year of Andronicus' play, doubtless fixed by consular date recording the *ludi* for which it was performed; so, rightly, W. Suerbaum, *Untersuchungen zur Selbstdarstellung alterer römischer Dichter* (Hildesheim, 1968), 299-300, with bibliography. The most elaborate defense of Accius' dating appears in G. Marconi, *MemAccadLinc*, 8.12 (1966), 125-213, who argues that the rival Varronian chronology stems from a tendentious tradition favoring Ennius and making of Andronicus a very early and therefore rude, uninfluential predecessor of the true course of Latin literature. The thesis is ingenious but altogether unfounded and unpersuasive. To establish Andronicus' primacy would hardly be to denigrate him. Mar-

shared the general view that Livius Andronicus headed the list of Latin poets and dramatists.[9] Production of the first Roman drama in the year 240 can be taken as established.

The event constitutes a milestone in Rome's literary history, but the implications carry wider meaning still: a link from the outset between artistic creation and state policy. The timing can be no accident. Livius' play was performed in the year that followed Rome's triumphant conclusion of the First Punic War. The games of which it formed part plainly served to celebrate that national victory.[10] The poet, we may presume, was commissioned for the purpose, a man who had already established his reputation. Rome's officialdom made the decision, shaped the event, and selected its man.

Wherein lay Livius' repute prior to 240? Extant biographical details are too sketchy or disputed to generate much confidence. Accius' statement that Livius was brought to Rome as a Tarentine captive in 209 can be safely discarded. And the modern idea that he came as prisoner from Tarentum after the Pyrrhic War in 272 rests on no ancient testimony whatever.[11] A notice in Jerome makes him a slave in the household of Livius Salinator, then manumitted for services in the education of Salinator's children.[12] That may rest on no more than an inference from late Republican practices, a time when Greek tutors in Roman households were regularly freedmen or slaves. The idea of Andronicus as captive and servile instructor remains questionable. The shifting sands offer little ground for a foothold. A few central items, however, warrant

---

coni's argument is adequately demolished by Suerbaum, *op. cit.*, 297-299, who also provides a useful bibliographic survey. See further Waszink, *ANRW*, I.2 (1972), 873-874. A different speculative reconstruction by R.E.A. Palmer, *Roman Religion and Roman Empire* (Philadelphia, 1974), 94-108. The recent suggestion of M. Drury, *Cambridge History of Class. Lit.*, II, 801, that there may have been two Livii Andronici, father and son, will be welcome only to those desperate to save Accius' credibility.

[9] Cicero's refutation in *Brutus*, 73, appears to take this common ground for granted. See quotation above, n. 7. *Contra*: D'Anna, *RendIstLomb*, 87 (1954), 119-124. The ancient consensus on Andronicus' primacy is reflected also in Cic. *Tusc. Disp.* 1.3; Livy, 7.2.8; Horace, *Epist.* 2.1.69-71; Val. Max. 2.4.4; Charisius, in Kiel, *GL*, 1.84.8-9; Gellius, 17.21.42; Cassiodorus, *Chron.* ad ann. 239.

[10] Cf. Gellius, 17.21.42: *pace cum Poenis facta...primus omnium L. Livius poeta fabulas docere Romae coepit.*

[11] The idea, often repeated in handbooks, was long ago discredited by W. Beare, *CQ*, 34 (1940), 11-19. Drury, *Cambridge History of Class. Lit.*, II, 800-801, claims it still as general scholarly opinion. Note, e.g., E. Flores, *Letteratura latina e ideologia del III-II a.C.* (Naples, 1974), 14-15, who asserts it without discussion.

[12] Jerome, *Chron.* Olymp. 148.2: *L. Livius tragoediarum scriptor clarus habetur, qui ob ingenii meritum a Livio Salinatore, cuius liberos erudiebat, libertate donatus est.* Observe, however, that Andronicus evidently did not take the *praenomen* of his supposed manumitter M. Livius Salinator; Jerome, *ad loc.*, Cassiodorus, ad ann. 239; Gellius, 6.7.11, 17.21.42.

emphasis. The Tarentine connection is plausible enough. Andronicus' name, in any case, is patently Greek, and a thorough knowledge of Greek drama and literature generally are prerequisites for his subsequent career in Rome.[13] When he came to Rome and why continue to elude inquiry—and are perhaps unimportant.[14] What matters is the commission for 240. Andronicus had obviously established a reputation in Rome that made him a likely candidate for the assignment. Patronage by the family of the Livii makes sense. The *nomen* adopted by Andronicus attests to it, perhaps acquired upon elevation to Roman citizenship.[15] But his attainments went beyond instructing the children of Livius Salinator. Andronicus, as bilingual intellectual, taught in both Greek and Latin, at home and in public, interpreting Greek texts and reading aloud from his own compositions in Latin.[16] When Rome's leadership decided to celebrate victory over Carthage with festivities that included a full-blown dramatic performance, they knew to whom to turn. Recommendation may have come from Livius Salinator. But it was the judgment of the senate to entrust so visible a public function to a Greek writer and dramatist.[17]

---

[13] The suggestion of P. Grimal, *Le siècle des Scipions* (Paris, 1953), 27-28, that Livius acquired his learning from Greek emigrés in Rome, has little to recommend it.

[14] Beare, *CQ,* 34 (1940), 17-19, suggests that he was summoned to Rome in 240 itself, precisely for the purpose of producing a play for the occasion. An unlikely idea. How would he have come to Roman notice? The Tarentine connection is questioned, indecisively, by Palmer, *Roman Religion and Roman Empire*, 97, 108.

[15] Accius indirectly alludes to the Livian connection, even though he has Fabius Maximus bring Andronicus to Rome. The play he produced in 197, according to Accius, was for games vowed by Livius Salinator; Cic. *Brutus*, 72-73.

[16] Suet. *De Gramm.* 1.

[17] It has often been surmised that Livius Andronicus earlier composed a hymn on public commission for the first *ludi saeculares* in 249. Ps.-Acro on Horace, *Carm. Saec.* 8, citing Verrius Flaccus, affirms that such a hymn was commissioned. And Varro in Censorinus, 17.8, refers to the games as *ludi Tarentini*. A hymn of Andronicus is cited in connection with rites in 200, recalled *patrum memoria*; Livy, 31.12.10. Those texts buttress the theory that Andronicus already held prominence as cultural servant of the state in 249. So, C. Cichorius, *Römische Studien* (Leipzig, 1922), 1-7; K. Barwick, *Philologus*, 88 (1933), 203-221; M. Lenchantin, *Athenaeum*, 14 (1936), 36-44. But the reconstruction is a house of cards. The hymn in 249 is nowhere ascribed to Andronicus. The *ludi Tarentini* have reference to a site on the Campus Martius and may have little or no association with Tarentum; cf. K. Latte, *Römische Religionsgeschichte* (Munich, 1960), 246-248; but see H. Erkell, *Eranos*, 67 (1969), 166-174. Livy's phrase, *patrum memoria*, need not imply that Andronicus' hymn belonged to a previous generation. The meaning may be that no other model for the hymn in 200 could be recalled apart from that of Andronicus; so Lenchantin, *op. cit.*, 41; or *patrum memoria* is reckoned from Livy's own day; J. Cousin, *RHR*, 126 (1942-3), 39-40; or, more likely, the term *patres* refers to senators, rather than ancestors; J. Briscoe, *A Commentary on Livy, Books XXXI-XXXIII* (Oxford, 1973), 91. In any event, the reed is too slender to build a case on. The hypothesis was satisfactorily disposed of by Marconi, *MemAccadLinc*, 8.12 (1966), 147-178. Further speculation by Mattingly, *Gnomon*, 43 (1971), 685-687.

The commissioning of Livius possessed both cultural and political con-notations. The poet's play was staged at the venerable Ludi Romani.[18] Entertainments of a dramatic sort had been part of the Ludi Romani in the past: variety shows, mime, brief playlets, comic dialogue, with actors and accompanying music. Andronicus, it is said, first applied a real story line to the performances, a full-scale drama rather than fragmentary pieces.[19] But the change had even larger reverberations. The Ludi Romani of 240 celebrated termination of the First Punic War, emblematic of Rome's ascendancy as prime power in the western Mediterranean. Livius was engaged as a Greek to adapt a Greek play for a national celebration at Rome. The decision set a precedent. Dramatic performances became a regular feature of the Ludi Romani, and were gradually introduced into other annual festivals, like the Ludi Plebeii, the Ludi Apollinares, the Ludi Megalenses, and the Ludi Cereales, by the end of the 3rd century.[20] The first occasion, however, had special over-tones. Rome's officialdom embraced the Hellenic artistic tradition and utilized it in the expression of their own national achievement. Victory in the First Punic War not only confirmed Roman ascendancy in Hellenic south Italy but extended it to Hellenic Sicily. The accomplishment would be marked by elevation of the ludi to a cultural event that announced Rome's participation in the intellectual world of the Greeks.[21] The national ceremony acquired an international dimension. And that dimension in turn highlighted the attainments of the nation. Livius Andronicus' visibility and esteem rose to the public level. The state was both patron and beneficiary.[22]

Andronicus was responsible for still another literary milestone, an even more renowned one: a rendering of Homer's *Odyssey* into Latin. This task did not come on public commission. Nor, on the other hand, did

---

[18] Cassiodorus, *Chron.* ad ann. 239: *his coss. ludis Romanis primum tragoedia et comoedia a L. Livio ad scaenam data.* That two plays were produced may be questioned, an item nowhere else corroborated.

[19] The background is presented in a confused mixture by Livy, 7.2.3-13; cf. Val. Max. 2.4.4.

[20] L.R. Taylor, *TAPA*, 68 (1937), 285-291.

[21] Cf. Waszink, *Mnemosyne*, 13 (1960), 21-22. Note that Hiero, the powerful ruler of Syracuse, came to Rome in 239 to attend the games, bringing a handsome grain donative; Eutrop. 3.1.

[22] Aediles took responsibility for supervising the games and for purchasing the theatrical scripts; cf. Terence, *Eun.* 20. But it would be erroneous to characterize their influence as patronage. They held office for just one year and would not likely have fur-ther occasion to promote the playwright's work. A dramatist, in fact, would do well not to link himself too closely to particular noble families, lest members of other clans hold the aedileship when he peddles his wares. The aedile's sponsorship of play and playwright came not as individual patron but as state official.

the work serve merely as a text for instructing school children. The adaptation, as even the few extant fragments indicate, went beyond mere translation to the realm of artistic creativity.[23] Absence of the public dimension takes it outside the area of our inquiry. But the choice of subject may not be altogether irrelevant. That Livius elected to translate the *Odyssey* rather than the *Iliad* discloses the orientation of the western Greek in Rome. The *Iliad* was Hellas' national epic; the *Odyssey* had resonance in the western Mediterranean. Odysseus was an Adriatic prince, and his wandering expanded Hellenic horizons in a western direction. Further, and more important, Greek legends on the origins of Rome included versions that incorporated Odysseus as companion of Aeneas or the sons of Odysseus and Circe as founders of Italian cities, Rome among them.[24] One will not conclude that Livius Andronicus translated the *Odyssey* to propagate a particular version of Rome's beginnings. But the selection of that epic betokened both the Hellenic heritage ascribed to Rome and the Italian connections of the hero. The epic, like the poet, represented a cultural amalgam: the Hellenic nourishment that fostered a national sensibility.[25]

A public commission came once more, in Andronicus' old age. Grave circumstances, rather than celebratory ones, dictated the appointment. It was a pivotal time in the Second Punic War, the year 207. Word had recently arrived that the army of Hasdrubal was poised to cross the Alps, nothing but winter in its way.[26] Entrance into Italy would mean a link with Hannibal's forces and promised the most serious Carthaginian thrust of the war. A time of anxiety prompted prodigies in number, sighted or reported in various parts of Italy. The need for expiation was urgent, and the religious establishment at Rome mobilized as never before. *Haruspices* were called from Etruria and directed the eradication of one monstrous portent. Roman pontiffs decreed a procession of 27 virgins chanting a hymn composed for the occasion. Then, when lightning allegedly struck the temple of Juno Regina on the Aventine, further rites were organized. The *haruspices* advised that an expensive gift be offered to the goddess by Roman matrons, who were then summoned by edict of the aediles and financed the gift from their own dowries. And still

---

[23] See, most recently, K. Büchner, *SO*, 54 (1979), 37-70. Note also Livius' acquaintance with Hellenistic literary theory and linguistic practice; G. Sheets, *AJP*, 102 (1981), 58-78.

[24] Dion. Hal. 1.72.2, 1.72.5. Cf. E.D. Phillips, *JHS*, 73 (1953), 53-67. *Contra*: Marconi, *MemAccadLinc*, 8.12 (1966), 127-129.

[25] Cf. Grimal, *Le siècle des Scipions*, 28-31. Flores' view, *Letteratura latina e ideologia*, 18-25, that Livius' *Odyssey* expressed the interests of the philhellenic and expansionist Scipionic party, rests purely on imagination.

[26] Livy, 27.36.3-4.

another sacrifice to Juno was proclaimed, this time by the decemvirs, to be brought by an elaborate procession that included the 27 singing virgins and the decemvirs themselves, bedecked in ritual finery.[27] The diverse combination of religious and secular officials was unprecedented in Roman history: *haruspices*, priests, decemvirs, and aediles. The gravity of the situation called forth extraordinary measures. Alien rites were drawn upon, as well as domestic ones. The *haruspices* were experts in Etruscan lore, and the decemvirs had charge of the Sibylline Books which contained Hellenic religious counsel. The procession itself appears to have derived from Greek religious practices. It was an eclectic collaboration, designed to appease the divinities and to ward off the Punic menace.[28]

As part of this collaboration the state invited the venerable Livius Andronicus to compose a hymn for the procession of maidens. Livius discharged the task and thus had a hand in winning the divine favor that issued in victory at the Metaurus.[29] The choice of that poet is symbolic and significant. This was no empty honor accorded a retired bard. Circumstances were too grave for mere ceremonial distinctions. Livius Andronicus embodied that blend of Hellenic culture and Roman national interest exemplified by the expiatory rites of 207. The Tarentine Greek who had become dean of Latin letters, signified for Rome and her

---

[27] Livy, 27.37. The effort of Barwick, *Philologus*, 88 (1933), 204-212, to excise this whole narrative as a doublet of the similar expiatory rites in 200, is drastic and unpersuasive. Cf. the criticisms of Cousin, *RHR*, 126 (1942-3), 37-39. And see further E. Flores, *Letteratura latina e società* (Naples, 1973), 7-22.

[28] The analysis of A. Boyce, *TAPA*, 68 (1937), 157-171, places too much stress upon rivalry and confusion among the various functionaries, for which the Livian text offers no explicit support. A more balanced and illuminating study by Cousin, *RHR*, 126 (1942-3), 15-41. B. MacBain, *Prodigy and Expiation: A Study in Religion and Politics in Republican Rome* (Brussels, 1982), 65-71, rightly emphasizes the Etruscan elements in Rome's reaction and the need to shore up defenses and morale in Etruria. But he plays down other dimensions in this elaborate set of religious performances. On the Hellenic character of the procession itself, see G. Wissowa, *Religion und Kultus der Römer*, 2nd ed. (Munich, 1912), 191. Barwick, *Philologus*, 88 (1933), 206-208, rightly cites Phlegon, *Mirab.* 10 = *FGH* IIB, 257, for a closely parallel expiatory ritual authorized by a Sibylline Oracle. The ritual, established for the first time in 207, set a precedent for subsequent expiations of androgynous portents, which occurred with some frequency in the next century and more. The evidence is conveniently collected now by MacBain, *op. cit.*, 127-135.

[29] Livy, 27.37.7; Festus, 446, L. Skepticism about the likelihood of Livius' still being alive in 207 is unwarranted. Cicero has the Elder Cato remark that Livius survived *usque adulescentiam meam; De Sen.* 50. But that need not imply a date of death well before 207; as, e.g., Barwick, *Philologus*, 88 (1933), 220-221; Mattingly, *CQ*, 51 (1957), 161. Cato was born in 234, and the term *adulescentia* is elastic. The authenticity of Cato's remark is, in any case, unverifiable. Attestation of Andronicus' hymn in 207 comes independently from Livy and Festus. No hypothetical reconstruction has shaken that testimony.

allies the union of cultural and religious traditions that would win divine beneficence for their cause.[30]

The battle of the Metaurus proved to be Rome's salvation. Livius earned his reward and received it—either shortly thereafter or posthumously. The state accorded him a signal honor: not a personal prize but a living and enduring monument. Public declaration authorized the establishment of a guild of writers and actors, with a locus in the Aventine temple of Minerva and the right to assemble and make offerings. The guild obtained official state sanction, an explicit distinction for Livius who was both playwright and actor.[31]

The commemoration of Livius' services is intelligible. But why in this peculiar fashion? No information survives on the organization of dramatic artists in Italy prior to this time. The Greek background, however, does emerge from the texts—and that background is critical. Hellenic artists, writers, actors, singers, and all other functionaries associated with dramatic performances had for some decades gathered themselves in guilds, based in certain cities or regions and under the auspices of the god Dionysus. These Dionysiac *technitai* gained considerable exposure and popularity throughout most of the Greek world, their corporations officially recognized and granted privileges by civic authorities and Hellenistic kings.[32] One may infer without difficulty that such guilds spread to the Greek communities of Sicily and southern Italy, notably the cultural center at Tarentum, the home town of Livius Andronicus.[33] When Rome called upon Livius to produce a play for the Ludi Romani in 240, the organization of performers was already in place. The poet must have drawn from and based his personnel upon the Greek companies. As dramatic performances became an increasingly frequent feature of Roman festivals in the next generation, Hellenic artists

---

[30] Flores, *Letteratura latina e società*, 19-22, sees the choice of Livius as a political maneuver by the Scipionic group, an unduly narrow interpretation. The argument depends on the personnel of the pontifical college in 207—a college which, even on Flores' analysis, had only a minority of Scipionic supporters.

[31] Festus, 446, L: *itaque cum Livius Andronicus bello Punico secundo scribsisset carmen quod a virginibus est cantatum, quia prosperius respublica populi Romani geri coepta est, publice adtributa est ei in Aventino aedis Minervae in qua liceret scribis histrionibusque consistere ac dona ponere; in honorem Livi, quia is et scribebat fabulas et agebat.* Festus draws perhaps on the Augustan writer Verrius Flaccus, but the information, and even the wording, goes back to an official document; see R. Till, *Neue Jahrbücher*, 115 (1940), 166-167.

[32] Evidence collected by Poland, *RE*, VA2 (1934), "Technitae," 2473-2558. A convenient summary by E.J. Jory, *Hermes*, 98 (1970), 224-225, who rightly recognizes the importance of these groups for understanding the Roman situation.

[33] The testimony is indirect but telling. See Jory, *Hermes*, 98 (1970), 228, n. 2, with bibliography. Cf. B. Gentili, *Theatrical Performances in the Ancient World: Hellenistic and Early Roman Theater* (Amsterdam, 1979), 15-41; P. Grimal, *IXᵉ Congrès Int. de Rome de l'Assoc. Budé* (1973), I, 252-255.

probably became an increasingly familiar part of the Roman scene. Some Romans may have joined the associations, but the membership doubtless remained predominantly Greek and the structure of the societies surely adopted the model of the Greek *technitai*.[34]

Important consequences follow with regard to the Roman decree of 206 or thereabouts. The *technitai* had hitherto been dedicated to Dionysus. The decree gave them official recognition, set them up on the Aventine, and sheltered them under the authority of a Roman deity, Minerva. What was the significance of this change? It has been surmised that growing disfavor shown to foreign cults imperilled the Dionysiac artists. A *senatus consultum* of 213 had suppressed alien observances. Association of the guilds with Minerva would give them new respectability.[35] That analysis misconceives Roman attitudes. The *s.c.* of 213 addressed itself to a temporary hysteria during the war, not a reflection of general Roman hostility to alien rites. More to the point is the transfer of Cybele's cult to Rome at about the same time as recognition of the *technitai*. The atmosphere was one of receptiveness to foreign institutions.[36]

It is Rome's advantage that needs to be explained in this affair. A recent suggestion assesses the decree as an attempt to regulate artistic production by placing it under state control: the measure curbed private activity by *poetae clientes* for individual patrons, thus serving the collective interest of the senatorial oligarchy.[37] But the text betrays no hint of regulation or restrictions: *scribae* and *histriones* receive public sanction, gain access to a sacred shrine for their meetings, and secure the right to make offerings to the goddess. The positive rather than the negative aspects stand out. Official recognition of the guild elevated its status and gave it a bond with the state religion. But the greater benefit came to the state itself. Dramatic performances had become part of Roman annual festivities, ceremonies of religious character and political celebration.

---

[34] The acute discussion of Jory, *Hermes*, 98 (1970), 228-233, is essential reading on this score. On the lively theatrical traditions in the towns of Latium and Campania, see the evidence cited by E. Rawson, *PBSR*, 53 (1985), 97-113—almost all of it, however, from the late Republic.

[35] So Jory, *Hermes*, 98 (1970), 229-230; N. Horsfall, *BICS*, 23 (1976), 81. The senatorial decree of 213: Livy, 25.1.6-12.

[36] Horsfall, *BICS*, 23 (1976), 80, oddly sees the transfer of the guild to Minerva's temple on the Aventine as reflection of Roman scorn for the artists, by associating them with dishonored *mercenarii*, the tradesmen also under Minerva's patronage. If this implication existed, it would be a distinctly peculiar honor for Andronicus and the dramatic artists. Minerva was, to be sure, patroness of various trades' guilds—but also of the arts and crafts; cf. Latte, *Römische Religionsgeschichte*, 166, n. 1; Jory, *Hermes*, 98 (1970), 227.

[37] M. Martina, *Labeo*, 26 (1980), 169-170; *DialArch* (1981), 66-67; cf. L. Ferrero, *Mondo Classico*, 11 (1941), 230.

The guilds shed their Dionysiac heritage and entered the embrace of Minerva, not because they required protection but because the act signified the appropriation of Hellenic traditions for Roman national purposes. As Livius Andronicus' hymn had helped to appease the gods, and would serve as a model for future expiatory rites, so the Greek dramatic companies for which Livius wrote and acted and which enhanced Roman festivals would become part of the cultural and religious order of the community.[38] The distinction accorded Livius was an appropriate one.

The subsequent history of the guild eludes our grasp. Fragmentary bits of information have confused rather than enlightened understanding. We have record of a *collegium poetarum* in the late 2nd century, an organization to which Accius belonged and whose meetings appear to have been held in the temple of Hercules of the Muses in the Campus Martius.[39] The relationship of the *collegium poetarum* with the association of *scribae* and *histriones* installed on the Aventine ca. 206 cannot be established. Some have seen the poets' guild as direct successor to the company of writers and actors, simply shifting its locus after 187, others imagine the two organizations functioning simultaneously at two separate sites, still others find no connection at all between them.[40] Much of the objection to a link between the groups rests on the assumption that scribes and actors were held in low esteem—so much so that poets would be eager to separate themselves through an organization of their own. But those prejudices against *scribae* and *histriones* belong to the late Republic.[41] They may not have held in the 3rd century. As Festus observes, the ancients

---

[38] Martina, *Labeo*, 26 (1980), 167-175, rightly stresses the religious element, but goes beyond the evidence in seeing the artists' guild confined only to those who contributed to religious ceremonies and in regarding Andronicus himself as a religious functionary.

[39] Only a single text explicitly refers to the *collegium poetarum*; Val. Max. 3.7.11—in an anecdote concerning Accius. The poet, we are told elsewhere, installed a statue of himself in the temple of the Camenae, the Latin equivalent of the Muses; Pliny, *NH*, 34.19. That temple, it may be surmised, corresponds to the *aedes Herculis Musarum*, either built or added to by M. Fulvius Nobilior who installed statues of the Muses captured from Ambracia in 187 and who also placed therein a bronze *aedicula Camenarum*; Pliny, *NH*, 35.66; Servius, *Ad Aen.* 1.8; Eumenius, *Pan. Lat.* 9.7.3; Martina, *DialArch* (1981), 49-58. Poetic contests are attested for a later period and situated in the *aedes Musarum*; Porphyrio on Horace, *Sat.* 1.10.38 and Horace, *Epist.* 2.2.91; Juvenal, *Sat.* 7.38. The evidence is clearly presented by B. Tamm, *Opuscula Romana*, 21 (1961), 157-161; rather more intricately by Horsfall, *BICS*, 23 (1976), 82-86. The study of the *collegium poetarum* by E.G. Sihler, *AJP*, 26 (1905), 1-21, contains some suggestive ideas and much speculation. Nothing substantive is added by N.B. Crowther, *Latomus*, 32 (1973), 575-580.

[40] For various hypotheses, see Sihler, *AJP*, 26 (1905), 20-21; Tamm, *Opuscula Romana*, 21 (1961), 166; Jory, *Hermes*, 98 (1970), 234-236; Horsfall, *BICS*, 23 (1976), 81-82; K. Quinn, *ANRW*, II.30.1 (1982), 173-176; Gold, *Literary Patronage*, 44-45.

[41] E.g., Nepos, *Praef.* 5; *Eum.* 23; Livy, 7.2.12.

applied the term *scribae* both to *librarii* and to *poetae*; only later did it confine itself to *librarii*, public clerks.[42] He proceeds to offer as apparent
illustration the tribute paid to the *scribae* and *histriones* in authorizing their
association on the Aventine. The logic of that passage may be questionable, but it is clear enough that *scribae*, whether poets or clerks, did
not engender contempt in the 3rd century. Nor apparently did actors.
Festus' note that Andronicus himself was both playwright and actor
drives home the point.[43] And the evidence on *scribae* in the 3rd and 2nd
centuries shows that they were often men of substance, indeed some
reached high magistracies.[44] Continuity between the guild organized ca.
206 and the *collegium poetarum* is a permissible postulate. In fact, there
may be continuity of a sort even into the early Empire. An inscription
of late Republican or Augustan date provides some intriguing information. The document records the career of a freedman, P. Cornelius
Surus, who, among other positions, held the office of *magister scribarum
poetarum*.[45] That may have been the title of the *collegium* from its inception.[46] Literary figures retained their association and their pride in it.
Whether actors still participated in the same organization cannot be
ascertained. Their stock had declined by the late Republic. But the
institution endured, testimony to the vitality of tradition.

The vitality stemmed in part from proud origins. The guild of poets
and artists had its genesis in a commemorative act. Livius' hymn had
contributed to Rome's rescue in a dark hour. And his entire career had
been emblematic of Hellenic arts adapted to Roman needs. The poet's
achievements as writer, actor, and producer were instrumental in
creating a new blend of Greco-Roman drama that took a prominent
place in religious ceremonies and national celebrations. It was only fitting that the artists' collective, Greek in origin and character, should gain

---

[42] Festus, 446, L: *scribas proprio nomine antiqui et librarios et poetas vocabant: at nunc dicuntur
scribae equidem librari, qui rationes publicas scribunt in tabulis.*

[43] Festus, 448, L: *is et scribebat fabulas et agebat;* cf. Livy, 7.2.8: *idem scilicet—id quod omnes
tum erant—suorum carminum actor.*

[44] Examples collected by Martina, *Labeo*, 26 (1980), 165-167.

[45] *Editio princeps* by B. Andreae, *ArchAnz* (1957), 235-236. See the improvements of
Jory, *BICS*, 15 (1968), 125-126, and the thorough treatment by J.H. More, *Grazer
Beiträge*, 3 (1975), 241-252.

[46] Festus, 446, L, gives no title. And the sole reference to *collegium poetarum*, Val. Max.
3.7.11, may be non-technical. That *collegium scribarum poetarum* was the original title is
suggested by Jory, *Hermes*, 98 (1970), 236; E. Badian, *Entretiens Fondation Hardt*, 17
(1972), 190-191; More, *Grazer Beiträge*, 3 (1975), 247-248. Jory, however, detaches it
from the guild established ca. 206, on the ground that actors are not mentioned. Horsfall,
BICS, 23 (1976), 89-91, goes further and questions all continuity—unpersuasively. He
offers instead a questionable hypothesis on the attachment of *poetae* to *scribae* in the title.
Whether *poetarum* is adjectival or substantive is indeterminable.

official favor from Rome. It served to memorialize the accomplishments of Livius Andronicus and to advertise the liaison between Hellenic crafts and the Roman religious and political establishment.[47]

Andronicus enjoyed the patronage of the *gens Livia*. His *nomen* reflects their beneficence and, it may be inferrred, his career profited from their support. If Jerome is to be believed, Andronicus earned credit by teaching the children of Livius Salinator.[48] The person in question is likely to be M. Livius Salinator, *decemvir sacris faciundis*, who presided at the secular games in 236.[49] His activities in that year suggest comparable ones in 240: Salinator doubtless promoted Andronicus for the job of introducing Greek drama into the Ludi Romani which celebrated the national victory over Carthage. Three decades later, in 207, when next we hear of a public commission for the poet, it can be no accident that the consul in office was M. Livius Salinator.[50] This individual too, we may be certain, was a member of Rome's religious officialdom: his son, the future consul of 188, had already been selected for the pontificate.[51] The choice of Andronicus to compose the expiatory hymn in 207 was a natural one—and a propitious one. The glorious victory at the Metaurus followed. Salinator commanded a consular army, earned chief credit, and celebrated a triumph. One will not be far wrong in detecting his hand behind the creation of the guild of writers and dramatic artists as a commemorative honor to Livius Andronicus. The honor would also reflect upon the *triumphator*. Association with a family in Rome's political and religious establishment advanced the career and gave lustre to the name of the poet.

---

[47] It is usually assumed that Andronicus was dead before 200, when another poet, P. Licinius Tegula, was chosen to write an expiatory hymn; Livy, 31.12.10. But there is no reason to believe that Andronicus would have been commissioned for every public hymn. He may, for all we know, have survived until 187, the year under which he is recorded by Jerome; cf. Palmer, *Roman Religion and Roman Empire*, 95, 97-98.

[48] Jerome, *Chron.* Olymp. 148.2; cf. Cic. *Brutus*, 73.

[49] *Fast. Cap.* fr. 49 = *CIL*, I², 1, 29, fr. 46. The authenticity of these games is in dispute; see J.B. Pighi, *De Ludis Saecularibus populi romani quiritium* (Amsterdam, 1965), 5-6.

[50] The consul of 219 and 207 was very probably son of the decemvir of 236. Palmer, *Roman Religion and Roman Empire*, 95-96, amalgamates the two men. But observe the M. Livius, ambassador to Carthage in 218 and described at that time as among the *maiores natu*; Livy, 21.18.1. If already elderly in 218, he is not easily identifiable with the consul of 207 who fought a vigorous campaign in that year, continued to command armies as proconsul in Etruria and Gaul for three years thereafter and proceeded to a contentious censorship in 204; Broughton, *MRR*, I, 294, 300, 303, 306, 308. The latter absented himself from public affairs anyway in 218; Livy, 27.34.3-4; Val. Max. 4.2.2.; *Vir. Ill.* 50.1.

[51] Livy, 26.23.7-8.

Patronage by the *gens Livia* helped elevate Andronicus to prominence. But it ought not to be misunderstood. Nothing suggests that the Livii dictated the themes and orientation of the artist. Nor should Andronicus be reckoned as publicity agent for a particular aristocratic household. His translation of the *Odyssey*, his initiation of a dramatic tradition at the Roman games, and his hymn to appease divine wrath in 207 brought Hellenic culture to the service of a larger Roman national interest.

For Cn. Naevius, events on the public stage played a dominant role. The poet was a participant in Rome's military enterprises and a keen observer of her political scene. Only scattered pieces of information survive on his career and attitudes, a spur to speculation but an obstacle to understanding. Misinterpretation beclouds his legacy. Naevius is customarily adjudged a figure of controversy, embroiled in politics, disciplined by aristocrats, and punished by law.[52] That reputation needs reassessment. The significance of his impact lay in its national character, rather than in political parochialism.

Naevius stemmed from Campania. His native language may well have been Oscan, and the region of his birth gave him close contact with Hellenic traditions.[53] The cultural mix clearly proved beneficial. Campanian origins meant that the poet was, in all probability, a *civis sine suffragio*. We know at least that he fought for Rome in the First Punic War, perhaps in a *legio Campana*, thus gaining exposure to Roman institutions and attitudes. Naevius records the fact of his military services in his own poetry, a measure of the pride he took in it.[54] Participation in that contest yields a birthdate of ca. 280-265, thus making him a close contemporary of Livius Andronicus. Literary activity began shortly after the close of the war, the first plays produced in 235.[55]

---

[52] So, e.g., E. Marmorale, *Naevius Poeta*[2] (Florence, 1950), *passim*; H.D. Jocelyn, *Antichthon*, 3 (1969), 32-47; Flores, *Letteratura latina e ideologia*, 27-34; G. Williams, in Gold, *Literary and Artistic Patronage*, 4-5; Gold, *Literary Patronage*, 47-48.

[53] Gellius, in commenting on Naevius' epitaph, allegedly self-composed, remarks that it was full of Campanian arrogance; 1.24.2: *plenum superbiae Campanae*. Whether Naevius did, in fact, compose the epitaph is questionable; see Marmorale, *Naevius*, 137-143, with earlier bibliography; H. Dahlmann, *Studien zu Varro, De Poetis* (Wiesbaden, 1963), 65-100; Suerbaum, *Untersuchungen*, 31-42, makes a cautious case for authenticity. Gellius probably drew the text from Varro, *De Poetis*, as he did that of Plautus' epitaph; 1.24.3. The comment on *superbia Campana*, however, may be his own. What weight to give it? The idea that "Campanian swagger" was a proverbial expression and had no territorial connotation is rightly rejected. When alluded to elsewhere it refers primarily to Capua's defection during the Hannibalic war; Livy, 9.6.5, 23.5.1; Cic. *De Leg. Agrar.* 1.18-22, 2.76-98. There is no good reason to doubt Gellius' report of Campanian roots, whether or not he derived the notice from Varro's work; Marmorale, *Naevius*, 15-21; H.T. Rowell, *MAAR*, 19 (1949), 17-21; O. Skutsch, *CR*, 65 (1951), 174.

[54] Gellius, 17.21.45. On the civic status of the Campanians, see Livy, 8.14.10, 23.5.9; Marmorale, *Naevius*, 21-26.

[55] Gellius, 17.21.44-45, also drawn from Varro's *De Poetis*.

The Campanian writer may or may not have been a Roman citizen, i.e. a *civis sine suffragio*, by birth. He certainly became one in spirit and advocacy. The experience of the First Punic War eventually issued in an epic poem, a work of the highest importance in Roman literary history. The *Bellum Punicum* gave voice to national achievements and aspirations, the first epic to celebrate specifically Roman deeds in a Roman context. At the same time Naevius put on record traditions of the city's origins, thereby to afford a contrast with the deadly enemy Carthage. Fragments of the poem make clear that its author transmitted the Trojan legend as the inception of Roman history, thus providing both a link with and a distinction from Hellas.[56]

The patriotic character of Naevius' work takes on still clearer focus in another area. The poet had a hand in the creation of a whole new genre of tragic drama. The *fabula praetexta* took its subject matter not from Greek tragedy but from Roman legend and history. Special significance attached here to Naevius' play *Clastidium*, a drama that has prompted confident but flawed analysis of the poet's aims and inclinations. *Clastidium* had as its subject the celebrated Roman victory at the town of that name in 222, critical turning point in the war against the Gauls. M. Claudius Marcellus, consul and commander, earned the plaudits, not only for leading his forces to triumph, but for personally defeating the Gallic chieftains in battle and thus winning the coveted *spolia opima*.[57] Naevius' drama appears to have been referred to both as *Clastidium* and as *Marcellus*, an indication that the consul was central figure and his accomplishments a principal reason for the production.[58] Scholarship conventionally dates the play to 208, the year of Marcellus' death and his funeral games, or to 205 when the temple of *Honos et Virtus*, vowed by Marcellus, was at last dedicated.[59] The customary conclusion seems natural enough: Naevius wrote his *fabula praetexta* to honor the great

---

[56] Naevius, *Bell. Pun.* fr. 1-18, Strzelecki. Cf. W. Richter, *Gymnasium*, 69 (1962), 294-296. Composition of the *Bellum Punicum* is commonly set late in Naevius' life, on the basis of Cic. *De Sen.* 49-50: *nihil est otiosa senectute iucundius...quam gaudebat Bello suo Punico Naevius*. Even if the statement rests on good authority—which is uncertain—it need not mean that Naevius began the poem in old age, only that he completed or polished it then. The view of Beare, *CR*, 63 (1949), 48, that Naevius' pleasure derived from reading his own work as an elderly man, is implausible and untenable. Cicero's language, *quid in levioribus studiis, sed tamen acutis*, rules it out. *Studia acuta* can hardly refer to a mere reading of one's own works.

[57] Sources in Broughton, *MRR*, I, 233.

[58] Varro gives the title *Clastidium; LL*, 7.107, 9.78. In the formulation of Diomedes, it is *Marcellus*; Keil, *GL*, I, 490. That those are titles of two separate plays, as sometimes conjectured, seems quite unlikely.

[59] The death of Marcellus in 208: Polyb. 10.32.1-6; Livy, 27.27; Plut. *Marc.* 29-30; the fulfillment of the vow in 205: Livy, 27.25.6-10, 29.11.13.

Marcellus, thus gaining, or rather exhibiting, the patronage of the Marcelli; the poet was a client of that noble house.[60] On the face of it, the *Clastidium* supplies a telling instance of artistic clientage.

That conclusion is by no means compelling. The play commemorated a major Roman triumph, not simply a personal accomplishment by Marcellus. Rome had turned back the Gallic menace, had subdued the enemy, and appeared to have secured the north of Italy. Polybius' account of the battle, in fact, even omits mention of Marcellus' personal duel and gaining of the *spolia opima*.[61] Nothing demands placement of the play in 208 or 205 as direct tribute to Marcellus. Naevius could have appropriately produced it at a date closer to 222, a pointer to collective success rather than a celebration of the individual.[62] The drama acquires greater meaning as parallel to the *Bellum Punicum*. Epic and *praetexta* both extolled national triumphs, the submission of Rome's most serious foreign foes, the salvation and exaltation of the state. Naevius' aims went beyond partisanship to patriotism.[63]

Naevius does not fit the image of a *poeta cliens*. In fact, documentation on his career and work, scanty though it is, might suggest a man of combative personality, outspoken in his opinions, and harsh in his judgments—to the point of provoking retaliation and ruin. How plausible is that portrait? The evidence needs to be reviewed with some circumspection.

Aulus Gellius stigmatized Naevius' epitaph as exhibiting Campanian arrogance.[64] And several fragments from the poet's works give *prima facie* indication of political dissent and critique of the contemporary scene. A character in the comedy *Agitatoria* ostensibly expresses a fierce commitment to autonomy: "I have ever placed much greater value on liberty

---

[60] So, e.g., F. Cassola, *I gruppi politici romani nel III secolo a. C.* (Trieste, 1962), 327-330; H.D. Jocelyn, *Antichthon*, 3 (1969), 34; Williams, in Gold, *Literary and Artistic Patronage*, 4-5. A more moderate interpretation by Marmorale, *Naevius*, 129-131, 153-154, who sees a connection established by the play and benefits subsequently enjoyed by the author. The reconstruction by Mattingly, *Historia*, 9 (1960), 432-438, is fanciful.

[61] Polyb. 2.34.

[62] Marmorale, *Naevius*, 130, rules out any date earlier than Marcellus' death in 208, on the basis of Cic. *De Rep.* 4.10.12 = Aug. *CD*, 2.9: *veteribus displicuisse Romanis vel laudari quemquam in scaena vivum hominem vel vituperari*. That testimony, however, says nothing about legal or moral prohibition—and may, in fact, imply that living persons were depicted on the stage with some frequency.

[63] Cf. H. Zehnacker, in *Théatre et spectacles dans l'antiquité*, Actes du Colloque de Strasbourg (1981), 41, 44, 46-47, who, however, believes that *praetextae* were only staged after the death of persons depicted therein. N. Zorzetti, *La pretesta e il teatro latino arcaico* (Naples, 1980), 53-73, sees the *praetexta* as celebration of divine sanction for the exercise of Roman *imperium* in legend and history.

[64] Gellius, 1.24.2.

than on cash.''[65] Elsewhere, a slave takes pride in his right to register approval by applause in the theater, a privilege that no ruler dares abrogate, and boasts that his servile status in this respect is preferable to others' liberty.[66] The remark has lent itself to substantive interpretation. Naevius, so it is surmised, here chafes against restrictions imposed upon playwrights by the authorities: dramas are best judged by free applause, even when tendered by slaves.[67] Specific political allusions are not easily detected in the brief fragments that survive. But the determined can find contemporary connotations in the dialogue of another of Naevius' comedies: ''Tell me, how did you ruin so mighty a state so quickly?'' ''New style orators came forth, nothing but silly youth.''[68] And one can add still another line from an unidentified work: ''at Liber's feast we enjoy free speech.''[69] The cumulative effect leaves a strong impression: the artist who guarded his independence and spoke his mind.[70]

Perhaps so. Yet it would be prudent to avoid over-interpretation. The authenticity of Naevius' epitaph remains in question; and Gellius' characterization of it probably represents his own judgment anyway. But even if Naevius composed the text and Gellius' ascription of *superbia* to it were accurate, the poet's boast refers to literary achievement, not to political stance.[71] As for the extracts from comic dramas or other works, they lack context and setting, thus precluding confidence and promoting guesswork. One can hardly identify lines uttered by characters with opinions of the author when neither the character nor the circumstances are known.[72] None of them buttresses the hypothesis that Naevius employed the stage for political advocacy.

---

[65] Charisius, in Keil, *GL*, I, 210: *Semper pluris feci ego/ potioremque habui libertatem multo quam pecuniam.*

[66] Charisius, in Keil, *GL*, I, 216: *quae ego in theatro hic meis probavi plausibus,/ ea non audere quemquam regem rumpere,/ quanto libertatem hanc hic superat servitus.*

[67] Cf. Marmorale, *Naevius*, 43-44; Suerbaum, *Untersuchungen*, 29-31. Cf. the line in *Agitatoria* which may also represent the playwright; Charisius, in Keil, *GL*, I, 208: *nimio arte colligor. Cur re inquaesita colligor?*

[68] Cic. *De Sen.* 20: *Cedo qui vestram rem publicam tantam amisistis tam cito?....proveniebant oratores novi, stulti adulescentuli.*

[69] Paulus-Festus, 83, L: *Libera lingua loquimur ludis Liberalibus.*

[70] So, e.g., Flores, *Letteratura latina e ideologia*, 27-34, who regards Naevius as representative of democratic elements, small farmers, and the urban plebs, in opposition to the ruling oligarchy.

[71] Gellius, 1.24.2: *Immortales mortales si foret fas flere./ Flerent divae Camenae Naevium poetam./ Itaque postquam est Orcho traditus thesauro,/ Obliti sunt Romae loquier lingua Latina.* See above, n. 53.

[72] See the salutary reminders by J. Wright, *RhM*, 115 (1972), 239-242, on Charisius, in Keil, *GL*, I, 216, and *idem, Dancing in Chains: The Stylistic Unity of the Comoedia Palliata* (Rome, 1974), 55-56, on Paulus-Festus, 83, L. For J.C. Dumont, in *Les bourgeoisies municipales italiennes aux II et 1er siècles av. J.C.*, Colloques Int. du Centre Nat. de la

The hypothesis receives support from apparently more solid—and certainly more notorious—information: the supposed feud between Naevius and the prominent house of the Caecilii Metelli. A celebrated line of the poet directed itself against that family: *fato Metelli Romae fiunt consules*. The phrase was evidently well known in the late Republic, well enough so that Cicero could allude to it in a speech before a senatorial jury and expect recognition from his audience. The orator taunted his contemporary Q. Metellus, consul-elect in 70, with a claim allegedly made by Verres: Metellus had reached the consulship *non fato*, like the rest of his family, but by Verres' own efforts.[73] A late antique commentator on the *Verrines* supplies us with the verse ascribed to Naevius, which Cicero took for granted, and adds also that the consul Metellus replied in kind to the playwright: *dabunt malum Metelli Naevio poetae*.[74] The reply is attested also by the scholar-poet Caesius Bassus of the 1st century A.D. For Caesius, the Metelli, frequently attacked in the verses of Naevius, responded with that sharp line of their own.[75] That constitutes the sum of our evidence on this abrasive interchange.

Naevius, however, had other targets for his abuse—or so it is generally believed. Even the mighty Scipio Africanus was reckoned as victim of the poet's verses. Preserved lines mock a man now preeminent in accomplishment and reputation, but once hauled away from his mistress in humiliating fashion, clad only in a *pallium*, and dragged home by his father.[76] Aulus Gellius preserves the passage and identifies its object as Africanus, an identification he attributes also to Valerius Antias in the early 1st century B.C.[77]

The pointed barbs may have struck home, and the poet, so report has it, did not escape unscathed. Gellius tells the tale. Naevius' persistent insolence and verbal assault upon the *principes* provoked retribution. The *triumviri capitales* hauled him off to prison where he languished for a time, until composition of two new plays wiped out the ill effects of his previous offenses and impudence, and induced the tribunes to release him.[78] A

---

recherche scientifique, n. 609 (Paris, 1983), 335-338, references to *libertas* in Naevius' lines represent advocacy of Dionysiac rites and their connection to the origins of the theater in southern Italy.

[73] Cic. *Verr.* 1.29: *nam hoc Verrem dicere aiebant, te non fato, ut ceteros ex vestra familia, sed opera sua, consulem factum.*

[74] Ps.-Ascon. 215, Stangl.

[75] Caesius Bassus, in Keil, *GL*, VI, 266: *optimus est quem Metelli proposuerunt de Naevio, aliquotiens ab eo versu lacessiti: malum dabunt Metelli Naevio poetae.*

[76] Gellius, 7.8.5: *etiam qui res magnas manu saepe gessit gloriose,/ cuius facta viva nunc vigent, qui apud gentes solus praestat,/ eum suus pater cum pallio uno domum ab amica abduxit.*

[77] Gellius, 7.8.5-6.

[78] Gellius, 3.3.15.

puzzling passage of Plautus is often taken as reference to Naevius' unhappy jail term. The playwright depicts a character with chin resting on his arm, and offers the metaphor of a building supported by a column. He then has the character insert an aside: *nam os columnatum poetae esse inaudivi barbaro,/ quoi bini custodes semper totis horis occupant.*[79] In a gloss on the word *barbari*, Festus supplies the name of a poet so labelled by Plautus: it was Naevius.[80] The passage can therefore be interpreted as allusion to Naevius' confinement, his head propped on a pillory while two guards kept him under constant surveillance.

Nor was that the end of Naevius' travails. The poet concluded his days in exile, if credit be given to a tradition recorded by St. Jerome. The Christian scholar notes that Naevius was driven out of Rome by a faction of nobles, the Metelli prominent among them, and departed for Utica in North Africa where he died in 201.[81]

A composite picture takes shape: Naevius, the feisty, outspoken writer who castigated Roman political leaders, fell afoul of the aristocratic establishment, suffered imprisonment until his artistic talents brought him temporary reprieve, and was finally banished to foreign shores for the remainder of his life. If the reconstruction holds, it implies that Naevius utilized literature for partisan politics, prompted official reaction, and felt the heavy hand of political censorship.

Does it hold? In fact, every link in the chain is weak. The phrase from which all discussion originates, *fato Metelli Romae fiunt consules*, is itself in dispute as to intent, significance, and authenticity. Some have adjudged the remarks as subsequent inventions, employed in verbal attack against the Metelli of the later 2nd century, when the clan garnered an extraordinary number of consulships.[82] That goes too far. Chief prop for the argument, the plural *Metelli*, carries little weight. The statement possesses (at least) a mildly ironic and mocking tone. Use of the plural to generalize from a single instance would be appropriate and not uncommon.[83] It requires faith to believe that the verse was invented at

---

[79] Plautus, *Miles*, 209-212.

[80] Festus, 32, L: *Barbari dicebantur antiquitus omnes gentes, exceptis Graecis. Unde Plautus Naevium poetam Latinum barbarum dixit.*

[81] Jerome, *Chron. Olymp.* 144.3: *Naevius comicus Uticae moritur, pulsus Roma factione nobilium, ac praecipue Metelli.*

[82] The genuineness of the verses was denied long ago by G. Wissowa, *Genethliakon für C. Robert* (1910), 51-63; F. Leo, *Geschichte der römischen Literatur* (Berlin, 1913), I, 78, n. 5. The cautious discussion of Jocelyn, *Antichthon*, 3 (1969), 42-47, commits only to the belief that the verses go back to Republican times, preserved by oral tradition among the Metelli. Similar caution is expressed most recently by Drury in *Cambridge History of Class. Lit*, II, 802: "in 1st c. B.C. there was an evidently widespread story..."

[83] So, rightly, F. Marx, *SitzSächsGes*, 63 (1911), 59-61, with examples. See, especially, Macrob. *Sat.* 7.3.10.

a time several generations removed from Naevius. What motives then would there be in ascribing it to that poet? The query remains without satisfactory answer. Other interpretations accept the line as Naevian but deny that it represents criticism of the Metelli; rather it was appropriated to that end by political figures for their own purposes, and at a very different time. The hypotheses are ingenious, but far-fetched and unpersuasive.[84] Should one then accept the tale as given? Did Naevius issue verbal assault on a scion of the Metellan *gens*, thus evoking reaction and retaliation?[85] A major obstacle stands in the way of acceptance. Scipio Aemilianus, in Cicero's *De Republica*, contrasted Roman comedy favorably with Greek in regard to vituperation against prominent individuals: "It was no more seemly that Pericles be attacked from the stage than if Plautus or Naevius had insulted the Scipios or Caecilius had attacked Cato." The passage allows for little ambiguity. It implies that as late as Cicero's day the idea that Naevius would give offense to Roman *nobiles* was unthinkable.[86]

The import of the notorious line continues to baffle inquiry. Inconclusive debate has raged on the meaning of *fato*. Does it signify "fate," "divine will," "necessity"? Or "chance," "luck"? Or "misfortune"? Or "prophecy," "oracular pronouncement"?[87] The connotation in Cicero's day, with its Stoic overtones, may be quite different from the meaning it carried a century and a half earlier. Definitive solution is unlikely and perhaps unnecessary. The verse suggests at least that the Metelli owed consulships to something beyond their own exertions.

A comment to that effect would fit suitably within the lifetime of Naevius. Q. Caecilius Metellus reached the consulship for 206 in circumstances that left a strong odor of political manipulation. Elections for

---

[84] Marmorale, *Naevius*, 58-91, sees Naevius' line as a favorable reference to L. Metellus' successes in the First Punic War, only later applied—and with the poet's consent—against Q. Metellus, consul in 206. That theory depends on reading the line as a saturnian rather than a senarius, thus to allow its placement in the *Bellum Punicum*. But the premise is shaky and the conclusion improbable; see O. Skutsch, *CR*, 65 (1951), 175. For Mattingly, *Historia*, 9 (1960), 427-432, Naevius intended *metelli*, not Metelli, an allusion to humble citizens, but his verse was expropriated and used against the noble family in the later 2nd century. That inventive idea has found no takers.

[85] The tradition is defended by, e.g., Marx, *SitzSächsGes*, 63 (1911), 57-68; E. Fraenkel, *RE*, Suppl. 6 (1935), "Cn. Naevius," 622-624; Rowell, *MAAR*, 19 (1949), 24-30.

[86] Cic. *De Rep.* 4.10.11 = Aug. *CD*, 2.9: *sed Periclen....violari versibus, et eos agi in scaena non plus decuit, quam si Plautus noster voluisset aut Naevius Publio et Gnaeo Scipioni aut Caecilius Marco Catoni maledicere.* Rightly stressed by Mattingly, *Historia*, 9 (1960), 415-417.

[87] For various interpretations, see Wissowa, *Genethliakon für C. Robert* (1910), 52-53; Marx, *SitzSächsGes*, 63 (1911), 61-64; T. Frank, *AJP*, 48 (1927), 106-108; Fraenkel, *RE*, Suppl. 6 (1935), "Cn. Naevius," 623; Marmorale, *Naevius*, 81-85; Jocelyn, *Antichthon*, 3 (1969), 44-47.

that year took place in the wake of Rome's glorious and momentous victory at the Metaurus. The two consuls of 207, C. Claudius Nero and M. Livius Salinator, successful commanders at the Metaurus, returned to popular acclaim and an outpouring of joyous emotion.[88] They seized the moment to work their will upon the electoral results by promoting actively the candidacies of two men who had served as legates in the military campaign: Q. Caecilius Metellus and L. Veturius Philo. Nor did they stop at mere canvassing. Nothing was left to chance. Nero named his colleague Livius dictator to hold the elections, and Livius, in turn, appointed Metellus as his *magister equitum*. The electorate predictably returned Metellus and Veturius, the former moving directly from dictator's deputy to consul.[89] It was a smooth operation, and obviously well planned. What intrigues lay behind it and what motives impelled it remain subject to speculation—with little sign of scholarly consensus. The matter need not be decided here.[90] What counts is the well orchestrated maneuver that elevated Metellus to the consulship. The new chief magistrate obtained that post despite the absence of a praetorship on his record and a relatively undistinguished career in general.[91] His

---

[88] Livy, 28.9.3-6.

[89] Livy, 28.9.19-28.10.2: *a M. Livio dictatore creati consules L. Veturius Q. Caecilius, is ipse qui tum erat magister equitum.* Frank, *AJP*, 48 (1927), 106-107, uses this election as support for his view that Naevius' *fato* means "fortuitously." He points to the "happy chance" whereby Metellus had been one of the messengers to deliver news of the Metaurus in 207, thus winning the popular favor that carried him to election; Livy, 27.51.1-10. But Livy draws no connection between the announcement of the military victory and the elections for the next year. Frank omits altogether the evidence on political maneuvering. Metellus' election was anything but "fortuitous."

[90] H.H. Scullard, *Roman Politics, 220-150 BC* (2nd ed., Oxford, 1973), 73-74, sees reconciliation between the two consuls, Nero and Salinator, and a joint promotion of favored candidates in order to check the faction of the Fabii. But the supposed reconciliation may be a sham. Livy's account reveals continued friction; 28.9.18, 29.37.8-17. Military motives prevailed, according to A. Lippold, *Consules* (Bonn, 1963), 196-197: the need to restore commanders to the army as quickly as possible, for both consuls were in Rome; a dictatorship would assure swift elections. In fact, however, there was no urgency in the military situation at that time. Had there been, the *patres* could easily have kept one consul in the field; cf. Livy, 28.9.1-2. J. Jahn, *Interregnum und Wahldiktatur* (Kallmünz, 1970), 139, raises the possibility of the dictatorship as symbolic of a political healing, with the two consuls of the next year representing a national consensus to complete the defeat of Carthage. For R. Rilinger, *Der Einfluss des Wahlleiters bei den römischen Konsulwahlen von 366 bis 50 v. Chr.* (Munich, 1976), 192-200, the procedures followed in 207 all had good precedent and simply confirmed convention. But he has to concede that the naming of a dictator when both consuls were in Rome and capable of presiding over the elections was hardly conventional. The purpose, in Rilinger's view, was to assure election of the plebeian Metellus. So also R. Develin, *Athenaeum*, 55 (1977), 423-425; *idem, The Practice of Politics at Rome, 366-167 B.C.* (Brussels, 1985), 163-164.

[91] The customary assignment of Metellus to the Scipionic faction may be premature. The major figure in 207 was clearly M. Livius Salinator. He had gained a triumph for the Metaurus, his colleague Claudius only an *ovatio*; Livy, 28.9.7-10. He presided over

connections and associations made it possible—a reason perhaps for pride rather than embarrassment. And Naevius' line can be readily understood with reference to that episode: not censure or indictment, but a wry allusion to the contemporary scene.

A corresponding interpretation might elucidate the Metellan reply. *Dabunt malum Metelli Naevio poetae* need not have sinister overtones. If intended as a serious threat, why was it couched in verse? Other means could be found to intimidate the poet. A literal reading of the line renders it blunt and heavy-handed—hardly sparkling repartee. In fact, the author employs the language of comedy, phraseology often signifying punishment for slaves and unsavory characters.[92] Viewed from that perspective, the verse contains some wit, a lighter tone, and perhaps parody—possibly even self-parody. It would not have been unsuitable in the prologue of one of Naevius' own comedies.[93] A later generation transformed the droll exchange into a political quarrel.

The supposed reprimand of Scipio is equally problematical. Naevius' lines derided a prestigious figure of world renown who had once suffered the embarrassment of being snatched from his *amica*'s boudoir by his father and led through the street while dressed in a *pallium*.[94] Gellius reports that a near consensus believed the verses to have been directed against Scipio Africanus and postulates that those lines led Valerius Antias to deliver an adverse judgment on Scipio's character.[95] Uncertainty abounds here. The text does not specify Scipio, Gellius concedes that there is less than total agreement on its object, and the idea that Valerius Antias took it as damaging to Scipio is simply conjecture. Models can readily be found in Greek literature, notably a closely parallel passage in Bacchylides, and the extraction of the young man from his mistress's home by the *senex* is a stock comic scene. Naevius, in

---

the elections as dictator, appointed Metellus as *magister equitum*, and assured his election as consul. Metellus had very likely served as Livius' legate in the war; see Livy, 27.50.2, 27.51.3. And the outcome boosted Livius' stock further. His *imperium* was prorogued; Claudius, who had expected prorogation, did not get it; Livy, 28.9.17, 28.10.4-5, 28.10.11. Cf. Jahn, *Interregnum und Wahldiktatur*, 139-140.

[92] E.g., Plautus, *Amph.* 563; *Most.* 655; *Poen.* 928; *Pseud.* 1130; acutely noted by Marx, *SitzSächsGes*, 63 (1911), 67, who, however, takes it as an authentic threat by Metellus.

[93] Cf. Plautus, *Poen.* 55-58; *Truc.* 1-8. Fraenkel, *RE*, Suppl. 6, "Cn. Naevius," 623-624, argued that Caesius Bassus' phraseology, *optimus est quem Metelli proposuerunt*, suggests a public posting of the reply; Keil, *GL*, VI, 266. But we can be sure only that it was so represented. The verse was probably not conceived by the grave and moralistic Q. Metellus; cf. Val. Max. 7.2.3.

[94] Gellius, 7.8.5. See above n. 76.

[95] Gellius, 7.8.5-6.

short, need not have had a contemporary figure in view.[96] And, as Cicero indicates, no one could imagine Naevius castigating Scipio Africanus.[97]

The doubts are legitimate. Yet there is more to be said. Even adaptation of a stereotypical comic scene and character does not exclude the possibility that audiences might detect a contemporary allusion. Scipio, and he alone, qualifies as a man who "stands out among the nations" during the lifetime of Naevius. His preeminence preceded Zama. Victories in Spain made him a celebrity in Rome, and the adulation of Spanish tribes lifted him to a unique position. Furthermore, Scipio gained reputation for his amatory adventures as well. The jibes of the poet might be apposite.[98] And an unobserved item in the record should be noticed here. Controversy and notoriety swirled about Scipio in 205. His victories in Spain helped earn him election as consul for that year. Heated argument followed, however, over political assignment and military strategy: the bitter debate between Fabius and Scipio, arising out of an effort to curb the soaring ambitions of the latter.[99] Criticism of Scipio mounted in the next year, particularly with regard to the activities of his subordinate Q. Pleminius in southern Italy.[100] Among the criticisms levelled against Africanus was his Hellenic posturing at Locri: he had sauntered about the gymnasium, spent time with Greek books and exercises, and had appeared in public wearing a *pallium*.[101] That is a clue no scholar should have missed. The comedy that paraded a prominent military and political figure in a *pallium* could easily evoke contemporary musings.

It would be rash to conclude that Naevius spoke for the political opponents of Scipio Africanus. The lines may be perfectly innocuous, no more than conventional comic characterization, only later interpreted as anti-Scipionic by someone who discerned a connection with Scipio's *pallium* episode. But one ought not rule out the possibility that Naevius took pleasure in indirect allusion of current import. In that event, the passage represents an amusing glance at the contemporary scene, not the

---

[96] The parallel with Bacchylides, fr. 19 (Snell) was alertly noted by B. Warnecke, *Philologus*, 71 (1912), 567-568. For W. Beare, *The Roman Stage* (3rd ed., N.Y., 1963), 40, the character in question may be a standard *miles gloriosus*. Cf. also Wright, *Dancing in Chains*, 56-57, who doubts Gellius' identification of Scipio.

[97] Cic. *De Rep.* 4.10.11 = Aug. *CD*, 2.9. See above, n. 86.

[98] Adulation by Spaniards: Polyb. 10.38.3, 10.40.2-9; amatory reputation: Polyb. 10.19.3-7; Val. Max. 6.7.1; Plut. *Mor.* 196b. A good discussion by Jocelyn, *Antichthon*, 3 (1969), 39-41. See also Marmorale, *Naevius*, 91-100.

[99] Livy, 28.38-45.

[100] Livy, 29.16-20.

[101] Livy, 29.19.11-12.

expression of a political stance.[102] It is even possible that Scipio, like the "Metelli", answered with a joke of his own. In any case, a pun of Scipio's stands on record, making sport of Naevius' name. That it applies to the poet remains conjectural—though perfectly plausible.[103] This is, at most, jocular repartee, not politics.

The facts are few. But learned speculation or inventive imagination manufactures elaborate tales. Gellius speaks of repeated insults and insolence directed at *principes civitatis* by Naevius—probably no more than an extrapolation from the supposed quarrel with the Metelli. And a more dramatic episode followed: the *principes* rounded on Naevius and the *triumviri capitales* threw him into jail, where he composed two plays, made atonement for his sins, and was released from confinement by the tribunes.[104] How much credit does that narrative deserve?

Acceptance of its truth is widespread, usually without argument. Indeed the assumption has spawned subtle debate about the legal ground for indictment and conviction. The Twelve Tables are commonly brought into the reckoning. A provision in that venerable document prescribed the capital penalty for anyone who sang or composed verses that brought dishonor or shame upon another.[105] For some, that clause applied initially to incantation, the summoning of magic, and the casting of spells, extended later as an ad hoc maneuver to cover Naevius' verses and terminate his career.[106] Others find the incarceration entirely legitimate, the relevant portion of the Twelve Tables aimed from the start at slanderous and defamatory songs.[107] The Twelve Tables them-

---

[102] W. Kroll, *Hermes*, 66 (1931), 472, described the verses as "ein harmloses Scherz," a view that has been unfairly dismissed; e.g. Fraenkel, *RE*, Suppl. 6 (1935), "Cn. Naevius," 622-623; Marmorale, *Naevius*, 101-104. But Kroll's further conclusion, that Naevius belonged to Scipio's *clientela*, has neither foundation nor plausibility.

[103] Cic. *De Orat.* 2.249: *quid hoc Naevio ignavius? severe Scipio.* A plausible argument can be made that the poet is here meant; P. Fraccaro, *Opuscula* (Pavia, 1956), I, 276-277; Jocelyn, *Antichthon*, 3 (1969), 38-39.

[104] Gellius, 3.3.15.

[105] Cic. *De Rep.* 4.10.12 = Aug. *CD*, 2.9: *nostrae contra duodecim tabulae cum perpaucas res capite sanxissent, in his hanc quoque sanciendam putaverunt, si quis occentavisset sive carmen condidisset.*

[106] So Frank, *AJP*, 48 (1927), 108-110; L. Robinson, *Freedom of Speech in the Roman Republic* (Baltimore, 1940), 3-6, with earlier bibliography. Marmorale, *Naevius*, 53-57, accepts the interpretation of the clause, but rejects its application to Naevius' case. Pliny, *NH*, 28.18, offers ostensible support for the argument by giving *qui malum carmen incantassit* as a clause in the Twelve Tables. But the phrase is not identical in wording or sense to the clause reported by Cicero.

[107] Fraenkel, *Gnomon*, 1 (1925), 185-200; A. Momigliano, *JRS*, 32 (1942), 120-122; R.E. Smith, *CQ*, 45 (1951), 169-170. Other references, direct or indirect, to the provision against slanderous songs: Cic. *Tusc. Disp.* 4.4; Horace, *Epist.* 2.1.152; *Sat.* 2.1.82; Porphyry on Horace, *Epist.* 2.1.152; on *Sat.* 2.1.82; Paulus, *Sent.* 5.4.6; Arnobius, *Adv. Gent.* 4.34; Cornutus, in Pers. *Sat.* 1.137. That Cicero's *occentavisset* referred to defamatory songs and not to magical incantation is confirmed by Festus, 190, L.: *"occentassit" antiqui dicebant quod nunc "convicium fecerit" dicimus.*

selves, however, may be irrelevant and the argument otiose. Nothing in the evidence connects Naevius' imprisonment with the archaic code. If it were applicable, one would expect a capital penalty or exile to escape it, not a stretch in prison. In fact, no evidence exists to show that anyone ever suffered conviction under that clause.[108] Other legal mechanisms have been excogitated to explain Naevius' confinement.[109] But the efforts all lack point unless the basic question is settled. Must one believe in Naevius' confinement at all?

Commentators comfort themselves with a postulate that the account derives from Varro's researches.[110] That itself would be no absolute guarantee of authenticity. But Gellius's source, in any case, escapes sure detection. He cites Varro in the preceding paragraph on a very different matter, and then shifts gears: *sicuti de Naevio quoque accepimus.*[111] An alternative tradition had Naevius exiled abroad, where he died, rather than imprisoned, released, and forgiven, and the former version may have stemmed from Varro.[112] That leaves the origin of the prison tale in a questionable limbo.

In fact, Gellius' account gives off the suspicious aroma of fictional biography. The idea of the poet thrown in jail, then producing two plays which mollified his foes and earned his liberation, has less to do with Roman penal practice than with literary convention.[113] The narrative centers upon the two plays supposedly written in prison. The author of

---

[108] Only two cases are known, from the later 2nd century, both involving defamatory statements from the stage, levelled against literary figures, Lucilius and Accius; *Ad Herenn.* 1.24, 2.19. But they fell under the rubric of *iniuria*, evidently governed by the Praetor's Edict, not by the Twelve Tables. Cf. Ulpian, *Dig.* 47.10.15.25-27; *Ad Herenn.* 4.35; T. Mommsen, *Römisches Strafrecht* (Leipzig, 1899), 794-795; Smith, *CQ,* 45 (1951), 171.

[109] For Marx, *SitzSächsGes*, 63 (1911), 71-72, Naevius was held in *libera custodia*, thereby giving him the opportunity to write more plays. Marmorale, *Naevius*, 104-112, sees the imprisonment as an act of *coercitio* exercised by Q. Metellus while dictator in 205. Both suggestions are pure conjecture—and both assume the truth of Gellius' narrative.

[110] So, e.g., Marmorale, *Naevius*, 108; Rowell, *MAAR*, 19 (1949), 30.

[111] Gellius, 3.3.15. Mattingly, *Historia*, 9 (1960), 421-422, is rightly skeptical.

[112] Jerome, *Chron.* Olymp. 144.3, who places Naevius' death in 201. Varro, as we happen to know, challenged the report that Naevius died in 204 and had him survive for some time thereafter; Cic. *Brutus*, 60. He may, therefore, be the authority for Jerome's story, and thus hardly a likely source for Gellius. Rowell, *MAAR*, 19 (1949), 22-23, acknowledges that Varro's studies lie behind this version, but does not see the conflict with Gellius. Marx, *SitzSächsGes*, 63 (1911), 68-80, accepts both by positing two separate trials and convictions of Naevius—a desperate solution.

[113] Imprisonment generally served the purpose of holding a defendant for trial or detaining him prior to execution; cf. Mommsen, *Strafrecht*, 48-49, 301-305, 930, 960-963. W. Eisenhut, *ANRW*, I.2 (1972), 268-282, has shown that it was occasionally resorted to as a penalty. But none of the instances cited approximates the case of Naevius.

the tale had those two works before him, and perhaps little else. Inference, ingenuity, and embellishment filled out the remainder.[114]

Naevius' alleged detention while uncomfortably fastened to a pillory has even less to be said for it. That is not even an ancient conjecture, but a purely modern concoction. Plautus, in the *Miles Gloriosus*, provides some obscure and nearly impenetrable lines about a *poeta barbarus* in a peculiar posture (*os columnatum*) under the watchful eye of *bini custodes*.[115] Festus notes that the playwright somewhere described Naevius as a *poeta barbarus*.[116] But not necessarily in the *Miles Gloriosus*. So even a connection between the two passages is far from certain. Further speculation becomes increasingly pointless—though by no means deterred. Most regard the Plautine testimony as evidence for the imprisonment of Naevius, set in stocks with two *custodes* either as guards or fetters.[117] The inference does not bear examination. Placement of prisoners in the stocks or a pillory was hardly standard practice. *Os columnatum* does not easily lend itself to literal interpretation, despite numerous efforts to construe it in that fashion.[118] A metaphorical meaning might be more suitable. But any association with Naevius, let alone with penal confinement, rests on imaginative reconstruction. To employ it as an item in the poet's biography is methodologically illegitimate.

One final notice ostensibly points to political engagement and retribution. Jerome reports that Naevius died at Utica in 201, having been driven from Rome by an aristocratic cabal headed by Metellus.[119] How much trust is to be placed in that information? The detail that specifies Utica would not have been invented or deduced. It stems most probably from Suetonius' *De Viris Illustribus*, behind which we may detect a reference in Varro's *De Poetis*.[120] The date, however, engendered dispute

---

[114] Questions about the story were raised long ago by Leo, *Hermes*, 24 (1889), 67, n. 2. Cf. Fraenkel, *RE*, Suppl. 6 (1935), "Cn. Naevius," 625; Jocelyn, *Antichthon*, 3 (1969), 37-38.

[115] Plautus, *Miles*, 209-212.

[116] Festus, 32, L. See above, n. 80.

[117] See Marmorale, *Naevius*, 112-116, with bibliography; Jocelyn, *Antichthon*, 3 (1969), 35-37. Mattingly, *Historia*, 9 (1960), 422-426, offers the extravagant hypothesis that the *custodes* were there to protect rather than to confine the poet and that the poet in question was Ennius! Quite apart from general implausibility, Mattingly makes no effort to interpret *os columnatum*.

[118] See previous note. The most elaborate reconstruction, purely speculative, by F.D. Allen, *HSCP*, 7 (1896), 37-64. More recently, J.F. Killeen, *CP*, 68 (1973), 53-54, sees sexual connotations in the phrase.

[119] Jerome, *Chron.* Olymp. 144.3.

[120] Cf. A. Rostagni, *Suetonio de poetis e biografi minori* (Turin, 1944), v-xxiv; Rowell, *MAAR*, 19 (1949), 22-23. Dahlmann, *Studien zu Varro, De Poetis*, 58-59, questions the ascription to Varro. Marmorale, *Naevius*, 132-133, sees Nepos as Jerome's ultimate source, on insufficient grounds.

even in antiquity. The *veteres commentarii* set Naevius' death in 204, a particular rejected by Varro who gave the poet a somewhat longer life. The former document, or an inference from it, may have assumed the year of death from the year of the last play. Varro knew better. He assigned Naevius some more years, doubtless aware of his sojourn at Utica, a city to which he could not have come before 201 when peace had been concluded with Carthage and the region was no longer enemy territory.[121] Varro himself did not specify a date of death, and evidently did not know it. Jerome's year of 201 could derive from independent testimony or, more likely, a guess associated with the year of Naevius' emigration to Utica. His information does not warrant implicit faith.[122] Corresponding doubt attaches to the assertion that Naevius was victimized by Metellus and a faction of *nobiles* and expelled from Italy. The testimony may represent no more than extrapolation from the tale of the Metellan quarrel with the poet. The reason for Naevius' trip to Africa does not repay conjecture.[123] More to the point is Cicero's description of Naevius in old age as happily working away at the *Bellum Punicum*.[124] That hardly suits the portrait of a broken poet languishing in exile as victim of his own political indiscretions.

Naevius was neither *poeta cliens* nor dissenting critic of the establishment. He wrote of Rome's national achievements, and he could comment wryly on her public affairs. Allusions to Metellus and Scipio would take on particular point at a time not long after the political campaigning and spirited debates of 206-204. It may not be coincidence that an event of high importance occurred at about that very time: public recognition for the guild of dramatic writers and artists now installed on the Aven-

---

[121] Cic. *Brutus*, 60: *his enim consulibus* [204] *ut in veteribus commentariis scriptum est, Naevius est mortuus; quamquam Varro noster diligentissimus investigator antiquitatis putat in hoc erratum vitamque Naevi product longius.* See Fraenkel, *RE*, Suppl. 6 (1935), "Cn. Naevius," 625-626; Suerbaum, *Untersuchungen*, 300; Badian, *Entretiens Fondation Hardt*, 17 (1972), 160-161. Against the bulk of scholarly opinion, L. Schaaf, *RhM*, 122 (1979), 24-33, holds that Cicero preferred the *veteres commentarii* to Varro on this point. Even if that were the case, however, it would not invalidate Varro's testimony.

[122] It has been argued that Naevius survived for many years after 201; L. Hermann, *Latomus*, 1 (1937), 29-30; Dahlmann, *Studien zu Varro, De Poetis*, 56-58. But the texts on which that view is based offer no support for it: Cic. *Brutus*, 60, 73; *De Sen.* 50.

[123] Jerome's explanation is rightly questioned by Leo, *Geschichte der römischen Literatur*, (Berlin, 1913), 80; Jocelyn, *Antichthon*, 3 (1969), 41-42. Alternative solutions have not been happy ones. Leo's idea that Naevius went to Africa for purposes of study has convinced few. Less plausible still is the view of Kroll, *Hermes*, 66 (1931), 472, that Scipio brought Naevius along on his invasion to serve as *laudator* of his accomplishments! Marmorale, *Naevius*, 133-135, postulates a semi-voluntary departure, the atmosphere in Rome no longer hospitable to him. Badian, *Entretiens Fondation Hardt*, 17 (1972), 161, n. 2, defends Jerome's account but offers no positive arguments.

[124] Cic. *De Sen.* 50: *quam gaudebat Bello suo Punico Naevius.*

tine.[125] The state's backing for this institution lifted the status of playwrights and their professional colleagues, lending an air of importance to the theater that it could not previously have claimed. The dramatic profession received official and conspicuous blessing. For Nacvius it was a spur and an opportunity.

The time is past due to remove from the handbooks the depiction of Naevius as embattled writer, sniping at aristocrats from the stage, and then clapped into jail or hounded into exile. The artist who celebrated his nation's exploits in epic, the *Bellum Punicum*, and in serious drama, the *Clastidium*, could also hint at its political foibles in comedy. He did not spend his force in assaults on a noble clan, let alone serve the interests of one. Cn. Naevius, encouraged by the cultural climate of the 3rd century, adapted Hellenic literary media to reflect and enhance the Roman public scene.[126]

The leading literary light of the next generation, Q. Ennius, enjoyed remarkable success in ingratiating himself with prominent members of the political classes. Evidence attests to associations with M. Cato, the Scipios, Servilius Geminus, Sulpicius Galba, and, especially, M. Fulvius Nobilior, an eminent and potent assemblage. Those connections give rise to a familiar portrait. Ennius appears as client-poet par excellence, moving from patron to patron or lending his services as panegyrist to various representatives of the aristocracy.[127] Was the artist now fettered to the needs of the nobility or to various families within it? The matter demands closer scrutiny.

Ennius' roots, like those of Livius Andronicus and Naevius, lay in a non-Latin community. The poet stemmed from Messapian Rudiae and held his roots dear, claiming descent from the legendary king Messapus.[128] Education and aspiration soon outgrew those origins.

---

[125] Festus, 446, L; see above, n. 31.

[126] Cf. the remarks, from a different vantage-point, of A. La Penna, *Fra teatro, poesia, e politica romana* (Turin, 1979), 49-71.

[127] See, e.g., Ferrero, *Mondo Classico*, 11 (1941), 227-231; Badian, *Entretiens Fondation Hardt*, 17 (1972), 182-183; Jocelyn, *ANRW*, I.2 (1972), 993: "an engaging courtier"; Flores, *Letteratura latina e ideologia*, 96: "l'adesione politica totale all'oligarchia anticatoniana di M. Fulvio Nobiliore e di Scipio Africano"; Martina, *QuadFilClass*, 2 (1979), 18-20: "il collaboratore prezisio, l'amico, il consigliere di un uomo politico, Marco Fulvio Nobiliore, al cui servizio egli pose il suo genio"; *DialArch* (1981), 63-68; Zehnacker, in *Théatre et spectacles*, 37-39, 42; Williams, in Gold, *Literary and Artistic Patronage*, 5; O. Skutsch, *The Annals of Quintus Ennius* (Oxford, 1985), 1-2; Gold, *Literary Patronage*, 48-49.

[128] Ennius, *Ann.* 376-377, Vahlen = 524-525, Skutsch: *nos sumus Romani, qui fuimus ante Rudini*; Cic. *Pro Arch.* 22; *De Orat.* 3.168; Strabo, 6.281; Servius, *ad Aen.* 7.691; Suidas, s.v. Ἔννιος; Sil. Ital. 12.393-397. On the birthplace, see P. Magno, *Quinto Ennio* (Fasano, 1979), 10-14, with literature.

Ennius gained extensive exposure to Greek culture, perhaps at Tarentum, and obviously acquired fluency in Latin as well. He took personal pride in being trilingual: Oscan, Greek, and Latin, an accomplishment he characterized as "having three hearts." [129] To the Romans, however, Ennius was simply Greek or semi-Greek, in any case regarded as representative of Hellenic culture. [130] Therein lay his appeal and desirability: an exponent of Greek classics and a creator in the Latin language. [131] The year of his birth stands on record, 239 B.C., thus a generation younger than Livius Andronicus and Naevius, and in a position to benefit from increased Roman encouragement for the life of letters. [132] It may not be irrelevant that Ennius eventually took up quarters on the Aventine hill, site of Minerva's temple, where the guild of poets and dramatic artists received recognition as a public honor bestowed upon Livius Andronicus. [133]

Ennius' early years are a blank. The veil lifts only in 204, and then just briefly—but most importantly. Young M. Porcius Cato, on service as quaestor in Sardinia, brought Ennius with him to Rome. So reports our one source: it was a deed as estimable as the grandest Sardinian triumph. [134] We have no explicit report of Ennius' activities in Sardinia, but surmise is permissible. The poet took part in a Calabrian contingent that helped to occupy Sardinia in the Hannibalic war. [135] The emigration to Rome, however, inaugurated the public career.

What did it mean? Did Cato transport Ennius as *laudator* of his accomplishments, the poet's first employment in the role of artistic client

---

[129] Gellius, 17.17.1: *Q. Ennius tria corda habere sese dicebat, quod loqui Graece et Osce et Latine sciret*; cf. Suerbaum, *Untersuchungen*, 140-142; Jocelyn, *ANRW*, I.2 (1972), 991; Skutsch, *Annals*, 749-750. Jerome, *Chron.* Olymp. 134.4, wrongly gives his birthplace as Tarentum, but may reflect a different fact: schooling in that Greek city. The imbibing of Latin, it is often surmised, came through the colony of Brundisium, planted by the Romans in 244 and a near neighbor of Rudiae. The inference is plausible enough, though it lacks attestation.

[130] Suet. *De Gramm.* 1; Festus, 412, L.

[131] Suet. *De Gramm.* 1: *et poetae et semigraeci erant—Livium et Ennium dico, quos utraque lingua domi forisque docuisse adnotatum est—nihil amplius quam Graecos interpretabantur, aut si quid ipsi Latine composuissent praelegebant.*

[132] Gellius, 17.21.43—drawing on Varro's *De Poetis*. So also Cic. *Brutus*, 12; *Tusc. Disp.* 1.1.3. Jerome, *Chron.* Olymp. 134.4, misses it by a year.

[133] Jerome, *Chron.* Olymp. 134.4. Other motives for the location of Ennius' residence are postulated by Badian, *Entretiens Fondation Hardt*, 17 (1972), 164-168.

[134] Nepos, *Cato*, 1.4: *Q. Ennium poetam deduxerat, quod non minoris aestimamus quam quemlibet amplissimum Sardiniensem triumphum*; Jerome, *Chron.* Olymp. 134.4.

[135] Silius Italicus, 12.393-416, invents heroic martial deeds for the poet during that war, a recognized fiction, but perhaps based on information attesting Ennius' military service; cf. Suerbaum, *Untersuchungen*, 138, n. 440. Jocelyn's view, *ANRW*, I.2 (1972), 993, that Ennius first learned Latin while in Sardinia, is unlikely.

to a political patron? Ennius certainly did sing Cato's praises, indeed lauded him to the skies.[136] And Cicero has the Censor, in old age, refer to Ennius as his *familiaris*.[137] Nonetheless, the idea that Cato anticipated glorification in verse and thus patronized the poet who would deliver it is patently false. The thirty year old quaestor had few accomplishments to provide poetic inspiration anyway. Further, Ennius' initial employment in Rome appears to have been that of schoolmaster. He earned his own way, no mere hireling of the Catonian household.[138] That Cato sought personal profit from the installation of Ennius in Rome is unattested and implausible. Praise for Cato presumably surfaced in the *Annales*, a work to which the poet only turned more than a decade later. And sponsorship of a poet as private client would fly in the face of Cato's own professed opposition to such practice.[139] Nothing suggests that Ennius became protégé and propagandist for the Censor. And we can discard the usual corollary as well: that Ennius later broke with Cato and transferred allegiance to a new patron.[140] The concept itself derives from false presuppositions. Ennius was not in harness. Cato's actions in 204 betray an interest in cultural matters that his subsequent posturing attempted—not quite successfully—to conceal.

A closer connection, it might be surmised, held between Ennius and the most celebrated figure of his time: P. Scipio Africanus. Cicero reports affection between the two men and alludes to the praise heaped upon Africanus by the poet.[141] Some of that praise, at least, appeared in a

---

[136] Cic. *Pro Arch.* 22: *in caelum huius proavus Cato tollitur.*

[137] Cic. *De Sen.* 10.

[138] Suet. *De Gramm.* 1. That Ennius taught Cato Greek literature is doubtless later invention or guesswork; *Vir. Ill.* 47.1. It has been doubted even that Cato sponsored Ennius' arrival in Rome at all. So Badian, *Entretiens Fondation Hardt*, 17 (1972), 154-163. But none of his arguments shakes Nepos' explicit testimony. The *argumenta e silentio*, based on Cic. *De Sen.* 10, *Tusc. Disp.* 1.3-2.1, and *Brutus*, 57-60, are quite indecisive, for the purpose of each of these passages demands no allusion to the Cato-Ennius story which would, in fact, be inappropriate to the contexts; see especially Jocelyn, *Entretiens Fondation Hardt*, 17 (1972), 200-201. Nor does it advance the cause to point to Plutarch's silence as well, as J.S. Ruebel, *LCM*, 2 (1977), 155-157, who does, at least, recognize the likelihood of Cato's service in Sardinia. The effort to discredit Nepos' testimony founders on a critical question: why should such a tale have been invented? Badian's answer, that it supplied a foil to Cato's later criticism of Fulvius Nobilior for taking Ennius with him to the East, will not do. The two stories are nowhere juxtaposed. And Nepos quite plainly finds the report of Ennius' transmission to be to Cato's credit; cf. Suerbaum, *Entretiens Fondation Hardt*, 17 (1972), 200.

[139] Gellius, 11.2.5; Cic. *Tusc. Disp.* 1.3. See below p. 116.

[140] The notion is recently reiterated by A.E. Astin, *Cato the Censor* (Oxford, 1978), 16-17.

[141] Cic. *Pro Arch.* 22: *carus fuit Africano superiori noster Ennius...eis laudibus certe non solum ipse qui laudatur, sed etiam populi Romani nomen ornatur.*

poetic panegyric entitled *Scipio*.[142] Extant fragments of that work and other verses as well lavish tribute upon the great general. He is addressed in the poem as *Scipio invicte*, his deeds described as surpassing any statue or monument that might be erected to celebrate them.[143] Ennius even has Scipio himself proclaim that the world has no one who can equal his accomplishments and that if mortal man can ascend to heaven the great portal lies open to him alone.[144] That is strong stuff. And it has led many to conclude that Ennius aimed at "heroization" of the general.[145] The conclusion is extreme and unwarranted. Prudence forbids an equation of poetic fancy with political calculation. No testimony suggests that Scipio Africanus engaged Ennius to prepare the way for elevation to superhuman status. The date of Ennius' *Scipio* is itself unknown, quite possibly after the death of its subject.[146] Of course, Ennius found in Scipio a source of poetic inspiration and judged his achievements to be of epic proportions. The conquest of Hannibal merited the loftiest laudation. Ennius reportedly expressed the sentiment that only Homer would be capable of singing Scipio's praises.[147] But Scipio's triumph was a

---

[142] For the title, see Gellius, 4.7.3; Macrob. *Sat.* 6.2.26. The genre of the work remains uncertain. The view of F. Skutsch, *RE*, V, "Ennius," n. 3, 2598-2599, that it was an epic, has been adequately refuted; see C. Pascal, *Athenaeum*, 3 (1915), 376. Others identify it as a drama, specifically a *praetexta*. More likely, it comprised one of Ennius' four books of *saturae*, or was perhaps an independent laudatory poem. For discussion, see Pascal, *op. cit.*, 369-375; J. Vahlen, *Ennianae Poesis Reliquiae* (Leipzig, 1928), ccxv-ccxvii; Suerbaum, *Untersuchungen*, 239-241, with bibliography; Richter, *Gymnasium*, 69 (1962), 301-302; Zehnacker, in *Théâtre et spectacles*, 37-39.

[143] Ennius, *Varia*, 1-3, Vahlen: *quantam statuam faciet populus Romanus,/ quantam columnam quae res tuas gestas loquatur.* Cf. 19-20, Vahlen: *hic est ille situs, cui nemo civis neque hostis/ quibit pro factis reddere opis pretium.*

[144] Ennius, *Varia*, 21-24, Vahlen: *A sole exoriente supra Maeotis paludes/ nemo est qui factis aequiperare queat./ Si fas endo plagas caelestum ascendere cuiquam est,/ mi soli caeli maxima porta patet.* The two couplets derive from different sources. Their conjunction is possible, but undemonstrable. For purposes of the present discussion, it makes no difference.

[145] A. Elter, *Donarem pateras* (Bonn, 1907), *passim*; A.R. Anderson, *HSCP*, 39 (1928), 31-37; R.M. Haywood, *Studies on Scipio Africanus* (Baltimore, 1933), 19-21; G.K. Galinsky, *TAPA*, 97 (1966), 227-230; F.W. Walbank, *PCPS*, 13 (1967), 56-58; Flores, *Letteratura latina e ideologia*, 90-91. Somewhat more cautious is H.H. Scullard, *Scipio Africanus: Soldier and Politician* (London, 1970), 247-248, n. 11.

[146] Vahlen, *Ennianae Poesis Reliquiae*, ccxvi-ccxvii, puts it shortly after Scipio's triumphant return from Africa; supported, most recently, by U.W. Scholz, *Hermes*, 112 (1984), 193-195. Pascal, *Athenaeum*, 3 (1915), 376-380, prefers a date late in Scipio's lifetime and after his trials in the 180s. No hard evidence backs either view. Skutsch, *Annals*, 3, cites Suidas, s.v. Ἔννιος, to argue that the *Scipio* preceded the *Annales*—also inconclusive. Martina, *QuadFilClass*, 2 (1979), 17-18, opts for a date after Scipio's death. But the lines he adduces from the *Annales*, 312-313, Vahlen = 312-313, Skutsch, even if they do refer to Scipio, need not imply his demise. And his assertion that Ennius can only have spoken well of Scipio after his patron Fulvius Nobilior entered the Scipionic group in 180 takes a narrow view of the poet's freedom—and of the Roman political scene.

[147] Suidas, s.v. Ἔννιος: Σκιπίωνα γὰρ ᾄδων καὶ ἐπὶ μέγα τὸν ἄνδρα ἐξᾶραι βουλόμενός φησι μόνον ἂν Ὅμηρον ἐπαξίους ἐπαίνους εἰπεῖν Σκιπίωνος.

national triumph—and Ennius celebrated his nation's time of glory. As Cicero discerned, the poet's praises of the individual enhanced the renown of the state. That held both for Ennius' panegyric of Africanus and for his exaltation of Cato.[148] His verses provided the most powerful and enduring monuments to Rome's leadership.[149] That is very far from being in thrall to a particular house of the *nobilitas*.

The relationship, in fact, had a quite different character. Not only did Ennius enjoy close relations with the Scipiones, but the association engendered mutual respect and a relaxed informality that ignored class lines. An engaging anecdote brings the fact to light. P. Scipio Nasica, probably the consul of 191, paid a call upon Ennius but was turned away by his slave girl on the transparently false pretext that her master was away from home. When Ennius returned the visit a few days later, Nasica himself shouted from within that he was not at home. Ennius, of course, recognized the voice and demanded a reason for this charade. Nasica gave a witty and pointed response: ''I believed your servant when she told me you were away; will you not believe the same of me when I tell you personally?''[150] The truth of the tale cannot be guaranteed. But the very fact of its attachment to the poet and the eminent patrician gives insight into their relationship. The camaraderie implicit in the interchange suggests that Ennius stood on an independent footing and had easy access to Scipionic society.[151] A similar inference can be drawn from the report that a statue of Ennius was included in the tomb of the Scipios. Cicero supplies the earliest notice of that report, duly labelling it as con-

---

[148] Cic. *Pro Arch.* 22: *at eis laudibus certe non solum* [Scipio] *ipse qui laudatur, sed etiam populi Romani nomen ornatur. In caelum huius proavus Cato tollitur; magnus honos populi Romani rebus adiungitur.*

[149] Horace, *Carm.* 4.8.13-20. The text, as it stands, gives special emphasis to Ennius' *laudes* of Scipio. But the structure of the poem and the logic of those lines have long troubled commentators. The attractive solution of C. Becker, *Hermes*, 87 (1959), 212-222, drawing on earlier suggestions, excises lines 15-19, thereby giving Ennius as *laudator* of Roman *duces*—as indeed he was—without specific allusion to Scipio: *non incisa notis marmora publicis,/ per quae spiritus et vita redit bonis/ post mortem ducibus...clarius indicant/ laudes quam Calabrae Pierides.* Cf. Sil. Ital. 12.410-411: *hic canet illustri primus bella Itala versu/ attolletque duces caelo.* See the full examination by Suerbaum, *Untersuchungen*, 176-248.

[150] Cic. *De Orat.* 2.276: *ego cum te quaererem, ancillae tuae credidi te domi non esse: tu mihi non credis ipsi?*

[151] Authenticity of the anecdote is plausibly defended by Badian, *Entretiens Fondation Hardt*, 17 (1972), 171-172. He prefers to see the protagonist as Scipio Nasica, consul 162, 155, rather than his father, the consul of 191, on grounds that the familiarity better suits association with a younger man, perhaps a pupil, than a contemporary where differences in status would be more conspicuous. The presumption of a teacher-pupil relationship, however, is unsupported and perhaps anachronistic—reflecting a subsequent generation when Hellenic teachers were imported as captives or hostages from abroad.

jecture. Similar caution appears in Livy's text.[152] The circumspection disappears thereafter. Subsequent authorities take the tale as fact, embellishing it further to make Scipio Africanus arrange for Ennius' burial in the family tomb—even though the general died a decade and a half before the poet.[153] The story carries marks of invention and elaboration.[154] Yet it can hardly have arisen without some basis. Ennius had obviously earned the affection and respect of the Scipios, and a ready entrance to their company. Mutual regard rather than clientage appears to have marked the association.

A comparable connection held between the poet and another patrician house, that of the Sulpicii Galbae. Only a fleeting allusion attests to it, but that suffices. Ser. Sulpicius Galba was Ennius' neighbor, their properties adjacent or near to one another on the Aventine. And the two men evidently enjoyed one another's company in walks on their grounds.[155] Here too the evidence leaves an impression of cordial familiarity and easy interchange that crossed social barriers. The poet commanded high esteem.

Ennius himself gives the most eloquent testimony to this form of relationship. The celebrated "Good Companion" passage, quoted by Gellius from Book VII of the *Annales*, presents a vivid and invaluable portrait. The lines derive from a section devoted to Servilius Geminus who in a respite from fighting turned to confide in a trusted friend. Ennius' portrayal of the latter is described by Gellius as an exemplary depiction of the virtues desired in a man who serves as refuge and solace for one higher in status and fortune.[156] In the opinion of L. Aelius Stilo,

---

[152] Cic. *Pro Arch.* 22: *itaque etiam in sepulcro Scipionum putatur is esse constitutus ex marmore*; Livy, 38.56.4: *Romae extra portam Capenam in Scipionum monumento tres statuae sunt, quarum duae P. et L. Scipionum dicuntur esse, tertia poetae Q. Ennii.*

[153] Ovid, *Ars Amat.* 3.409-410; Val. Max. 8.14.1; Pliny, *NH*, 7.114; Schol. Bob. 178, Stangl; Jerome, *Chron.* Olymp. 153.4. The texts are conveniently set out by Suerbaum, *Untersuchungen*, 210-211.

[154] Its dubious character was recognized by Vahlen, *Ennianae poesis reliquiae*, xix. See also Skutsch, *RE*, V, "Ennius," n. 3, 2590-2591; Suerbaum, *Untersuchungen*, 210-213. On the archaeological evidence, see F. Coarelli, *DialArch*, 6 (1972), 36-105. The laureate head excavated at the tomb of the Scipios is surely not that of Ennius; T. Dohrn, *MdI*, 69 (1962), 76-95. The tale, surprisingly, is still accepted, without discussion, by some moderns; e.g. Galinsky, *TAPA*, 97 (1966), 228; Scullard, *Scipio Africanus*, 237.

[155] Cic. *Acad. Prior.* 2.51: *num censes Ennium cum in hortis cum Servio Galba vicino suo ambulavisset dixisse: 'visus sum mihi cum Galba ambulare?'* That Ennius dwelled on the Aventine is recorded by Jerome, *Chron.* Olymp. 134.4. On the location of the property, see Badian, *Entretiens Fondation Hardt*, 17 (1972), 163-168. Badian identifies Galba with the consul of 144 and cautiously suggests a teacher-pupil relationship here as well; *op. cit.*, 171-172. There is no explicit testimony. Galba, the praetor of 187 and a man closer in age to Ennius, is an alternative possibility.

[156] Gellius, 12.4.1: *ad muniendas vitae molestias fomentis, levamentis, solacis amicum esse conveniat hominis genere et fortuna superioris.*

writing in the late 2nd century, Ennius' characterization of the "good companion" had none other than himself directly in mind.[157] Scholars divide on the troublesome questions raised by this passage. Is it authentic autobiography? Which Servilius Geminus is the subject being treated? Did Ennius have an attachment to the family of the Servilii Gemini as *amicus* or *cliens*? The state of the evidence prevents decisive answers. Yet some tentative and cautious conclusions are permissible. Stilo, in all probability, relied on more than sheer guesswork in declaring the passage to be self-portrayal by Ennius. The specific Servilius Geminus in question may escape detection. But the inference by Stilo that Servilius' companion is the poet suggests that association between Ennius and the house of the Servilii was an understood presumption. Whether or not the passage intends an accurate self-portrait matters little. The presentation of close friendship between a cultivated intellectual and a man of superior social standing applied to Ennius' circumstances—as the poet was well aware. The "good companion," if not Ennius himself, serves as a reasonable facsimile.[158]

The passage itself demands attention. It is consistently interpreted by moderns as describing a faithful client's relation to his noble patron.[159] That interpretation misplaces the emphasis. What stands out, despite the acknowledged difference in social status, is mutual trust and candor. Servilius frequently and eagerly shared both meals and personal conversa-

---

[157] Gellius, 12.4.4: *L. Aelium Stilonem dicere solitum ferunt Q. Ennium de semet ipso haec scripsisse picturamque istam morum et ingenii ipsius Q. Ennii factam esse.*

[158] The judgment of Stilo that the portrayal is basically autobiographical has been accepted by most; e.g., A.D. Leeman, *Mnesmosyne*, 11 (1958), 318-321; O. Skutsch, *Studia Enniana* (London, 1968), 92-94; Badian, *Entretiens Fondation Hardt*, 17 (1972), 180-182; Martina, *Labeo*, 26 (1980), 158-160. The fact that Ennius ascribed no name to the "good companion" supports that view. More skeptical are Suerbaum, *Untersuchungen*, 142-143, n. 455, and Jocelyn, *ANRW*, I.2 (1972), 993-994. Servilius Geminus is generally identified with P. Geminus, cos. 252, or C. Geminus, cos. 217, who perished heroically at Cannae. See the discussion, with bibliography, by Badian, *op. cit.*, 174-177, 180, who opts for the former. Skutsch, *Annals*, 447-448, prefers the latter. In neither case, of course, can the poet be referring to a literal friendship, for he did not come to Rome until 204, well after the death of both men. Two other Gemini were contemporaries of Ennius, the consuls of 203 and 202. But Book VII of the *Annales* can hardly have contained reference to them, and a resort to emendation is not clearly justified; *contra:* Skutsch, *Annals*, 447-448. The anonymous "good companion" can, in any event, represent Ennius' view of himself masked as an invented friend of Geminus. For Skutsch, *Studia Enniana*, 92-94, it is an idealized representation of the poet's relationship with Fulvius Nobilior. So also Jocelyn, *loc. cit.*, who sees it as response to Cato's criticism of Fulvius for having Ennius accompany him to the East.

[159] Cf. Skutsch, *Studia Enniana*, 94; Badian, *Entretiens Fondation Hardt*, 17 (1972), 171-172, 182-183: "a footing of inferiority and clientship"; Jocelyn, *ANRW*, I.2 (1972), 994: "clients of the leaders of the state"; and, especially, Martina, *QuadFilClass*, 2 (1979), 74; *Labeo*, 26 (1980), 158-160: "il personaggio enniano è un *poeta cliens*."

tions with his "companion".[160] To him he spoke out boldly in matters great and small, in jest or seriousness, spewing forth language both reputable and disreputable, relying implicitly on his friend's discretion, a man with whom he shared many a pleasure and joy, whether openly or secretly.[161] The "companion" in turn is depicted as learned, trustworthy, charming, eloquent, self-content, happy, and well-informed.[162] He was a man of few words—but suitable and timely ones—who held to ancient practices long buried by time, respected customs both old and new, and observed the laws of gods and men.[163] He knew what information to express—and what to keep to himself.[164] This is no description of a deferential and submissive client.[165] Ennius presents the "companion" as a cultivated and accomplished individual, a staunch and reliable friend, whose intimacy with the powerful demonstrated his character, not his dependence. The glorified portrait may reflect more aspiration than realization. But the relationship it delineated corresponds closely to that which Ennius enjoyed with *amici* in the *nobilitas*.[166]

A more conspicuous bond tied the poet to M. Fulvius Nobilior, the consul of 189. Here the issue of patronage arises in starkest form. Fulvius is generally seen as Ennius' principal patron and protector, whose interests the poet advanced with energy and enthusiasm.[167] Testimony on the connection offers apparent support to the idea that it contained political implications. When Fulvius drew Aetolia as his consular *provincia* in 189, he went east with Ennius as companion. The writer, we may safely assume, was expected to chronicle the campaign, perhaps to

---

[160] Ennius, *Annales*, 234-236, Vahlen = 268-270, Skutsch = Gellius, 12.4.4: *quocum bene saepe libenter/ mensam sermonesque suos rerumque suarum/ comiter inpertit.*

[161] Ennius, *Annales*, 239-242, Vahlen = 273-276, Skutsch = Gellius, 12.4.4: *cui res audacter magnas parvasque iocumque/ eloqueretur et cuncta malaque et bona dictu/ evomeret si qui vellet tutoque locaret,/ quocum multa volup/ guadia clamque palamque.*

[162] Ennius, *Annales*, 244-246, Vahlen = 279-281, Skutsch = Gellius, 12.4.4: *doctus, fidelis,/ suavis homo, facundus, suo contentus, beatus,/ scitus.*

[163] Ennius, *Annales*, 246-249, Vahlen = 281-284, Skutsch = Gellius, 12.4.4: *secunda loquens in tempore, commodus, verbum/ paucum, multa tenens, antiqua sepulta vetustas/ quae facit; et mores veteresque novosque tenentem,/ multorum veterum leges divumque hominumque.*

[164] Ennius, *Annales*, 250, Vahlen = 285, Skutsch = Gellius. 12.4.4: *prudentem, qui dicta loquive tacereve posset.*

[165] The only term employed that might suggest deference is *commodus*; 246, Vahlen = 281, Skutsch. But, in the context, it should more probably be rendered "agreeable" than "accommodating."

[166] On *amicitia* between poets and members of the *nobilitas* in later periods, see W. Allen, *CP*, 3 (1938), 167-181; White, *JRS*, 68 (1978), 74-92; Saller, *CQ*, 33 (1983), 246-257; R.L. Hunter, *Hermes*, 113 (1985), 480-486. Evidence from the late Republic and from the Empire, however, cannot easily serve to elucidate circumstances in the early stages of Latin literature.

[167] Cf. Badian, *Entretiens Fondation Hardt*, 17 (1972), 182; Martina, *QuadFilClass*, 2 (1979), 20; Skutsch, *Annals*, 1, 144, 502.

embellish the command which, Fulvius anticipated, would bring the
Aetolian war to a successful conclusion. Cato, of course, denounced the
move, probably objecting to the exploitation of literary talent by an
individual commander.[168] Ennius did indeed chronicle the campaign. It
comprised the fifteenth book of the *Annales*, designed to climax and conclude the great epic.[169] And he composed a separate work, the *Ambracia*,
perhaps a *fabula praetexta*, devoted to the siege of that state conducted by
M. Fulvius Nobilior. It can hardly be coincidence that Nobilior came
under heavy fire in Rome for his conduct of the siege, his enemies seeking to block his triumph in 187 and claiming that his attack on Ambracia
was unprovoked, inhumane, and brutal.[170] Ennius' composition plainly
aimed to defend the reputation and justify the triumph of M. Nobilior.
Signal praise from the poet enhanced an already glorious victory.[171] The
vindication of Nobilior brought rewards for Ennius. Among the spoils
transported by Nobilior from Greece were statues of the Muses, to be followed by Nobilior's dedication of the temple of Hercules of the Muses,
thereby establishing a cult of those divinities, a bold tribute to poetry
itself. The temple would become the new site for the *collegium poetarum*.
And there can be little doubt that Ennius played a role in Fulvius'
benefactions.[172] In 184 the poet acquired an even more tangible prize:
Roman citizenship, awarded through the good offices of Nobilior's son
in his capacity as colonial commissioner in that year.[173] The accumula-
tion of evidence appears to form a collective portrait: Ennius as *poeta cliens*
of the house of Fulvius Nobilior.

---

[168] Cic. *Tusc. Disp.* 1.3: *oratio Catonis, in qua obiecit ut probrum M. Nobiliori, quod is in
provinciam poetas duxisset; duxerat autem consul ille in Aetoliam, ut scimus, Ennium.* Ennius'
accompaniment of Fulvius is noted also by Cic. *Pro Arch.* 27, and *Brutus,* 79—although
one need not take literally the phrase that Ennius *militaverat.* See also Symmachus, *Epist.*
1.20.2.

[169] For the content of Book XV, see Vahlen, *Ennianae poesis reliquiae,* cxcix; Skutsch,
Annals, 553-563. Ennius later changed his mind and composed additional books; Pliny,
NH, 7.101.Cf. Skutsch, *Studia Enniana,* 19-20.

[170] Livy, 38.43-44, 39.4.5.

[171] *Vir. Ill.* 52.2-3: *quam victoriam per se magnificam Ennius amicus eius insigni laude celebravit.*
Extant fragments of the *Ambracia,* very few in number, with ancient references to the
work, are collected by Vahlen, *Ennianae poesis reliquiae,* 188-189. It is not certain whether
the reference in *Vir. Ill.* 52.3 is to the *Ambracia* or to Book XV of the *Annales.*

[172] That is stated explicitly by *Pan. Lat.* 9.7.3: *aedem Herculis Musarum in circo Flaminio
Fulvius ille Nobilior ex pecunia censoria fecit, non id modo secutus quod ipse litteris et summi poetae
amicitia duceretur.* There may be indirect allusion to Ennius' involvement by Cic. *Pro Arch.*
27: *ille, qui cum Aetolis Ennio comite bellavit, Fulvius, non dubitavit Martis manubias Musis con-
secrare;* but see Martina, *DialArch* (1981), 55-58. Skutsch, *Studia Enniana,* 18-19, finds an
even more indirect allusion in Symmachus' report that Fulvius gave the poet nothing
from the spoils of Ambracia except a single cloak; Symmachus, *Epist.* 1.20.2; cf. Servius,
ad Aen. 1.8. On the *collegium poetarum,* see above pp. 87-90.

[173] Cic. *Brutus,* 79; cf. Livy, 39. 44.10.

That evidence, however, admits of a different interpretation. Cultural motives take precedence here, relegating political implications to a secondary category. M. Fulvius Nobilior had authentic intellectual interests, no mere puffery or publicity. His promotion of the cult of the Muses is but one indication. Fulvius produced a work on the *Fasti*, a learned calendrical study requiring astronomical and perhaps philosophical investigations, the finished version of which was installed in the temple of Hercules of the Muses.[174] Ennius, for his part, had either recently embarked or was soon to embark upon his epic, the *Annales*. He must certainly have contemplated the project before his decision to accompany Fulvius to Greece.[175] The poet could already visualize the war's end, a conclusion to the cycle of Hellenic wars that demonstrated Roman supremacy in the eastern Mediterranean. Participation in the final campaign could give the experience and inspiration that had helped to launch Naevius' *Bellum Punicum*. Fulvius' motives, to be sure, were far from unselfish. He could anticipate a featured role in Ennius' treatment of the Aetolian war. But one need not confine his purpose to pure personal promotion. The encouragement of artistic and intellectual endeavors gave special satisfaction to Fulvius Nobilior.

Ennius nowhere suffers criticism for being the hired instrument of political ambition. Cato levelled stern rebuke at Fulvius, not at the

---

[174] Macrob. *Sat.* 1.12.16; Varro, *LL*, 6.33; cf. P. Boyancé, *RevPhil*, 29 (1955), 172-192.

[175] The time of composition of the *Annales* is a notoriously insoluble puzzle. Some scholars have placed the inception of the work shortly after Ennius' arrival in Rome in 204, and the scheme conceived even earlier; see citations in Jocelyn, *ANRW*, I.2 (1972), 997. That seems far-fetched. Ennius refers in Book IX to M. Cornelius Cethegus, in terms that imply that his contemporaries belonged to an earlier generation, and he wrote of his death. Cethegus' death, in fact, came in 196; Cic. *Brutus*, 57-58; Livy, 33.42.5. For most scholars, that serves as *terminus post quem* for the *Annales*; e.g. Skutsch, *RE*, V, "Ennius," n. 3, 2613; Suerbaum, *Untersuchungen*, 114. Actually it serves as *terminus post quem* only for Book IX. Suerbaum, *op. cit.*, 115, takes Ennius' appeal to *cives* in *Annales*, 16, Vahlen = *op. inc.* 1, Skutsch, as evidence that he already had Roman citizenship—which would date the poem after 184. But that fragment may not, in fact, come from the *Annales*; Skutsch, *Annals*, 750-751. For Jocelyn, *op. cit.*, 997-998, the invocation of the Muses suggests a time after the Aetolian war and Fulvius' promotion of the temple of Hercules Musarum. Nothing like certainty is possible. Gellius, 17.21.43, quotes Varro's *De Poetis* for Ennius' composition of Book XII at age 67, i.e. 172 BC, on Ennius' own authority. But we know that the poet died in 169 at age 70, the year in which he produced his tragedy *Thyestes*; Cic. *Brutus*, 78; *De Sen.* 14. That he also completed the first edition of the *Annales* with books XIII through XV, then later resumed the work and wrote three new books, all between 172 and 169, is unlikely in the extreme. Hence, as is now generally acknowledged, the number in Gellius' text must be emended; see Suerbaum, *op. cit.*, 117-120; Skutsch, *Annals*, 674-676. This does not, unfortunately, help to fix the date at which the *Annales* were begun. That the idea of the epic was not conceived until after Ennius returned from Aetolia, however, is difficult to believe.

writer. He attacked the principle of Roman officials taking poets in their
entourage, an unwelcome precedent that would distort or demean their
proper functions as servants of the state.[176] Ennius could hardly be
faulted for seizing the opportunity offered. Cato harbored no ill feelings
for the poet and was even presented in old age as referring to Ennius as
familiaris noster.[177]

Cato's criticisms had a different objective. The stern moralist declared
in his *Carmen de Moribus* that the poetic art once lacked credit and that
those who were avid for it and plied their trade at banquets were
regarded as *grassatores*.[178] The term, plainly derogatory, often means
vagabond or idler, but another meaning better suits the context: flat-
terer.[179] His speech against Fulvius Nobilior expressed a similar sentiment:
the practice of celebrating the deeds of famous men in song had lost all
esteem when a general brought his own poets along on a provincial
assignment.[180] The moral indignation of the Censor, as so often, exag-
gerates and distorts the issue. Other evidence provides corrective. Cato's
own *Origines* portrayed the ancient custom of praising great men at banquets in a positive light. Indeed, he himself promoted discussion of
Rome's worthy and virtuous men at his dinner table.[181] And the claim
that literary artistry suffers disrepute stands at variance with the honors
bestowed upon Livius Andronicus and the privileges awarded to the
guild of writers and actors. Cato is plainly not issuing a blanket condemnation of poetry. His strictures have a narrower focus, and the *ars poetica*
has a special meaning here: the use of poetic hirelings summoned to flatter the egos of their patrons.[182] In his own historical work Cato even
made a point of narrating events without naming names—an exercise in
purist posturing.[183] He set himself against the employment of literary art

---

[176] Cic. *Tusc. Disp.* 1.3: *probrum M. Nobiliori, quod is in provinciam poetas duxisset.*

[177] Cic. *De Sen.* 10. Jocelyn, *ANRW*, I.2 (1972), 995, oddly understands this to mean
that Cato did not take his own public statement on Fulvius and Ennius seriously.

[178] Gellius, 11.2.5: *Poeticae artis honos non erat. Si quis in ea re studebat aut sese ad convivia
adplicabat, "grassator" vocabatur.*

[179] See Festus, 86, L.: *grassari antiqui ponebant pro adulari.* For discussion of the Catonian
passage, see Till, *Neue Jahrbücher*, 115 (1940), 165-166; J. Préaux, *Latomus*, 25 (1966),
710-725; Martina, *Labeo*, 26 (1980), 161-164.

[180] Cic. *Tusc. Disp.* 1.3: *Quamquam est in Originibus solitos esse in epulis canere convivas ad
tibicinem de clarorum hominum virtutibus, honorem tamen huic generi non fuisse declarat oratio
Catonis, in qua obiecit ut probrum M. Nobiliori, quod is in provinciam poetas duxisset.*

[181] Plut. *Cato*, 25.3; Cic. *Tusc. Disp.* 1.3, 4.3; *Brutus*, 75.

[182] Notice the *huic generi* in Cic. *Tusc. Disp.* 1.3, thus singling out a particular form of
the poetic art for censure, by implied contrast with others. So, rightly, Ferrero, *Mondo
Classico*, 11 (1941), 208-209. Martina, *Labeo*, 26 (1980), 163, is misleading on this.

[183] Nepos, *Cato*, 3.4.

by individual *nobiles* for personal or political gain.[184] The attack was not aimed at Ennius, nor at the practice of poetry in general.

Ennius' *Ambracia* doubtless defended the actions of Fulvius, legitimated the siege, and augmented the victory. But its aim reached beyond political partisanship. Cato's continued affection for the poet demonstrates that adequately enough. Ennius' writings paid high tribute to Cato, as they did to another political foe of Nobilior, M. Aemilius Lepidus—with special commendation to Lepidus for his reconciliation with Nobilior.[185] The poet applauded political unity, rather than abetting divisiveness. If the *Ambracia* took up Fulvius' cause, it did so as much to rally opinion around a national victory as to provide an apologia for the commander.[186] Ennius concentrated on patriotic, not partisan, themes.

The self-advertisement of M. Fulvius Nobilior is subsumed in the larger cultural meaning of his association with Ennius. The victor in the Aetolian war returned with the statues of the Muses and installed them in a new or enlarged temple of Hercules of the Muses.[187] Into that structure he also placed the small *aedicula Camenarum* attributed to Numa which had earlier been struck by lightning and was temporarily housed in the shrine of Honos and Virtus.[188] The Camenae, sacred deities of hoary Latin tradition, had been invoked by both Livius Andronicus and Naevius. Ennius, by contrast, opens the *Annales* by an invocation to the Hellenic Muses and their stomping grounds on Mt. Olympus.[189] The symbolic character of these developments can hardly be missed. Fulvius assimilated the Latin deities of song to the Greek Muses, an amalgam

---

[184] Cf. Ferrero, *Mondo Classico*, 11 (1941), 208-211, 220-231, in a somewhat confusing discussion. A more pointed treatment by Martina, *Labeo*, 26 (1980), 161-165.

[185] The tribute to Cato: Cic. *Pro Arch.* 22; the praise for Lepidus: Cic. *De Prov. Cons.* 21. Martina's elaborate hypothesis, *QuadFilClass*, 2 (1979), 21-37, that Ennius praised Lepidus here to cover up what was really Fulvius' ignominious initiative for reconciliation, is purely speculative and implausible, though endorsed now by Skutsch, *Annals*, 572-574. If Ennius' purpose were to advance the interests of his "patron," he could as easily have represented him as the great reconciler.

[186] It is unnecessary to assume that the *Ambracia* was produced either for Fulvius' *ludi votivi* in 186 or for his funeral games, as does Zehnacker, in *Théâtre et spectacles*, 42. On the *praetexta* as a means of extending sacral celebrations of achievements associated with *imperium* into a period when they came under attack, see the (highly abstract) comments of Zorzetti, *La pretesta*, 75-92.

[187] Whether this was done shortly after his return to Rome in 187 or during his censorship in 179 remains uncertain. The evidence of Cic. *Pro Arch.* 27 and Pliny, *NH*, 35.66 inclines to the former, though indecisively; *Pan. Lat.* 9.7.3 indicates the latter. Martina, *DialArch* (1981), 49-58, makes a vigorous argument for the later date.

[188] Servius, *ad Aen.* 1.8. Servius refers to it as an *aedicula* of the Muses, reflecting the long-standing identification of the two sets of divinities.

[189] Ennius, *Annales*, 1, Vahlen = 1, Skutsch: *Musae, quae pedibus magnum pulsatis Olympum.* Cf. *Annales*, 326, Vahlen = 322, Skutsch. For the appeal of Andronicus and Naevius to the Camenae, see Gellius, 1.24.2, 18.9.5.

that would bring Hellenic inspiration to a Roman setting. Ennius' sum-
moning of the Muses had similar implications: not a rejection of the
Camenae but their absorption into a larger Greco-Roman concept. The
Hellenic models were once again appropriated for Roman purposes.[190]
No less important as a symbol was the combination of Hercules and the
Muses. The most powerful of divine spirits would provide protection for
poetry, and the Muses in turn would sing of the exploits of Hercules.[191]
The association of martial prowess and poetic genius received dramatic
display in the new shrine. The *aedes Herculis Musarum*, future home of the
collegium poetarum, honored artistic creativity in the service of the state.
And Ennius' epic performed precisely that function of applying the
imagination of the poet to the exploits of the nation. The collaboration
of Fulvius and Ennius went well beyond a client's advancement of his
patron's private ambitions.[192] It is fitting that Ennius' accomplishments
earned him Roman citizenship. Nobilior's son may have been the agent,
but the nation itself bestowed the award.[193] Q. Ennius was no mere time
server of the Fulvian *gens*.[194]

---

[190] It is customarily supposed that Ennius' invocation of the Muses signified turning
his back on the Camenae, a conspicuous reproof to his poetic predecessors; e.g. J.H.
Waszink, *ClMed*, 17 (1956), 145; Skutsch, *Studia Enniana*, 3-5, 18-21; Palmer, *Roman
Religion and Roman Empire*, 99; A. Ronconi, in *Poesia latina in frammenti* (Genoa, 1974), 16-
17; Martina, *DialArch* (1981), 68. Badian, *Entretiens Fondation Hardt* 17 (1972), 191-195,
gives what is surely the right interpretation: the Camenae are enhanced rather than
disparaged by having them take on the name of the Hellenic patronesses of song. Cf.
Ennius, *Annales*, 2, Vahlen = 487, Skutsch: *Musas quas memorant, nosce nos esse Camenas*—a
controversial line, which cannot here be discussed; cf. Skutsch, *op. cit.*, 20-21; Suerbaum,
Untersuchungen, 347-349, with bibliography.

[191] *Pan. Lat.* 9.7.3: *signa...Camenarum ex Ambraciensi oppido translata sub tutela fortissimi
numinis consecravit, ut res est, quia mutuis opibus et praemiis iuvari ornarique deberent. Musarum
quies defensione Herculis et virtus Herculis [et] voce Musarum*. On the artistic representations
of this group, see M.T.M. Moevs, *Bolletino d'Arte*, 66 (1981), 1-58.

[192] Best discussions of the *aedes Herculis Musarum* by Tamm, *Opuscula Romana*, 21
(1961), 157-167; Badian, *Entretiens Fondation Hardt*, 17 (1972), 187-191; Martina, *DialArch*
(1981), 62-68. But Martina's view that Fulvius sponsored the new building to transform
patronage of the arts from a public function to a private venture is unacceptable.

[193] Cic. *Pro Arch*. 22: *ergo illum, qui haec fecerat, Rudinum hominem, maiores nostri in civitatem
receperunt*. Even the fact of the younger Nobilior's effecting the franchise grant has been
called into question by Badian, *Entretiens Fondation Hardt*, 17 (1972), 183-185. But,
although he demonstrates that the *triumvir* for colonial assignations cannot have been Q.
Fulvius Nobilior, cos. 153, the possibility remains open that he was M. Nobilior, cos.
159, brother of the former. In any case, Cicero's remark in this context also draws attention to the political association; *Brutus*, 79: *Q. Nobiliorem M.f. iam patrio instituto deditum
studio litterarum, qui etiam Q. Ennium...civitate donavit*.

[194] Badian, *Entretiens Fondation Hardt*, 17 (1972), 185-187, argues that Ennius added
Book XVI to the *Annales* in order to oblige M. Fulvius Nobilior: the book served to vin-
dicate Fulvius' political ally, A. Manlius Vulso, who had come under sharp criticism for
his conduct of the Istrian war in 178 and 177. Martina, *QuadFilClass*, 2 (1979), 37-44,
goes further still and suggests that Ennius knowingly retailed false propaganda, even

Ennius belonged to the generation that succeeded Livius Andronicus and Naevius. The difference is notable. Ennius' ties to individual houses of the *nobilitas* were more conspicuous and, no doubt, more important than those of his predecessors. The phenomenon, however, should not be misconceived. It signals a greater interest in learning and literature on the part of the Roman upper classes—not a drive to manipulate literary output. The patronage of the powerful was compatible with the freedom of the artist.

Ennius found favor with the mighty without compromising his independence. He reached Rome in 204, through the initiative of Cato, not long after the guild of writers and actors had been installed by public act in the Temple of Minerva on the Aventine. It is pertinent that the poet took up residence in the vicinity of that establishment.[195] He would add lustre to the artistic community in Rome, a consideration that obviously carried weight with Cato and others. The promotion of literary activity took on increasing importance in these years, as Rome struggled for articulation of her national character. And the very fact of Ennius' residence is noteworthy. He did not enter the household of Cato or of any other Roman aristocrat. His income came through teaching: the interpretation of Greek literature and the presentation of his own compositions.[196] Tradition has it that Ennius' dwelling was humble, his needs minimal, and his acceptance of poverty, even in old age, cheerful.[197] Such tales—or rather conventions—regularly attach themselves to ancient biographies of poets and need not be taken seriously. As we have seen, Ennius' home was frequented by Scipio Nasica and his grounds the site of pleasant walks with Sulpicius Galba. A loyal maidservant, moreover, guarded his privacy.[198] These were hardly poverty-stricken circumstances. And they betoken the poet's autonomy.

---

inserting Istri into Book XV as allies of the Aetolians to authenticate Vulso's supposed justification for initiating the war; cf. Macrob. *Sat.* 6.2.30; Florus, 1.26.1. All of this is unfounded speculation, with no trace of support in the texts. Skutsch, *Annals*, 559, 569-570, is duly skeptical. More strained still is Martina's hypothesis, *op. cit.*, 45-61, that Ennius exaggerated the role of L. Aemilius Regillus in the Antiochene war, thereby to accomodate M. Aemilius Lepidus, recently reconciled to Nobilior. The conjecture, surprisingly, is adopted by Skutsch, *Annals*, 552-553.

[195] Jerome, *Chron.* Olymp. 134.4.

[196] Suet. *De Gramm.* 1: *antiquissimi doctorum, qui iidem et poetae et semigraeci erant—Livium et Ennium dico, quos utraque lingua domi forisque docuisse adnotatum est—nihil amplius quam Graecos interpretabantur, aut si quid ipsi Latine composuissent praelegebant.*

[197] Cic. *De Sen.* 14: *ita ferebat duo quae maxima putantur onera, paupertatem et senectutem, ut eis paene delectari videretur*; Jerome, *Chron.* Olymp. 134.4: *habitavit in monte Aventino, parco admodum sumptu contentus, et unius ancillae ministerio.* Cf. also Symmachus' notice that Ennius received only a single cloak from the spoils of Ambracia; *Epist.* 1.20.2.

[198] Cic. *De Orat.* 2.276; *Acad. Prior.* 2.51.

Concentration on Ennius' connections with public figures can easily obscure an important fact: the volume of his output that is quite unrelated to politics or the affairs of state. He produced at least twenty tragedies, three comedies, four books of *saturae*, a gastronomic poem, the *Epicharmus* based on the Greek philosopher-poet of that name, a fanciful version of the *historia sacra* ascribed to Euhemerus, various epigrams and other minor works either translated or adapted from the Greek.[199] The time, energy, and commitment lavished upon this productivity precludes any notion that he ministered primarily to the needs of private or political ambitions.

The roster of Roman luminaries with whom Ennius shows some association itself refutes the idea of dependence on a particular sponsor. Cordiality bordering on intimacy characterized Ennius' relations with eminent Romans of the most diverse political interests and alliances: Cato, Scipio Africanus, Scipio Nasica, Servilius Geminus, Sulpicius Galba, Fulvius Nobilior. It is ludicrous to imagine Ennius hopping from patron to patron, shedding old sponsors and latching onto new ones when changed political conditions demanded it. Nothing in the evidence implies any break with backers or transfer of allegiance. Ennius enjoyed the confidence or sang the praises of many individuals whose public life set them at odds with one another. His tributes did not derive from partisanship. The *Annales* celebrated the deeds of numerous leaders who had earned the gratitude of their countrymen. Q. Fabius Maximus received encomia as generous as those bestowed by Ennius upon Fabius' rival and the poet's *amicus* Scipio Africanus.[200] Fragments or references reveal warm praise also for the eloquence of M. Cornelius Cethegus, cos. 204, the acute intellect of Sex. Aelius Paetus, cos. 198, and the graciousness of M. Aemilius Lepidus, cos. 187, in burying his *inimicitia* with Fulvius Nobilior.[201] We are told even that Ennius decided to resume work on the *Annales*, after completing a first edition, because of his special admiration for T. Caecilius Teucer and his brother, whose achievements he wished to chronicle. The motive seems inadequate for the composition of three

---

[199] Discussion of the evidence by Vahlen, *Ennianae poesis reliquiae*, cc-ccxxiv.

[200] As is obvious, *inter alia*, from the celebrated line in Book XII, *unus homo nobis cunctando restituit rem*; 370, Vahlen = 363, Skutsch.

[201] Cethegus: Cic. *Brutus*, 57-58; Paetus: Cic. *De Rep.* 1.30; *De Orat.* 1.198; *Tusc. Disp.* 1.18; *Digest*, 1.2.2.38; Lepidus: Cic. *De Prov. Cons.* 21. With regard to Cethegus, Cicero comments that Ennius published his lines after Cethegus' death, lest he be suspected of fabrication because of *amicitia*. Martina, *QuadFilClass*, 2 (1979), 16, unjustifiably takes this to imply that partisanship and propaganda suffused the *Annales*. The relationship between Ennius and Aelius Paetus seems to have been one of mutual respect; cf. R.A. Bauman, *Lawyers in Roman Republican Politics* (Munich, 1983), 123-126. Bauman's reconstruction of close ties to the Aelian family generally, however, is largely speculative.

new books, but there is no reason to doubt Ennius' affection for and desire to celebrate the exploits of men otherwise unknown to history.[202]

Ennius was *laudator* of a collective effort: *moribus antiquis res stat Romana virisque*.[203] But it was by no means an anonymous one. Heroes in number graced the pages of the *Annales*. As Cicero observed, accolades for the individual only enhanced the lustre of the commonwealth.[204] Ennius himself reportedly composed lines, perhaps for a sepulchral bust, which summed up his achievement: "Behold, citizens, the sculpted portrait of aged Ennius—he who recorded the greatest feats of your ancestors."[205] The characterization may be idealized, perhaps a touch romanticized. But it corresponds in essence to the testimonia on Ennius' aims, associates, and accomplishments.

The poet arrived in Rome at a time when its leadership was reaching out to Hellenic culture, encouraging literary activity, and prodding intellectuals to shape a national image. Ennius flourished in that setting and fulfilled expectations. The heady atmosphere that pervaded Rome at the end of the Hannibalic war and the years of spectacular military and diplomatic success in the East that followed could only intensify incentive. The guild of writers and dramatic artists on the Aventine may have offered comfortable collegiality. But greater stimulus came from association with public figures and the leadership of the state. The *Annales* grew out of that association, not to advance the dignity of particular families but, through them, to give a sense of national goals and successes. The offer to accompany Fulvius abroad gave the opportunity for direct participation in what promised to be the culminating phase of Rome's demonstration of supremacy in the East. Fulvius' victory corresponds to Ennius' vision—which is why the poet felt it necessary to defend the victor, justify his triumph, and appeal for political unity. And Ennius' work corresponded similarly to the vision of Fulvius. That vision was

---

[202] Pliny, *NH*, 7.101: *Q. Ennius T. Caecilium Teucrum fratremque eius praecipue miratus propter eos sextum decimum adiecit annalem.* The identities of these men continue to baffle scholars. Their names are probably incorrectly transmitted. Observe the *Caelius tribunus* who served in the Istrian war and appears in Ennius' verses in Book XVI, according to Macrob. *Sat.* 6.3.3, and the T. and C. Aelii recorded as participants in the fighting by Livy, 41.1.7, 41.4.3. Various combinations and emendations have been suggested; see Suerbaum, *Untersuchungen*, 146-151; Badian, *Entretiens Fondation Hardt*, 17 (1972), 196-199; Bauman, *Lawyers*, 125. Skutsch, *Annals*, 569-570, holds to the text.

[203] Ennius, *Annales*, 500, Vahlen = 156, Skutsch.

[204] Cic. *Pro Arch.* 22: *At eis laudibus certe non solum ipse qui laudatur, sed etiam populi Romani nomen ornatur...Omnes denique illi Maximi, Marcelli, Fulvii, non sine communi omnium nostrum laude decorantur.* Cf. Horace, *Carm.* 4.8.13-20; Prop. 3.3.5-12; Sil. Ital. 12.410-411.

[205] Cic. *Tusc. Disp.* 1.34: *Aspicite, o cives, senis Enni imaginis formam;/ hic vestrum panxit maxima facta patrum.* Cicero's comment is apt: *mercedem gloriae flagitat ab iis, quorum patres adfecerat gloria.* Cf. Suerbaum, *Untersuchungen*, 208-215.

implemented by the Temple of Hercules of the Muses. The juxtaposition of power and poetry held important symbolic value. Artistic energy would find expression in celebration of national success. And that success in turn would nourish the creative imagination. A larger cultural collaboration too was implied. Statues of the Muses came from Hellas to grace the new *aedes Herculis Musarum*. And transfer of the Camenae to that site as well denoted fusion of the Latin deities with the Greek patronesses of poetry. The Hellenic Muses could now be invoked by the Roman poet—and their new habitation signified that Rome would be sponsor of their cult and subject of their song. Ennius both encouraged and fulfilled that vision.

The coordination of politics and poetry stamped Latin literature from its beginnings. The boundaries of the first two generations can be conveniently marked by Andronicus' commemoration of Roman superiority in the West and Ennius' paean to Roman supremacy in the East. Hellenic inspiration and public objectives promoted the emergence of Latin letters.

Cultural patronage was indispensable for the nurturing of literature in Rome. Livius Andronicus hailed from Tarentum, Naevius from Campania, and Ennius from Calabria. Teaching might supply a modest living, but artistic success required more potent support and backing. This form of patronage, however, ought not to be misconstrued as the binding of the artist to the interests of individual aristocrats or aristocratic groups. The caveat is critical. Andronicus may have benefited from the assistance of the Livii Salinatores, but nothing indicates that his productivity attended to their special needs or political ends. The career of Cn. Naevius betrays no obligations to houses of the *nobilitas*. Indeed he could even indulge in occasional drollery at their expense and gained a reputation, however ill deserved, of being a thorn in their side. Ennius, by contrast, gained welcome admittance to the embrace of a whole range of political families. But the very diversity of that assemblage, which included personages at sharp variance with one another on the public scene, shows that Ennius can hardly have acted as spearhead for partisan purposes. Cato's complaints about poets recruited to flatter the egos of individual aristocrats may have had some legitimate targets. But they do not apply—and are probably not meant to apply—to Andronicus, Naevius, and Ennius. The major literary figures had aims other than the promotion of patrons.

The political character of early Latin literature has a broader meaning. Rome's establishment strove to apply Hellenic cultural institutions to the task of articulating Roman goals and accomplishments. The government commissioned Livius Andronicus to adapt Greek drama to celebrate Rome's successful conclusion of the First Punic War and elevation to principal power in the West. The play both helped to announce the international stature of the city and set a precedent for future ceremonies that would combine Hellenic and Latin features for Roman self-congratulation. Equally pivotal was Andronicus' hymn in 207 that providentially anticipated divine delivery of Rome in a dark hour of the Hannibalic War. That too was a public commission and resulted in public approbation for the guild of writers and dramatic artists who would now gain official status in the Roman cultural community. Naevius advanced national causes in analogous ways. The new genre of the *fabula praetexta* allowed him to commemorate a glorious triumph in the *Clastidium*, and the bold innovation of an epic poem with Roman themes and a Roman narrative gave voice to the nation's pride. Ennius took inspiration from those efforts and obtained even greater encouragement for his own. The *Scipio* and the *Ambracia* underscored the deeds of men responsible for the state's climactic triumphs in West and East. And the *Annales*, with their striking adaptation of the Hellenic hexameter, highlighted Roman accomplishments through the centuries and the honor roll of leaders who made them possible. It was fitting tribute that the *aedes Herculis Musarum* provided symbolic union of artist and statesman—and that it blended Greek and Latin inspirers of song.

The poets gave shape to the national image and expression to national aspirations. Incitement, opportunity, and perhaps subsidy came from the officialdom. State demands, however, did not create literature. The dramatic events of 3rd and early 2nd century Roman history provided stimulus enough for the imagination of the artist. Andronicus, Naevius, and Ennius understood that the fledgling intellectual life of the Republic called for a poetry that could articulate, celebrate, and perhaps even mildly fabricate the national character.

CHAPTER FOUR

PLAUTUS AND THE PUBLIC STAGE

The fragments of early Latin literature invite groping in the dark. They stimulate imagination and give rise to attractive speculation. But the pieces are too few and isolated, the context too cloudy to permit clear vision. Livius Andronicus, Naevius, and Ennius remain shadowy and elusive. By contrast, the comedies of Plautus pull us from the dusky realm of the fragments to the radiance of literature. Twenty Plautine plays constitute the extant corpus, dwarfing the remains of poetic predecessors and contemporaries. The very richness of the material holds out promise of fuller insight into the relationship between artist and political society.

But the endeavor has its own hazards. A different set of obstacles stands in the way. Plautus' life and career are nearly a blank to us, thus blocking knowledge of the condition and associations that governed his work. Most or all of the plays themselves derive from Greek originals, adaptations of New Comedy that create grave difficulties in extracting the Roman elements embedded in the Hellenic texture.[1] And more frustrating still to the historian, neither an absolute nor a relative chronology of the dramas can be established with any degree of precision. Hence, despite a plethora of material, the fundamental question remains open: what relationship did Plautine drama bear to the Roman public scene? Did the dramatist hold up his contemporaries to analysis—or derision?

The question is tough but not intractable. Much depends upon the methodology employed in approaching it. Efforts to ferret out the sequence and dating of the plays have exhibited considerable ingenuity, yet frequently fall into the trap of question-begging and circular reasoning. Historical events discerned in Plautine allusions owe more to the discerner than to the dramatist. Plautus, in fact, nowhere makes explicit and unambiguous reference to a contemporary event. Only conjecture can find correspondence, and the conjectures mount, building upon one another to create a shaky edifice without solid foundation. Individual suggestions are often acute and appealing, but the notion that scholarship

---

[1] The possibility that the *Epidicus*, and perhaps some other Plautine plays, may not rest on Hellenic originals has recently been raised by S.M. Goldberg, *TAPA*, 108 (1978), 81-91.

has developed a reasonably reliable chronology of the plays is an illusion.[2] Too much energy has been expended in identifying specific episodes and personages supposedly intended by Plautine allusions, as if the poet were some Roman Lycophron inviting readers to puzzle over recondite references. That approach misconceives Plautus' purposes. The absence of distinct pointers to contemporary incidents is deliberate—not surely to tempt readers into a guessing game, but because the specifics are irrelevant. Plautus' topicality has to be assessed on a broader level.

The existence of decidedly Roman elements in the plays that cannot have derived from Greek originals has long been recognized. Plautus regularly introduces Roman legal, political, and religious institutions, with conscious or inadvertent echoes of Italian usages and practices foreign to the Greek setting.[3] These aspects have been much studied, with considerable profit. They provide invaluable enlightenment on Roman society in the late 3rd and early 2nd century, especially on matters like slavery, business relations, and private law.[4] But they give only limited access to the disposition of the poet. And they do not address the critical question of comic drama's relationship to contemporary public life. A different angle of vision is needed. The present investigation proposes neither to mine the texts for information on Roman social history, nor to guess at particular identifications that might yield conjectural dates for the plays. Instead, a different method and purpose: to examine

---

[2] There is little point in registering the host of studies that have contributed to the debate on Plautine dating. Among the more important, see J.N. Hough, *CP*, 30 (1935), 43-57; *TAPA*, 70 (1939), 231-241; *AJP*, 60 (1939), 422-435; W.B. Sedgwick, *CQ*, 24 (1930), 102-105; *AJP*, 70 (1949), 376-383; C.H. Buck, *A Chronology of the Plays of Plautus* (Baltimore, 1940), 25-107; K.H.E. Schutter, *Quibus annis comoediae plautinae primum actae sint quaesitur* (Groningen, 1952), *passim*; A. de Lorenzi, *Cronologia ed evoluzione plautina* (Naples, 1952), *passim*; F. della Corte, *Da Sarsina a Roma* (Genoa, 1967), 51-97. P. Harvey, *Athenaeum*, 59 (1981), 480-489, expresses salutary skepticism about proposing dates for the comedies on the basis of supposed historical allusions, but succumbs to the same temptation himself. His broader observations in *CW*, 79 (1986), 297-304, stressing the value of Plautus for illuminating the general Roman atmosphere, point in the right direction.

[3] See especially F. Leo, *Plautinische Forschungen*, 2nd ed. (Berlin, 1912); E. Fraenkel, *Plautinisches in Plautus* (Berlin, 1922), and the revised Italian edition, *Elementi plautini in Plauto* (Florence, 1960); K.M. Westaway, *The Original Element in Plautus* (Cambridge, 1917); G. Jachmann, *Plautinisches und Attisches* (Berlin, 1931); a brief summary with more recent bibliography by K. Gaiser, *ANRW*, I.2 (1972), 1088-1093. Extensive compilations of Plautine scholarship can be found in J.D. Hughes, *A Bibliography of Scholarship on Plautus* (Amsterdam, 1975), and D. Fogazza, *Lustrum*, 19 (1976), 72-296. See also the surveys by J.A. Hanson, *CW*, 59 (1965-6), 103-107, 126-148; E. Segal, *CW*, 74 (1980-81), 353-433.

[4] See, e.g., J. Andreau, *MEFRA*, 80 (1968), 461-526; A. Watson, *Roman Private Law around 200 B.C.* (Edinburgh, 1971), *passim*; P.P. Spranger, *Historische Untersuchungen zu den Sklavenfiguren des Plautus und Terenz*[2] (Stuttgart, 1984), *passim*. For a recent particular example, with profitable results, see M. McDonnell, *AJAH*, 8 (1983), 54-80.

Plautus' presentation of issues and attitudes prominent on the Roman public scene, thus to gain insight into relations between contemporary developments and the comic stage. Relevant allusions in the plays are plentiful, not so much disguised as indirect. Plautus did not reproduce current events, but called attention to their implications.

The writer's own opinions are deftly masked. Comic characters and situations supplied convenient camouflage. Plautus could screen himself behind the conventions of the theater while simultaneously giving voice to matters of contemporary concern and discussion. But which was the poet's voice?

A reliable biography would help. But none issued from antiquity. The few details we possess are disputed and dubious, nothing to allow conclusions on character or attitude. Tradition located Plautus' birthplace at Sarsina in Umbria.[5] That itself causes problems. Where did the poet learn Greek and gain mastery of Hellenic dramatic conventions? Hardly in Umbria. When and why did he come to Rome? And how did he establish a reputation? Unanswerable questions for the most part.[6] But a clue resides in the peculiar tale preserved by Gellius and drawn from Varro's researches on the lives of the poets. Plautus, so it was recorded, earned a livelihood through employment associated with the theater, lost his savings in a commercial enterprise, and had to resort to work in a mill where he wrote his first comedies.[7] Assessments of the story range from complete acceptance to total rejection.[8] The idea of Plautus as merchant entrepreneur is hard to swallow—not to mention the image of the poet laboring at a mill while scribbling comedies in his spare time. But the notice of work in the theatrical profession has some logic and plausibility. Just what kind of work invites hypothesis but escapes certainty. Gellius' language is vague: Plautus might have been actor,

---

[5] Festus, 274, L; Jerome, *Chron.* Olymp. 145.1.

[6] Even the dramatist's name, T. Maccius Plautus, is a subject of controversy, variously given in the text, and its origin uncertain. See Festus, 275, L. Other references and discussion by Schutter, *Quibus annis*, i-iv; della Corte, *Da Sarsina a Roma*, 15-21; A.S. Gratwick, *CQ*, 67 (1973), 78-84.

[7] Gellius, 3.3.14.

[8] Leo, *Plautinische Forschungen*, 70-71, reckoned it as invention on the model of the fabricated lives of Greek literary figures. Its authenticity is defended by F. Marx, *Zeitschr. f. Österr. Gymn.* (1898), 385ff; similarly, Buck, *Chronology*, 1-24; Schutter, *Quibus annis*, vi-ix. A more moderate position is taken by della Corte, *Da Sarsina a Roma*, 23-50. Skepticism of an extreme variety may be found now in M. Drury, *The Cambridge History of Classical Literature*, II (Cambridge, 1982), 808-809, who doubts every item in the tale and even questions the tradition on Plautus' birthplace. On fictitious literary biographies generally, see J. Fairweather, *AncSoc*, 5 (1974), 231-275; M. Lefkowitz, *Lives of the Greek Poets* (London, 1981), *passim*.

playwright, impresario, or stage-hand.[9] Or, more probably, a combination of the above. A sharp differentiation of roles would not have been characteristic of the early theater. Livius Andronicus was both author of and actor in his own plays.[10]

Experience in a dramatic troupe also provides the easiest answer to another puzzle: Plautus' acquaintance with Greek drama. That experience may already have been broad and deep before his arrival in Rome, with a reputation that preceded him. The travelling Dionysiac *technitai* perhaps offered opportunities and nourished his skills as playwright and producer.[11] Precisely when Plautus reached Rome escapes record, but the later years of the 3rd century would be a safe estimate.[12]

The atmosphere in Rome at that time was especially congenial to the theater. Livius Andronicus had given it respectability, and state encouragement allowed it to flourish. The Ludi Romani provided the initial setting for dramatic performances as part of national celebration, the occasion for Livius Andronicus' production in 240. In the last quarter of the 3rd century and the beginning of the 2nd century new festivals came into being and included theatrical performances as part of their offerings: the Ludi Plebeii, the Ludi Apollinares, the Ludi Megalenses, the Ludi Cereales. The number of days set aside for plays multiplied, increased still further by the practice of *instauratio*, the repetition of games called for by religious improprieties. Such circumstances markedly enhanced the desirability of popular playwrights.[13] And official

---

[9] Gellius, 3.3.14: *in operis artificum scaenicorum*. The idea of Plautus as miller may be inference from the playwright's own frequent allusions to mills and mill workers; e.g. *Bacch.* 2, 781; *Capt.* 808; *Epid.* 145; *Men.* 975; *Most.* 17; *Pers.* 22; *Poen.* 827, 1152; *Pseud.* 494, 499-500; see L.A. Moritz, *Grain-Mills and Flour in Classical Antiquity* (Oxford, 1958), 67-73.

[10] Livy, 7.2.8: *idem scilicet—id quod omnes tum erant—suorum carminum actor*; Festus, 448, L: *is et scribebat fabulas et agebat*.

[11] The common notion that Plautus only gained familiarity with Greek after reaching Rome and joining Hellenic circles there has no foundation. Cf. Schutter, *Quibus annis*, viii-ix, with literature. On the Dionysiac *technitai*, see above pp. 87-88.

[12] Cicero dates Plautus' death in the consular year of 184; *Brutus*, 60. If derived from Varro, that may represent inference from the date of his last play. In any case, the death is presumably not much later. Plautus was a *senex* when he produced the *Pseudolus* (Cic. *De Sen.* 50), a play independently dated to 191 by the didascalic notice. This implies a birthdate some time in the mid 3rd century—though there is no ancient authority for the commonly given date of 254. Drury's hyper-criticism, *Cambridge Hist. of Class. Lit.*, II, 809, does not give credence even to Cicero's report of the year of death and thus leaves open the altogether improbable idea that Plautus was born a decade after Cato.

[13] On the expansion of the *ludi* and its impact upon dramatic performances, see L.R. Taylor, *TAPA*, 68 (1937), 284-304; Buck, *Chronology*, 10-18; della Corte, *Da Sarsina a Roma*, 33-40. Buck, however, goes too far in claiming that Plautus' popularity was itself responsible for the jump in number of dramatic performances.

imprimatur was stamped on the profession ca. 206 when the guild of writers and actors gained public recognition, special privileges, and a conspicuous site in Minerva's temple on the Aventine.[14] The occasion honored Livius Andronicus, but the beneficiaries included all those engaged in the composition and production of drama. The climate was exceedingly favorable. Plautus' profession secured state sponsorship, and the playwright enjoyed public acclaim.[15]

Did the favors of the officialdom and the public help to mold the creativity of the artist? Did the patronage of the powerful exercise an influence on the content of drama? In short, was there a political tinge to Plautine comedy? Numerous studies interpret the writer's inclinations in terms of factional or ideological conflicts prevalent in his day. The game is a seductive one, and it has led to a plethora of mutually inconsistent hypotheses. Plautus has been reckoned as an advocate of Scipio Africanus, as a sympathizer with Cato and adversary of Scipio, or as having moved from the Scipionic camp to the Catonian party, as supporter and then opponent of philhellenic movements in Rome, as adherent or critic of Fulvius Nobilior, or as antagonist of Flamininus.[16] The suggestions rest more on ingenuity than on testimony. Plautus does not parade his political orientation. The playwright puts no contemporary figures on the stage, and makes no forthright comment on contemporary affairs. He wished to avoid the fate of Naevius, so it is commonly said: hence, the comments are veiled, the names unexpressed, the allusions indirect. That analysis misdirects inquiry. The dubious stories on Naevius' demise provide too shaky a foundation for hypothesis. Plautus deliberately chose a genre that avoided political embroilment: not the overt topicality of Aristophanic comedy which savaged the most prominent figures of the day but the dramas of ordinary life peopled by the stock characters of New Comedy. The conventions of the genre rather than the fate of Naevius governed this feature of the Plautine

---

[14] Festus, 446, L; see above pp. 87-89.

[15] Cf. Plautus, *Casina*, 11-20; *Men.* 1-4.

[16] As supporter of Scipio: A.F. West, *AJP*, 8 (1887), 15-33. As adversary of Scipio: T. Frank, *AJP*, 53 (1932), 152-156; L. Herrmann, *AntCl*, 17 (1948), 317-322. As transferring allegiance from Scipionic philhellenism to Catonian anti-hellenism; Frank, *Anatolian Studies presented to W.H. Buckler* (Manchester, 1939), 85-88; Buck, *Chronology*, 105-107, and *passim*; I. Lana, *RivFilol*, 75 (1947), 47-51; della Corte, *Da Sarsina a Roma*, 79-93. As backer of Fulvius: L. Halkin, *AntCl*, 17 (1948), 297-304. As antagonist of Flamininus: A. Archellaschi, *REL*, 56 (1978), 119-133. G.K. Galinsky, *TAPA*, 97 (1966), 203-235, finds numerous "Scipionic themes" in Plautus' *Amphitryon*, but no clear pattern of praise or hostility. For E. Flores, *Letteratura latina e ideologia del III-II a.C.* (Naples, 1974), 57-81, Plautus represents a democratic, populist attitude, one that is anti-Hellenic and resistant to Roman imperialism.

plays—several of which may have preceded Naevius' last years. The dramatist's choice itself must be given due significance: he elected to steer clear of engagement with political personalities, factions, and programs. To foist them upon him posthumously seems singularly misguided. The scholarly pastime of identifying public figures or current events lurking surreptitiously in Plautus' scripts violates his own purposes. A different approach is called for.

Not that the comedies are devoid of political meaning. Nor did their author strive to suppress personal sentiments. Plautus was alive to issues that engaged his contemporaries on the public scene in an age of overseas expansion and rapid internal change. The models of New Comedy had little place for direct political commentary or a one-to-one correspondence between characters or events and their real-life counterparts. But the plays could serve as vehicles to address, promote, mock, or satirize items that held public attention or provoked public debate. At that level Plautus' topicality, neither Aristophanic nor Menandrian, takes shape. The subjects of public discourse, rather than particular persons or incidents, find an appropriate outlet on the stage. And the great popularity of comic drama gave that outlet a special importance. Plautus had a medium with which to expand awareness and augment discussion.

Numerous themes course through the plays, yielding insight into matters that captured Roman attention around the turn of the 3rd century. Only a selective sample can here be treated. But enough to give a sense of how the dramatist could both articulate and denigrate the issues that exercised his contemporaries.

The feats of the soldier dominated the era. The expulsion of Hannibal and conquest of Carthage gave the nation her finest hour, followed by dramatic expansion to the north, the west, and, most especially, to the Hellenistic East. It was a time of pronounced display of Roman power abroad, the influx of staggering amounts of wealth, and the opportunity for unprecedented authority by successful individuals.

Prime illustration of these developments comes over the quest for a triumph. The public celebration of one's military accomplishment had long been the most coveted of honors for Rome's leaders. Claims to a triumph and disputes over the legitimacy of those claims reached new levels of intensity in this period. The political stakes were high and the competition keen.

A flood of instances exemplifies the trend. Scipio Africanus himself requested a triumph in 206, after return from his extraordinarily successful campaign in Spain. The honor was richly deserved in view of his accomplishments: Scipio had chased the Carthaginians from the Iberian peninsula, the real turning point of the Hannibalic War. And he spoke eloquently in defense of his claim. But the senate denied his request on formal grounds. Scipio was technically a *privatus*, never elected to any magistracy with *imperium*, and no one in that position had ever sought or received a triumph. He wisely withdrew the request. To press the point would have been fruitless.[17] A different technicality had blocked M. Claudius Marcellus' petition for a triumph in 211: failure to bring back his army from Sicily.[18] Marcellus received an *ovatio* instead and further advertised his achievement by taking triumph on the Alban Mount—but not one sanctioned by the state. Rome's most lauded heroes, in short, ran into resistance from their peers. That experience proved to be portentous.

Once the Hannibalic War ended, the scramble for triumphs grew fiercer and the restraints upon them more controversial. The next decade and a half, i.e. to the end of Plautus' life, witnessed repeated debates over the rights and eligibility of *triumphatores*. L. Cornelius Lentulus applied for a triumph in 200, after six years of distinguished service in Spain. The senate acknowledged that his accomplishments merited a triumph, but raised the same technicality that had held against Scipio Africanus: his status as *privatus* precluded the triumph. This time, however, discussion issued in a compromise: Lentulus could have an *ovatio*.[19] The outcome was reasonable enough, but the discrepancy is revealing. The *patres* granted to Lentulus what they had denied Scipio. Elevation of Scipio had troubling implications; an *ovatio* for the lesser man Lentulus would not have the same political repercussions. Arguments that the decision lacked all precedent were overriden.[20] The senate would set new precedents to reward achievements—especially as a means to balance distinctions within their own ranks.

In the same year of 200 L. Furius Purpureo laid claim to a triumph for victories over the Gauls. The request provoked new problems and divisions. Furius' victories came as praetor, while temporarily heading an army that was really, so some argued, under the consul's authority. Further, he had raced to Rome to seek his honor before the consul could return and challenge his right to it. Complaints about violation of prece-

---

[17] Livy, 28.38.2-4; Val. Max. 2.8.5; Dio, 17.57.56. The tradition preserved in Polyb. 11.33.7 and Appian, *Iber.* 38, that Scipio did celebrate a triumph, is plainly mistaken. See J.S. Richardson, *JRS*, 65 (1975), 52.

[18] Livy, 26.21.1-3; Plut. *Marc.* 22; *Vir. Ill.* 45.6. A political pretext, according to Richardson, *JRS*, 65 (1975), 54-55; a sound constitutional decision, according to R. Develin, *Klio*, 60 (1978), 432. The matter need not be decided here.

[19] Livy, 31.20.1-7.

[20] Livy, 31.20.5-6.

dent surfaced again. And again a senatorial majority overrode them: Furius became the first praetor to earn the distinction of a triumph.[21] But that decision did not establish a pattern. Five years later, a senatorial debate cost M. Helvius a triumph, though awarding an *ovatio*, on the ground that his victories in Spain had been fought under another's auspices and in another's province.[22]

The *patres* followed no formula. They prevailed upon a tribune to withdraw his veto in order to award Lentulus his *ovatio* in 200.[23] But they let another tribunician veto stand in 199, thus blocking an *ovatio* for L. Manlius Acidinus who had served in a capacity identical to that of Lentulus in Spain.[24] *Ad hoc* circumstances governed decisions, creating confusion and unpredictability. C. Cornelius Cethegus received a triumph in 197, but Q. Minucius Rufus was refused one, despite the fact that both had fought the Gauls as consuls and that Cethegus himself had recommended a dual triumph.[25] A comparable situation arose in the next year when two commanders returned from Spain. One obtained an *ovatio* rather than a triumph, the other declined to seek either, evidently convinced that his claims would not persuade his colleagues.[26] L. Cornelius Merula's bid for a triumph after campaigns in Gaul in 193 was sabotaged by a letter from one of his officers maintaining that Merula's achievements did not warrant the honor. Merula pressed his case, but two tribunes intervened, and the matter was dropped. The claimant went away empty.[27] By contrast, the senate overbore a tribunician veto in 191 when they endorsed Scipio Nasica's application for a triumph to celebrate successes in Gaul. This time the martial feats outweighed any technicalities.[28]

Battles over military honors became still more frequent and more heated in the aftermath of the Antiochene war. Q. Minucius Thermus' application for a triumph after campaigns in Liguria in 190 ran into stiff opposition. M. Cato rose to denounce it in a blistering speech entitled *De Falsis Pugnis*, evidently asserting that Thermus had fabricated victories to justify a triumph.[29] Thermus never got it.[30] Similar criticisms were

---

[21] Livy, 31.47.6-31.49.3, 31.49.8-11.
[22] Livy, 34.10.3-7.
[23] Livy, 31.20.6.
[24] Livy, 32.7.4.
[25] Livy, 33.22-23.
[26] Livy, 33.27.1-4.
[27] Livy, 35.8.2-9
[28] Livy, 36.39.4-36.40.14.
[29] Gellius, 10.3.17. The one extant fragment from the speech attacks Thermus for brutal treatment of Roman allies; *ORF*, Cato, fr. 58. Commentary on the fragment in M.T.S. Cugusi, *M. Porci Catonis Orationum Reliquiae* (Turin, 1982), 194-205.
[30] Livy, 37.46.1-2.

levelled against Q. Fabius Labeo in 188 when he sought recognition for a naval command in Crete during the war on Antiochus. Opponents alleged that, far from earning a triumph, he had not so much as laid eyes on the enemy. Labeo, however, did get his triumph.[31] The *inimici* of M. Fulvius Nobilior organized a major campaign to deny him that distinction in 187, after he had closed out the Aetolian war and captured Ambracia. They even imported Ambraciote representatives to attest to Fulvius' atrocities, to allege that he had attacked them without provocation, and to charge him with having carried off every art object in the state. They also steered a resolution through a rump senate stating that Ambracia did not appear to have been taken by force—a rebuff to Fulvius' claims on a triumph.[32] Cato reiterated the point in a later speech.[33] When Fulvius returned, however, his arguments or *auctoritas* overcame the opposition. The senate acknowledged his successes in Aetolia and voted his triumph.[34] A still more bitter contest raged in 187 over the claims of Cn. Manlius Vulso who had conducted an aggressive and ruthless campaign against the Galatians. Political adversaries charged him with pursuing an undeclared and unauthorized war, then fighting it in reckless fashion.[35] Prevailing opinion stood against Manlius. But this time precedent was on his side. Supporters, friends, and relatives pointed out that commanders who decisively defeated the enemy, carried out their assignments, and led back their army were never denied triumphs. The statement was inaccurate—but true enough to make its point. The *patres* granted Manlius' request.[36] They knew the consequences of refusal: any one of them might be in Manlius' shoes in the future.

Debate and controversy over triumphs pervaded the period. Ambitions roused in the wars intensified them. The senate was evidently groping for ways to control the hunt for martial honors without discouraging the hunt itself—a quest in which every individual *nobilis* had a stake. Absence of a clear pattern is conspicuous. *Ad hoc* decisions prevailed. Triumphs were sometimes awarded for merit, sometimes denied on technicalities, tribunician vetoes were occasionally upheld and occasionally overridden, *ovationes* were substituted for triumphs in certain

---

[31] Livy, 37.46.1-2, 37.60.5-6.

[32] Livy, 38.43.1-38.44.6.

[33] *ORF*, Cato, fr. 148: *iam principio quis vidit corona donari quemquam, cum oppidum captum non esset aut castra hostium non incensa essent?* The speech probably belongs to 178; P. Fraccaro, *Opuscula* (Pavia, 1956), I, 247-253; H.H. Scullard, *Roman Politics, 220-150 B.C.*, 2nd ed. (Oxford, 1973), 266-267.

[34] Livy, 39.4.1-39.5.17.

[35] Livy, 38.44.9-38.46.15.

[36] Livy, 38.50.1-3.

situations but rejected in others. Competition and dissent forestalled the establishment of any clear guidelines.[37] Opportunities presented themselves for the mighty to become mightier, thereby generating increased opprobrium. Even well earned and undeniable triumphs could not prevent sniping from the sidelines. L. Scipio Asiagenus, victor over Antiochus the Great and conqueror of the Seleucid kingdom, felt their sting. Critics claimed that Asiagenus had encountered no serious resistance in the war: Antiochus was an easy mark; one battle sufficed, at Magnesia; in fact, the war had really been won a year earlier, at Thermopylae, before the Scipios even went east.[38] Asiagenus obtained his triumph, to be sure, but the cavils indicate that the more compelling the claim on honors, the more urgent the need to reassert the limits on individual ambition. The period of Plautus' *floruit* witnessed mounting criticism of would-be *triumphatores*, of their motives, methods, and claims. But that criticism also impelled them to articulate more forcefully their justifications for seeking distinctions, thereby augmenting the competition and intensifying the spirited character of discussion.

Public debate swirled with equal vehemence around another, related issue: control over the spoils of war. The amounts of cash and booty at the disposal of victorious commanders reached unprecedented levels. And the display of captured loot dazzled contemporaries. As often, Scipio Africanus set the pattern. After close of the Carthaginian war, he deposited 123,000 pounds weight of silver into the Roman treasury and distributed 400 asses each to his soldiery.[39] Escalation proceeded from that point. Cato's victories in Spain netted 25,000 pounds of silver bullion, 123,000 silver *bigati*, 540,000 Oscan silver coins, and 1400 pounds of gold. His soldiers got 270 asses each, and the cavalrymen twice that amount.[40] More spectacular still was the triumph of T. Flamininus in 194, which put on show 18,270 pounds of silver, 84,000 tetradrachms, 3714 pounds of gold, 14,514 gold coins, plus countless art objects. He distributed 250 asses to each infantryman, 500 to centurions, and 750 to *equites*.[41] It was a game of one-upmanship, with very large sums being played. L. Scipio's triumph in 189 attained new heights of extravagance: 137,420 pounds of silver, 224,000 tetradrachms, 321,700 cistophori,

---

[37] The fluidity of this period undermines any search for patterns, despite the efforts of Richardson, *JRS*, 65 (1975), 50-53, and Develin, *Klio*, 60 (1978), 429-438; *The Practice of Politics at Rome, 336-167 B.C.* (Brussels, 1985), 207-213.

[38] Livy, 37.58.7-8: *erant qui fama id maius bellum quam difficultate rei fuisse interpretarentur: uno memorabili proelio debellatum, gloriamque eius victoriae praefloratam ad Thermopylas esse.*

[39] Livy, 30.45.3.

[40] Livy, 34.46.2-3.

[41] Livy, 34.52.4-11; Plut. *Flam.* 14.

140,000 gold coins, 1423 pounds of engraved silver vases, 1023 pounds of gold vases—not to mention 234 gold crowns, 1231 ivory tusks, and 134 models of towns. Soldiers were no longer paid in bronze, but in silver: 25 *denarii* to each *miles*, 50 to centurions, 75 to horsemen.[42] These were staggering sums—and recorded in loving detail. The parade of captured spoil augmented the prestige of the *triumphator*, and the allocation of cash to the troops reinforced his influence. The ambitious found opportunity to make political capital. But, inevitably, they also provoked challenge.

Long standing tradition in Rome gave generals the right to dispose of booty as they saw fit.[43] Roman aristocrats knew the advantages that it brought and had no intention of depriving themselves of those advantages. But convention suffered strains on this score in the early 2nd century. The vast amounts gathered as spoils created tensions and demanded some consideration of means to effect restraint.

The issue surfaced unmistakably in connection with the triumph of M'. Acilius Glabrio, the victor at Thermopylae. Shortly after his triumph in 189, two tribunes lodged an accusation against him, alleging that part of the money and booty seized in Antiochus' camp had failed to turn up in the procession and had not found its way into the treasury.[44] The redoubtable Cato appeared as witness for the prosecution, testifying that he had seen gold and silver vessels among the captured loot which then never appeared in the triumph.[45] The precise legal charge against Glabrio remains obscure. Nothing suggests that there were statutory restrictions upon the general's authority to dispose of booty. And the case, in any event, never came to completion, for the tribunes dropped their charge once Glabrio abandoned his candidacy for the censorship.[46] The fact of the trial itself, however, carries real significance. Factional politics may be involved. But the implications exceed those bounds. By shining the glare of publicity upon Glabrio and embarrassing him, through allegation that he had appropriated booty for personal use, the instigator of the trial could move toward some moral, if not legal restraints upon commanders' powers in the distribution of spoils.[47]

---

[42] Livy, 37.59.3-6.

[43] See I. Shatzman, *Historia*, 21 (1972), 177-205, with reference to earlier literature. His treatment is preferable to the extended study by F. Bona, *SDHI*, 26 (1960), 105-175.

[44] Livy, 37.57.12: *quod pecuniae regiae praedaeque aliquantum captae in Antiochi castris neque in triumpho tulisset, neque in aerarium rettulisset.*

[45] Livy, 37.57.13-14: *is testis, quae vasa aurea atque argentea castris captis inter aliam praedam regiam vidisset, ea se in triumpho negabat vidisse.*

[46] Livy, 37.57.15-37.58.1.

[47] Shatzman, *Historia*, 21 (1972), 191-192, minimizes the case by suggesting that the prosecutors wanted only to have Glabrio submit a report of the distribution—a view unfortunately endorsed by A.E. Astin, *Cato the Censor* (Oxford, 1978), 63.

A broader thrust followed in 187. Cn. Manlius Vulso came under attack for extortions made not only from Antiochus but from other kings and peoples of Asia.[48] That assault coincided with the notorious trials of the Scipios for actions in the Antiochene war, cases which also raised the troubling question of misappropriation of funds by commanders abroad. This, of course, is not the place to probe the details of those murky and confused hearings. But the fact that both L. Scipio and Cn. Manlius were charged in the same tribunal needs to be stressed.[49] The issue plainly stands outside the realm of mere factional politics. Larger matters were here at stake: the prerogative of commanders to control moneys garnered in foreign wars. The precise legal category of the accusation against L. Scipio Asiagenus need not be decided and makes little difference. An argument holds that Asiagenus could not have been cited for allocation of loot, since commanders had a free rein in that regard.[50] But that analysis misses the main point. It was precisely such free rein which had now come under challenge—an effort to define the limits of commanders' authority. The testimony of Aulus Gellius, drawn from Nepos, makes the matter clear: accusers demanded an accounting both of *pecunia Antiochina* and of *praeda*.[51] We do know that the cash exacted from Antiochus by L. Scipio, 500 talents, intended as first installment on the king's indemnity, in fact went to provide double pay to Scipio's troops.[52] At the very least, the general was playing fast and loose with cash that ought to have been destined for the treasury. And one might note that Manlius Vulso also used the opportunity to give double pay as a bonus to his soldiers.[53] Some effort to set limits on this sort of activity before it got out of hand seemed imperative.

---

[48] Livy, 38.54.7: *latius rogandum censebat, non quae ab Antiocho modo pecuniae captae forent, sed quae ab aliis regibus gentibusque, Cn. Manlium inimicum incessens.*

[49] Association between the judicial attacks on Manlius and the Scipios is clear from Livy, 39.6.3-5: Manlius was accused by the same *quaestio* that convicted L. Scipio; cf. D. Kienast, *Cato der Zensor* (Heidelberg, 1954), 57-67. The fact is confirmed by the sums reportedly at stake in the hearings. Polybius, 23.14.9, gives a figure of 3000 talents. We know, in fact, that only 500 talents were turned over to L. Scipio by Antiochus as down payment on his indemnity; Polyb. 21.17.5. Manlius, however, collected 2500 talents in 188 at the time of the peace of Apamea; Polyb. 21.41.8. The investigation evidently sought an accounting of all the cash appropriated from Antiochus, by both Manlius and the Scipios.

[50] Shatzman, *Historia*, 21 (1972), 192-194.

[51] Gellius, 4.18.7-8: *desiderabant in senatu instantissime ut pecuniae Antiochinae praedaeque in eo bello captae rationem redderet.* Shatzman's effort to discard this testimony is unconvincing; *Historia*, 21 (1972), 193. There is ample evidence that the investigation included both payments made by Antiochus and moneys captured from him; Livy, 38.54.3, 38.55.5-8; Gellius, 6.19.8; Val. Max. 5.3.2c, 8.1.damn.1; Dio, fr. 63; Zon. 9.20.

[52] Livy, 37.59.6.

[53] Livy, 39.7.2.

Not that these trials succeeded in establishing any firm regulations. The accusation against Glabrio dissolved when the defendant offered a political concession. The case against Manlius too evidently came to naught: nothing further is heard of it. And the celebrated trials of the Scipios, as is well known, became so enmeshed with political maneuvering that confusion over charges, court, and outcome still reigns.[54] Certainly no clear-cut guidelines emerged from the smoke of those battles. Posturing rather then substance prevailed. The contests spawned considerable debate and little resolution. But the debate counted. The issue of financial accountability by military leaders now received public airing. And Rome's aristocracy began to grapple with the consequences of conquest.

The heated character of public discussion can be read in the words and actions of Cato the Elder. He took a leading role in prompting and pressing the attacks on the Scipios. A speech delivered during those proceedings survived at least to Livy's day, sporting the title *De Pecunia Regis Antiochi*. According to Valerius Antias, the speech supported a bill which commissioned the *quaestio* to try L. Scipio.[55] Unfortunately, no fragments are extant. But the title indicates its purpose: to challenge the use or misuse of funds obtained in the Antiochene war. Another Catonian speech, of uncertain date and context, addressed a similar issue. Its heading, "that booty be brought to public account," discloses Cato's stance clearly enough. The one surviving fragment castigates those who adorn their private dwellings with statues seized as plunder.[56] Cato—and doubtless not he alone—probed for means to restrict the authority of commanders over the spoils of war. On a different occasion the Censor made proud boast of never assigning booty for the profit of his friends— an apparent reference to standard practice, or at least his characterization of it. That address censured allocation of loot to private parties, not to soldiers who, he implied, deserved it.[57] But another Catonian oration directed itself to the latter practice as well, so its title reveals: *De Praeda Militibus Dividenda*. A memorable fragment of that work observes that those who steal private property lead out their lives in chains and

---

[54] The most important studies on the Scipionic trials, none of them fully satisfactory, are T. Mommsen, *Römische Forschungen* (Berlin, 1879), II, 417-510; Fraccaro, *Opuscula*, I, 263-415; Scullard, *Roman Politics*, 290-303; G. Bandelli, *Index*, 3 (1972), 304-342.

[55] Livy, 38.54.11.

[56] *ORF*, Cato, fr. 98: *miror audere atque religionem non tenere, statuas deorum, exempla earum facierum, signa domi pro supellectile statuere*. The speech is often assigned to Cato's censorship, but without good reason. Discussion and bibliography in Cugusi, *Catonis Orationum Reliquiae*, 248-251.

[57] *ORF*, Cato, fr. 203: *numquam ego praedam neque quod de hostibus captum esset neque manubias inter pauculos amicos meos divisi ut illis eriperem, qui cepissent*. Cf. Cugusi, *op. cit.*, 406-412.

imprisonment, those who take public funds luxuriate in gold and purple.[58] So Cato, it appears, was prepared to advocate restrictions even
upon commanders' prerogatives in assigning the fruits of plunder to their
troops.

Evidence for contention over these matters abounds. Leadership and
commons were regaled by disputes over the merits of *triumphatores*, the
diversion of public funds to private use, and the appropriation of the
prizes of war. The controversies began to be heard at the end of the 3rd
century and gained in momentum during the first two decades of the
2nd—precisely the time of Plautus' prominence. If the dramatist paid
any heed to current events, these debates should find reflection. The
plays do not disappoint.

The clever slave Chrysalus in Plautus' *Bacchides* compares his successful deception with military victory. His words are pregnant with
meaning for Romans attuned to public affairs in the early 2nd century.
Chrysalus represents himself as marching along laden with booty—and
ovans. The word was not selected at random. It refers to an *ovatio*, alternative to a triumph, an institution resorted to with greater frequency in
these years to deflect claims on a triumph.[59] Allusion to debates over such
matters is reinforced by the lines that follow. Chrysalus acknowledges
that his conquest came through deceit but he has marched his army home
intact.[60] Objection to triumphs, it will be recalled, sometimes focused on
the general's inability to withdraw his army.[61] And Chrysalus concludes
by dismissing concern for a triumph: there were too many of them
anyway, the institution had been cheapened by mediocrity.[62] One need
not assume that Plautus pointed to a particular occasion.[63] But the echoes

---

[58] *ORF*, Cato, fr. 224: *fures privatorum furtorum in nervo atque in compedibus aetatem agunt, fures publici in auro atque in purpura.* Cf. Cugusi, *op. cit.*, 425-428.

[59] Plautus, *Bacch.* 1068-1069: *bellule/ mi evenit, ut ovans praeda onustus incederem.*

[60] Plautus, *Bacch.* 1070-1071: *salute nostra atque urbe capta per dolum/ domum redduco integrum omnem exercitum.*

[61] See above p. 130.

[62] Plautus, *Bacch.* 1072-1073: *sed, spectatores, vos nunc ne miremini/ quod non triumpho: pervolgatum est, nil moror.*

[63] Lines 1072-1073 are often taken as establishing a date of 189 for the play—a year in which four triumphs were supposedly held. The suggestion goes back to F. Ritschl, *Parerga Plautina et Terentiana* (Leipzig, 1845), 423-427. Endorsed by Buck, *Chronology*, 41-47, who supplies further arguments, and Schutter, *Quibus annis*, 30-38, with a valuable summary of other opinions. Add also de Lorenzi, *Cronologia*, 184-187; della Corte, *Da Sarsina a Roma*, 63-64; D. Gagliardi, *Le Parole e le idee*, 5 (1965), 174, n. 13. But this narrows Plautus' intent artificially and misleadingly. Controversy over triumphs marked the
entire period, and their frequency was illustrated by more than a single year. Properly
skeptical is G. Williams, *Hermes*, 84 (1956), 447. Earlier skepticism, on different grounds,
by Fraenkel, *Elementi plautini*, 226-231. Cf. C. Questa, *T. Maccius Plautus: Bacchides*
(Florence, 1975), 1-8. None of the commentators, however, has noted the significance
of the *ovans*—or the emphasis on return of the army.

of contemporary debates are unmistakable. Plautus' audience could find in the scramble for triumphs a subject for amusement.

Ambition for honors and resistance to them provoked exaggerated claims on the part of those seeking distinctions. Cato's fulminations taxed Q. Minucius Thermus in 190 with seeking a triumph on the basis of *falsae pugnae*.[64] The identical phrase reappears in Plautus' *Truculentus*, put in the mouth of the *miles gloriosus* Stratophanes. The captain remarks that mendacity has become a commonplace among soldiers and that countless men have been condemned *falsis de pugnis*.[65] That Plautus took his cue from Cato or referred specifically to the case of Thermus would be unwarranted deduction.[66] The phenomenon was a more general one. Stratophanes' remarks can be taken in conjunction with those of Sosia in the *Amphitryon* who contemplated the report he was to make of a military campaign fought abroad: he would invent some of it—as was his wont.[67] Plautus pointed beyond the specific. It gives him less than his due to consider the theme merely as reference to Greek mercenaries or as lifted directly from the stereotypes of New Comedy. More probably, the playwright mirrors public awareness, perhaps exasperation, with the distortions and hyperbole engaged in by *imperatores* avid for distinction.[68]

The vast sums accruing from foreign conquests and the repercussions they had upon the influence of the *imperator* also find reflection in the pages of Plautus. Distribution of spoils to soldiers as a means to popularity became more common and conspicuous. Amphitryon's vic-

---

[64] *ORF*, Cato, fr. 58.

[65] Plautus, *Truc.* 484-486: *Scio ego multos memoravisse milites mendacium:/ et Homeronida et postilla mille memorari potest,/ qui et convicti et condemnati falsis de pugnis sient.*

[66] As Th. Beyk, *Beiträge zu lateinische Grammatik* (Halle, 1870), 139-140; P.J. Enk, *Plauti Truculentus* (Leiden, 1953), I, 28-30; II, 117-119; O. Musso, *StudItalFilolClass*, 41 (1969), 135-138. More strained still is the hypothesis that Homeronides refers to Ennius and that Plautus parodies Ennius' celebration of Fulvius Nobilior's victory in his *Ambracia*; Frank, *Anatolian Studies Presented to W.H. Buckler* (Manchester, 1939), 86-87; Buck, *Chronology*, 103-104. See the sensible remarks of de Lorenzi, *Cronologia*, 168-170.

[67] Plautus, *Amph.* 197-198: *ea nunc meditabor quo modo illi dicam, quom illo advenero,/ si dixero mendacium, solens meo more fecero.*

[68] On the relevance of Plautus' *miles gloriosus* to Roman society generally, see the astute remarks of J.A. Hanson, in T.A. Dorey and D.R. Dudley, *Roman Drama* (New York, 1965), 51-67. Other allusions to triumphs, in the mouths of slaves and with comic irony, underscore Plautus' irreverence; cf. *Asin.* 269, 278-279; *Epid.* 208-218. It is tempting to interpret the mention of envoys from Ambracia in *Stich.* 490-491 as reference to the witnesses brought from that state to testify against Fulvius' bid for a triumph in 187; Livy, 38.43. So A. Boutemy, *REA*, 38 (1936), 29-30. That interpretation, however, depends upon assuming later insertions in the text, for the didascalic notice dates the *Stichus* to 200 B.C. H.B. Mattingly's effort to discredit the Plautine *didascaliae* is unjustified; *Athenaeum*, 35 (1957), 78-88. In any case, Plautus may well have taken the Ambraciote envoys directly from his Greek original; Schutter, *Quibus annis*, 139-140. Nothing in the passage implies a specific Roman context.

tory at Thebes made beneficiaries of his soldiers: they acquired booty, land, and glory.[69] The expectation of material awards could now be assumed. Chrysalus in the *Bacchides* depicts himself as laden with spoils and announces a handsome reception for his soldiers.[70] The wily and resourceful slave of the *Persa*, Toxilus, also portrays his successful duplicity in military terms: victory allows him to carry off the spoils, to share them with his partisans, and to host them lavishly.[71] Closely comparable language appears in a heady speech of Pseudolus, boasting of his chicanery: he will now pile on the booty for himself and his partisans.[72] The phrases recall Cato's proud claim that he never distributed plunder to his *amici*—thereby indirectly censuring contemporaries who followed a different practice.[73] The latter practice is strikingly illustrated in a Plautine line. The courtesan in *Truculentus* induces a youth to collaborate with her for purposes of profit, urging him *saltem amicus mi esto manubiarius*. The term *manubiarius* is otherwise unattested, but the meaning clear enough: "a friend in plunder."[74] It does not follow that Plautus acted as ally or sympathizer of Cato the Elder.[75] But he plainly underscored contemporary uneasiness about the arbitrary disposal of foreign spoils by Rome's generals.

The importance of the issue for Plautus manifests itself further in an indirect way: the great frequency with which he employs the term *praeda* or its equivalent as a metaphor for the object of schemes by crafty slaves and double dealing characters.[76] The playwright does not announce his attitude. But the association of shady maneuvers and intrigues with the acquisition of spoils gave signals to an audience responsive to public affairs.

---

[69] Plautus, *Amph.* 193: *praeda atque agro adoriaque adfecit popularis suos*. For the usage of *populares* as soldiers, see Harvey, *Athenaeum*, 59 (1981), 486, n. 28, with bibliography. Harvey's general argument, *op. cit.*, 480-489, about land distribution places a heavy burden upon the single word *agro*.

[70] Plautus, *Bacch.* 1069, 1074.

[71] Plautus, *Pers.* 757-758: *nunc ob eam rem inter participes dividam praedam et participabo;/ ite foras; his volo ante ostium et ianuam meos participes bene accipere*.

[72] Plautus, *Pseud.* 588: *inde me et simul participes omnis meos praeda onerabo atque opplebo*. Cf. also *Truc.* 522: *filium peperisti, qui aedis spoliis opplebit tuas*. The soldier's expectation is indicated also in *Poen.* 802-803.

[73] *ORF*, Cato, fr. 203.

[74] Plautus, *Truc.* 880. A felicitous rendering by the Loeb translator: "a bootiful friendship." On the passage, see Enk, *Plauti Truculentus*, II, 197. Musso, *StudItalFilolClass*, 41 (1969), 136-138, rightly draws attention to the Catonian line for comparison. But he goes well beyond the evidence in having both refer to the trial of Acilius Glabrio in 190.

[75] As is argued, in general, by O. Jurewicz, in J. Irmscher and K. Kumaniecki, *Aus der altertumswissenschaftlichen Arbeit Volkspolens* (Berlin, 1959), 52-72.

[76] See, e.g., Plautus, *Asin.* 269-271, 294-295, 317; *Bacch.* 709-712, 968-969; *Casina*, 113-114; *Epid.* 381, 393; *Men.* 134-136, 434, 441; *Merc.* 498; *Rud.* 1261-1262.

Criticism of commanders for misappropriation of moneys and questionable disposition of prizes spilled over into the courts. Special notoriety, as we have seen, attached to the trials of Glabrio, Manlius, and the Scipios. The question of how to set bounds to the *imperator*'s authority gained widespread attention. To what extent Plautus made reference to criminal hearings on this score is unclear. No explicit mention can be discerned. But a few hints bear notice. The slave Libanus' bold assertion in the *Asinaria* that he aspires to sequester public funds and then to deny and foreswear the deed may have struck familiar chords.[77] So perhaps did Chrysalus' dodges in *Bacchides* when questioned about cash brought from abroad: he evaded the inquiry and claimed ignorance of the amount involved. The resort to obfuscation had evocative parallels to the blurring of distinctions between public and private control over the proceeds of conquest.[78] One may note also Chrysalus' later boast about carrying off booty: he announced that he would deliver it directly to the quaestor.[79] That passage plainly speaks to increasing emphasis on the treasury's claims to foreign spoils. Official registration would forestall criticism and perhaps avert prosecution. Otherwise, witnesses and informers were only too ready to testify on purported infractions and to reap personal advantage. Plautus provides suggestive references to false testimony and over-zealous informers.[80]

The comedies, in short, take definite notice of concern over the effects of expansion. Power in the hands of *imperatores*, intense competition for triumphs, opportunities to lavish favors upon partisans, the ambiguous character of public control over military spoils, the attacks on returning commanders, the tensions created by prosecutions or by fear of prosecution permeated the public scene at the beginning of the 2nd century. Plautus, to be sure, did not propose solutions. He was comic dramatist, not political reformer. But the plays had a contemporary resonance that reached beyond the fantasies of the stage. They mocked ambition, lampooned exaggerated claims, deflated conquerors, and likened the acquisition of plunder to the duplicitous guile of slaves. The medium of comedy itself and the popularity of Plautus served to keep these issues before a broader public.

---

[77] Plautus, *Asin.* 321-322: *rapere cupio publicum;/pernegabo atque obdurabo, periurabo denique.*
[78] Plautus, *Bacch.* 297-326. For A.E. Anspach, *Neue Jahrbücher*, 139 (1889), 355-358, the passage refers specifically to the Scipionic trials. Buck, *Chronology*, 42-43, prefers the trial of Glabrio. Schutter, *Quibus annis*, 35-36, is rightly dubious. The lines cannot serve to date the play.
[79] Plautus, *Bacch.* 1075: *nunc hanc praedam omnem iam ad quaestorem deferam.*
[80] Especially Plautus, *Pers.* 62-73; cf. *Curc.* 470; *Men.* 838-839.

Political pressures and the desire to maintain an internal equilibrium within the ruling class deterred reform. No legislation surfaced, no tangible measures obtained a consensus for curbing the prerogatives of generals and instituting firm criteria on triumphs or financial responsibility. On such matters the Romans resorted to *ad hoc* actions, allowing *mos* to develop and shunning *leges*. The evidence of comic drama reinforces the conclusion that this drift failed to alleviate the problems.

On other matters, by paradoxical contrast, the reverse situation held. Lawmakers proposed and passed legislation on a variety of fronts—yet the presence of *leges* proved as ineffective as their absence. Such, at least, is the impression delivered by the Plautine plays. The dramatist who derided behavior unrestrained by statute could be equally derisive when dealing with statutes that were unenforced or unenforceable. Plautus found irony either way.

The themes recur with some frequency in the scripts. Plautus, as usual, avoided the specific. He directed his aim not at a particular piece of legislation but at the fact of legislation. Lawmakers in the plays are busy and harried, but also foolish, with much ado about very little. Father and son in the *Asinaria* are both belittled as expending their labors in senate and legislative activity to no good purpose: the activity debilitates those who engage in it, and the legislation appeals to the debauched.[81] The parasite Peniculus in the *Menaechmi* vents his fury at public *contiones* which usurp the time of busy men and keep them from more important matters—like lunch.[82] In *Epidicus*, the *senex* duped by the slave berates himself and takes consolation only in the fact that his friend was equally bamboozled, despite a reputation for expertise in the fashioning of laws and legal principles.[83]

The Plautine legislator, shallow and fatuous, wastes his own time and others'. And the fruits of his labors are equally ineffectual. Plautus several times alludes to legislation that is ignored, unenforced, or violated with impunity. A character in the *Poenulus* makes reference to laws passed repeatedly by the people against the same offense—an offense committed again in the play. The statutes were obviously without force.[84] Labrax, the pimp in the *Rudens*, expresses contempt for *leges* designed to restrain his activities: he will pursue his operation in defiance of them.[85] The

---

[81] Plautus, *Asin.* 599-602, 871-875.

[82] Plautus, *Men.* 451-459.

[83] Plautus, *Epid.* 517-523: *quid nunc? qui in tantis positus sum sententiis.../ei seic data esse verba praesenti palam!/atque me minoris facio prae illo, qui omnium/ legum atque iurum fictor, condictor cluet.*

[84] Plautus, *Poen.* 725: *rem advorsus populi saepe leges.*

[85] Plautus, *Rud.* 724-725: *mihi cum vostris legibus/ nihil est commerci.*

parasite Curculio, himself hardly of the most distinguished occupation, excoriates pimps and bankers, lumping them together as practitioners of the most unsavory professions and levelling his harshest assaults upon the latter. Curculio blasts bankers for breaking every law passed to hold them in check. They can always find a loophole—like waiting for boiling water to cool down. Again it is the repeated passage of laws for the same purpose—and their futility—at which Plautus takes aim.[86] A slave's scorn rises to the level of indignation when he denounces laws which would only be obeyed by those who were themselves worthless and intemperate.[87] The most extensive tirade is placed in the mouth of another slave, Stasimus in the *Trinummus*, who laments the loss of *veteres mores*, replaced now by *mores mali* which sanction every form of deplorable behavior: contemporary practice runs roughshod over laws; *leges* are without force, subservient to *mos*; whatever custom endorses is released from the authority of law.[88]

Plautus underlines the inefficacy of legislation by having two characters in two separate plays propose transparently ludicrous bills. Eutychus at the close of the *Mercator* frames a measure prohibiting all men over sixty, whether married or single, from affairs with courtesans—and fur-

---

[86] Plautus, *Curc.* 509-511: *rogitationes plurumas propter vos populus scivit,/ quas vos rogatas rumpitis; aliquam reperitis rimam,/ quasi aquam ferventem frigidam esse, ita vos putatis leges.* Cf. Fraenkel, *Elementi plautini*, 108-109. The passage cannot be safely used for chronology— i.e. as reference to the *lex Sempronia* of 193; Livy, 35.7.2-5, see Schutter, *Quibus annis*, 63-64. Gratwick, *Mnemosyne*, 34 (1981), 331-342, has recently made a compelling case for dating the *Curculio* prior to the *Trinummus*. But that does not establish an absolute chronology. Reference to the "new aediles" in *Trinummus*, 990 by no means fixes 194 as a *terminus post quem* for that play, despite Schutter, *op. cit.*, 143-144, and N.W. Slater, *AJP*, 108 (1987), 264-269.

[87] Plautus, *Asin.* 601-602: *qui sese parere apparent huius legibus, profecto/ numquam bonae frugi sient, dies noctesque potent.*

[88] Plautus, *Trin.* 1028-1044; see especially 1032-1033: *nam nunc mores nihili faciunt quod licet, nisi quod lubet;/ ambitio iam more sanctast, liberast a legibus*; 1037: *mores leges perduxerunt iam in potestatem suam*; 1043-1044: *neque istis quicquam lege sanctumst: leges mori serviunt,/ mores autem rapere properant qua sacrum qua publicum.* Frank, *AJP*, 53 (1932), 153-154, takes the speech as reflecting the current debate between Cato and Scipio over the latter's questionable activities in Asia, a view accepted, in one form or other, by several subsequent studies; A. Rostagni, *La letteratura di Roma repubblicana ed augustea* (Bologna, 1939), 81; Buck, *Chronology*, 100-101; D. Gagliardi, *Le parole e le idee*, 5 (1965), 172; D.C. Earl, *Historia*, 9 (1960), 235. Salutary doubts are expressed by Schutter, *Quibus annis*, 145-146, and de Lorenzi, *Cronologia*, 136. Nothing in the text ties these remarks to a particular and unmistakable occasion. More recently, E. Segal, *AJP*, 95 (1974), 260-264, stressed the praise of *mos maiorum*, a conservative position taken by Plautus and designed to appeal to his financial backers. If so, one wonders why Plautus did not deem it necessary to cater to those financial backers in other plays. Segal's analysis does not deal with the implications for Plautus' attitude toward *leges*. W.S. Anderson, *Traditio*, 35 (1979), 333-345, more plausibly suggests that the play caricatures self-righteous moralism—although he does not discuss Stasimus' lines.

ther debarring them from interference with their sons' wenching! A classic instance of the unenforceable law.[89] Equally preposterous is the *lex* conceived by Saturio, the parasite in the *Persa*. Saturio denounces the practice of informing and suggests a remedy: a measure that requires the successful informer to yield up half his earnings to the public coffers and permits any defendant to sue his accuser for the same sum sought from himself, thus to appear before the *tresviri* on equal terms.[90] Implementation of such an ordinance was plainly unthinkable. The proposals perhaps parodied extant legislation that could command no obedience.

What type of legislation came under censure here? The dramatist, once again, refrains from explicit designation. But certain areas offer suggestive possibilities. Sumptuary laws, for example, warrant notice. They did not lend themselves to easy enforcement.

The *lex Oppia* demands attention, a notorious and controversial measure. The assembly, on tribunician initiative, passed the bill in 215, while gripped by the intensity of the Hannibalic war.[91] Its provisions prohibited any woman from having more than a *semuncia* of gold, from wearing colorful garb, and from riding in a carriage in Rome or any town within a mile.[92] What was the purpose of the enactment and how effective was it? On the surface, it would appear to be a wartime measure designed to rally the community and rescue the treasury.[93] If so, however, the provisions are most peculiar. Prohibition of fancy clothing and carriages would provide no material benefits to the war effort. And the restrictions on gold would be of only limited benefit. The state needed silver. Nothing in the *lex Oppia* would provide it. The law, it has been suggested, would protect the less well-to-do by removing the need to compete or the shame of failing to compete. All would be put on an equal footing.[94] Yet the measure could hardly wipe out distinctions of wealth or class. The war effort received a genuine transfusion in 210 when senators contributed gold, silver, and bronze to the common cause, each retaining

---

[89] Plautus, *Merc.* 1015-1024.

[90] Plautus, *Pers.* 62-76.

[91] Livy, 34.1.3: *in medio ardore Punici belli*. On the date, see A. Haury, *Mélanges Heurgon* (1976), I, 427-436.

[92] Livy, 34.1.3: *ne qua mulier plus semunciam auri haberet neu vestimento versicolori uteretur neu iuncto vehiculo in urbe oppidove aut propius inde mille passus nisi sacrorum publicorum causa veheretur.* Evidence on the *lex Oppia* and the debate over its repeal is contained in Livy, 34.1.8. The rest of the testimony is derivative or adds little; Zon. 9.17.1; Val. Max. 9.1.3; Tac. *Ann.* 3.33-34; Gellius, 10.23, 17.6; *Vir. Ill.* 47.6; Orosius, 4.20.14.

[93] Cf. Livy, 34.6.16: *cui non apparet inopiam et miseriam civitatis, quia omnium privatorum pecuniae in usum publicum vertendae erant, istam legem scripsisse.*

[94] Cf. Livy, 34.4.12-13: *pessimus quidem pudor est vel parsimoniae vel paupertatis; sed utrumque lex vobis demit, cum id quod habere non licet non habetis*; D. Daube, *Aspects of Roman Law* (Edinburgh, 1969), 117-128, esp. 125.

only a token for his household.[95] And three years later Roman matrons, to expiate ill omens, selected twelve in their number to draw on their own dowries for a gift to Juno.[96] Does this imply that enforcement of the *lex Oppia* was lax from the start? Perhaps. But that conclusion depends on the premise that the bill was a confiscatory measure, a view shared by most commentators.[97] The premise, however, is mistaken. The heated debate over repeal of the law in 195 nowhere breathes a hint that the wives are to receive back any cash—or that there is any to receive. Their demands concentrated only on the freedom to deck themselves out in finery once again. The Oppian law was a *lex sumptuaria*, not a means of economic relief.[98] As such, its principal value was symbolic rather than pragmatic. The appearance of women, bedecked and bejewelled, in public would be offensive at a time of economic hardship and national crisis. The *lex* imposed a patriotic uniformity.

Retention of the measure after the end of the war, therefore, created an anomaly. Cato might argue that the moral welfare of the community would continue to benefit from an enactment which held women's extravagance in check. But the argument did not prevail for long. The women themselves engaged in vociferous demonstration in 195, gained support (or encouragement) in high circles, and generated heated dispute. The matter received considerable public visibility and issued in repeal of the statute.[99] Its symbolic value had eroded away, once the constraints of the Hannibalic war were lifted. The vigorous complaints of its victims exposed the measure's hollowness.

Plautus' comedies contain recurrent references to female luxury and display. The oft-cited lines of the *senex* Megadorus in the *Aulularia* berate the arrogance and extravagance of wives who bring handsome dowries to their marriages. They parade about in polished carriages and purple finery, reducing their husbands to servitude.[100] The needs of their ward-

---

[95] Livy, 26.36.5-12.

[96] Livy, 27.37.8-10.

[97] E.g., A. Boyce, *TAPA*, 68 (1937), 168; C. Herrmann, *Le rôle judiciaire et politique des femmes sous la republique romaine* (Brussels, 1964), 54-57; S. Pomeroy, *Goddesses, Whores, Wives, and Slaves* (New York, 1975), 177-181; Astin, *Cato the Censor*, 25; J. Briscoe, *A Commentary on Livy, Books XXXIV-XXXVII* (Oxford, 1981), 44; G. Clemente, in *Società romana e produzione schiavistica*, III (1981), 5-6. Haury, *Mélanges Heurgon* (1976), I, 431-432, sees the *lex Oppia* as an economic measure designed to check luxury imports.

[98] Note the language of Zon. 9.17.1: μήτε χρυσοφορεῖν τὰς γυναῖκας. Women were forbidden to wear gold—not to possess it. Livy, 34.1.2, should be interpreted in this sense as well. This was rightly seen by I. Sauerwein, *Die leges sumptuariae als römische Massnahme gegen den Sittenverfall* (Hamburg, 1970), 40-46. So also Ph. Culham, *Latomus*, 41 (1982), 786-793, evidently unaware of Sauerwein's work.

[99] See sources listed above, n. 92.

[100] Plautus, *Aul.* 167-169.

robe and cosmetics keep an army of merchants in business.[101] Rich dowries encourage ostentation and allow wives to lord it over their spouses.[102] Those lines have traditionally served to date the *Aulularia*: Megadorus' strictures show close parallels to those of Cato, and the argument seems to mirror the debate on repeal of the law in 195: hence the play was produced in 194 or thereabouts.[103] The conclusion is unverifiable and unpersuasive. Speeches for and against repeal of the law stem from Livy's narrative and his own composition. How near or far they are to the arguments actually expressed in 195 we shall never know. A case can be made for seeing them as reflecting the atmosphere of the Augustan age.[104] Whatever one makes of that, it is methodologically unsound to employ the Livian text as a means of dating Plautus' comedy. The playwright, in fact, harps on the practice of luxurious living by women in numerous plays. That theme is not confined to a date or an occasion.

Pampered women appear with frequency in the comedies. Dowries support only a portion of them. Others are indulged by their husbands who provide maids, jewelry, linen, purple garments, and luxury items of all sorts.[105] Nor are wives alone the beneficiaries of this generosity. Courtesans too sport jewelry and elegant raiments supplied by lovers.[106] Their households include wardrobe mistresses, masseuses, bookkeepers, custodians of accessories, numerous flunkies, and every variety of garment—to the despair or ruin of their benefactors.[107] Special irony

---

[101] Plautus, *Aul.* 505-522.

[102] Plautus, *Aul.* 475-502.

[103] So, e.g., W. Wagner, *De Plauti Aulularia* (Bonn, 1874), 24; Buck, *Chronology*, 37; Schutter, *Quibus annis*, 21-23; Culham, *Latomus*, 41 (1982), 790. Harvey, *CW*, 79 (1986), 300-301, rightly demurs.

[104] So F. Hellmann, *NJADB*, 4 (1940), 81-86. That may be extreme. But the idea that the speeches in this debate were framed by Livy and not based on any originals has now received general acknowledgment. See, e.g., Fraccaro, *Opuscula*, I, 120-122, 179-181; Scullard, *Roman Politics*, 257; Sauerwein, *Leges sumptuariae*, 59-66; Haury, *Mélanges Heurgon* (1976), I, 434-435; Astin, *Cato the Censor*, 25; Cugusi, *Catonis Orationum Reliquiae*, 511-512. The efforts of Kienast, *Cato der Zensor*, 21-22, to establish the authenticity of Cato's speech have not found favor. One could argue against the dating of Plautus' *Aulularia* also from a different direction: that the railing against luxury was actually drawn from the Greek model and not Roman experience; cf. della Corte, *Da Sarsina a Roma*, 60-61. But the Roman character of this portion was convincingly established by Fraenkel, *Elementi plautini*, 130-132.

[105] Plautus, *Men.* 120-121, 801-804; *Stich.* 373-388. Boutemy, *REA*, 38 (1936), 31-32, takes the last passage as specific reference to Manlius Vulso's return from his Asian campaign with magnificent luxury items. The drive to find specificity in Plautus distracts rather than advances understanding. See also above, p. 138.

[106] Plautus, *Curc.* 344; *Miles*, 980-981, 1147; *Most.* 282; *Truc.* 530-544.

[107] Plautus, *Epid.* 222-236; *Trin.* 247-254. On the relevance of the *Epidicus* passage to the dating of that play, much disputed, see the survey of opinions in G.E. Duckworth, *T. Macci Plauti Epidicus* (Princeton, 1940), 239-240.

attaches to the remarks of the Carthaginian woman Adelphasium in *Poenulus*, who plays the part of moralist and censures her own sex for excessive devotion to luxury and pampering, thus causing endless trouble to men. The sentiments closely parallel those of Megadorus in the *Aulularia*.[108] To interpret this as Plautus embracing Catonian conservatism misses the mark. By placing analogous comments in the mouths of both *meretrix* and *senex*, the playwright surely parodies the moralism that frowns on luxury but is powerless to check it.[109] Composition of these lines need not have awaited the specific debate over repeal of the *lex Oppia*. The very fact of legislation on the books that had outstripped its usefulness, antagonized its constituents, and contravened both public opinion and public practice provided a target for the playwright's wit. Plautus is neither moralist nor political partisan. The comic writer delights in the incongruity of rhetoric and reality.[110]

Another type of legislation may also have prompted Plautine parody. Laws on usury made an appearance in the early 2nd century, with some frequency and reiteration. Livy speaks, under the year 193, of *multae leges* on the subject. They had curbed greed but also stimulated moneylenders to find loopholes and ply their trade in indirect ways. Hence the assembly promulgated still another measure in that year, closing one of the loopholes exploited by *faeneratores* and relieving the burden of high interest payments.[111] The bill engendered numerous prosecutions and the resultant fines paid for lavish public monuments.[112] But the problem

---

[108] Plautus, *Poen.* 210-231; cf. *Aul.* 167-169, 475-522. See the intriguing analysis of P.A. Johnston, *TAPA*, 110 (1980), 143-159, who rightly notes the parallels. Her efforts to tie them closely to Cato's position on the *lex Oppia*, however, are less compelling. Nor is it clear that Plautus intended to call attention to the relationship between Rome and Carthage.

[109] Notice Adelphasium's noble pronouncement that good character requires no outward adornment and that the courtesan should prefer *pudor* to *purpura*; Plautus, *Poen.* 301-304: *bono med esse ingenio ornatam quam auro multo mavolo;/ aurum, id fortuna invenitur, natura ingenium bonum;...lmeretricem pudorem gerere magis decet quam purpuram*. The lines are certainly not to be taken seriously. Observe the remarks of the courtesan's maid in *Most.* 289-292: *pulchra mulier nuda erit quam purpurata pulchrior;...lnam si pulchra est, nimis ornata est*.

[110] Other allusions to sumptuary matters are few or hard to detect. The majority of laws on luxury post-dated Plautus' death in any case. But the poet does supply reference to a *lex alearia*, which restricted gambling, a *lex* otherwise unattested. And the passage may imply that that measure is honored in the breach; *Miles*, 164-165: *atque adeo ut ne legi fraudem faciant aleariae,/ adcuratote ut sine talis domi agitent convivium*. Sauerwein, *Leges sumptuariae*, 47-50, identifies the law with a *lex Publicia* on gambling, named but not dated by *Dig.* 11.5.3, and identifies the author as C. Publicius Bibulus, tribune 209 and sponsor of a measure limiting the gifts that a client could confer on his patron; Macrob. 1.7.33. The identifications are tempting but unverifiable. Mentions of lavish living also occur elsewhere in the Plautine corpus; *Most.* 42-46, 908-911; *Trin.* 468-471.

[111] Livy, 35.7.2-5; cf. Briscoe, *Commentary*, 153-154.

[112] Livy, 35.41.9-10.

of usury did not evaporate. The money-lenders rechanneled their activities and found other means whereby to evade restrictions—or so it may be inferred from the passage of a new usury law, the *lex Junia de feneratione* not long thereafter. Cato voiced opposition to the bill, perhaps as being insufficiently severe.[113] It was, in any case, hardly more effective than its predecessors. Still another measure needed to be passed, the *lex Marcia*, perhaps in the 180s.[114] Usury did not readily succumb to legislation.

The subject lent itself to comic treatment. Bankers, money-lenders, and usurers abound in Plautus' scripts. Nothing surprising in that, of course. The Greek models will account for most of them, essential as they often are to the plot or intrigues of the play. But not always. Curculio's broadside against the whole tribe of *faeneratores* has a sweeping character that removes it from the realm of the plot. The assault matches pimps with bankers as objects of revilement: the first tear men apart with baneful solicitation and debauchery, the second with oppressive interest charges. Bankers, if anything, are worse: pimps at least conduct business in private, the *faeneratores* in the open forum. And, most important, the latter have scornfully violated a multitude of laws passed by the people against them; they count on ineffectiveness and escape clauses.[115] The lines almost certainly have contemporary resonance—and deliberately so. They attack both the profession and the futile measures taken to curb it. An illustration of the loophole comes in the same play. The banker Lyco's initial entrance onto the stage brings a monologue in which he contemplates means of evading his own creditors: if they should put on too much pressure, he would seek a praetor's judgment, evidently confident in the outcome.[116]

The theme of bankers forever dunning their debtors but eluding their creditors recurs in the comedies. The prologue of the *Casina* presents it with word play. The *ludi* allow men to forget their debts, but the bankers have their own *ludus*: they dun no one at the games, and they repay no one after the games.[117] A conventional literary charge against *faeneratores*? Possibly. But a passage in the *Pseudolus* suggests something more topical. Calidorus complains that no loans are obtainable. Pseudolus concurs and

---

[113] *ORF*, Cato, fr. 56-57; see the discussion by Astin, *Cato the Censor*, 321-323, with bibliography. Add Cugusi, *Catonis Orationum Reliquiae*, 188-193.

[114] Gaius, *Inst.* 4.23.

[115] Plautus, *Curc.* 506-511, quoted above, n. 86.

[116] Plautus, *Curc.* 373-376: *dives sum, si non reddo eis quibus debeo;.../verum hercle vero quom belle recogito,/si magis me instabunt, ad praetorem sufferam.* See also *Curc.* 683-684.

[117] Plautus, *Cas.* 25-28: *ludi sunt, ludus datus est argentariis;/ tranquillum est, Alcedonia sunt circum forum;/ ratione utuntur, ludis poscunt neminem,/secundum ludos reddunt autem nemini.* Cf. *Curc.* 377-379.

explains: from the time that the bankers, having satiated themselves and closed up shop, called in their debts but paid none of their creditors, everyone is too cautious and distrusting to lend any money.[118] The allusion has a concreteness that goes beyond the world of fantasy. Plautus may attend to tight credit and straitened economic circumstances that prevailed in the aftermath of the Hannibalic war.[119] Comparable allusions occur elsewhere in the texts—to economic hardship, to the high cost of living, to the cornering of the grain market.[120] The playwright need not simply be copying out his Greek models here. Strictures against money-lenders have a ring of authenticity. A reputation for untrustworthiness clings to them.[121] They are swift to find more moneys due from debtors.[122] They are notoriously relentless in pressing for repayment.[123] But if any cash is entrusted to them, they vanish faster than a liberated hare.[124] No sure criteria distinguish the Plautine money lenders who derive from New Comedy and those rooted in the Roman scene.[125] But Plautus had an eye for the vexatious issues of his time.[126] The troublesome circumstances of debt and tight credit, the greed and untrustworthiness of money-lenders, and the frustration engendered by inept and fruitless legislation all find place in the comedies, and touched chords familiar to Plautus' countrymen.

Contemporary reflections in the plays extend beyond the realms of the military and the political. Plautus catches the echoes of the key cultural

---

[118] Plautus, *Pseud.* 296-300: *heus tu, postquam hercle isti a mensa surgunt satis poti̦ viri,/ qui suom repetunt, alienum reddunt nato nemini,/ postilla omnes cautiores sunt, ne credant alteri.*

[119] The didascalia dates *Pseudolus* to 191, but there is no reason to believe that historical allusions in the text must refer to that year. Cf. also *Asin.* 428-429.

[120] Plautus, *Aul.* 373-376; *Epid.* 227; *Miles,* 733-735; *Pseud.* 188-191; *Stich.* 179; *Trin.* 484.

[121] Plautus, *Most.* 532-535, 657-658: *nullum edepol hodie genus est hominum taetrius/ nec minus bono cum iure quam danisticum.*

[122] Plautus, *Aul.* 527-531.

[123] Plautus, *Epid.* 53-54, 114-115; *Most.* 536-538.

[124] Plautus, *Persa,* 435-436: *ubi quid credideris, citius extemplo a foro,/ fugiunt quam ex porta ludis quom emissust lepus.*

[125] A worthy effort to draw the distinctions is made by J. Andreau, *MEFRA,* 80 (1968), 461-526—but not with full success. Andreau, for example, follows G.P. Shipp, *Glotta,* 34 (1955), 139-152, in finding that the Greek and Latin terms used by Plautus for banker, *trapezita* and *argentarius,* signal a Greek and a Roman context respectively. But that thesis does not always work. Lyco is seven times termed a *trapezita* in the *Curculio;* 341, 345, 406, 420, 560, 618, 712. Yet he is plainly regarded as among the *argentarii; Curc.* 679-682. And Andreau himself recognizes Curculio's tirade against Lyco as reflecting a Roman situation; *Curc.* 506-511. The terminological distinction between *trapezita* and *argentarius* is far from firm.

[126] Allusion is made also to a *lex* on electoral bribery—but without clear indication of its enforceability; Plautus, *Amph.* 69-74. And the lines may be a post-Plautine interpolation; Mattingly, *Latomus,* 19 (1960), 237-240; M. McDonnell, *AJP,* 107 (1986), 564-576.

development of his time: the adaptation of Hellenism by the intellectual leadership of Rome. The comedies themselves, of course, exemplify it— the classic instance of a Greek medium converted for the Roman scene. The overlap of Roman elements on the Hellenic form, setting, characters, and techniques has long been subject to dissection and analysis.[127] That topic, already extensively explored, needs no further investigation here. A somewhat different inquiry has relevance to the present study: Plautus' own allusions to the Roman reception of Hellas.

The comic dramatist, as usual, does not supply direct and straightforward commentary on this or any other matter. Meaning often needs to be extracted from ambiguity, irony, and parody. A select number of texts offer illustration.

A striking passage in the *Bacchides* provides an opening. The conniving *servus* Chrysalus compares his wheedling of cash out of old man Nicobulus to the capture of Troy and downfall of Priam through the chicanery of Odysseus.[128] The lines have stimulated political interpretation: Plautus here parodies the expedition of the Scipio brothers against Antiochus the Great, which included a pilgrimage to the citadel of Ilium and a sacrifice to the goddess as reminder of Rome's Trojan heritage. The dramatist's stance, on this view, was anti-Scipionic, a shot fired on behalf of the Catonian party.[129] Nothing in the text lends support to that sort of hypothesis.[130] Chrysalus' comic analogy of the fall of Troy and the outwitting of a *senex* hardly qualifies as commentary on foreign policy or senatorial rivalries. The implausibility of narrow political interpretation stands out starkly here. One may leap to the other extreme and deny all

---

[127] Most notably by Fraenkel, *Elementi plautini*. Among more recent works, see della Corte, *Da Sarsina a Roma*; R. Perna, *L'originalità di Plauto* (Bari, 1955); Gaiser, *ANRW*, I.2 (1972), 1027-1113.

[128] Plautus, *Bacch.* 925-974, 987. On problems with the text, not relevant here, see H.D. Jocelyn, *HSCP*, 73 (1969), 135-152. Other bibliography in Questa, *Plautus: Bacchides*, 54-68; A. Primmer, *Handlungsgliederung in Nea und Palliata: Dis Exapaton und Bacchides* (Vienna, 1984), 85, n. 151.

[129] For the Scipionic sacrifice at Troy, see Livy, 37.37.2-3. The political interpretation derives from Frank, *Anatolian Studies presented to W.H. Buckler* (Manchester, 1939), 85-86. Plautus' line, *Bacch.* 933: *o Troia, o patria, o Pergamum, o Priame periisti senex*, it can be argued, has as model a verse of Ennius, *Andromache*, 99, Vahlen: *o pater, o patria, o Priami domus*; so Fraenkel, *Elementi plautini*, 63. For Frank, Ennius' tragedy honored his patron Scipio and his eastern campaign, a tragedy then mocked by Plautus, a converted Catonian. Cf. also de Lorenzi, *Cronologia*, 186, for whom the *Bacchides* is suffused by an anti-Scipionic spirit. Schutter, *Quibus annis*, 37-38, expresses doubt but does not argue the case.

[130] Chrysalus does begin his *canticum* with the words *Atridae duo fratres*; Plautus, *Bacch.* 925; cf. 946. But to see this as hidden reference to the Scipio brothers strains belief. The Scipios came to claim Trojan heritage, not to sack Troy. And the central figure in Chrysalus' speech, in any event, is Odysseus-Ulysses. The Atridae receive but passing mention.

contemporaneity to the passage. Plautus is merely being playful: Chrysalus ineptly confuses various episodes from the Trojan war, thus making the more ridiculous his ascription of epic grandeur to a scheme of rogueish thievery.[131] An easy explanation, but not fully compelling.

Chrysalus' words strike a responsive note. The native city of Priam is termed Pergamum. Troy, Ilium, and Pergamum are interchangeable names.[132] That equation may not be inadvertent or accidental. Association between Rome and Pergamum had important diplomatic implications in the late 3rd and early 2nd centuries, the association fortified through use of the Trojan legend that both gave Rome a foothold in the Greek East and permitted her to claim an identity apart from the Hellenic. King Attalus I of Pergamum was principal *amicus* of the Republic, joint benefactor of Delphi, transmitter of the Magna Mater from Mt. Ida to Rome, ally in two Macedonian wars, signatory with Ilium of the Peace of Phoenice, and collaborator in the propaganda that connected Rome to the tale of Troy.[133] Plautus' sensitivity to cultural and diplomatic cross-currents perhaps comes into play here.[134] In his customary fashion, the poet does not parade his own attitudes—nor, on the other hand, does he altogether conceal them. Chrysalus' monologue parodies the Trojan story by reducing it to the level of a trickster's intrigue. The analogy between the taking of the city and the schemes of a *servus* appears elsewhere in the plays as well.[135] Plautus' irreverence inclines to mockery, a burlesque of contemporary manipulations of the Trojan legend for purposes of international relations.[136] Roman adaptation of the Hellenic tradition to advance her diplomatic standing may not have impressed the poet.

Another Hellenic feature transplanted to Italian soil met with disfavor as well: the worship of Bacchus. The Bacchantes appear several times in Plautus' scripts. To what extent mention of them represents the dramatist's opinion or mirrors public perception cannot be determined.

---

[131] Fraenkel, *Elementi plautini*, 9, 63-70; Gagliardi, *Le parole e le idee*, 5 (1965), 170-172; N.W. Slater, *Plautus in Performance: The Theater of the Mind* (Princeton, 1985), 110-113.

[132] Plautus, *Bacch.* 926: *Priami patriam Pergamum*; 933: *o Troia, o patria, o Pergamum*; 1053-1054: *fit vasta Troia, scindunt proceres Pergamum;/scivi ego iam dudum fore me exitio Pergamo.*

[133] On all this, see the discussion above pp. 15-33.

[134] Explicit reference to Attalus, as well as to Philip of Macedon, comes in Plautus, *Persa*, 339-340, just possibly an indirect allusion to Rome's actions on behalf of those kings—not necessarily to her own advantage: *mirum quin regis Philippi causa aut Attali/ te potius vendam quam mea, quae sis mea.*

[135] Plautus, *Miles*, 1025-1026; *Pseud.* 1063-1064, 1244.

[136] One might compare, in this connection, Pseudolus' parody of the Delphic Oracle—conceivably also an allusion to the use of that Hellenic institution in the interest of diplomatic associations; Plautus, *Pseud.* 480-487.

But the plays demonstrate graphically the low esteem in which the sect was held, valuable testimony that helps to supply the context for its victimization in 186.

Bacchic cells were secretive, as Plautus' evidence shows. The *ancilla* Milphidippa of the *Miles Gloriosus* speaks of a password as exemplifying membership of the Bacchic cult.[137] Secrecy generated suspicion. Rumors attached themselves to the sect, assumptions that violence pervaded its meetings. The cook who was chased headlong from Euclio's house by the miser in the *Aulularia* complains of his cudgeling in terms of being caught in a Bacchanalian ritual.[138] Young Pistoclerus expresses fear of the den of Bacchantes, comparing it to the establishment of the two Bacchides, a darkened spot.[139] The slave Lydus in the same play even infers that participants in the rites suck the blood of men.[140] The image of Bacchic celebrants was that of raving revellers. Such is the description made by Sosia in the *Amphitryon*.[141] The myth of Bacchants tearing Pentheus to pieces seems to have been familiar to Roman audiences. Charinus makes reference to the tale in the *Mercator*.[142] Plautus even employs the verb *bacchor* to mean revel and carouse.[143] The sect had clearly made an impression in Rome—and largely a negative one.[144]

Plautus reflects public distrust, suspicion, and hostility. Whether he ever gave notice of the state's campaign against the celebrants is uncertain, though generally assumed. Scholars point to a line in the *Casina* which purportedly implies that Bacchic rites were no longer practiced.[145]

---

[137] Plautus, *Miles*, 1016: *cedo signum, si harunc Baccharum es.* Cf. E. Riess, *CQ*, 35 (1941), 151.

[138] Plautus, *Aul.* 408-409: *neque ego umquam nisi hodie ad Bacchas veni in Bacchanal coquinatum,/ ita me miserum et meos discipulos fustibus male contuderunt.*

[139] Plautus, *Bacch.* 53: *quia, Bacchis, bacchas metuo et bacchanal tuom*; 56: *latebrosus locus.* de Lorenzi, *Cronologia*, 187-189, argues unconvincingly that this helps date the play to 189, for it presumes female dominance in the cult and suggests a time of proselytizing of males; cf. Livy, 39.10.6, 39.13.8, 39.13.14. Even less plausible is his view that Plautus shows sympathy for the sect, an attitude nowhere suggested by the texts.

[140] Plautus, *Bacch.* 371-372: *Bacchides non Bacchides, sed bacchae sunt acerrumae;/ apage istas a me sorores, quae hominum sorbent sanguinem*—evidently a reference to rumors of human sacrifice; cf. Livy, 39.13.11; Riess, *CQ*, 35 (1941), 151.

[141] Plautus, *Amph.* 703-704: *non tu scis? Bacchae bacchanti si velis advorsarier,/ ex insana insaniorem facies, feriet saepius.* Cf. also *Men.* 828-841.

[142] Plautus, *Merc.* 469: *Pentheum diripuisse aiunt Bacchas.* Cf. *Vid.* fr. 1, Lindsay. Familiarity with the myth may derive from exposure to Euripides' *Bacchae.*

[143] Plautus, *Miles*, 856: *ubi bacchabatur aula*; 857-858: *vos in cella vinaria/ bacchanal facitis.*

[144] Boutemy, *REA*, 38 (1936), 32-33, finds in Gelasimus' complaints about dangers in the streets a reference to the excesses of the Bacchantes; Plautus, *Stichus*, 606-607; cf. *Amph.* 152-153. But the sect receives no explicit mention here, and the suggestion is too speculative to build upon.

[145] Plautus, *Casina*, 980: *nam ecastor nunc Bacchae nullae ludunt.* This is taken as an indirect allusion to the *senatus consultum* of 186. The idea stems from J. Naudet, *JSav* (1838), 406-407, and has been followed by almost all commentators; e.g. Ritschl, *Parerga*,

If so, it is the only such indication in the comedies, and a remark so bland as to carry no impact. Had Plautus wished to draw attention to the vigorous state action and extensive publicity set in motion against the Bacchantes in 186, this would hardly do the job.[146] He concerns himself with the general reputation of the sect, not the particular occasion of its suppression—typical of his approach and technique. The playwright gives voice to popular fears, suspicions, and dislike of this alien cult and of Hellenic intrusion. As he offered cynical observations on Roman use of Greek legends, so he cast an unfavorable light on Roman reception of a Greek religious sect.

The Umbrian poet, who was steeped in Greek, who chose to work in a medium that was thoroughly Greek, and who depended upon Greek models, nevertheless had reservations about things Hellenic. The commingling of cultures was not an unmixed blessing. The ambivalence felt by so many Roman intellectuals who both embraced Hellenism and strove to keep it at arm's length manifests itself strikingly in Plautus.

The plays of Plautus present an amalgam: the tight interweaving of Hellas and Italy. Generations of scholars have found it devilishly difficult to disentangle the Greek and Roman elements therein. The reason is simple enough: they were not meant to be disentangled. Plautus employed the Hellenic setting and characters partly to elucidate his countrymen's perception of an alien people, and partly to reflect back on the characteristics of his own society and contemporaries. The comic stage supplied a suitable vehicle for this overlay of elements. Irony and irreverence combine with serious intent. Roman actors in Greek garb possess the necessary detachment to comment wryly on both societies, a convenient means for the poet to capture attitudes on the interplay of the cultures.

192; Buck, *Chronology*, 55-56; Schutter, *Quibus annis*, 49-50; della Corte, *Da Sarsina a Roma*, 76-77; de Lorenzi, *Cronologia*, 197-198; W.T. MacCary, *Hermes*, 103 (1975), 459-463; W.T. MacCary and M.M. Willcock, *Plautus: Casina* (Cambridge, 1976), 11, 207. Yet the use of *nunc*, rather than *iam*, is emphatic. Plautus refers to an absence of Bacchic rites at that time, not necessarily to a termination of them; see J.C. Dumont, in *Les bourgeoisies municipales italiennes aux II et Ier siècles au J.C.* (Colloques Int. du Centre Nat. de la recherche scientifique, n. 609) (Paris, 1983), 341.

[146] A rather different passage could, *prima facie*, be taken as pointing to the hunting down of the sect's membership: Eutychus' statement in the *Mercator* regarding application to the praetor for *conquaestores* in every district of the city; Plautus, *Merc.* 664-665: *post ad praetorem ilico/ ibo, orabo, ut conquistores det mi in vicis omnibus*; cf. Livy, 39.13.9-10. But Bacchantes are not named here. And the *Mercator* is placed by almost all scholars among Plautus' early plays, and well before 186; P.J. Enk, *Plauti Mercator* (Leyden, 1932), 1, 28-29; Buck, *Chronology*, 75-79; Schutter, *Quibus annis*, 87-93; de Lorenzi, *Cronologia*, 112-117, 220-221. Dumont's view, *op. cit.* (n. 145), 339-343, that Plautus is a promoter of the Bacchic cult has no foundation. R. Rousselle, *CJ*, 82 (1987), 196-197, by contrast, regards Plautus' plays as contributing to public hostility toward Bacchic practices.

A famous aside by Stichus reminds his audience that they are witness-
ing the peculiar practices of the Greeks—not to be confused with Roman
behavior. "Don't be surprised," he admonishes, "to find insignificant
little slaves drinking, making love, and giving dinner parties. We can do
all of that—in Athens."[147] The passage is conventionally taken as an
apology: Plautus seeks to get off the hook, lest anyone complain that he
distorts or disparages Roman mores. But the words have ironic intent,
unmistakably so.[148] Plautus' purpose is not to escape the censor's wrath
or to avoid offense to his audience. If they needed reminder that a Greek
locale explained the actions of the characters, it was because Plautus'
palliata generally blurred the lines between the two cultures. Stichus'
disclaimer on the one point only underscored the absence of sharp
distinction on all others.[149]

Plautus' characters were both acting out an illusion and self-conscious
about doing so.[150] That ironic detachment permitted them to deliver
strictures upon themselves and upon those they represented. Plautus
employs the device to convey an unflattering portrayal of Hellenic
temperament. The playwright resorts to the terms *pergraecari* and *con-
graecari* to signify loose-living and dissipation. Grumio in the *Mostellaria*
berated his fellow *servus* Tranio for wild extravagance at his master's
expense: continual drinking, buying and liberating prostitutes, supporting parasites, sumptuously feasting, in short, "acting the Greek"—
pergraecamini.[151] Another slave in the same play expostulates in similar
fashion: a nearly uninterrupted binge of wining, wenching, and musical
entertainment, tantamount to *pergraecari*.[152] The *advocati* in the *Poenulus*
supply a closely parallel conjunction of terms: sensual pleasures, women,
drink, and *pergraecare*.[153] They appear also in the letter dictated by

---

[147] Plautus, *Stich.* 446-448; *atque id ne vos miremini, homines servolos/ potare, amare atque ad
cenam condicere;/licet haec Athenis nobis.*

[148] This is correctly perceived by E. Segal, *Roman Laughter* (Cambridge, Mass., 1968),
31-34.

[149] The prologue to the *Casina* makes a similar disclaimer. Slave marriages are
acknowledged as alien to Rome, yet justifiable on stage, for they occur in Greece and
other places with customs unacceptable in Rome; Plautus, *Casina*, 67-72. Cf. also the prologue to the *Truculentus*, announcing at the outset that Plautus is bringing Athens onto
the stage; *Truc.* 1-3: *Perparvam partem postulat Plautus loci/ de vostris magnis atque amoenis
moenibus,/ Athenas quo sine architectis conferat.*

[150] See Slater, *Plautus in Performance*, *passim*, especially 118-146, his illuminating study
of the *Pseudolus*.

[151] Plautus, *Most.* 22-24: *dies noctesque bibite, pergraecamini,/ amicas emite liberate, pascite/
parasitos, opsonate pollucibiliter*; 64-65: *bibite, pergraecamini, este, ecfercite vos, saginam caedite.*

[152] Plautus, *Most.* 959-961: *triduom unum est haud intermissum hic esse et bibi,/ scorta duci,
pergraecari, fidicinas tibicinas/ ducere.*

[153] Plautus, *Poen.* 601-603: *oraveris,/ liberum ut commostraremus tibi locum et voluptarium,/
ubi ames, potes pergraecere.*

Chrysalus for his master and composed to deceive his father: money is promised to purchase prostitutes and to squander in debauchery "in Greek fashion."[154] The phrase, evidently a favorite, can be found elsewhere in the comedies, with the same connotation. "Playing the Greek" denotes intemperate revelling.[155]

Athens, of couse, is the vice capital of Hellas. Charinus in the *Mercator* makes the point more in sorrow than in anger: in Athens morals become the worse daily, a place where loyal and faithless friends are indistinguishable.[156] Stichus too, in a more positive vein, reckons Athens as the exemplary locale for festivity and excess: abandon all foreign association, let's cherish Athens.[157]

The Greece of the comedies induces belittlement, not emulation. The less appealing characteristics of its people receive principal emphasis, an untrustworthy lot: *Graeca fides*.[158] Plautus repeatedly has fun at their expense. The *senex* Periplectomenus of the *Miles Gloriosus* boasts of his own urbanity and congeniality by contrast with spitters, coughers, and snifflers, uncivilized behavior which the Ephesian gentleman associated with the stereotyped center of boorishness: Apulia.[159] That fact lends special amusement to a passage in the prologue to the *Casina*. There the institution of slave weddings, unthinkable to the Romans, is ascribed to three, obviously inferior, societies: Greece, Carthage, and Apulia![160] Greeks may regard themselves as at the furthest remove from Apulians. From the Roman vantage-point they could be lumped together and jointly derided.

A reasonable conclusion would seem to follow. Plautus holds the Greek world up to scorn. The corrupt, self-seeking, and immoral society that appears on the stage would enhance by contrast the Roman sense of superiority. A fundamentally anti-Hellenic strain runs through the plays. Or so, at least, interpretations often propose.[161] That is reductionism and

[154] Plautus, *Bacch.* 742-743: *atque id pollicetur se daturum aurum mihi,/ quod dem scortis quodque in lustris comedim congraecem.*
[155] Plautus, *Bacch.* 812-813; *Truc.* 88.
[156] Plautus, *Merc.* 837-839: *ab Atticis abhorreo,/ nam ubi mores deteriores increbrescunt in dies,/ ubique amici, qui infideles sient nequeas pernoscere.* Segal's view, *Roman Laughter,* 32, 185, n. 56, that the lines were meant to refer to Rome does not persuade.
[157] Plautus, *Stich.* 669-670: *volo eluamus hodie, peregrina omnia/ relinque, Athenas nunc colamus.* Cf. 446-448, quoted above, n. 147.
[158] Plautus, *Asin.* 199; *cetera quae volumus uti Graeca mercamur fide.* Cf. also *Stich.* 226-227: *unctiones Graecas sudatorias/ vendo*—whatever that means; H. Petersmann, *T. Maccius Plautus: Stichus* (Heidelberg, 1973), 131.
[159] Plautus, *Miles,* 641-648.
[160] Plautus, *Casina,* 67-72.
[161] Cf. e.g., P. Grimal, *Le siècle des Scipions* (Paris, 1953), 96-97; Perna, *L'originalità,* 227-231; Jurewicz, in Irmscher and Kumaniecki, *Aus der altert. Arbeit Volkspolens,* 58-72; Flores, *Letteratura latina e ideologia,* 61-67.

simplification. And it overlooks the fact that the prejudicial characterizations of Hellas issue from the mouths of Greeks themselves. The ironic twist is deliberate and pointed. To be sure, one might infer that cognoscenti in Plautus' audience would smile and nod knowingly at such remarks delivered by Roman actors in Latin about Greeks. The attitude suited Roman prejudice. But it need not have been Plautus' attitude. By setting the criticism of Hellenic character in the mouths of Greeks, indeed usually Greek slaves, the playwright did not so much reinforce Roman bias as mock it.

Plautus could also turn the tables. His Greek characters indulged Hellenic prejudice against the "barbarian." Non-Greeks were objects of scorn, rude and uncultured, a foil for the urbane Hellene—even for the servile Hellene. Olympio, a *servus* in the *Casina*, sneers at tasteless foreign fare, another in the *Mostellaria* at inferior foreign workmanship.[162] Elsewhere Greek figures, whether slaves, parasites, or free men, denigrate barbarian foolishness, barbarian law, and barbarian cities.[163] Naevius, if indeed it is he, is referred to as *poeta barbarus*.[164] And Plautus even describes his own renderings of Greek plays as turning them into a "barbaric tongue."[165] Only once are Romans mentioned as such, and then in the most disparaging terms: the *miles* Antamonides of *Poenulus* blasts Hanno for smelling more foully than a bunch of Roman oarsmen.[166] But there is no question that most, if not all, of the references to *barbarus* or *barbari* point to the Romans.[167] In Plautus' comedies the joke is not only on the Greeks but on the Romans as well. The playwright invited spectators to observe with a form of double vision. They witnessed Roman actors in Greek garb deprecating Greeks—and they witnessed Greek characters, played by Romans, deprecating Romans. Plautus himself remains above the fray.

The dual derision manifests itself also in a different form. Greek intellectuals are frequent targets of abuse in the plays. Curculio the parasite delivers the lengthiest tirade. He debunks those cloaked Greeks who wander about with covered heads, their clothes stuffed with books,

---

[162] Plautus, *Casina*, 748; *sed lepide nitideque volo, nil moror barbarico bliteo; Most.* 828: *non enim haec pultiphagus opifex opera fecit barbarus.*

[163] Plautus, *Bacch.* 121-124; *Capt.*, 492, 884; *Poen.* 598.

[164] Plautus, *Miles*, 211. The identification is made by Festus, 32, L—though not necessarily with reference to this passage.

[165] Plautus, *Asin.* 11: *Demophilus scripsit, Maccus vortit barbare*; *Trin.* 19: *Philemo scripsit, Plautus vortit barbare.*

[166] Plautus, *Poen.* 1313-1314: *tum autem plenior/ ali-ulpicique quam Romani remiges.*

[167] That is obvious in allusions to Latin translations; Plautus, *Asin.* 11; *Trin.* 19. Also in the explicit mention of Italian cities; *Capt.* 881-884. See W.M. Lindsay, *The Captivi of Plautus* (London, 1900), 319. Cf. too the aside to the audience by the *advocati* in *Poen.* 597-598.

or stand around talking away, blocking one's path, and offering unwanted opinions.[168] Philosophers or philosophizing gain mention several times in the plays and always in derogatory fashion. Philosophizing is generally equated with idle prattling.[169] Cultivated Greeks plainly serve as the butts of ridicule. Yet there is an inversion here as well. Not just that the strictures are delivered by Greeks. Plautus scores some indirect hits at Roman intellectuals too, especially those who ostentatiously parade their Greek learning. The prologue to the *Menaechmi* distances Plautus from most comic poets who conventionally announce that the settings of their plays are in Athens—thus to make everything seem the more Greek; he will not "Atticize"; the play is Sicilian not Athenian.[170] The barb seems directed at the pretensions of those who put on display their familiarity with Hellenic culture. Ridicule of this form of snobbishness can be read in the numerous occasions in which Plautine characters, including slaves and parasites, lapse into Greek—often in the most unlikely and implausible situations.[171] Plautus thereby not only twits bookish Greeks but makes light of pompous philhellenism among Romans.

The playwright's posture is complex and elusive. He does not propose a campaign of resistance to Greek culture and denunciation of Romans who succumb to it—like some comic Cato. That would be preposterous for a poet deeply imbued with the traditions and techniques of Hellenic drama, and one who made no secret of his adaptation of Greek plays. Nor does Plautus take the role of moral preacher, underscoring the character flaws of the Greeks and warning his countrymen of their baneful influence. Interpretations of that sort miss the comic irony. Greeks render negative verdicts upon fellow-Greeks, a parody of Roman attitudes and a signal that the dramatist does not subscribe to them—or take them seriously. Plautine lampoons embrace Romans too. Depending upon perspective, they can be viewed as rude *barbari* or pretentious intellectuals. All is grist to the comic mill. Plautus is not intent upon

---

[168] Plautus, *Curc.* 288-291: *tum isti Graeci palliati, capite operto qui ambulant,/ qui incedunt suffarcinati cum libris, cum sportulis,/ constant, conferunt sermones inter sese drapetae,/ opstant, opsistunt, incedunt cum suis sententiis.*

[169] Plautus, *Capt.* 284; *Merc.* 147; *Pseud.* 687, 974; *Rudens,* 986.

[170] Plautus, *Men.* 7-12; cf. *Persa,* 394-395.

[171] Plautus, *Bacch.* 1162; *Capt.* 880-882; *Casina,* 728-732; *Most.* 972; *Persa,* 159; *Poen.* 137; *Pseud.* 210-211, 443, 482-488, 653-654, 700-712, 1010; *Stich.* 707; *Trin.* 187, 418-419, 705-706; *Truc.* 558. See Perna, *L'originalità,* 230-235, who also calls attention to *Bacch.* 239-240 and *Men.* 779, which may be relevant. The view of G.B. Shipp, *WS,* 66 (1953), 105-112, that Plautus used Greek to mark servile status or merely for humor, is unconvincing. W.R. Chalmers, in Dorey and Dudley, *Roman Drama,* 39-41, considers the frequent use of Greek terms as evidence for their importation into Latin by Plautus' day—a strained interpretation.

delivering a message, whether moral, political, or philosophical. The dramatist's ear is attuned to public attitudes and sensibilities: to Greek impressions of Romans and Romans' of Greeks, to the heady welcome of Greek culture in Rome and the corresponding uneasiness and resistance to it.[172] Plautus touches the essence of those attitudes and, through the medium of mockery, maintains a safe and sardonic distance.

Contemporaneity permeates the plays of Plautus. The comic dramatist is neither political commentator nor moral reformer. Topicality operates at a different level. Caricature, spoof, and parody punctuate the vicissitudes of public affairs and the foibles of public figures. Plautine wit penetrates the rivalries over military honors, the scramble for triumphs, the private ambitions of conquerors, the lavish ostentation of wealth, the impact upon political society of the spoils of war. The comedies also heighten public awareness of fatuous moralism and futile legalism as manifested in sumptuary laws or attempted curbs on financial abuses.

More important still, Plautus illuminates and elucidates the central cultural experience of his age: the tension created by interaction between the Greek world and Roman sensibilities. The playwright turns a jaundiced eye on Roman manipulation of Hellenic tradition and, conversely, on Hellenic incursions into Roman traditions. Confrontation and interpenetration of the two cultures form the principal motif of the plays. Plautus mocks Greek stereotypes of Romans and Roman misapprehensions of Greeks. He directs audience laughter as much at foolish philhellenes as at suspicious philistines. The comedies reflect attitudes and temperaments, reactions and impressions that commingled in that confused time of cultural permutation. Plautus does not wear his heart on his sleeve. But he exhibits a keen sensitivity to the issues of his time and the dispositions of his contemporaries. The plays address both the implications of those issues and the fatuity of those dispositions. Therein lies their true topicality. They remain our chief document for the cultural convergence of Hellas and Rome.

---

[172] On the sophistication of Plautus' audience, see J.-P. Cèbe, *REL*, 38 (1960), 101-106; Chalmers, *op. cit.*, 121-150; E.W. Handley, *Dioniso*, 46 (1975), 117-132.

CHAPTER FIVE

PHILOSOPHY, RHETORIC, AND ROMAN ANXIETIES

Philosophy and rhetoric were not native to Italian soil. The wellsprings of those disciplines lay in the land of the Greeks. Romans acknowledged the debt, benefited from the seeds that were planted, cultivated and nurtured their growth, and disseminated the fruits. Yet their attitudes toward those realms of knowledge remained ambiguous and problematical for generations. Greek scholars and teachers gained access to Roman households, and Roman intellectuals gained increasing familiarity with the philosophical and rhetorical precepts of Hellas. But the path was far from smooth or untroubled. The same years that marked the gradual assimilation of Hellenic teachings also witnessed periodic expulsion of Hellenic philosophers, orators, and professors, and outbursts against Hellenic intellectual traditions. The absorption of alien culture brought its own strains and tensions. A number of hostile eruptions punctured the process and intensified the paradox. Those very eruptions, however, when closely scrutinized, can provide the best means for understanding the peculiar confrontation of Roman mentality and Greek learning.

In the course of a century, expulsions of intellectuals ceased. Public manifestations of hostility to Hellenism no longer seemed urgent or even advantageous. The cultural scene had undergone transformation. A more mature Roman self-consciousness permitted not only acknowledgment of but accolades for Greek learning. Inadequate testimony prevents retrieval of the process of change. But as select episodes disclose the tensions of the 2nd century, so an official act of the early 1st century documents a marked maturation.

Legend traced a fascinating connection back into the mists of early Roman history. A striking tale linked two celebrated figures and, through them, two separate cultures. Numa Pompilius, the second king of Rome, had been a pupil, so it was widely believed, of that wisest of Greeks, Pythagoras of Samos. As the story had it, Numa was studying philosophy at the feet of Pythagoras in Croton when summoned to become Rome's monarch.[1] An inner logic recommended the tale: Numa,

---

[1] Dion. Hal. 2.59.1; Diod. 8.14; Ovid, *Fasti*, 3.151-154; *Met.* 15.1-8, 15.60-72, 15.479-484.

the gentle ruler who taught Rome the arts of peace, gave her laws, and established her religious institutions, had much in common with the renowned Pythagoras, who counselled abstinence, advocated concord and harmony, promoted religious precepts, and discerned the laws of the universe. The story had inherent appeal and apparent plausibility.

In fact, it was a chronological absurdity. Cicero pointed out that Numa Pompilius, by the reckoning of the chronographers, died 140 years before Pythagoras even reached the shores of Italy. Dionysius of Halicarnassus reiterated the discrepancy of dates and added the argument that Croton itself did not exist in the time of Numa. And Livy cleared away lingering doubts by asserting that, even if the dates fitted, Pythagoras' repute could hardly have reached as far as Sabine country, and language barriers would have precluded communication anyway.[2]

The truth of the tale matters little. What counts is its remarkable tenacity. The fact that Cicero, Dionysius, and Livy take pains to refute it in the later years of the Roman Republic shows that belief was current even then.[3] The chronological argument ought to have sufficed. Yet confidence in the association between Numa and Pythagoras still prevailed in many cities. It was too good to give up. Ovid recounts it as if transparently true and unquestioned. Whatever his personal opinion of the matter, the poet's presentation suggests that his readers' acceptance of the tale could be taken for granted.[4] Even those who recognized the impossibility of the connection searched for ways to rationalize the legend. Some postulated that another Pythagoras, also a philosopher, preceded his more renowned namesake by a century and a half and served as teacher of the Roman king.[5] Others imagined a Spartan Pythagoras, an Olympic victor in the time of Numa, who made a trip to Italy and advised Numa on the governance of Rome.[6] Plutarch, of course, knew full well that the chronological obstacle was insurmountable. Yet he could not quite relinquish the idea of an association between Roman ruler and Greek philosopher. Ancient chronology, he asserts rather lamely, is inconclusive, dependent upon Olympic victor lists compiled long after the event.[7] That line, however, could not be pursued very

---

[2] Cic. *De Rep.* 2.28-29; Dion. Hal. 2.59.1-2; Livy, 1.18.1-3.

[3] Note the forcefulness of Scipio Aemilianus' remarks in Cic. *De Rep.* 2.28: *falsum est enim...id totum, neque solum fictum, sed etiam imperite absurdeque fictum.* To be sure, that dialogue is set in 129 B.C. But belief in the contemporaneity of Numa and Pythagoras appears also in the *De Oratore*, set in 91; *De Orat.* 2.154: *quidam Numam Pompilium, regem nostrum, fuisse Pythagoreum ferunt.* The accounts of Dionysius and Livy clearly imply the need to disprove present misconceptions.

[4] Ovid, *Fasti*, 3.151-154; *Met.* 15.1-8, 15.60-72, 15.479-484; *Pont.* 3.3.41-44.

[5] Dion. Hal. 2.59.4.

[6] Plut. *Numa*, 1.3.

[7] Plut. *Numa*, 1.4.

far. Plutarch falls back on parallels and similarities: Numa and Pythagoras shared an interest in religious institutions; the Pythagoreans placed a premium on silence, Numa gave high honor to the Musa Tacita; Numa's ban on images of the gods corresponded to Pythagorean belief that the supreme deity could not be represented; both sage and ruler discouraged blood sacrifices; Numa's circular temple to Vesta enclosing the sacred fire parallels Pythagorean belief that the universe revolves about a central fire.[8] Never mind that these comparisons are rather far-fetched or erroneous.[9] They reveal the lengths to which Plutarch's sources went in order to maintain some connection between the revered Roman king and the teachings of a Greek philosophical sect.[10]

The origins of the tale remain elusive. But a plausible milieu can be surmised. Aristoxenus of Tarentum, a student of Aristotle but fervid admirer of Pythagoras, composed a biography of the latter in the late 4th or early 3rd century. The writer lavished praise upon Pythagoras and observed, among other things, that distant peoples came to take his advice and hear his words of wisdom, including Lucanians, Peucetians, Messapians—and Romans.[11] Aristoxenus further awarded credit to Pythagoras for instruction of the famed law-givers of southern Italy, Charondas and Zaleucus.[12] It would be a relatively small step to appropriate for Pythagoras the law-giver of Rome as well.[13] Hellenic literary imperialism of this sort has many parallels. The legend of Numa and Pythagoras then would derive from Greek historiography or biography, the Roman figure being but one of many statesmen depicted as protegés of the Samian sage and responsible for establishing institutions and harmonious government in the state of Italy. The story has as chief design enhancement of Pythagoras' repute and that of his sect. Romans embraced the tale rather than invented it.

When did Rome embrace the legend? Involvement with the Greeks of Magna Graecia began in the later 4th century, stepped up with increased intensity during the 3rd century as consequence of the Pyrrhic war. Acquaintance with the area and its traditions brought Pythagoras to Roman attention. Hence, it is often stated, Romans adopted the legend

---

[8] Plut. *Numa*, 8.2-8, 11.1-2. Cf. Clem. Alex. *Strom.* 1.71.

[9] Cf. G. Garbarino, *Roma e la filosofia greca dalle origini alla fine del II secolo a.C.* (Turin, 1973), II, 223.

[10] Cf. Plut. *Numa*, 22.3-4: τοῖς εἰς τὸ αὐτὸ Πυθαγόρᾳ Νομᾶν φιλοτιμουμένοις συνάγειν ἐπὶ τοσαύταις ὁμοιότησιν.

[11] Diog. Laert. 8.14; Porphyry, *Vita Pythag.* 22; Iamblichus, *Vita Pythag.* 241. See S. Mazzarino, *Il pensiero storico classico* (Bari, 1968), II.1, 96-99.

[12] Diog. Laert. 8.16.

[13] So E. Gabba, *Entretiens Fondation Hardt*, 13 (1967), 157-158, 161-163.

with alacrity around the end of the 4th century.[14] That may be premature. Evidence for the conclusion is thin and inadequate. Cicero, in a dialogue set in 129, labels belief in an association between Numa and Pythagoras as an *inveteratus error*.[15] But this hardly brings us back to the late 4th century. The renown of Pythagoras had indeed made itself known to Romans around that time. Report has it that a consultation of Pythian Apollo during the Samnite wars brought back the response that Rome should erect statues to the bravest and to the wisest of Greeks. The senate chose Alcibiades in the first category, Pythagoras in the second, duly commissioning their statues and installing them in the comitium.[16] How seriously to take that story? A trip to Delphi as early as the end of the 4th century or beginning of the 3rd is questionable. Roman connections did not yet reach that far. Erection of the statue, however, need not be doubted; nor is there good reason to question the date.[17] But even if the tale is accepted wholly as given, this speaks only to the reputation of Pythagoras and the impression left upon the Romans in their dealing with Magna Graecia. Numa goes unmentioned here. That connection had yet to be made. A search in the *annales* on Rome's early history failed to turn up evidence to confirm a link between king and philosopher.[18] Aristoxenus may have invented the link around 300, but nothing suggests that Romans were reading learned treatises on Greek philosophers.[19]

A fascination with Pythagoras, however, persisted. The statue in the comitium stood as evidence, causing later Romans to wonder why the

---

[14] E.g., L. Ferrero, *Storia del pitagorismo nel mondo romano* (Turin, 1955), 142-147; Gabba, *Entretiens Fondation Hardt*, 13 (1967), 159-163; Garbarino, *Roma e la filosofia greca*, II, 230-238.

[15] Cic. *De Rep.* 2.29.

[16] Pliny, *NH*, 34.26; Plut. *Numa*, 8.10. See above, Chapter 1, n. 18.

[17] G. Vitucci, *Problemi attuali di scienza e di cultura, AccadLinc*, 473 (1976), 154-157, puts it some time in the first half of the 3rd century, on no compelling grounds.

[18] Cic. *De Rep.* 2.28: *neque vero satis id annalium publicorum auctoritate declaratum videmus.* The statement is not free of ambiguity. Gabba, *Entretiens Fondation Hardt*, 13 (1967), 155-156, takes it to mean that the *annales* reported the tradition but failed to comment on its veracity; so also Garbarino, *Roma e la filosofia greca*, 235, n. 2. That inference is possible, but, in the context, unlikely. Cicero sets the *annales* apart from the sources of the story, which he identifies as oral tradition and popular belief: *saepe enim hoc de maioribus natu audivimus et ita intellegimus vulgo existimari.*

[19] Little can be made of the supposedly "Pythagorean" poem composed by Ap. Claudius Caecus in the late 4th century. That label derived from Cicero who thought that the *carmen* seemed Pythagorean; *Tusc. Disp.* 4.4: *mihi quidem etiam Appii Caeci carmen...Pythagoreum videtur.* His comment may refer more to form than to content; see Garbarino, *Roma e la filosofia greca*, 224-226. The attempt of Ferrero, *Pitagorismo*, 152-174, to interpret Ap. Claudius' whole career and personality in terms of Pythagorean teaching is quite fanciful.

patres rated Pythagoras ahead of Socrates as wisest of Greeks.[20] He evidently possessed a special attraction. The presence of Pythagoras on Italian soil and the spread of his teachings in Italy must hold part of the explanation. It was reported even that Rome had awarded citizenship to the philosopher—a report that Plutarch takes as evidence for the Numa-Pythagoras association.[21] In fact, it contains no such evidence. The tale warrants little credence in itself and, in any case, omits mention of Numa. Just when the affiliation of Pythagoras and Numa entered the Roman tradition remains beyond our grasp. But the appeal of that invention is easily understood. Cicero's brief sketch sums it up neatly enough: Pythagoras' fame as a man preeminent in wisdom took hold among Romans as they gained acquaintance with the traditions of Magna Graecia; and the analogy with Rome's own founding father whose reputation for justice and sagacity excelled all was too hard to resist. The legend of Numa's education at the feet of Pythagoras thus had its genesis.[22] Whether Roman intellectuals discovered the traditions in Aristoxenus' work or conceived it on their own is indeterminable and unnecessary to determine.[23] The effect, in any case, was compelling.[24] The fable perhaps gained circulation in the later years of the 3rd century which witnessed increased Roman acquaintance with matters Hellenic.[25] Its force in the early 2nd century can be documented unambiguously.

----

[20] Pliny, *NH*, 34.26. A. Alföldi, *Early Rome and the Latins* (Ann Arbor, 1963), 346, suggests that Rome curried the favor of Italian Greeks in the Samnite wars by paying homage to Pythagoras. That, however, ignores the other evidence on Pythagoras' appeal for the Romans, unconnected to the Samnite context. Cf. Ferrero, *Pitagorismo*, 137-141; H.D. Jocelyn, *BRL*, 59 (1977), 324, 329.

[21] Plut. *Numa*, 8.9. The story is ascribed to Epicharmus, the 5th century Sicilian comic poet, a highly questionable ascription, perhaps based on nothing more than the tradition that Epicharmus was a pupil of Pythagoras; Diog. Laert. 8.78; cf. Ferrero, *Pitagorismo*, 138.

[22] Cic. *Tusc. Disp.* 4.2-3: *erat enim illis paene in conspectu praestanti sapientiae nobilitate Pythagoras...nam cum Pythagorae disciplinam et instituta cognoscerent regisque eius aequitatem et sapientiam a maioribus suis accepissent...eum, qui sapientia excelleret, Pythagorae auditorem crediderunt fuisse.*

[23] The theory of Gabba, *Entretiens Fondation Hardt*, 13 (1967), 163, that Timaeus had corrected Aristoxenus' chronology and exploded the tale of a Numa-Pythagoras connection is purely speculative. If he did do so, the refutation obviously had no impact upon the Romans who held firmly to the connection.

[24] The noble house of the Aemilii traced their ancestry back to Mamercus, son of Numa, a name supposedly adopted in imitation of a like-named son of Pythagoras; Plut. *Numa*, 8.9-10; *Aem. Paul.* 2.1; Festus, 22, Lindsay. Cf. Gabba, *Entretiens Fondation Hardt*, 13 (1967), 159-161.

[25] One story even had Cato seek instruction from the Pythagorean Nearchus at Tarentum in 209; Cic. *De Sen.* 41; Plut. *Cato*, 2.3. But the tale may be a much later invention; cf. A.E. Astin, *Cato the Censor* (Oxford, 1978), 8, n. 15; 160, n. 7. *Contra*: A. Mele, *AION*, 3 (1981), 69-77.

A bizarre and intriguing event in 181 provides the evidence. Its peculiar, indeed unique, character arrests attention. And it demands more careful scrutiny than has hitherto been accorded. The *Annales* of L. Cassius Hemina, composed within a generation of the event, provide the earliest narrative. Excavation at the estate of a Roman *scriba* on the Janiculum turned up the coffin of Numa Pompilius. And in it were discovered ancient books containing the philosophical doctrines of the Pythagoreans. According to the *Commentarii* of L. Calpurnius Piso, cos. 133, the chest disclosed seven volumes of pontifical law and a like number of Pythagorean philosophy. Variations occcur in subsequent versions, but broad agreement prevails on the essentials of the tale. Livy's account, drawing on Valerius Antias, but not uncritically, transmits the fullest story. The *scriba*, in his narrative, uncovered two stone chests, each inscribed in Greek and Latin. The lettering identified one as the coffin of Numa Pompilius, the other as container of his writings. The first, when opened, revealed nothing, evidently the result of total decomposition over the years. The second produced two sets of writing, works on pontifical law in Latin, and on philosophy in Greek (the latter characterized as Pythagorean by Valerius Antias). The owner of the property read through the material, then circulated it to friends and other interested parties. At some point, the matter came to the attention of Q. Petilius, urban praetor in 181. Petilius found the books destructive of Roman religion and announced an intention to burn them. He provided an opportunity for their discoverer to inquire of his rights to the documents. Appeal went to the tribunes who turned the question over to the senate. When Petilius offered to swear an oath that the books ought not to be read or saved, the *patres* decreed their burning. Compensation was offered to the man who had uncovered them, but he declined. In public display in the comitium the *libri* were consigned to the flames.[26]

The impact must have been stunning. How to explain it? Precedents do not help. One may point to government action in 213 when addiction to alien rites had allegedly reached mass proportions, prompting a senatorial decree and praetorian edict which ordered confiscation of all writings on prayers, prophecies, and sacrifice.[27] That, however, was a wartime measure, conceived in an emergency, and executed hastily. No wartime fear motivated matters in 181, and the episode gives every evidence of advance planning. It needs examination in its own terms and context.

---

[26] Livy, 40.29.2-14. The works of Hemina, Piso, and some later writings are cited by Pliny, *NH*, 13.84-88. See also Val. Max. 1.1.12; Plut. *Numa*, 22.2-5; *Vir. Ill.* 3.2; Festus, 178, Lindsay; Lactantius, *Div. Inst.* 1.22.5-6; Augustine, *CD*, 7.34.

[27] Livy, 25.1.6-12.

Near unanimity prevails in the scholarship on this subject. The "Pythagorean" writings of Numa Pompilius have been taken seriously by moderns. That is, although obviously concocted for the occasion, the books had a serious purpose: a Pythagorean movement to reform and rationalize Roman religion, providing it with a philosophical basis, perhaps an injection of Euhemerism and a naturalistic interpretation of divine phenomena. Variations on this thesis appear in the literature. The Pythagoreans, it has been argued, went underground as a result of attacks on the Bacchanalian cult. Fearful of persecution themselves, they resorted to subterfuge in order to authenticate their beliefs by association with Numa and to recast Roman religious concepts by reference to Greek philosophy. Whatever the details, a general consensus holds on the essentials: virtually all treatments see a genuine effort to bring traditional religion into line with philosophic precepts, an effort thwarted by conservative fears in Rome. Government action upset the attempt, burned the writings, and halted the movement.[28]

The interpretation has gone unchallenged. Yet it is surely preposterous. Can one really imagine that Pythagorean devotees, whether from fear of persecution or zeal for proselytizing, expected to remodel traditional religion in accordance with their own teachings? Could they hope to take in Roman authorities by a transparent hoax, dazzle them by the reputation of Numa, and induce them to graft Pythagorean precepts upon ancestral practices? The idea is absurd on the face of it, and ought to have been impugned long ago.

A clue lurks in the tradition which opens the way to a different solution. Livy gives the name of the clerk on whose property the two stone

---

[28] The most elaborate treatment by A. Delatte, *BullAcadRoyBelg*, 22 (1936), 19-40, who provides a speculative reconstruction of the books' contents. For Delatte, the Pythagoreans endeavored to transform Roman religion through the doctrines of Euhemerism and naturalistic interpretations. K. Latte, *Römische Religionsgeschichte* (Munich, 1960), 269-270, suggests metempsychosis or the introduction of bloodless sacrifices. Others are more cautious about specifics but concur in seeing a genuine Pythagorean movement behind the episode; e.g., J. Gagé, *Apollon romain* (Paris, 1955), 328-334; Ferrero, *Pitagorismo*, 231-235; Mazzarino, *Il pensiero*, 515-516, n. 393; K.R. Prowse, *Greece and Rome*, 11 (1964), 36-42; Garbarino, *Roma e la filosofia greca*, 244-256. K. Rosen, *Chiron*, 15 (1985), 77, is properly skeptical. Alternative hypotheses have occasionally surfaced, but none that deserves serious attention. G. Dumézil, *Archaic Roman Religion* (Chicago, 1970), II, 521-525, describes the whole affair as the private scheme of an "overingenious scribe." T. Frank, *CQ*, 21 (1927), 132, pins the blame on a Greek refugee from Tarentum who brought his Pythagorean books with him and hastily buried them when the senate conducted its Bacchanalian investigation, hoping to be spared by shielding the books with Numa's reputation. For F. Della Corte, *Maia*, 26 (1974), 3-20, the affair belongs to a broader tradition associating Numa with wizardry and black magic. The analysis of E. Peruzzi, *Origini di Roma* (Bologna, 1973), 123-143, actually accepts the authenticity of the writings as derived from Numa's time!

chests were discovered as L. Petilius. That scribe, so the historian continues, later turned over the books, upon request, to the urban praetor
Q. Petilius with whom he had a personal connection: Q. Petilius, during
his quaestorship, had enrolled him into the guild of public clerks.[29] The
information is almost certainly erroneous. The earliest source on the
episode, the mid 2nd century annalist L. Cassius Hemina, reports the
name of the *scriba* as Cn. Terentius. And the same appears in the work
of the assiduous scholar Varro.[30] We can go further. The root of Livy's
error is detectable. The version on which he drew, whether at first or
second hand, quite probably stated that the buried chests were found *in
agro scribae Petilii*. It would be reasonable enough to translate "in the land
of the clerk Petilius"—but perhaps more accurate to render it "in the
land of a clerk of Petilius." This eliminates the anomaly of *scriba* and
praetor with the same name and confirms the testimony of our most
reliable authors, Cassius Hemina and Varro.[31] More important, it
verifies the connection between *scriba* and praetor that had held when the
latter was quaestor. The notion that Terentius endeavored to propagate
Pythagoreanism, an endeavor then exposed and squelched by Q.
Petilius, becomes quite untenable. The two worked hand in hand.

The events that brought the "writings of Numa" to light and promptly extinguished them reinforce that conclusion. The clerk, or his
laborers, dug them up. The books were then distributed to friends and
steps taken to spread the word of their contents. Q. Petilius intervened
at the proper moment, when the existence of the works had become
public knowledge.[32] His acquisition of them from his own *scriba* and

---

[29] Livy, 40.29.3, 40.29.9: *Q. Petilius praetor urbanus studiosus legendi libros eos a L. Petilio
sumpsit; et erat familiaris usus, quod scribam eum quaestor Q. Petilius in decuriam legerat.* Valerius
Maximus, 1.1.12, plainly drawing on Livy or on Livy's source, also gives the name as
L. Petilius. Lactantius, *Div. Inst.* 1.22.5, has *Petilius*.

[30] Hemina is cited by Pliny, *NH*, 13.84. The reference to Varro comes from
Augustine, *CD*, 7.34. The clerk is also identified as Terentius in Festus, 178, Lindsay;
cf. *Vir. Ill.* 3.2.

[31] See Livy, 40.29.3: *in agro L. Petilii scribae sub Ianiculo*; Lactantius, *Div. Inst.* 1.22.5:
in agro scribae Petili sub Ianiculo. The point is acutely made by L. Herrmann, *Latomus*, 5
(1946), 87-90. In his view, Livy arbitrarily added the *praenomen* Lucius. More probably,
he found it in a late annalistic source who bears responsibility for the error; F. Münzer,
RE, 19.1, "Petillius", n. 11, 1151. Herrmann, unfortunately, sets aside the evidence of
Hemina and Varro, preferring the manuscript tradition of *Vir. Ill.* 3.2, which gives *a
Tarentino quodam* instead of *a Terentio quodam*, and goes on to identify the Tarentine as the
poet Ennius who engineered the entire episode, a wholly conjectural and improbable
idea. That conclusion was adumbrated, though in much more circumspect fashion, by
Gagé, *Apollon romain*, 333. Peruzzi, *Origini di Roma*, II, 114-115, seeks to reconcile the
traditions by making both Cn. Terentius and L. Petilius *scribae* and having the one as
tenant, the other as proprietor of the land in question!

[32] Livy, 40.29.9: *primo ab amicis qui in re praesenti fuerunt libri lecti: mox pluribus legentibus
cum volgarentur, Q. Petilius praetor urbanus studiosus libros eos a L. Petilio sumpsit.*

beneficiary can hardly be coincidental. It was prearranged.[33] Subsequent developments bear out that inference. Petilius put on the proper posture of legality. He offered Terentius the option of seeking redress for his lost property through appropriate channels. The *scriba* magnanimously declined.[34] It is difficult to evade the conclusion that all had been orchestrated in advance. The principals took pains to assure propriety. And the outcome was foreordained. The tribunes deferred to the senate, and the senate to the praetor. No dissenting voice was heard. Even the clerk, in effect, endorsed the verdict by foregoing compensation. Q. Petilius' judgment held without argument, an impressive show of unanimity. The books, it seems, were ''discovered'' precisely in order to be burned.

What was the purpose of this charade? One avenue of approach suggests itself readily. Perhaps Romans resisted the expropriation of Numa Pompilius by the Pythagoreans. The episode of 181, it might be surmised, strove to disassociate the Roman ruler from Hellenic traditions: Numa's inherent wisdom and justice had no need of Greek philosophy; Rome's legal and religious institutions grew out of native soil. That is certainly the line taken by later writers on the subject. Cicero makes the point with emphasis. Chronological research decisively detached Numa from Pythagoras, with salutary results: it was now clear that the Roman ruler was the greater man, having learned the skill of fashioning a state nearly two centuries before the Greeks ever experienced its birth; the Romans owed their intellectual maturation to native virtues, not to alien imports.[35] The same national pride swelled in Livy who took a position identical to that of Cicero: release of Numa from the Pythagorean legend allows the deduction that his excellent character derived not from foreign teachings but from the stern discipline of the ancient Sabines, a people unsurpassed in integrity.[36] By the late Republic, as is obvious, Romans claimed Numa's qualities as indigenous to Italy and independent of Hellas. It is tempting to see the affair of 181 as an early step in the nationalizing of Numa.

---

[33] Augustine, *CD*, 7.34, even has Terentius bring the books directly to Q. Petilius, an obvious foreshortening of events.

[34] Livy, 40.29.10-13. Other sources on the subject unfortunately omitted these details. Plutarch's variant version, *Numa*, 22.4-5, even has the chests dislodged and exposed by torrential rains, leaving all human agency out of account.

[35] Cic. *De Orat.* 2.154: *quo etiam maior vir habendus est, quoniam illam sapientiam constituendae civitatis duobus prope saeculis ante cognovit, quam eam Graeci natam esse senserunt; De Rep.* 2.29: *non esse nos transmarinis nec importatis artibus eruditos, sed genuinis domesticisque virtutibus.*

[36] Livy, 1.18.4: *suopte igitur ingenio temperatum animum virtutibus fuisse opinor magis instructumque non tam peregrinis artibus quam disciplina tetrica ac tristi veterum Sabinorum, quo genere nullum quondam incorruptius fuit.*

The idea seems sound in principle. But it is erroneous in fact. The events of 181 take the affiliation between Numa and Pythagoras for granted. Far from throwing it into question, they make no sense except on the assumption of that interrelationship. The episode itself constitutes our best evidence for public confidence in the tradition by the early 2nd century. Nothing else can explain the unearthing of Greek philosophic texts juxtaposed with Latin volumes on pontifical law, Numa's specialty. The conjunction of king and sage was uncontested at the time—indeed, so far as we can tell, for some time thereafter. Cassius Hemina, writing around the middle of the 2nd century, evidently accepted it. The annalist Piso, consul in 133, certainly did.[37] And a generation later, Valerius Antias' history reaffirmed faith in the association by repeating the tale of the two sets of books.[38] The tradition had compelling authority. We cannot be sure that it received challenge before the age of Varro and Cicero.[39] The vigor of Cicero's refutation suggests that the tale commanded wide belief even at that time. Popular conceptions died hard. Ovid repeats the legend as if no chronological difficulties ever stood in the way. And Plutarch is reluctant to give it up still another century later.[40]

---

[37] Cassius Hemina, strictly speaking, is quoted by Pliny only for the philosophical *libri*, found in the same coffin with Numa's body; *NH*, 13.84-86; cf. Garbarino, *Roma e la filosofia greca*, II, 248-249. But Hemina plainly associates Numa with Pythagorean philosophical writings: the books were "his books," *libros eius*. Piso explicitly records both the volumes on pontifical law and the Pythagorean treatises; Pliny, *NH*, 13.87. Rosen's effort, *Chiron*, 15 (1985), 66-78, to see Piso's work as revising Hemina and unjustifiably inserting Pythagoreanism into the story is strained and unconvincing. On the much maligned Piso in general, see the judicious treatment by E. Rawson, *Latomus*, 35 (1976), 702-713.

[38] Pliny, *NH*, 13.87; Livy, 40.29.7-8; Plut. *Numa*, 22.4. Pliny cites C. Sempronius Tuditanus, cos. 129, as speaking of twelve volumes of "Numa's decrees." It does not follow, however, that Tuditanus omitted any mention of the philosophic texts, let alone that he denied a connection between Numa and Pythagoras; as Garbarino, *Roma e la filosofia greca*, II, 248-249. Plutarch, *Numa*, 1.1-2, refers to a certain "Clodius" (Κλώδιός τις), whose work on chronology denied the authenticity of any documents purporting to date earlier than the sack of the city in 390, thus implicitly impugning the books uncovered in 181 and the link between Pythagoras and Numa. But Clodius' date and identity remain uncertain. General scholarly consensus sees a revision of the chronology and a refutation of the Numa-Pythagoras bond occurring in the later 2nd century; see Ferrero, *Pitagorismo*, 145; Mazzarino, *Il pensiero*, II.1, 521-522, n. 431; Garbarino, *op. cit.*, II, 232-233, 242-243. If so, the revision did not impress itself upon Valerius Antias.

[39] It is not clear that Varro's account even mentioned philosophical books. The citations of his work refer only to Numa's religious and institutional writings; Pliny, *NH*, 13.87; Augustine, *CD*, 7.34. Livy, 40.29.7, records the two sets of books: *septem Latini de iure pontificum erant, septem Graeci de disciplina sapientiae quae illius aetatis esse potuit*. The same in Val. Max. 1.1.12; Lactantius, *Div. Inst.* 1.22.5. But Livy implicitly questions whether these were Pythagorean texts, and ascribes that idea to Valerius Antias who follows erroneous opinion linking Numa to Pythagoras; 40.29.8. Plutarch knows Antias'

One cannot avoid a strange and most surprising conclusion. The authorities in 181 were prepared to throw out the baby with the bathwater. Since Numa and Pythagoras were indissoluble, the destruction of the books carried an implicit censure of the king.[41] Of course, the Romans did not repudiate Numa Pompilius. His reputation remained as high after as before. But the machinations of 181 entailed a public disapproval of Hellenic elements that may have influenced the religious and institutional changes associated with the king. The ruling class once again asserted its cultural independence.

Like the affair of the Bacchanalians, this episode must be seen as posture and demonstration, not a genuine effort to root out evil. Pronouncements by the authorities were studiously vague and indefinite. Q. Petilius asserted that many of the writings tended to erode and undermine traditional religion.[42] Numa's treatise supposedly dealt with the origins of Roman religious institutions. In so far as they owed their origins to philosophic precepts and Hellenic influence, Roman officials declared the need for suppression.[43] But they rigorously avoided specifics. No individual institutions are singled out as infected by Hellenism or ripe for reform. Indeed, Roman leaders took steps to avoid any tampering with institutions. The books were to be burned unread.[44] The point was not to purge Roman religion of Hellenic elements—a task that would be chaotically disruptive and ultimately quite impossible. It was disavowal in principle, not a call to action. St. Augustine read the situation clearly: the Romans would not condemn the religion of their forefathers, nor openly castigate Numa. Destruction of the books made their point: since maintenance of traditional religion was essential, it was

---

version, but accepts only the pontifical volumes of Numa; Plut. *Numa*, 22.2-4; cf. *Vir. Ill.* 3.2. The hesitation of Livy and Plutarch, and probably of Varro, is readily explicable, stemming no doubt from their awareness of the chronological gap that demolishes any connection between Numa and Pythagoras.

[40] See above pp. 159-160.

[41] It is noteworthy that Valerius Maximus, 1.1.12, seeks to escape that conclusion by having the Latin books preserved while the Greek writings were burned. A somewhat similar view in Lactantius, *Div. Inst.* 1.22.5-6. It is a transparent effort to evade an unpalatable fact.

[42] Livy, 40.29.11: *pleraque dissolvendarum religionum esse*; Val. Max. 1.1.12: *ad solvendam religionem pertinere existimabantur*; Lactantius, *Div. Inst.* 1.22.5: *religionem non eas modo quas ipse instituerat, sed omnes praeterea dissoluit.*

[43] Augustine, *CD*, 7.34: *sacrorum institutorum scriptae erant causae...cur quidque in sacris fuerit institutum; Vir. Ill.* 3.2: *quia leves quasdam sacrorum causas continebant, ex auctoritate patrum cremati sunt.* Cassius Hemina gives as reason for burning the mere fact that the books were philosophical; Pliny, *NH*, 13.86.

[44] Plut. *Numa*, 22.5: μὴ δοκεῖν αὐτῷ θεμιστὸν εἶναι λέγων μηδὲ ὅσιον ἔκπυστα πολλοῖς τὰ γεγραμμένα γενέσθαι; Livy, 40.29.12: *praetor se iusiurandum dare paratum esse aiebat, libros eos legi servarique non oportere.*

preferable that men not know its particular defects rather than cause civic upheaval in attempting to correct them.[45]

Why was the whole affair engineered? To imagine that a Pythagorean movement genuinely threatened Roman orthodoxy or that the establishment feared such a movement borders on absurdity. The creed can hardly have attracted devotees in menacing numbers. Pythagoras enjoyed great repute as a sage—but surely not because his treatises were read and studied in Rome. Nothing in our evidence suggests that Pythagoreans foisted their doctrines upon Roman religious practices or had the slightest intention of doing so. It has been held that the affair represents another conservative thrust against philhellenic factions in Rome. The name of the urban praetor who played a central role in the events provides a tempting hint: Q. Petilius, identical with or related to one of the Petilii who as allies of Cato the Elder levelled charges against the Scipios in 187.[46] That Cato had a hand in it may well be true. But interpretations of the episode as a contest between philhellenic and antihellenic forces misses the mark. As in the case of the Bacchanalian affair, no friction or dissent within the ruling class surfaces anywhere in the testimony. Unanimity rather than divisiveness prevails. The event was well orchestrated to display the solid front of the nobility.

A different approach offers better prospects. The early years of the second century witnessed increasing Roman familiarity with Greek culture and increasing fascination for it. The intermingling of Hellenic and Roman traditions, indeed the artificial grafting of the one upon the other, commanded ingenuity and earned popularity. A paradoxical—or perhaps not so paradoxical—consequence manifested itself. As Roman individuals embraced Hellenic intellectual imports in ever greater numbers, the community felt a correspondingly greater need to define itself as distinct from those imports. The Numa-Pythagoras legend had

---

[45] Augustine, *CD*, 7.34: *senatus autem cum religiones formidaret damnare maiorum et ideo Numae adsentiri cogeretur, illos tamen libros tam perniciosos esse iudicavit, ut...iuberet...flammis aboleri nefanda monumenta ut, quia iam necesse esse existimabant sacra illa facere, tolerabilius erraretur causis eorum ignoratis quam cognitis civitas turbaretur.*

[46] The connection is often noted. See, e.g., Ferrero, *Pitagorismo*, 232-233; Garbarino, *Roma e la filosofia greca*, II, 256. Cf. Vitucci, *Problemi attuali di scienza e di cultura, AccadLinc*, 473 (1976), 158-160. The fanciful reconstruction of Della Corte, *Maia*, 26 (1974), 16-20, excogitates an economic struggle between pastoralists headed by Cato and agricultural reformers who promoted the image of Numa as an advocate of land distribution. A. Grilli, in M. Sordi, *Politica e religione nel primo scontro tra Roma e l'Oriente* (Milan, 1982), 186-197, sees the affair as engineered by anti-Scipionic political forces and molded by a historiographic tradition beginning with Cassius Hemina ca. 146—when Scipio Aemilianus was the chief focus of attention. For Rosen, *Chiron*, 15 (1985), 83-90, the conservative aristocracy sought to checkmate what it took to be a political move by M. Fulvius Nobilior—an ingenious reconstruction but altogether speculative.

taken hold, flattering at first no doubt, but a growing embarrassment. It implied that some of Rome's most venerable and hallowed institutions owed their origins to Greek inspiration. To challenge the legend would be difficult if not pointless; it was too firmly fixed in popular conception. The establishment took a different path: rather than discredit the tradition, they exploited it to their own purposes. The writings of Numa, with their Greek philosophic counterparts, hitherto a mere phantom, would miraculously materialize, come to public view—and then be eliminated for good. Official scrutiny of the "documents" pronounced them unfit for public consumption: they would undermine religious belief and practice. That pronouncement seems baffling at first glance, but meaningful upon reflection. It intimates that the *mos maiorum* had outgrown its origins, that Roman religious tradition had separated itself from Hellenic underpinnings. To confront the Greek component was to expose its estrangement. Rome's spokespersons declared that the archaic writings no longer suited the modern circumstances, indeed could be destructive of them. Best to eradicate material that recalled a time of cultural dependence, prior to maturation of the national character. It was a form of exorcism. Burning of the books represents renunciation not of Numa but of Numa's Hellenism. The event signified avowal of native values inherent in the community.

Public display stood at the heart of this episode. It was a collective cultural statement. As such, it calls to mind a comparable and near contemporary statement. In the year prior to the Numa-Pythagoras affair, the tribune C. Orchius, acting on a senatorial decree, sponsored a law before the assembly of the people. The *populus* approved the bill, the *lex Orchia*, the first sumptuary law to impose restrictions on the lavishness of the dinner table.[47] The measure, in fact, limited the number of guests that could legitimately be invited—and did so with excessive verbiage.[48] On any sober reckoning, the issue is peripheral and the tangible accomplishment meager. It would not be easy to enforce such a measure and little likelihood that it was enforced. Why then a solemn decree of the senate, advocacy by a tribune, and public approval by the assembly? The bill hardly set a genuine levelling process in motion. It imposed no drastic limitation on the wealthy noble who might outstrip his peers, nor did it provide much protection for the less affluent aristocrat. It would be unlikely to arrest any supposed moral decline, and it would have little

[47] Macrob. *Sat.* 3.17.2: *prima autem omnium de cenis lex ad populum Orchia pervenit.*
[48] Macrob. *Sat.* 3.17.2: *cuius verba quia sunt prolixa praetereo, summa autem eius praescribebat numerum convivarum.*

impact on the style and stability of the political class.[49] Extended discussion of the *leges sumptuariae* would here be out of place. But it would not be rash to suppose that posture, once again, may be more important than substance. The eastern wars had brought the luxury goods of the Greek world into Rome, a fact noted with dismay by moralists who saw the seeds of internal decay in the import of foreign opulence.[50] Sumptuary laws, it can be suggested, represented, in part at least, a symbolic resistance to Hellenic influence in the public character.[51]

Twenty years elapsed before the next recorded instance of Roman action against the intake of Hellenism. And it may not be wholly coincidental that the same year also witnessed the next known example of a *lex sumptuaria*. The senate in 161 discussed a motion by the praetor M. Pomponius regarding philosophers and rhetors and then passed a decree authorizing Pomponius to rid the city of those professors.[52] Satisfactory explanation for that deed has eluded scholarship. An influx of academics from the Greek world after the close of the Third Macedonian War in 167 may have made them conspicuous.[53] But why expel them from the city? That the philosophers and rhetors engaged in duplicitous reasoning and rhetorical trickery that prompted their removal is an unverifiable and unnecessary hypothesis.[54] To be sure, Cato, in his gruff moods, railed against philosophers and mocked rhetors: students of Isocrates' school took so long to complete their training that they were fit only to declaim in Hades.[55] The fact remains, however, that Cato's own

---

[49] For these interpretations of the *leges sumptuariae*, see D. Daube, *Aspects of Roman Law* (Edinburgh, 1969), 117-128; I. Sauerwein, *Die Leges Sumptuariae als römische Massnahme gegen den Sittenverfall* (Berlin, 1970), *passim*, and on the *lex Orchia*, 70-76; G. Clemente, in *Società romana e produzione schiavistica* (1981), III, 1-14, 301-304. For W.V. Harris, *War and Imperialism in Republican Rome, 327-70 B.C.* (Oxford, 1979), 89, the laws endeavored to curb illicit influences in elections.

[50] Livy, 39.6.7-9; Pliny, *NH*, 34.14—from Calpurnius Piso; cf. Val. Max. 9.1.3.

[51] Cf. M. Bonamente, *Tra Grecia e Roma* (1980), 67-91. Efforts to repeal or amend the *lex Orchia* followed at some time thereafter, with Cato apparently opposed to the repeal. But fragments of his speech or speeches on the subject are too sketchy and ambiguous to reveal a clear position; *ORF*, Cato, fr. 139-146. Discussion in P. Fraccaro, *Opuscula* (Pavia, 1956), I, 233-237; H.H. Scullard, *Roman Politics, 220-150 B.C.*[2] (Oxford, 1973), 265-266; M.T.S. Cugusi, *M. Porci Catonis Orationum Reliquiae* (Turin, 1982), 348-352. Cf. also another measure in 182 restricting expenditure on games sponsored by Roman officials; Livy, 40.44.12.

[52] Suetonius quotes the *senatus consultum; Rhet.* 1.2: *ut M. Pomponius praetor animadverteret curaretque, ut si ei e re publica fideque sua videretur, uti Romae ne essent.* The same in Gellius, 15.11.1, who wrongly assumes that these are Latin philosophers and rhetors. Practitioners of those disciplines in the early 2nd century were all Greek. Cf. Garbarino, *Roma e la filosofia greca*, 370.

[53] Cf. Polyb. 31.24.6-7; Plut. *Aem. Paul.* 6.4-5, 33.3.

[54] The idea is suggested by G. Kennedy, *The Art of Rhetoric in the Roman World, 300 B.C.-A.D. 300* (Princeton, 1972), 53-54. Similarly, Astin, *Cato the Censor*, 154.

[55] Plut. *Cato*, 23.1-3.

household included a Greek tutor.[56] And the celebrated philologist Crates, envoy of the Pergamene court, who broke a leg while in Rome, taught his subject undisturbed during the period of his convalescence, probably in the early 160s.[57] Catonian conservatism does not suffice as explanation for the move against Greek professors in 161.[58] It strains credulity to imagine them as a threat to subvert traditional teaching for Roman youth.

A more promising avenue lies again in comparison with sumptuary measures. A *senatus consultum* issued from the *patres* in the very year of 161, setting limits upon expenditures by *principes* upon dinners for entertainment at the Megalensian games. The measure specified 120 asses per meal, exclusive of vegetables, bread, and wine, 100 pounds weight of silverware, and native wine only.[59] A law of the assembly followed, sponsored by the consul himself, C. Fannius Strabo. It provided even greater specificity—and considerable detail. Officials could spend no more than 100 asses a day at the Ludi Romani, the Ludi Plebei, and the Saturnalia, 30 asses on another ten days a month, and only 10 on all remaining days.[60] Such were the restraints on public functions. In the private sphere, the *lex Fannia* prohibited entertainment of more than three persons outside the family or more than five on the *nundinae*. Maximum expenditures were spelled out for daily purchases, and limits also on annual outlays for particular items like smoked meat and green vegetables.[61] The measure even went so far as to ban poultry dishes, beyond a single hen per meal—and then only if it had not been artificially fattened.[62]

The detailed prescriptions are impressive in their specificity, but to what end? Fragments of a speech in support of the *lex Fannia* stress the heedless luxury and irresponsibility of Roman youth, a moral failure to be corrected by restraint upon prodigality.[63] Public pronouncements undoubtedly did take this line. It put the best face upon sumptuary legislation: restraint by the wealthy and powerful upon their own excesses in order to promote communal welfare. The *nobiles* came out in force,

---

[56] Plut. *Cato*, 20.3.

[57] Suet. *Gramm.* 2; cf. F. Della Corte, *RivFilol*, 12 (1934), 388-389; Garbarino, *Roma e la filosofia greca*, 356-362.

[58] As Garbarino, *Roma e la filosofia greca*, 370-372.

[59] Gellius, 2.24.2.

[60] Gellius, 2.24.3-6; Macrob. *Sat.* 3.17.5.

[61] Athenaeus, 6.274c.

[62] Pliny, *NH*, 10.139.

[63] Macrob. *Sat.* 3.13.13, 3.16.14-16. The speech is assigned to C. Titius, a contemporary of Lucilius, and thus probably not an advocate of the *lex Fannia* at the time of its passage. Cf. Cic. *Brutus*, 167. He may have delivered the oration to thwart a later attempt at repeal of the measure. The moral aspects and motives are stressed by Sauerwein, *Die Leges Sumptuariae*, 76-89.

elected officials and others, mobilizing support in numbers and strength to show public solidarity on the measure.[64] Yet one can hardly conclude that the morals of the community would be reformed or improved by restricting expenses on green vegetables or limiting the numbers to be invited to the family table. It is no more plausible to suppose that these prescriptions applied a brake to the political usages of wealth in assembling *clientelae*.[65] Enforcement of the various known clauses—we do not even know them all—would present endless difficulties. It might be possible to police expenditures by officials on the public games, but hardly to check on the annual costs of smoked meat for the household, let alone on fattened chickens at dinner. The conclusion imposes itself that Fannius' law was more important for the message than for the content. A decree of the senate laid the groundwork, the consul himself introduced the bill, large numbers turned out to endorse it, and the popular assembly passed it into law. The whole event represented an assertion by the community's leadership that they could control and contain the influence of eastern opulence on the national character.[66]

A comparable assertion is implicit in the eviction of philosophers and rhetors in that same year. The ban was surely unenforceable at the level of the private household, and understood to be so from the start. Rhetorical schools advertising their wares and organized philosophical instruction would certainly suffer. But there can have been few established educational structures in the subjects of philosophy and rhetoric. What counted was the public perception. The years after the conclusion of the Third Macedonian War witnessed the migration or importation of Greek professors to Italy in noticeable numbers. A throng of teachers and pedagogues followed the triumphal train of Aemilius Paullus, brought as captives after the defeat of Macedon.[67] Education of Roman youth was almost entirely in the hands of Greek grammarians, intellectuals, and trainers.[68] Polybius himself offered to oversee the political tuition of Scipio Aemilianus, resigning all other matters of learning to the crowd of academics streaming into Rome from Greece.[69] The relegation of rhetors and philosophers in 161 may have had few practical conse-

---

[64] Macrob. 3.17.4: *lex Fannia...ingenti omnium ordinum consensu pervenit ad populum, neque eam praetores aut tribuni ut plerasque alias, sed ex omnium bonorum consilio et sententia ipsi consules pertulerunt.*

[65] As Clemente, in *Società romana e produzione schiavistica*, III, 8-9.

[66] Bonamente, *Tra Grecia e Roma* (1980), 75-77, 81-83, recognizes the implications but sees sumptuary legislation as almost exclusively the province of Cato and the Catonians.

[67] Plut. *Aem. Paul.* 33.3: διδασκάλων καὶ παιδαγωγῶν δεδακρυμένων ὄχλος.

[68] Plut. *Aem. Paul.* 6.4-5; Cic. *De Orat.* 1.14; cf. Pliny, *NH*, 35.135.

[69] Polyb. 31.24.6-7: πολὺ γὰρ δή τι φῦλον ἀπὸ τῆς Ἑλλάδος ἐπιρρέον ὁρῶ κατὰ τὸ παρὸν τῶν τοιούτων ἀνθρώπων.

quences. One will hardly imagine a thorough sweep through the city to gather up every Greek with academic pretensions in those disciplines. And indeed we know that learned men from Hellas continued to find a place in Rome. The measure, however, carried symbolic significance. Rome's *principes* had declared their determination to guard the nation's values and to exercise surveillance over intellectual infiltration from abroad.

A pattern is discernible. The cultural strains of the late 160s recall those of two decades earlier. Rome's successful wars in the Greek East had culminated in 188, bringing in their wake heightened exposure to Hellenic attitudes, art, and behavior. By the end of the decade, the establishment felt a need to reaffirm Roman cultural autonomy. "Discovery" of Numa's religious writings and their Pythagorean counterparts, followed immediately by their conspicuous destruction, advanced that purpose. Similarly, Rome's triumph in the war on Perseus in 168 occasioned a stream of learned migrants to Italy, intensifying the Hellenization of Roman education. Expulsion of the philosophers and rhetors in 161 may have had little tangible effect, but it reasserted confidence in native cultural traditions. Two sumptuary laws, the *lex Orchia* and the *lex Fannia*, respectively close in timing to those events, illuminate and reinforce them. A symbolic resistance to Greek morals and manners also strengthened trust in the virtues of the national character.

Philosophers were not, in fact, unwelcome at Rome. The notorious philosophic embassy from Athens in 155 proves it. The Athenians had suffered a damaging arbitral judgment in their dispute with Oropus: the city of Sicyon, to whom the case had been referred by Rome, imposed a stiff fine of 500 talents. Athens appealed that judgment to the Roman senate.[70] As spokesmen she selected the heads of three major philosophical schools: Carneades of the New Academy, Diogenes of the Stoa, and Critolaus the Peripatetic. The diplomatic stakes were high for Athens. She would hardly have dispatched men whose very professions found automatic disfavor in Rome. Cicero even inferred that the envoys, who had had no prior experience in public affairs, would surely not have been summoned from the ivory tower had there been no zeal for their discipline among Roman leaders.[71] The embassy came just six years after

---

[70] For the historical circumstances, see Paus. 7.11.4-8.

[71] Cic. *Tusc. Disp.* 4.5: *qui cum rei publicae nullam umquam partem attigissent...numquam profecto scholis essent excitati neque ad illud munus electi, nisi in quibusdam principibus temporibus illis fuissent studia doctrinae*. Appointment of the commission is recorded also by Cic. *De Orat.* 2.155; *Ad Att.* 12.23.2; Pliny, *NH*, 7.112; Gellius, 6.14.8-9, 17.21.48; Macrob. *Sat.* 1.5.14-15; Aelian, *VH*, 3.17; Plut. *Cato*, 22.1. Cicero's inference itself may go beyond the facts. The appointment of philosophers or other intellectuals on diplomatic missions was not itself unusual in the Greek world; see D. Kienast, *RE*, Suppl. 13 (1974), "Presbeia," 590-596.

the supposed ban on philosophers and rhetors. Obviously that ban was not taken by Greeks as a serious expression of displeasure with intellectuals.

The envoys went beyond a formal plea to the Roman senate. They offered public lectures and expounded the doctrines of their respective philosophical schools. The visit has gained notoriety in subsequent literature. It featured an encounter between the philosophers and the stern and censorious Cato. Carneades made the most lasting impression. His lectures were virtuoso performances, with a brilliant defense of justice on one day, followed by an equally compelling exposition of injustice the next. Cato stood in the audience and found the rhetorical dexterity disconcerting: one could not tell where the truth lay.[72] The elder statesman professed concern that Roman youth would be led astray, giving more weight to skill in speaking than to prowess in war, paying greater heed to seductive voices than to laws and magistrates.[73] Cato then pressed for swift conclusion of the ambassadors' business and their removal from Rome before the younger generation became infected by Hellenic verbal chicanery.[74]

How best to interpret the episode? It is too easily over-interpreted. Cato's involvement might suggest a clash of cultural values. And some have seen Carneades' lectures as critical of Rome, an exposure of the injustice inherent in Roman imperialism.[75] The inferences are faulty. Carneades would not undermine the very purpose of his mission, the winning of a diplomatic concession for Athens, by denouncing his hosts and condemning their foreign policy.[76] Cato's strictures have helped to make the event memorable. But they also distort it. One overlooks too

---

[72] Pliny, NH, 7.112: *illo viro argumentante quid veri esset haud facile discerni posset*; Plut. *Cato*, 22.2-3; Cic. *De Rep.* 3.8-12 = Lactantius, *Div. Inst.* 5.14.3-5.

[73] Plut. *Cato*, 22.4-5: οἱ νέοι τὴν ἐπὶ τῷ λέγειν δόξαν ἀγαπήσωσι μᾶλλον τῆς ἀπὸ τῶν ἔργων καὶ τῶν στρατειῶν. See also Quint. 12.1.35: *non minoribus viribus contra iustitiam dicitur disseruisse quam pridie pro iustitia dixerat*. The envoys' oratorical skills were commented on also by Polybius and Rutilius Rufus; Gellius, 6.14.9-10; Macrob. *Sat.* 1.5.15-16. Cf. Cic. *Acad. Prior.* 2.137.

[74] Plut. *Cato*, 22.4-5; Pliny, *NH*, 7.112.

[75] Fragments of Carneades' speech on injustice ostensibly lend themselves to that interpretation; Cic. *De Rep.* 3.21 = Lactantius, *Div. Inst.* 5.16.2-4; W. Capelle, *Klio*, 25 (1932), 86-89; H. Fuchs, *Der geistige Widerstand gegen Rom in der antiken Welt* (Berlin, 1938), 2-5; F.W. Walbank, *JRS*, 55 (1965), 12-13. The clash of values is stressed by Garbarino, *Roma e la filosofia greca*, II, 364-370.

[76] Cf. E.S. Gruen, *The Hellenistic World and the Coming of Rome* (Berkeley, 1984), 341-342. The suggestion of Garbarino, *Roma e la filosofia greca*, II, 368-369, that by pointing out the irrelevance of justice in international politics Carneades might legitimize Athens' actions against Oropus, is ingenious but dubious. That the extant fragments accurately represent what Carneades himself said is also questionable; see J.-L. Ferrary, *REL*, 55 (1977), 128-156.

easily the most important facts: the popularity of Carneades' lectures and the positive impression left upon Roman intellectuals. If Plutarch is to be believed, Roman youth were swept off their feet by Carneades' eloquence, his audiences packed with enthusiastic disciples, and other Romans delighted with the idea that the younger generation was partaking of Hellenic culture and enjoying the company of such remarkable men.[77] Plutarch may have embellished the scene, but the basic fact is confirmed by Cicero: Rome's *principes* expressed pleasure that Athens had chosen to send the most renowned philosophers as her diplomatic representatives and frequently joined the audiences at their lectures.[78] The persuasive powers of the ambassadors, moreover, affected the senate, which was not just swayed but compelled by their argument and eloquence.[79] Cato's complaints were swallowed up in the enthusiasm. One often forgets that Cato did not, in fact, drive the philosophic embassy out of Rome—indeed did not attempt to do so. It would have been futile. He endeavored only to hurry the decision of the senate on the envoys' request, thus to leave them with no further pretext for remaining in Rome.[80]

The event did not betoken a mighty confrontation between the cultures. Rather the reverse. The success of the philosophers discloses a markedly increased zeal for Greek learning among the Roman intelligentsia by the mid-2nd century. Athens had sent her eminent professors in the first instance in expectation that they would get a warm reception. The expectation was fulfilled, both in the lecture halls and in the *curia*. The *patres*, of course, insisted that proper formalities be observed as usual. When the envoys presented their case to the Roman senate, it had to be delivered in Latin translation, conveyed by the cultivated senator C. Acilius.[81] It was essential to maintain the distinction between private ardor for Greek culture and the official demeanor of the state. The *patres* conducted their deliberations in Latin and rendered their decisions in the interests of the *res publica*. When public business had been concluded, the Athenian representatives returned home. There had been no expulsion order. Cato succeeded only, if at all,

---

[77] Plut. *Cato*, 22.2-3: ταῦτα τοῖς μὲν ἄλλοις ἤρεσκε Ῥωμαίοις γινόμενα, καὶ τὰ μειράκια παιδείας Ἑλληνικῆς μεταλαμβάνοντα καὶ συνόντα θαυμαζομένοις ἀνδράσιν ἡδέως ἑώρων.

[78] Cic. *De Orat.* 2.155.

[79] Plut. *Cato*, 22.4-5: οἳ περὶ παντὸς οὗ βούλοιντο ῥαδίως πείθειν δύνανται; Aelian, *VH*, 3.17: οἵπερ οὖν ἐς τοσοῦτον ἐνέτρεψαν τὴν σύγκλητον βουλήν, ὡς εἰπεῖν αὐτοὺς "ἔπεμψαν Ἀθηναῖοι πρεσβεύοντας οὐ τοὺς πείσοντας ἀλλὰ γὰρ τοὺς βιασομένους ἡμᾶς δρᾶσαι ὅσα θέλουσιν."

[80] Plut. *Cato*, 22.5; Pliny, *NH*, 7.112.

[81] Gellius, 6.14.9; Plut. *Cato*, 22.4.

in speeding completion of the senatorial debate. The philosophers had accomplished their mission and left in high repute.

A token expulsion, it seems, came a year later. A *senatus consultum* decreed the ejection of two Epicurean philosophers, Alcaeus and Philiscus.[82] Nothing more is known. Circumstances, motivation, and even date remain obscure. Athenaeus specifies the consulship of L. Postumius, which suits either 173 or 154, each year having a consul by that name. Two considerations incline a choice towards the latter year. The aftermath of the Third Macedonian War noticeably multiplied the number of visiting or migrating Greek intellectuals. A singling out of Epicureans for removal shows a discrimination among the schools that more likely suits the mid 150s than a time two decades earlier. And proximity to the year 155, when the philosophic embassy from Athens had caused a sensation, also lends greater probability to the later date.[83]

What relationship held between the philosophic visit of 155 and the eviction of Epicureans in (perhaps) the following year? An answer demands resort to speculation. The texts indicate that Alcaeus and Philiscus were removed because they introduced unnatural pleasures to the young.[84] The charge may derive from a source hostile to Epicureanism which added the motive because of the negative stereotype attached to the school, rather than from the actual wording of the *senatus consultum*.[85] But it can also have stood in the decree itself. As plausible pretext it makes sense. Few Romans can have had any deep understanding of Epicureanism at this time. Its reputation as a sect promoting pleasure counted for more than any serious grappling with philosophic technicalities or detailed principles. The school of Epicurus had not been represented in the embassy of 155 which included a noble Stoic, a learned Peripatetic, and a rhetorically gifted Academic. Their presentations found welcome and even fervor. Perhaps too much so, at least in the eyes of Cato, who paraded his concern about youthful minds diverted from public responsibilities by the pleasures of philosophy.[86] The envoys left

---

[82] Athenaeus, 12.547a; Aelian, *VH*, 9.12; Suda, s.v. Ἐπίκουρος.

[83] Cf. the arguments of Garbarino, *Roma e la filosofia greca*, II, 374-377, with reference to modern works lined up on one side or the other—though none with extended discussion.

[84] Athenaeus, 12.547a: δι' ἃς εἰσηγοῦντο ἡδονάς; Aelian, *VH*, 9.12: ὅτι πολλῶν καὶ ἀτόπων ἡδονῶν ἐσηγητὰι τοῖς νέοις ἐγένοντο.

[85] See the discussion of Garbarino, *Roma e la filosofia greca*, II, 372-374.

[86] Note that Cato, in Plutarch's version, includes philosophy among the pleasures, indeed asserts that young men are losing interest in "other pleasures and activities" because of their passion for philosophy; Plut. *Cato*, 22.3: ὑφ' οὗ τῶν ἄλλων ἡδονῶν καὶ διατριβῶν ἐκπεσόντες ἐνθουσιῶσι περὶ φιλοσοφίαν. Absence of an Epicurean from the philosophic embassy may have been due to the Epicurean lack of interest in rhetoric.

shortly thereafter, but the enticements of their teaching lingered on. Upper class Romans did not deprive themselves of those intellectual pleasures. But they could at least take a stand against the one philosophy for which pleasure itself was the central principle. Rome's officialdom drew the line at Epicureanism. The decree of 154 (if that was the year) was no more than tokenism, hardly a concerted campaign. Only two philosophers were named for banishment. But tokens have their public value. The Epicureans, it can be suggested, served conveniently as scapegoats. By singling out that creed for censure and dismissal, the senate implicitly legitimized cultivation of the other philosophic disciplines. The measure both sanctioned Hellenic education and advertised Rome's differentiation among the sects.

It may be no coincidence that the year 154 also witnessed another official act that publicized Roman superiority to the more frivolous pursuits from Hellas. The censors of that year contracted for the building of a stone theater, the first such edifice in Rome. Construction was already under way when abruptly halted by a compelling speech of the ex-consul P. Scipio Nasica. Scipio deplored the effects of theatrical entertainment upon the character and morals of the Romans: it was altogether undesirable for Romans to become accustomed to Hellenic pleasures.[87] His objections carried the day, and the half-built theater was demolished. The decision delivers a message usefully comparable to expulsion of the Epicureans. Roman traditions could embrace instruction in the serious philosophic schools, but disdained the Epicurean doctrine of pleasure and the frivolities of the theater.

A flimsy record frustrates us for the next half century and more. Occasional state action against idle entertainments, however, can be inferred even from that record. One instance happens to be preserved in an unlikely source. Cassiodorus' chronicle, which lists consular years and periodically adds a stray comment, notes under the year 115 that the censors banned certain popular amusements from the city.[88] A periodic expression of scorn for light diversions reiterated public concern for the molding of national character. The same purpose was served by sumptuary laws which appear sporadically but not infrequently in the second half of the second century: the *lex Didia* of 143, the *lex Licinia* some years later, the *lex Aemilia* of 115, and the *lex Tappula* of the late second cen-

---

[87] Appian, *BC*, 1.28: οὐ χρήσιμον ὅλως Ἑλληνικαῖς ἡδυπαθείαις Ῥωμαίους ἐθίζεσθαι; Livy, *Per.* 48: *tamquam inutile et nociturum publicis moribus*; Val. Max. 2.4.2; Vell. Pat. 1.15.3; Orosius, 4.21.4; Augustine, *CD*, 2.5.

[88] Cassiodorus, *Chron.* ad ann. 115: *L. Metellus et Cn. Domitius censores artem ludicram ex urbe removerunt, praeter Latinum tibicinem cum cantore, et ludum talorum.* Observe the exception of the Latin *tibicen*. The measure seems directed against alien intrusions into these musical entertainments.

tury.[89] No source, however, attests any further government measures against Greek intellectuals.[90] If that silence is meaningful, it suggests a growing maturity and self-confidence in the Roman cultural scene. The officialdom frowned on shallow amusements that distracted men from serious pursuits, but pride in a national culture had ripened to the point that Hellenic learning could be acknowledged without risking a threat to Roman tradition.

The development of that self-confidence cannot be tracked in detail. But a revealing moment makes it manifest. A puzzling and much discussed event in the year 92, when examined in this context, acquires new and resonant meaning. The censors of that year, L. Licinius Crassus and Cn. Domitius Ahenobarbus, issued an edict that delivered stern criticism of the schools run by Latin rhetors. That pronouncement had no known precedents or models. And its implications repay careful scrutiny.

The edict itself has ostensibly survived verbatim. The censors declared that they had learned of a new form of education, organized by men who style themselves Latin rhetors, in whose schools young men while away their days: such schools—novel, unconventional, and at variance with the *mos maiorum*—deserve censure, as do those who administer them and those who attend them.[91] Authenticity of the decree has been questioned on various flimsy grounds, including the clumsiness of the style. None is compelling, and the text can be accepted as it stands, possibly drawn from the archives by Suetonius, who was in a position to do so.[92] The edict, it should be noted, did not direct disbandment or dispersal of the schools. Nothing in the text specifies actions to be taken or sanctions to be imposed. This constituted strictly moral censure, a pronouncement of deep disapproval by holders of Rome's most prestigious office.[93] As such,

---

[89] For sources and discussion, see Sauerwein, *Die Leges Sumptuariae*, 89-127. The *"lex Tappula"*, in fact, became the butt of mockery and ridicule; *ILS*, 8761; Lucilius, 1307, Marx; Festus, 363, Lindsay.

[90] The edict in 139, expelling astrologers and adherents of Sabazius from Italy, is not, of course, aimed at Greek intellectuals; Val. Max. 1.3.3.

[91] The decree is quoted by Suet. *Rhet.* 1.1. Identical wording appears in Gellius, 15.11.2, evidently drawn from Suetonius. Cf. Tac. *Dial.* 35.

[92] The text was challenged, though the fact of the decree accepted by F. Marx, *Incerti auctoris, de ratione dicendi ad C. Herennium* (Leipzig, 1894), 144-145. His arguments are weak and adequately refuted by G. Bloch, *Klio*, 3 (1903), 68-73. See also A. Manfredini, *SDHI*, 42 (1976), 100-103.

[93] Gellius, 15.11.2, wrongly infers that this was a decree *de coercendis rhetoribus Latinis*. Similarly Tac. *Dial.* 35.1: *claudere...ludum impudentiae iussi sunt*. Wording of the decree offers no support for that conclusion. The point is made at unnecessary length and with unhelpful legalistic discussion by Manfredini, *SDHI*, 42 (1976), 105-114. Cicero has Crassus claim that his edict had removed the Latin rhetors; Cic. *De Orat.* 3.93: *quos ego censor edicto meo sustuleram*. But the rhetors, in fact, continued to operate; see below p. 191.

it served as the token gesture *par excellence*, not meant for implementation but as enunciation of principle by spokesmen of the nation's conscience.[94]

To what end and with what meaning? A long favored interpretation finds party-political designs in the event. Most eminent of the Latin rhetors was L. Plotius Gallus, a friend and panegyrist of C. Marius. Hence, the political strains in the 90s B.C. between Marians and anti-Marians have been seen as lurking behind the edict of 92. The Latin rhetors represented a democratic element in the educational process, backed by Marius, the *novus homo*, enemy of Greek learning and aristocratic culture. L. Crassus, on this analysis, stood as champion of Hellenism, an advocate of the conservative strain in Roman politics, and the censorial decree aimed at demolition of the rhetorical schools that encouraged demagogy.[95]

The thesis is vulnerable on several counts. Plotius indeed held chief place among the Latin rhetors, a man to whom the keenest students flocked in numbers and whom Cicero himself considered as a potential

---

[94] The edict appeals to *maiores nostri* who had decided what their children should learn and what schools they should attend; Suet. *Rhet.* 1.1: *maiores nostri quae liberos suos discere et quos in ludos itare vellent instituerunt.* The statement is ostensibly at odds with a remark in Cicero's *De Republica* that Romans, unlike Greeks, did not want any education for the young fixed by law, publicly established, or uniform for all; *De Rep.* 4.3: *disciplinam puerilem ingenuis…nullam certam aut destinatam legibus aut publice expositam aut unam omnium esse voluerunt.* Marx, *Prolegomena*, 144-145, sees the statements as conflicting and mutually exclusive, a reason for rejecting the text of the edict. The solution of Bloch, *Klio*, 3 (1903), 69-70, that the Ciceronian dialogue, set in 129, refers to a time when no regulations applied, by contrast with the situation in 92, is lame and unconvincing. So also is the idea that Cicero speaks only of an elementary school level for young children and adolescents, thus inapplicable to a higher stage involving rhetoric to which the decree addresses itself; C. Barbagallo, *RivFilol*, 88 (1910), 482-484. The texts are, in any case, not in conflict. The censorial edict speaks in indistinct fashion of ancestral desires and demands, not of laws and institutions. Cf. Manfredini, *SDHI*, 42 (1976), 101-102.

[95] Marx, *Prolegomena*, 147-150; Bloch, *Klio*, 3 (1903), 72-73; Barbagallo, *RivFilol*, 88 (1910), 498-500; A. Gwynn, *Roman Education from Cicero to Quintilian* (Oxford, 1926), 60-66; Gabba, *Athenaeum*, 31 (1953), 269-271. For skepticism on this reconstruction, see, e.g., M.L. Clarke, *Rhetoric at Rome* (London, 1953), 12-13; A.E. Douglas, *CQ*, 54 (1960), 77; M. Gelzer, *Kleine Schriften* (Wiesbaden, 1962), I, 211-215; P.L. Schmidt, in E. Lefèvre, *Monumentum Chiloniense, Festschrift für Erich Burck* (Amsterdam, 1975), 187-201; Manfredini, *SDHI*, 42 (1976), 114-127; S.F. Bonner, *Education in Ancient Rome* (Berkeley, 1977), 71-74. The idea, in modified form, has been revived most recently by G. Calboli, *Entretiens Fondation Hardt*, 28 (1982), 70-99; cf. E. Rawson, *Intellectual Life in the Late Roman Republic* (Baltimore, 1985), 78. J.-M. David, *MEFRA*, 91 (1979), 135-181, stresses the growth of a *factio accusatorum* after C. Gracchus' legislation and especially after the Mamilian tribunal of 109. In this version of the older thesis, a popular movement encouraged *novi homines* and men from the municipalities who sought political careers in Rome and sharpened their oratorical skills to shake off hereditary allegiances, a movement promoted by the leadership and example of Marius and the rhetorical school of L. Plotius.

teacher.[96] And he won the affection of Marius who considered the rhetor worthy of celebrating his exploits.[97] But the evidence betrays no political connection between the men. Plotius, as we happen to know, survived the fall of Marius and the Sullan proscriptions, still active as a speech writer in the 50s.[98] He can not have been regarded as principal spokesman for Marius' political or educational philosophy.[99] One may go further. Marius' own anti-Hellenic pretensions, assumed as genuine by most scholars, are, in fact, suspect. The general professed to scorn the study of Greek literature: it brought no *virtus* to those learned in it.[100] But that was a pose struck by the *novus homo* who stressed his military credentials as against intellectuals whose martial prowess he questioned.[101] Marius, as Plutarch reveals, did not use Greek for any matter of seriousness—i.e. presumably in the course of public affairs. The implication is plain enough: Marius knew the language and made a public show of avoiding it.[102] He derided Greek culture as the product of a subject people, and he even deliberately sponsored Greek shows only to be able to walk out on them.[103] The behavior obviously forms a pattern. It was calculated showmanship, not authentic aversion to Hellenism. That hardly constituted a political program.

The basic construct is itself shaky. Too many analyses reduce the politics of the early 1st century to a contest between the factions of Marius and his opponents. The political scene was more ambiguous and more complex. Marius' ill-fated coalition with Saturninus had collapsed in 100, as the oligarchy coalesced against the tribune. Marius survived politically, but at the cost of setback and embarrassment. Much of the decade of the 90s witnessed efforts by the general to climb back into the center of the political stage through new alliances and compromises.

---

[96] Suet. *Rhet.* 2.1: *ad quem cum fieret concursus, quod studiosissimus quisque apud eum exerceretur*; Quint. 2.4.42; Seneca, *Contr.* 2, praef. 5; Jerome, *Chron.* Olymp. 173.1.

[97] Cic. *Pro Arch.* 19-20: *itaque ille Marius item eximie L. Plotium dilexit, cuius ingenio putabat ea quae gesserat posse celebrari*; cf. Schol. Bob. 178, Stangl.

[98] Suet. *Rhet.* 2.1. Rightly emphasized by Gelzer, *Kleine Schriften*, I, 214-215.

[99] Manfredini, *SDHI*, 42 (1976), 118-124, even denies the identification between Plotius the Latin rhetor and L. Plotius Gallus the friend of Marius. This goes too far and strains the evidence. Cicero's reference to the rhetor as *Plotium quendam* means only that he was unacquainted with him as a youth; Suet. *Rhet.* 2.1; so, rightly, Calboli, *Entretiens Fondation Hardt*, 28 (1982), 91-92. There is no reason to believe that Suetonius erroneously amalgamated two individuals. They are amalgamated also by Schol. Bob. 178, Stangl, a passage missed by both Manfredini and Calboli. Other references to Plotius the rhetor in Varro, *Men.* 251, Bol.; Quint. 11.3.143.

[100] Sallust, *Iug.* 85.32; cf. 63.3.

[101] Cf. Cic. *Pro Font.* 43.

[102] Plut. *Mar.* 2.2: μήτε γλώττῃ πρὸς μηδὲν Ἑλληνίδι χρῆσθαι τῶν σπουδῆς ἐχομένων.

[103] Plut. *Mar.* 2.2-3. θέας Ἑλληνικὰς παρέχων εἰς τὸ θέατρον ἐλθὼν καὶ μόνον καθίσας εὐθὺς ἀπαλλαγῆναι.

Details would here be out of place.[104] One alliance, however, needs emphasis. Some time in the 90s, probably before 95, Marius' nephew and adopted son married the daughter of L. Crassus.[105] The two men collaborated in a political trial of 95.[106] Marius established connections in that decade not only to Crassus, but to M. Antonius, Q. Mucius Scaevola, and the most eminent M. Aemilius Scaurus.[107] Links with *nobiles* of that stature and influence belie any effort to divide Roman politics into Marian democrats and anti-Marian conservatives. And the idea that Crassus' edict directed itself against a Marian movement based upon the demagogic tactics of Latin rhetors collapses.

Crassus himself falls into no obvious political camp. His career as senator, orator, and intellectual kept him in the public eye, but also evoked opinions on various subjects that show considerable malleability. A brief review of his most important stands will suffice to make the point. Crassus first came to public notice as prosecutor of the Gracchan renegade C. Papirius Carbo in 119, thus establishing a reputation for forensic skill and also earning credit with those who looked upon the Gracchan tradition with favor. A memorable intervention came a year or more later when Crassus delivered a vehement speech on behalf of the commercial colony at Narbo, with popular overtones, evidently favorable to equestrian interests, and critical of the senate. More celebrated still, however, was his brilliant oration in support of a judiciary law in 106 that reduced equestrian influence in the courts. Crassus' words this time excoriated the *equites* and lavished praise on the senate. As consul in 95, he lent his name to a bill that struck illegally enfranchised Italians from the registry rolls and instituted a *quaestio* to expose additional fraud. And in the last year of his life, 91, he served as a principal counselor to M. Livius Drusus, advocate of jury reform in the

---

[104] See the arguments and evidence presented by Gruen, *Historia*, 15 (1966), 32-64, especially 42-49, with extensive bibliography; *Roman Politics and the Criminal Courts, 149-78 B.C.* (Cambridge, Mass., 1968), 186-203. A different view in E. Badian, *Studies in Greek and Roman History* (Oxford, 1964), 34-70; cf. T.J. Luce, *Historia*, 19 (1970), 161-183; Gabba, *ANRW*, I.1 (Berlin, 1972), 783-785.

[105] Cicero, *Pro Balbo*, 49, asserts that Marius and Crassus were already *adfines* in 95, an assertion that can stand despite some scholarly objections; see Gruen, *Historia*, 15 (1966), 43. The *adfinitas* is alluded to also in Cic. *De Orat.* 1.66, 3.8; *Ad Att.* 12.49.1, 14.8.1. See now Manfredini, *SDHI*, 42 (1976), 124-134. Calboli, *Entretiens Fondation Hardt*, 28 (1982), 83-88, still prefers to see a breach between Marius and most of the *nobiles*.

[106] Cic. *Pro Balbo*, 49.

[107] See above, n. 104. On Marius and Scaurus, see Pliny, *NH*, 36.116, with Gruen, *Historia*, 15 (1966), 58. And cf. now R.L. Bates, *ProcAmerPhilosSoc*, 130 (1986), 271.

interests of the senate and of Italian enfranchisement.[108] He perished
shortly after delivering a powerful speech supporting senatorial *dignitas* in
the heated debate on Drusus' reforms.[109] Crassus had had a distinguished and often embattled career. But it was plainly not the career of
a committed ideologue.[110]

Both censors of 92 sponsored the edict on Latin rhetors. Crassus' colleague, Cn. Domitius Ahenobarbus, resists even more forcibly any
categorization as opponent of popular tastes and movements. As a fiery
tribune in 104, Domitius, in fact, rode a popular tide. He promoted and
implemented a bill directing that all priests be elected by the people in
tribal assembly. His own election to the priesthood followed passage of
the measure.[111] Domitius also engaged in a fierce altercation with the
princeps senatus M. Aemilius Scaurus whom he brought to trial before the
people.[112] Those activities do not themselves justify the label of a persistent and determined demagogue.[113] But they make it difficult to see
Domitius' sponsorship of the censorial edict in 92 as resistance to
democratic developments.

A striking fact requires attention. The censors of 92, far from joining
in political alliance, engaged in vitriolic public exchanges with one
another. Domitius levelled stinging charges against his colleague,
reproaching him for lavish and luxurious living. Crassus replied in kind,
his speech spiced with cutting wit. The repartee became notorious.
Crassus played maliciously on the name Ahenobarbus: Domitius' bronze
beard well suits his iron face and leaden heart. But Crassus' speech contained more than mere spite. Cicero regarded the retort to Domitius as

---

[108] Prosecution of Carbo: Cic. *De Orat.* 1.40, 3.74; *Brutus*, 159; Val. Max. 3.7.6, 6.5.6;
Tac. *Dial.* 34. Advocacy of Narbo: Cic. *Brutus*, 160; *Pro Cluent.* 140. Speech for judiciary
law: Cic. *Brutus*, 164; *Pro Cluent.* 140; *De Orat.* 1.225; cf. *Brutus*, 161. Consular bill: Cic.
De Off. 3.47; *De Orat.* 2.257; *Brutus*, 63; *Pro Balbo*, 48, 54; Asconius, 67-68, Clark; Schol.
Bob. 129, Stangl; Sallust, *Hist.* 1.20, Maur. Adviser to Drusus: Cic. *De Domo*, 50;
Asconius, 21, Clark; cf. Cic. *De Orat.* 3.2-5. Whether the backing of Drusus extended
to his franchise bill, however, as most assume, is uncertain; cf. Gruen, *Roman Politics*,
211-213.

[109] Cic. *De Orat.* 3.1-6.

[110] Crassus is seen as part of a "reformist party" by Manfredini, *SDHI*, 42 (1976),
127-134, and Calboli, *Entretiens Fondation Hardt*, 28 (1982), 83-88. This suggests more
system and consistency than the record readily allows. David, *MEFRA*, 91 (1979), 165-
168, also presents too monolithic a picture of Crassus' politics.

[111] Cic. *De Leg. Agrar.* 2.18; Asconius, 79-80, Clark; Suet. *Nero*, 2.1; Dio, 37.37.1.

[112] Asconius, 21, Clark; Cic. *Pro Deiot.* 31; Val. Max. 6.5.5; Dio, 27, fr. 92; Plut. *Ex
Inim. Util.* 9.

[113] Domitius was one of those who stood in opposition to the tribune Saturninus in
100; Cic. *Pro. Rab. Perd.* 21. And he supported the recall from exile of Marius' most bitter
opponent, the eminent Q. Metellus Numidicus, in 98; Gellius, 15.13.6, 17.2.7. Cf.
Schmidt, in Lefèvre, *Monumentum Chiloniense* (1975), 200-201, n. 53.

a classic. The contest between the censors reverberated, noted with some frequency in later literature.[114] Their antagonism persisted until abdication from office.[115] A deeper rivalry may lurk behind the mutual attacks.[116] The animosity, in any case, was unconcealed and public. This makes collaboration on the edict against Latin rhetors all the more remarkable. The explanation of factional politics plainly misses the mark: the two censors agreed on nothing but the edict alone. The very fact of their joint sponsorship gives this event singular significance, an act calculated to capture public notice. But what is that significance?

The political implications of this cultural change, it can be argued, went beyond mere factional politics. Substitution of Latin for Greek in rhetorical education democratized the process. The change provided access to oratorical tools for far larger numbers of aspiring leaders, thus threatening the control of the established elite.[117] The idea has superficial attraction. But it depends on the assumption that rhetorical training in Latin was available for the first time in the late 90s B.C.—a far from secure interpretation. In fact, there is good reason to believe that rhetors taught in Latin for some time prior to that decade. Grammarians certainly did, and, as Suetonius reports, the early grammarians offered instruction in rhetoric.[118] One such figure, Aurelius Opilius, moved from the teaching of philosophy to rhetoric and then to grammar, before abandoning Italy in 91.[119] The *grammaticus* L. Aelius Stilo also gained renown by composing speeches for many Roman orators and thus very probably taught rhetoric as well.[120] M. Antonius, reckoned together with Crassus as chief among orators in his generation, wrote up a pamphlet on oratory, published without his consent, and presumably employed in rhetorical training.[121] And Cicero's own youthful *De Inventione* appeared

---

[114] See, especially, Val. Max. 9.1.4; Pliny, *NH*, 17.1-6; Cic. *De Orat.* 2.45, 2.227, 2.230; *Brutus*, 164; Suet. *Nero*, 2. Other references collected in Broughton, *MRR*, II.17.

[115] *Fasti Antiates*, s.a. 95.

[116] See Badian, *Foreign Clientelae, 264-70 B.C.* (Oxford, 1958), 264-265; *Studies*, 93-94.

[117] So R. Pichon, *RÉA*, 6 (1904), 37-41; J. Kaimio, *The Romans and the Greek Language* (Helsinki, 1979), 196-198. In the formulation of A. Michel, *Rhétorique et philosophie chez Cicéron* (Paris, 1960), 64-70, the censors resisted change by the *populares* who would divert education away from the ideals cultivated by the circle of Scipio Aemilianus. A similar view is adopted by Bonner, *Education*, 72-74.

[118] Suet. *Gramm.* 4: *veteres grammatici et rhetoricam docebant.*

[119] Suet. *Gramm.* 6: *Aurelius Opilius, Epicurei cuiusdam libertus, philosophiam primo, deinde rhetoricam, novissime grammaticam docuit.* Opilius closed his school to accompany Rutilius Rufus into exile in 91.

[120] Cic. *Brutus*, 169, 205-207; Suet. *Gramm.* 3; cf. Gellius, 1.18.2.

[121] Cic. *De Orat.* 1.94, 1.206, 1.208, 3.189; *Brutus*, 163; *Orator*, 18; Quint. 3.1.19. On the date, probably between 102 and 91, see Calboli, *GiornItalFilol*, 24 (1972), 149-150; Manfredini, *SDHI*, 42 (1976), 138.

not long after 92, its composition indicating that a tradition of rhetorical handbooks was already in place.[122] Instruction in Latin rhetoric, therefore, did not emerge with suddenness in the 90s, thereby prompting immediate reaction.

Yet the edict of 92 did react against a novelty of some sort: *novum genus disciplinae*.[123] The Latin rhetors, we are told, established themselves for the first time in 93.[124] A recent phenomenon indeed. The evidence implies that prior education had been on an individual and personal basis, private rhetors attached to houses of the nobility. If change there was in 93, it must have involved the placement of rhetorical education on an organized footing. The objection raised to this development in 92, therefore, was not to rhetorical training as such, but to institutionalized rhetorical training. Establishment of formal schools to mold orators galvanized the resistance of the censors.

Why? A recent theory offers possible explanation. Demagogic activity mushroomed in the Gracchan era, so it is argued, a premium placed on persuasive skills before the assembly of the people. The agitation reached a peak in the last years of the 2nd century, with a concentration of activist tribunes and popular legislation, culminating in the turbulent tribunate of L. Saturninus. The momentum of this movement provoked educational innovation. Instruction in Latin rhetoric on a systematic basis would supply needed tools to the ambitious. The schools of L. Plotius and his compatriots answered that need. Crassus and Domitius responded swiftly and firmly in 92: the censorial edict, on this view, sought to dissolve the schools and preserve the traditional pattern of elitist higher education.[125]

---

[122] Cic. *De Invent.* 1.1. On the date of composition, see Kennedy, *Art of Rhetoric*, 106-110. The tradition might even go back to Cato the Elder; Quint. 3.1.19; Victorinus, in Halm, *Rhetores Latini*, 308. But it is uncertain that these passages refer to an actual book on rhetoric by Cato; Astin, *Cato the Censor*, 333-334. It will be prudent not to bring the *Rhetorica ad Herennium* into the reckoning. The date of the manual may be as late as the 50s; Douglas, *CQ*, 54 (1960), 74-78. But even if one places it in the 80s, it need not reflect attitudes against which the edict of 92 directed itself; cf. Manfredini, *SDHI*, 42 (1976), 135-140. The suggestions of G. Achard, *REL*, 63 (1985), 56-68, are highly speculative.

[123] Suet. *Rhet.* 1: *haec nova, quae praeter consuetudinem ac morem maiorum fiunt.*

[124] Cic. *De Orat.* 3.93: *Latini...hoc biennio magistri dicendi exstiterunt*—the dialogue is set in 91. The date is supported, though with less precision, by other testimony: Quint. 2.4.42: *extremis L. Crassi temporibus*; Seneca, *Contr.* 2, praef. 5: *puero Cicerone*; Tac. *Dial.* 35: *paulo ante Ciceronis tempora*; Suet. *Rhet.* 2.1: *pueris nobis* (Cicero).

[125] The thesis is developed by Schmidt, in Lefèvre, *Monumentum Chiloniense* (1975), 183-216, esp. 192-193, 208-211, 214-215. Schmidt accepts the view that only a single school, that of Plotius, is at issue here. Need for a censorial edict, however, becomes less intelligible on that analysis. David, *MEFRA*, 91 (1979), 135-181, emphasizes the increasing role of the new orators in the courts rather than in the assemblies: the *eloquentia popul[aris]* was more aggressive, unrestrained, and hostile to the traditional ties between

The theory is tempting and attractive, but it lacks support in the evidence. And other stumbling blocks stand in the way. If institutional education in rhetoric were invented in the 90s, it would surely have encompassed Hellenic as well as Latin teaching. Yet the decree addressed itself only to Latin rhetors. That gives immediate pause. And a still more important obstacle to the theory exists: the political climate of the 90s. The fall of Saturninus in 100 administered a severe setback to popular politics. Demagogy receded. Advocacy of measures in the broader interests of the community virtually vanished in the next decade. That period featured fierce contests within the aristocracy, strains between the senatorial and equestrian orders, and growing pressure for Italian enfranchisement, pressure that came to a head in the devastating Social War. It was not a time congenial for democratic advance.[126] Atmosphere, events, and attitudes conspired to discourage such advance. And they would hardly invite creation of rhetorical schools with populist overtones. Uneasiness may have been felt by the censors about training in Latin for practical oratory to the detriment of fundamental *techne* taught in Greek—thus allowing for readier manipulation of law and principle. But analysis in terms of a struggle between political groups or ideologies seems doomed to failure. The collaboration of Crassus and Domitius alone condemns it. Their otherwise conspicuous antagonism precludes political interpretation.

Various alternative explanations have found their way into the literature, paradoxical, strained, or fallacious. It has been held that, despite all appearances, the censorial decree had an anti-Hellenic, rather than pro-Hellenic character: the *rhetores Latini* simply adapted Greek rhetoric to the Latin language, and the aristocracy acted in fear of Hellenism as serving the cause of the *populares*.[127] Apart from flying in the face of the evidence, this idea leaves the stance of L. Crassus quite unintelligible. The learned scholar and orator, whose Greek was so fluent that it seemed to be his native tongue, would not strive to eradicate Hellenism from Roman education.[128] A similar objection holds against the view that the censors resisted a trend to remove rhetorical training

---

patrons and clients. David's assemblage of persons attested as *accusatores* from the Gracchi to the Social War is valuable. But he does not examine the edict of 92 closely, nor does he recognize the complexities of the political situation in the 90s.

[126] On the character of the 90s, see Gruen, *Roman Politics*, 185-214, with relevant references and bibliography.

[127] A.D. Leeman, *Orationis Ratio* (Amsterdam, 1963), I, 62-64. A variation on this by Schmidt, in Lefèvre, *Monumentum Chiloniense* (1975), 194-198, who sees a distrust of theory and doctrine brought into rhetorical training by Hellenization.

[128] On Crassus' knowledge of Greek, see Cic. *De Orat.* 2.2: *Graece sic loqui, nullam ut nosse aliam linguam videretur.*

from the forum to the schoolroom, a substitution of the dry *declamationes* for the practical experience of the political arena.[129] This suggestion too runs afoul of what we know of Crassus' career and inclinations. He sought advice and instruction on oratory wherever he could from Greek professors. And his basic orientation, as presented in the *De Oratore*, was not to advocate pragmatic training on the job, but to insist on a cultivation of broader learning for the making of a orator.[130] A very different thesis connects the attack on Latin rhetors with the movement to restrict the influence of non-Romans upon the social and political scene, thus an association with the *lex Licinia Mucia* of 95.[131] That finding rests on a mistaken identification of the *rhetores Latini* with Latins, i.e. non-Roman citizens. Some may perhaps have belonged to that category. But the fact is irrelevant. The edict directed itself against Latin rhetoric, not against Latins.[132] The diverse suggestions have failed to reach the heart of the matter.

A return to the texts will be salutary. The edict of the censors struck against men calling themselves Latin rhetors who had established a new form of training for the young, one which violated ancestral practice and provoked the censors to declare strong disapproval.[133] The novelty, as we have seen, was not the fact of teaching Latin rhetoric but the creation of *ludi*, organized schools, in which it was taught to the young.[134] The censors' decree administers rebuke but does not specify the grievance. What caused Crassus and Domitius to join in reprimand?

One ancient text offers reasons and must be attended to. Crassus himself, as interlocutor in Cicero's *De Oratore*, explains his motives and intent. He had been criticized for the edict, charged with seeking to check the honing of young minds. Crassus insisted that the reverse was true. He wished to prevent the blunting of their acuity. Rhetorical training had become too dense. The Greeks themselves could no longer retain it all. Latin teachers of rhetoric therefore stepped in to offer short cuts. Instruction by Greeks has its drawbacks, but they at least provide a

---

[129] So Manfredini, *SDHI*, 42 (1976), 141-148, relying largely on Tac. *Dial.* 34-35.

[130] Cic. *De Orat. passim*. For Crassus' interest in the company and advice of Greeks, see Cic. *De Orat.* 1.45-47, 1.62, 1.82, 1.93, 1.104, 2.2, 2.365, 3.75.

[131] E. Jullien, *Les professeurs de littérature dans l'ancienne Rome* (Paris, 1885), 96-98; Gruen, *Roman Politics*, 203. The possibility is considered but not embraced by Gabba, *Athenaeum*, 31 (1953), 270. Rightly rejected by Calboli, *Entretiens Fondation Hardt*, 28 (1982), 87.

[132] The decree is clear enough on that point; Suet. *Rhet.* 1.1: *homines qui novum genus disciplinae instituerunt*. And Cic. *De Orat.* 3.93 is decisive: the contrast is between Greek and Latin teachers, not between citizens and Latins.

[133] Suet. *Rhet.* 1: *haec nova, quae praeter consuetudinem ac morem maiorum fiunt, neque placent neque recta videntur.*

[134] Suet. *Rhet.* 1: *ad quos iuventus in ludum conveniat.*

theoretical basis and a cultivated tradition that goes beyond mere babble. The new masters teach nothing but effrontery and insolence, thus obliging the censors to halt their effort before they spread. The ancient and admirable wisdom of the Greeks can be adapted to Roman usage, a task that requires men of an erudition not yet produced by the Romans—though when they emerge, they will eclipse even the Greeks.[135] Such is the substance of Crassus' apologia.

Ostensibly this is a precious source. Yet it also creates a problem. Can we trust the passage as genuine reflection of Crassus' reasoning, or is it rather Cicero's invention for his own purposes? Did not the author devise an ideal Crassus to convey his own ideas on education and oratory? The matter has provoked substantial debate, without reaching consensus or resolution. One may concede that the portrait of Crassus as imbued with Greek learning contains exaggeration and idealization. The wide familiarity with rhetoric, philosophy, history, civil law, and constitutional traditions may reveal more of Cicero than of Crassus. And no one doubts that Crassus serves in part as mouthpiece for Ciceronian opinions.[136] But the character in the De Oratore is far from sheer creation. Cicero strove for accuracy in the historical details of his philosophical and rhetorical treatises.[137] His methodological statement near the beginning of Book II of the De Oratore declares his intent to reproduce the sentiments of Crassus and Antonius as closely as possible. A check existed on too much deviation: contemporaries of those men survived to challenge any obvious inventions.[138] Cicero apparently even endeavored to approximate the oratorical styles of Crassus and Antonius.[139] The dialogue paid due heed to the historical personalities.

The Crassus of this passage is not cut from a mold fashioned by Cicero and duplicated mechanically throughout the dialogue. Elsewhere Crassus

---

[135] Cic. De Orat. 3.93-95.

[136] The fullest treatment by R.D. Meyer, *Literarische Fiktion und historischer Gehalt in Ciceros De Oratore* (Stuttgart, 1970), 24-96, who accepts much of the Ciceronian portrait, with due caution and qualification, but balks at the idea that Crassus had much grasp of Greek philosophy. More skeptical are A.D. Leeman and H. Pinkster, *M. Tullius Cicero, De Oratore Libri III* (Heidelberg, 1981), I, 90-96; more credulous is Schmidt, in Lefèvre, *Monumentum Chiloniense* (1975), 207-208. An inconclusive discussion by R.E. Jones, *AJP*, 60 (1939), 318-320. Meyer is rather too confident that he can distinguish the historical from the invented characteristics of Crassus. On relations between Crassus and Cicero, see E. Rawson, *PCPS*, 17 (1971), 82-88.

[137] Cf. Cic. *Ad Att.* 12.20.2; *Brutus*, 218-219.

[138] Cic. De Orat. 2.7-9. In the view of A.D. Leeman, H. Pinkster, and H.L.W. Nelson, *M. Tullius Cicero, De Oratore Libri III* (Heidelberg, 1985), II, 186-188, Cicero's claim of authenticity is a literary device to give concreteness to the fiction.

[139] Cic. De Orat. 3.16; cf. N. Martinelli, *La rappresentazione dello stilo di Crasso e di Antonio nel De Oratore* (Rome, 1963); and on Crassus in particular, Meyer, *Literarische Fiktion*, 88-96.

affected scorn for Hellenic learning and claimed to prefer the wisdom of his countrymen to that of the Greeks in every regard.[140] The attitude contrasts sharply with that articulated in the passage under scrutiny, indeed nearly a reversal: Greek wisdom, described as venerable and outstanding, is imported for Roman usage but has yet to find a Roman with the competence to graft it onto the native culture.[141] The latter sentiments more faithfully represent the man, a devotee of the Greek language and of Hellenic culture.[142] To be sure, Crassus occasionally sniped at "Greeklings", repeating standard stereotypes about their loquaciousness and their preference for argument over truth.[143] And he claimed for the Twelve Tables greater authority than the libraries of all Greek philosophers.[144] That was obligatory posturing for a Roman statesman. Reservations about the Greeks, in fact, find echoes even in the present passage.[145] But Crassus' Hellenic credentials were impeccable. The presentation by Cicero is complex and artful, not a simplistic reproduction of himself. Its reliability holds in essentials.

The care taken by the author lends confidence in the result.[146] The methodological principle expressed in Book II is meant to apply generally through the work. And there is reason to see its applicability with regard to the edict. Reference to criticism of Crassus for sponsoring the measure, thus inducing him to respond, rings true. It would be a gratuitous addition if merely fabricated.[147] The forecast at the end of the passage that looks ahead to learned Romans who could adapt Greek wisdom to national purposes may indeed have Cicero himself in mind.[148] But the plausibility of the sentiments expressed in the passage as a whole remains unaffected. It is one thing to amplify Crassus' intellectual attainments or to employ him as spokesman for Ciceronian ideals in

---

[140] Cic. De Orat. 2.4: ut Crassus non tam existimari vellet non didicisse, quam illa despicere, et nostrorum hominum in omni genere prudentiam Graecis anteferre.

[141] Cic. De Orat. 3.95: patitur enim et lingua nostra et natura rerum veterem illam excellentemque prudentiam Graecorum ad nostrum usum moremque transferri.

[142] Cic. De Orat. 1.45-47, 1.93, 2.2, 2.365, 3.75.

[143] Cic. De Orat. 1.47, 1.102, 2.17-18. Cf. Leeman, Pinkster, and Nelson, Cicero De Oratore, II, 211-212.

[144] Cic. De Orat. 1.195. Cf. also his high-handed treatment of the Athenians; Cic. De Orat. 3.75.

[145] Cic. De Orat. 3.93: rerum est silva magna, quam cum Graeci iam non tenerent; 3.94: apud Graecos, cuicuimodi essent.

[146] Note, for example, Cicero's concern for the plausibility of Scaevola's participation in the dialogue; Cic. Ad Att. 4.16.3.

[147] Cic. De Orat. 3.93: non quo, ut nescio quos dicere aiebant, acui ingenia adulescentium nollem.

[148] Cic. De Orat. 3.95: sed hominibus opus est eruditis, qui adhuc in hoc quidem genere nostri nulli fuerunt; sin quando extiterint, etiam Graecis erunt anteponendi. Cf. Meyer, Literarische Fiktion, 70-73. Meyer does, however, concede the reliability of Crassus' statement on the motivation for this edict.

general, quite another to ascribe to him bogus opinions in a specific
historical event of which he was chief actor. Cicero would not likely com-
mit the latter offense. We can trust the substance of Crassus' remarks on
the edict of 92.

Those remarks, when coupled with the evidence of the edict, lead to
a startling conclusion. The *mos maiorum* defended by the censors had the
principles of Greek rhetoric at its core. Such a move by the moral
caretakers of the Roman system would have been unthinkable three
quarters of a century earlier. The confrontations of Greek and Latin
culture that followed Rome's eastern wars in the 180s and 160s
engendered nervous insistence on the superiority of native traditions.
The mentality that fabricated the Pythagorean books of Numa in order
to exorcize them, that expelled Greek rhetors and philosophers from the
city, that frowned on teaching by expatriate intellectuals, and that condemned Epicureans had largely faded by 92.[149] The declarations of
public officials had now come full circle. Domitius Ahenobarbus might
lash out at his rival Crassus for excessive luxury, adopting the conventions of sumptuary laws and perhaps emulating his father who had sponsored such a measure in 115.[150] But when he combined with Crassus in
their one joint decree, it delivered a very different message indeed. The
censors no longer rebuked Romans for succumbing to alien imports or
harried Greek intellectuals in the interests of an indigenous culture. The
edict of 92 used conventional language but aimed at a new target.

The Hellenic character of Roman higher education could now be taken
for granted. It had become the *mos maiorum*; it defined the schools which
maiores nostri had approved for their children.[151] Use of Latin in rhetorical
training at an organized level was the innovation, a cheapening of the
process, a stripping away of humane culture and erudition for mere prat-
tle and impudence.[152] Such a stance might, of course, be expected of the
cultured intellectual L. Crassus. It appears also in the advice given to
young Cicero when he inclined to join the pupils flocking to the Latin
rhetor L. Plotius: the most learned men convinced him that his talents

---

[149] It is noteworthy, for example, that the grammarian Aurelius Opilius, who also
taught rhetoric and philosophy, was himself freedman of an Epicurean; Suet. *Gramm.* 6.

[150] Cassiodorus, *Chron.* ad ann. 115.

[151] Suet. *Rhet.* 1: *maiores nostri, quae liberos suos discere et quos in ludos itare vellent,
instituerunt.*

[152] Cic. *De Orat.* 3.94: *nam apud Graecos, cuicuimodi essent, videbam tamen esse praeter hanc
exercitationem linguae doctrinam aliquam et humanitate dignam scientiam, hos vero novos magistros
nihil intellegebam posse docere nisi ut auderent.* This may also, of course, reflect a certain snob-
bery and intellectual conservatism on the part of those who had been educated in an
earlier tradition.

would best be nurtured through training in Greek recitations.[153] But the
attitude did not confine itself to private opinion among the refined elite.
A censorial edict delivered official doctrine. And it was delivered in conjunction by two men otherwise notorious for their mutual animosity. The
decree castigated teachers of Latin, and upheld the virtue and tradition
of Hellenism in Roman rhetoric. Public policy had taken a very different
turn.

The act, like its predecessors, gave greater weight to gesture than to
implementation. It is uncertain that any rhetorical schools shut their
doors in consequence of the censors' declaration. Cicero refers to crowds
of students who signed up to work with L. Plotius, and gives no hint that
his courses were interrupted.[154] Rhetorical training in both Greek and
Latin was available in Cicero's youth.[155] Certainly the rhetors M.
Antonius Gnipho and L. Voltacilius Plotus plied their trade with
impunity in the years after the edict.[156] If a break occurred, it cannot
have been for long. But here too, as in the earlier instances, the purpose
was less to effect a practical change than to enunciate a principle.

The principle warrants reiteration, for it reveals a changed cultural
world at the beginning of the 1st century. Censors took as their charge
the protection of institutions and traditions. Domitius and Crassus found
common ground in deploring the inroads made on traditional education
by vulgarizers who would cut it adrift from its Hellenic moorings. The
censors cannot have expected eradication of the Latin rhetorical schools.
But they gave official voice to the precept that the teachings of rhetoric
must remain rooted in the humane tradition of Greek learning.

The official acts and pronouncements previously discussed contrasted
quite starkly with the edict of 92. Measures taken early in the 2nd century asserted the autonomy of native values and reminded Romans of the
enervating effect of Hellenic infiltration. The burning of "Numa's
Pythagorean books" signified that Rome's religious institutions had
transcended Greek influence and would no longer stay in its shadow. The
series of sumptuary laws declared public displeasure with the effects of
eastern opulence on the national character. Expulsion of philosophers
and rhetors denoted a still abiding cultural insecurity that demanded a

---

[153] Suet. *Rhet.* 2.1: *continebar autem doctissimorum hominum auctoritate, qui existimabant
Graecis exercitationibus ali melius ingenia posse.*

[154] Suet. *Rhet.* 2.1: *ad quem cum fieret concursus, quod studiosissimus quisque apud eum
exerceretur.* Other references to Plotius also fail to mention any halting of his operation;
Seneca, *Contr.* 2, praef. 5; Quint. 2.4.42; Jerome, *Chron.* Olymp. 173.1.

[155] Cic. *Brutus*, 310; cf. *De Orat.* 1.16.

[156] Suet. *Gramm.* 7; *Rhet.* 3; Jerome, *Chron.* Olymp. 174.4.

symbolic removal of the alien presence. Not coincidentally, these expressions of national concern tend to concentrate in the 180s, in the aftermath of eastern wars that exposed Rome to Hellas, and in the 160s, which saw a notable increase of Greek intellectuals in Italy.

Token gestures that represented a communal posture could not, however, restrain the expansion of Hellenism in Rome's upper class society and education. The visit of the Athenian embassy in 155 and the success of Carneades epitomized that expansion. Banishment of Epicureans was tokenism once again, only this time the tokenism served to validate other Greek intellectual strands in Rome by singling out Epicureanism. The Hellenic component in the schooling of Roman intellectuals swelled in the next half century. And the relative absence of official resistance signals a noteworthy growth in national self-confidence. The censorial edict of 92 supplies the most revealing signpost. Its rebuke fell not upon alien intrusion but upon native tampering with the educational process. An amalgam of Greco-Roman culture had now received official embrace. It was the truest token of Rome's cultural maturity.

BIBLIOGRAPHY

Accame, S. "Il senatus consultum de Bacchanalibus." *RivFilol* 66 (1938): 225-234.
Achard, G. "L'auteur de la Rhétorique a Herennius." *REL* 63 (1985): 56-68.
Alföldi, A. *Early Rome and the Latins.* Ann Arbor, 1963.
Allen, F.D. "On 'Os Columnatum' (Plaut. M.G. 211) and Ancient Instruments of Confinement." *HSCP* 7 (1896): 37-64.
Allen, R.E. *The Attalid Kingdom: A Constitutional History.* Oxford, 1983.
Allen, W. "On the Friendship of Lucretius with Memmius." *CP* 3 (1938): 167-181.
Altheim, F. *A History of Roman Religion.* London, 1938.
Anderson, A.R. "Heracles and his Successors." *HSCP* 39 (1928): 7-58.
Anderson, W.S. "Plautus' 'Trinummus': The Absurdity of Officious Morality." *Traditio* 35 (1979): 333-345.
Andreae, B. "Archäologische Funde und Grabungen im Bereich der Soprintendenzen von Rom 1949-1956/1957." *ArchAnz* 72 (1957): 110-358.
Andreau, J. "Banque grecque et banque romaine dans la théâtre de Plaute et de Terence." *MEFRA* 80 (1968): 461-526.
Anspach, A.E. "Die Abfassungszeit der plautinischen Bacchides." *Neue Jahrbücher für Philologie und Paedagogie* 139 (1889): 355-358.
Archellaschi, A. "Politique et religion dans le Pseudolus." *REL* 56 (1978): 115-141.
Arciniega, A.P. and Sanahuja Yll, M.E. *Paganismo y cristianismo en el occidente del imperio romano.* Oviedo, 1983.
Astin, A.E. "The Atinii." *Hommages Renard* (1969) II: 34-39.
——. *Cato the Censor.* Oxford, 1978.
Aurigemma, S. "La protezione speciale della Gran Madre Idea per la nobilità romana e le leggende dell'origine troiana di Roma." *BullCommArchRoma* 37 (1909): 31-65.
Badian, E. *Foreign Clientelae, 264-70 B.C.* Oxford, 1958.
——. *Studies in Greek and Roman History.* Oxford, 1964.
——. "Ennius and his Friends." *Entretiens Fondation Hardt* 17 (1972): 151-208.
——. "*Nobiles amici*: Art and Literature in an Aristocratic Society." *CP* 80 (1985): 341-357.
Balsdon, J.P.V.D. *Roman Women.* London, 1962.
Bandelli, G. "I processi degli Scipioni: le fonti." *Index* 3 (1972): 304-342.
Barbagallo, C. "Stato, scuolo e politica in Roma repubblicana." *RivFilol* 88 (1910): 481-514.
Barwick, K. "Das Kultlied des Livius Andronicus." *Philologus* 88 (1933): 203-221.
Bates, R.L. "Rex in senatu: A Political Biography of M. Aemilus Scaurus." *ProcAmerPhilosSoc* 130 (1986): 251-288.
Bauman, R.A. *Lawyers in Roman Republican Politics.* Munich, 1983.
Bayet, J. *Histoire politique et psychologique de la religion romaine.²* Paris, 1969.
Beare, W. "When Did Livius Andronicus Come to Rome?" *CQ* 34 (1940): 11-19.
——. "The Date of the Bellum Punicum." *CR* 63 (1949): 48.
——. *The Roman Stage.³* New York, 1963.
Becker, C. "Donarem Pateras." *Hermes* 87 (1959): 212-221.
Béquignon, Y. "Observations sur l'affaire des Bacchanales." *RevArch* 17 (1941): 184-198.
Beyk, Th. *Beiträge zu lateinische Grammatik.* Halle, 1970.
Bickerman, E.J. "Les préliminaires de la seconde guerre de Macédoine." *RevPhil* 61 (1935): 59-81, 161-176.
——. "Origines Gentium." *CP* 47 (1952): 65-81.
Bitto, I. "Venus Erycina e Mens." *ArchStorMessinese* 28 (1977): 121-133.

Bloch, G. "De l'authenticité de l'édit censorial de 92 av. J. C. contre les rhéteurs latins." *Klio* 3 (1903): 68-73.

Bomati, Y. "Les légendes dionysiaques en Étrurie." *REL* 61 (1983): 87-107.

Bömer, F. *Rom und Troia*. Baden-Baden, 1951.

———. P. *Ovidus Naso, Die Fasten* II. Heidelberg, 1958.

———. "Kybele in Rom." *MdI* 71 (1964): 130-151.

Bona, F. "Sul concetto di 'Manubiae' e sulla responsibilità del magistrato in ordine alla preda." *SDHI* 26 (1960): 105-175.

Bonamente, M. "Leggi suntuarie e loro motivazioni." *Tra Grecia e Roma* (1980): 67-91.

Bonner, S.F. *Education in Ancient Rome*. Berkeley, 1977.

Boutemy, A. "Quelques allusions historiques dans le 'Stichus' de Plaute." *REA* 38 (1936): 29-34.

Boyancé, P. "Les origines de la légende troyenne de Rome." *REA* 45 (1943): 275-290.

———. "Cybèle aux Mégalésies." *Latomus* 13 (1954): 337-342.

———. "Fulvius Nobilior et le dieu Ineffable." *RevPhil* 29 (1955): 172-192.

———. *Études sur la religion romaine*. Rome, 1972.

Boyce, A.A. "The Expiatory Rites of 207 B.C." *TAPA* 68 (1937): 157-171.

Bremmer, J. "The Legend of Cybele's Arrival in Rome." In M.J. Vermaseren, *Studies in Hellenistic Religions*. Leiden, 1979: 9-22.

Briscoe, J. *A Commentary on Livy, Books XXXI-XXXIII*. Oxford, 1973.

———. *A Commentary on Livy, Books XXXIV-XXXVII*. Oxford, 1981.

Broughton, T.R.S. *The Magistrates of the Roman Republic*. New York, 1951-52.

Bruhl, A. *Liber Pater*. Paris, 1953.

Büchner, K. "Livius Andronicus und die erste künstlerische Übersetzung der Europäischen Kultur." *SO* 54 (1979): 37-70.

Buck, C.H. *A Chronology of the Plays of Plautus*. Baltimore, 1940.

Calboli, G. "L'oratore M. Antonio e la 'Rhetorica ad Herennium'." *GiornItalFilol* 24 (1972): 120-177.

———. "La retorica preciceroniana e la politica a Roma." *Entretiens Fondation Hardt* 28 (1982): 41-108.

Capelle, W. "Griechische Ethik und römischer Imperialismus." *Klio* 25 (1932): 86-113.

Capozza, M. *Movimenti servili nel mondo romano in età repubblicana*. Rome, 1966.

Cassola, F. *I gruppi politici romani nel III secolo a.C.* Trieste, 1962.

Cazanove, O. de. "Lucus Stimulae: les aiguillons des Bacchanales." *MEFRA* 95 (1983): 55-113.

Cèbe, J-P. "Le niveau culturel du public plautinien." *REL* 38 (1960): 101-106.

Chalmers, W.R. "Plautus and his Audience." In T.A. Dorey and D.R. Dudley, *Roman Drama*. New York, 1965: 21-50.

Cichorius, C. *Römische Studien*. Leipzig, 1922.

Cimma, M.R. *Reges socii et amici populi romani*. Milan, 1976.

Clarke, M.L. *Rhetoric at Rome*. New York, 1963.

Clemente, G. "Esperti ambasciatori del senato e la formazione della politica estera romana tra il III e il II secolo a.C." *Athenaeum* 54 (1976): 319-352.

———. "Le legge sul lusso e la società romana tra III e II secolo a.C." *Società romana e produzione schiavistica* 3 (1981): 1-14, 301-304.

Coarelli, F. "Il sepolcro degli Scipioni." *DialArch* 6 (1972): 36-105.

Cole, S.G. "New Evidence for the Mysteries of Dionysos." *GRBS* 21 (1980): 223-238.

Cornell, T.J. "Aeneas and the Twins: The Development of the Roman Foundation Legend." *PCPS* 201 (1975): 1-32.

della Corte, F. "L'ambasceria di Cratete a Roma." *RivFilol* 12 (1934): 388-389.

———. *Da Sarsina a Roma*. Genoa, 1967.

———. "Numa e le streghe." *Maia* 26 (1974): 3-20.

Cousin, J. "La crise religieuse de 207 avant J.-C." *RHR* 126 (1942-43): 15-41.

Cova, P.V. "Livio e la repressione dei baccanali." *Athenaeum* 52 (1974): 82-109.

Crowther, N.B. "The Collegium Poetarum at Rome: Fact and Conjecture." *Latomus* 32 (1973): 575-580.

Cugusi, M.T.S. *M. Porci Catonis Orationum Reliquiae*. Turin, 1982.

Culham, P. "The Lex Oppia." *Latomus* 41 (1982): 786-793.

Dahlheim, W. *Struktur und Entwicklung der römischen Völkerrechts im 3. und 2. Jahrhundert v. Chr.* Munich, 1968.

Dahlmann, H. *Studien zu Varro, De Poetis*. Wiesbaden, 1963.

d'Anna, G. "Contributo alla cronologia dei poeti latini arcaici: II⁰-la prima rappresentazione di una *fabula* di Livio Andronico." *RendIstLomb* 87 (1954): 117-128.

———. *Problemi di letteratura latina arcaica*. Rome, 1976.

———. "La leggenda delle origini di Roma nella più antica tradizione letteraria." *Cultura e Scuola* 17 (1978): 22-31.

Daube, D. *Aspects of Roman Law*. Edinburgh, 1969.

David, J-M. "Promotion civique et droit à la parole: L. Licinius Crassus, les accusateurs et les rhéteurs latins." *MEFRA* 91 (1979): 135-181.

Delatte, A. "Les doctrines pythagoriciennes des livres de Numa." *BullAcadRoyBelg* 22 (1936): 19-40.

De Robertis, F. *Il diritto associativo romano dei "collegia"*. Bari, 1938.

———. *Storia delle corporazione e del regime associativo nel mondo romano*. Bari, 1971.

De Sanctis, G. *Storia dei Romani* IV.1. Florence, 1969.

Develin, R. "The Elections of 207 B.C." *Athenaeum* 55 (1977): 423-425.

———. "Religion and Politics During the Third Century B.C." *Journal of Religious History* 10 (1978): 3-19.

———. "Tradition and the Development of Triumphal Regulations in Rome." *Klio* 60 (1978): 429-438.

———. *The Practice of Politics at Rome, 366-167 B.C.* Brussels, 1985.

Diels, H. *Sibyllinische Blätter*. Berlin, 1890.

Dihle, A. "Miszellen zum sc de Bacchanalibus." *Hermes* 90 (1962): 376-379.

Dohrn, T. "Der vatikanische 'Ennius' und der poeta laureatus." *MdI* 69 (1962): 76-95.

Douglas, A.E. "Clausulae in the Rhetorica ad Herennium as Evidence of its Date." *CQ* 54 (1960): 65-78.

———. *M. Tulli Ciceronis Brutus*. Oxford, 1966.

Drury, M. "Appendix of Authors and Works." In E.J. Kenney and W.V. Clausen, *The Cambridge History of Classical Literature, II: Latin Literature*. Cambridge, 1982: 799-935.

Duckworth, G.E. *T. Macci Plauti Epidicus*. Princeton, 1940.

Dumézil, G. *Archaic Roman Religion*. Chicago, 1970.

Dumont, J.C. "Les gens de théâtre originaires des municipes." In *Les bourgeoisies municipales italiennes aux II et Iʳ siècles av. J.C.* (Colloques lat. du Centre Nat. de la recherche scientifique n. 609). Paris, 1983: 333-345.

Earl, D.C. "Political Terminology in Plautus." *Historia* 9 (1960): 235-243.

Eisenhut, W. "Die römische Gefängnisstrafe." *ANRW* I.2 (1972): 268-282.

Elter, A. *Donarem pateras*. Bonn, 1907.

Enk, P.J. *Plauti Mercator*. Leyden, 1932.

———. *Plauti Truculentus*. Leyden, 1953.

Erkell, H. "Ludi saeculares und ludi Latini saeculares. Ein Beitrag zur römischen Theaterkunde und Religionsgeschichte." *Eranos* 67 (1969): 166-174.

Fairweather, J. "Fiction in the Biographies of Ancient Writers." *AncSoc* 5 (1974): 231-275.

Ferrary, J.-L. "Le discours de Philus (Cicéron, De Re Publica, III, 8-31) et la philosophie de Carnéade." *REL* 55 (1977): 128-156.

Ferrero, L. "Su alcuni riflessi del patronato nella letteratura romana del III secolo a.C." *Mondo Classico* 11 (1941): 205-231.

———. *Storia del Pitagorismo del mondo romano*. Turin, 1955.

Festugière, M.A.-J. "Ce que Tite-Live nous apprend sur les mystères de Dionysos." *MEFRA* 66 (1954): 79-99.

Flacelière, R. *Les Aitoliens à Delphes*. Paris, 1937.

Flores, E. *Letteratura latina e società*. Naples, 1973.

———. *Letteratura latina e ideologia del III-II a.C.* Naples, 1974.

Fogazza, D. "Plauto 1935-1975." *Lustrum* 19 (1976): 79-296.
Fontenrose, J. *The Delphic Oracle.* Berkeley and Los Angeles, 1978.
Fraccaro, P. *Opuscula.* Pavia, 1956.
Fraenkel, E. "Review of F. Beckmann, *Zauberei und Recht in Roms Frühzeit.*" *Gnomon* 1 (1925): 185-200.
———. *Elementi plautini in Plautus.* Florence, 1960.
———. *Plautinisches in Plautus.* Berlin, 1922.
———. "Senatus consultum de Bacchanalibus." *Hermes* 67 (1932): 369-396.
Frank, T. "Naevius and Free Speech." *AJP* 48 (1927): 105-110.
———. "The Bacchanalian Cult of 186 B.C." *CQ* 21 (1927): 128-132.
———. "Some Political Allusions in Plautus' Trinummus." *AJP* 53 (1932): 152-156.
———. "Plautus' Comments on Anatolian Affairs." *Anatolian Studies Presented to W.H. Buckler* (1939): 85-88.
Frézouls, E. "Rome et les Latins dans les premières décennies du IIe siècle av. J.-C." *Ktema* 6 (1981): 115-132.
Fronza, L. "De Bacanalibus." *Annali Triestini* 17 (1947): 205-227.
Fuchs, H. *Der geistige Widerstand gegen Rom in der antiken Welt.* Berlin, 1938.
Gabba, E. "Politica e cultura in Roma agli inizi del I sec. a.C." *Athenaeum* 31 (1953): 259-272.
———. "Considerazioni sulla tradizione letteraria sulle origini della Repubblica." *Entretiens Fondation Hardt* 13 (1967): 135-174.
———. "Mario e Silla." *ANRW* I.1 (Berlin, 1972): 764-805.
———. "Storiografia greca e imperialismo romano (III-I sec. a.C.)." *RivStorItal* 86 (1974): 625-642.
Gagé, J. *Apollon romaine.* Paris, 1955.
Gagliardi, D. "Aspetti del teatro comico latino: la 'politica' di Plauto." *Le parole e le idee* 5 (1965): 167-174.
Gaiser, K. "Zur Eigenart der römischen Komödie: Plautus und Terenz gegenüber ihren griechischen Vorbildern." *ANRW* I.2 (1972): 1027-1113.
Galinsky, G.K. "Scipionic Themes in Plautus' Amphitruo." *TAPA* 97 (1966): 203-235.
———. *Aeneas, Sicily, and Rome.* Princeton, 1969.
Gallini, C. *Protesta e integrazione nella Roma antica.* Bari, 1970.
Galsterer, H. *Herrschaft und Verwaltung im republikanischen Italien.* Munich, 1976.
Garbarino, G. *Roma e la filosofia greca dalle origini alla fine del II secolo a.C.* Turin, 1973.
Gelzer, M. "Die angebliche politische Tendenz in der dem C. Herennius Gewidmeten Rhetorik." *Kleine Schriften.* Wiesbaden, 1962. I:211-221.
———. "Die Unterdrückung der Bacchanalien bei Livius." *Hermes* 71 (1936): 275-287.
———. *Kleine Schriften.* 3 vols. Wiesbaden, 1962-64.
Gentili, B. *Theatrical Performances in the Ancient World: Hellenistic and Early Roman Theater.* Amsterdam, 1979.
Gérard, J. "Légende et politique autour de la mère des dieux." *REL* 58 (1980): 153-175.
Giovannini, A. "Téos, Antiochos III et Attale Ier." *MH* 40 (1983): 178-184.
Golan, D. "The Problem of the Roman Presence in the Political Consciousness of the Greeks before 229 B.C." *RivStorAnt* 1 (1971): 93-98.
Gold, B.K. (ed.) *Literary and Artistic Patronage in Ancient Rome.* Austin, 1982.
———. *Literary Patronage in Greece and Rome.* Chapel Hill, 1987.
Goldberg, S.M. "Plautus' Epidicus and the Case of the Missing Original." *TAPA* 108 (1978): 81-91.
Graillot, H. *Le culte de Cybèle, mère des dieux, a Rome et dans l'empire romaine.* Paris, 1912.
Gratwick, A.S. "Titus Maccius Plautus." *CQ* 67 (1973): 78-84.
———. "Curculio's Last Bow: Plautus, Trinummus IV. 3." *Mnemosyne* 34 (1981): 331-350.
——— "Drama". In E.J. Kenney and W.V. Clausen, *The Cambridge History of Classical Literature*, II: *Latin Literature.* Cambridge, 1982: 77-137.
Griffin, J. "Augustus and the Poets: 'Caesar qui cogere posset." In F. Millar and E. Segal: *Caesar Augustus: Seven Aspects.* Oxford, 1984: 189-218.

Grilli, A. "Numa, Pitagora e la politica antiscipionica." In M. Sordi, *Politica e religione nel primo scontro tra Roma e l'Oriente*. Milan, 1982: 186-197.

Grimal, P. *La siècle des Scipions*. Paris, 1953.

——. "Le théâtre à Rome." *IXᵉ-Congrès Int. de l'Assoc. Budé* (1973) I: 249-305.

Gruen, E.S. "Political Prosecutions in the 90's B.C." *Historia* 15 (1966): 32-64.

——. *Roman Politics and the Criminal Courts, 149-78 B.C.* Cambridge, Mass., 1968.

——. *The Hellenistic World and the Coming of Rome*. Berkeley and Los Angeles, 1984.

Guarducci, M. "Cibele in un' epigrafe arcaica di Locri Epizefiri." *Klio* 52 (1970): 133-138.

Günther, R. "Der politisch-ideologische Kampf in der römischen Religion in den letzten zwei Jahrhunderten v.u. Z." *Klio* 42 (1964): 209-297.

Gwynn, A. *Roman Education from Cicero to Quintilian*. Oxford, 1926.

Habicht, C. "Über die Kriege zwischen Pergamon und Bithynien." *Hermes* 84 (1956): 90-110.

——. *Studien zur Geschichte Athens in hellenistischer Zeit*. Göttingen, 1982.

Halkin, L. "La parodie d'une demande de triomphe dans l'Amphitryon de Plaute." *AntCl* 17 (1948): 297-304.

Handley, F.W. "Plautus and his Public: Some Thoughts on New Comedy in Latin." *Dioniso* 46 (1975): 117-132.

Hansen, E.V. *The Attalids of Pergamum²*. Ithaca, 1971.

Hanson, J.A. "Scholarship on Plautus Since 1950." *CW* 59 (1965): 103-107, 126-148.

——. "The Glorious Military." In T.A. Dorey and D.R. Dudley, *Roman Drama*. New York, 1965: 51-85.

Harris, W.V. "Was Roman Law Imposed on the Allies?' *Historia* 21 (1972): 639-645.

——. *War and Imperialism in Republican Rome, 327-70 B.C.* Oxford, 1979.

Harvey, P.B. "Historical Allusions in Plautus and the Date of the Amphitruo." *Athenaeum* 59 (1981): 480-489.

——. "Historical Topicality in Plautus." *CW* 79 (1986): 297-304.

Haury, A. "Une 'année de la femme' à Rome, 195 avant J.-C.?" *Mélanges Heurgon* (1976) I: 427-436.

Haywood, R.M. *Studies on Scipio Africanus*. Baltimore, 1933.

Hellman, F. "Zur Cato—und Valerius—Rede." *NJADB* 4 (1940): 81-86.

Henrichs, A. "Greek Maenadism from Olympias to Messalina." *HSCP* 82 (1978): 121-160.

——. "Changing Dionysiac Identities." In B.F. Meyer and E.P. Sanders, *Jewish and Christian Self-Definition*. Philadelphia, 1982. III: 137-160, 213-236.

——. "Male Intruders among the Maenads: The So-Called Male Celebrant." In H.D. Evjen, *Mnemai: Classical Studies in Honor of Karl K. Hulley*. Chico, Ca., 1984: 69-91.

Herrmann, C. *Le rôle judiciaire et politique des femmes sous la republique romaine*. Brussels, 1964.

Herrmann, L. "La date du "Miles Gloriosus' de Plaute et la fin de Naevius," *Latomus* 1 (1937): 25-30.

——. "Ennius et les livres de Numa." *Latomus* 5 (1946): 87-90.

——. "L'actualite dans l'Amphitryon de Plaute." *AntCl* 17 (1948): 317-322.

Herrmann, P. "Antiochos der Grosse und Teos." *Anatolia* 9 (1965): 29-159.

Heurgon, J. "Influences grecques sur la religion Étrusque: l'inscription de Laris Pulenas." *REL* 35 (1957): 106-126.

Hoffman, W. *Wandel und Herkunft der Sibyllinischen Bücher in Rom*. Diss. Leipzig, 1933.

——. *Rom und die griechischen Welt im 4. Jahrhundert*. Leipzig, 1934.

Holleaux, M. *Rome, la Grèce et les monarchies hellénistiques au IIIᵉ siècle avant J.-C. (273-205)*. Paris, 1935.

Horsfall, N. "The Collegium Poetarum." *BICS* 23 (1976): 79-95.

——. "Some Problems in the Aeneas Legend." *CQ* 29 (1979): 372-390.

Hough, J.N. "The Development of Plautus' Art." *CP* 30 (1935): 43-57.

——. "Link-monologues and Plautine Chronology." *TAPA* 70 (1939): 231-241.

——. "The Understanding of Intrigue: A Study in Plautine Chronology." *AJP* 60 (1939): 422-435.

Hughes, J.D. *A Bibliography of Scholarship on Plautus*. Amsterdam, 1975.

Hunter, R.L. "Horace on Friendship and Free Speech." *Hermes* 113 (1985): 480-490.

Jachmann, G. *Plautinisches und Attisches*. Berlin, 1931.

Jahn, J. *Interregnum und Wahldiktatur*. Kallmünz, 1970.

Janne, H. "L'Amphitryon de Plaute et M. Fulvius Nobilior." *RevBelge* 12 (1933): 515-531.

Jocelyn, H.D. "Chrysalus and the Fall of Troy (Plautus, Bacchides 925-978)." *HSCP* 73 (1969): 135-152.

——. "The Poet Cn. Naevius, P. Cornelius Scipio and Q. Caecilius Metellus." *Antichthon* 3 (1969): 32-47.

——. "Discussion on Badian, Ennius, and his Friends." *Entretiens Fondation Hardt* 17 (1972): 200-201.

——. "The Poems of Quintus Ennius." *ANRW* I.2 (1972): 987-1026.

——. "The Ruling Class of the Roman Republic and Greek Philosophers." *BRL* 59 (1977): 323-367.

Johnston, P.A. "Poenulus 1, 2 and Roman Women." *TAPA* 110 (1980): 143-159.

Jones, R.E. "Cicero's Accuracy of Characterization in his Dialogues." *AJP* 60 (1939): 307-325.

Jope, J. "The Fasti: Nationalism and Personal Involvement in Ovid's Treatment of Cybele." *EMC* 32 (1988): 13-22.

Jory, E.J. "P. Cornelius P.L. Surus: An Epigraphical Note." *BICS* 15 (1968): 125-126.

——. "Associations of Actors in Rome." *Hermes* 98 (1970): 224-253.

Jullien, E. *Les professeurs de littérature dans l'ancienne Rome*. Paris, 1885.

Jurewicz, O. "Plautus, Cato der Ältere und die römische Gesellschaft." In J. Irmscher and K. Kumaniecki, *Aus der Altertumswissenschaftlichen Arbeit Volkspolens*. Berlin, 1959: 52-92.

Kaimio, J. *The Romans and the Greek Language*. Helsinki, 1979.

Keil, J. "Das sogenannte Senatusconsultum de Bacchanalibus." *Hermes* 68 (1933): 306-312.

Kennedy, G. *The Art of Rhetoric in the Roman World, 300 B.C.-A.D. 300*. Princeton, 1972.

Kenney, E.J. and Clausen, W.V. *The Cambridge History of Classical Literature, II: Latin Literature*. Cambridge, 1982.

Kienast, D. *Cato der Zensor*. Heidelberg, 1954.

——. "Rom und die Venus vom Eryx." *Hermes* 93 (1965): 478-489.

Killeen, J.F. "Plautus Miles Gloriosus 211." *CP* 68 (1973): 53-54.

Köves, T. "Zum Empfang der Magna Mater in Rom." *Historia* 12 (1963): 321-347.

Kraemer, R.S. "Ecstasy and Possession: The Attraction of Women to the Cult of Dionysus." *HTR* 72 (1979): 55-80.

Krause, W. "Zum Aufbau der Bacchanal-Inschrift." *Hermes* 71 (1936): 214-220.

Kroll, W. "Der Tod des Naevius." *Hermes* 66 (1931): 469-472.

Kuiper, K. "De Matre Magna Pergamenorum." *Mnemosyne* 30 (1902): 277-306.

Kunkel, W. *Untersuchungen zur Entwicklung des römischen Kriminalverfahrens in vorsullanischer Zeit*. Munich, 1962.

Lambrechts, P. "Cybèle, divinité étrangère ou nationale?" *BullSocBelge d'anthropologie et de préhistoire* 62 (1951): 44-60.

Lana, I. "Terenzio e il movimento filellenico in Roma." *RivFilol* 75 (1947): 44-80, 155-175.

La Penna, A. *Fra teatro, poesia, e politica romana*. Turin, 1979.

Latte, K. *Römische Religionsgeschichte*. Munich, 1960.

Leeman, A.D. "The Good Companion (Ennius, *Ann.* v. 234-251 Vahlen)." *Mnemosyne* 11 (1958): 318-321.

——. *Orationis Ratio*. Amsterdam, 1963.

—— and H. Pinkster. *M. Tussius Cicero. De Oratore Libri III*. I. Heidelberg, 1981.

——, H. Pinkster, and H.L.W. Nelson. *M. Tullius Cicero. De Oratore Libri III*. II. Heidelberg, 1985.

Lefkowitz, M. *Lives of the Greek Poets*. London, 1981.

Lenchantin, M. "I due inni religiosi di Livio Andronico." *Athenaeum* 14 (1936): 36-44.
Leo, F. "Varro und die Satire." *Hermes* 24 (1889): 67-84.
——. *Plautinische Forschungen.*² Berlin, 1912.
——. *Geschichte der römischen Literatur.* Berlin, 1913.
Levi, M.A. "Bacchanalia, foedus e foederati." *Klearchos* (1969): 15-23.
——. *Il Tribunato della plebe.* Milan, 1978.
Lindsay, W.M. *The Captivi of Plautus.* London, 1900.
Lintott, A.W. "Provocatio. From the Struggle of the Orders to the Principate." *ANRW* I.2 (1972): 226-267.
Lippold, A. *Consules.* Bonn, 1963.
Littlewood, R.J. "Poetic Artistry and Dynastic Politics: Ovid at the Ludi Megalenses (Fasti 4.179-372)." *CQ* 31 (1981): 381-395.
de Lorenzi, A. *Cronologia ed evoluzione plautina.* Naples, 1952.
Luce, T.J. "Marius and the Mithridatic Command." *Historia* 19 (1970): 161-194.
Luisi, A. "La lex Maenia e la repressione dei Baccanali nel 186 a.C." In M. Sordi, *Politica e religione nel primo scontro tra Roma e l'Oriente.* Milan, 1982: 179-185.
MacBain, B. *Prodigy and Expiation: A Study in Religion and Politics in Republican Rome.* Brussels, 1982.
MacCary, W.T. "The Bacchae in Plautus' Casina." *Hermes* 103 (1975): 459-463.
—— and M.M. Willcock. *Plautus: Casina.* Cambridge, 1976.
Magie, D. *Roman Rule in Asia Minor.* Princeton, 1950.
Magno, P. *Quinto Ennio.* Fasano, 1979.
Manfredini, A. "L'editto 'de coercendis rhetoribus Latinis' del 92 a.C." *SDHI* 42 (1976): 99-148.
Manganaro, G. "Una biblioteca storica nel ginnasio di Tauromenion e il P. Oxy. 1241." *PP* 29 (1974): 389-409.
Manni, E. "Sulle più antiche relazioni fra Roma e il mondo ellenistico." *PP* 11 (1956): 179-190.
Marconi, G. "La cronologia di Livio Andronico." *MemAccadLinc* 8.12 (1966): 125-213.
Marmorale, E.V. *Naevius Poeta².* Florence, 1950.
Martina, M. "Ennio 'poeta cliens'." *QuadFilolClass* 2 (1979): 15-74.
——. "'Grassatores' e 'Carmentarii'." *Labeo* 26 (1980): 155-175.
——. "Aedes Herculis Musarum." *DialArch* (1981): 49-68.
Martinelli, N. *La rappresentazione dello stile di Crasso e di Antonio nel De Oratore.* Rome, 1963.
Marx, F. *Incerti auctoris, de ratione dicendi ad C. Herennium.* Leipzig, 1894.
——. *Zeitschr. Österr. Gymn.* (1898): 385ff.
——. "Naevius." *SitzSächsGes* 63 (1911): 39-82.
Mattingly, H.B. "The Date of Livius Andronicus." *CQ* 51 (1957): 159-163.
——. "The Plautine 'Didascaliae'." *Athenaeum* 35 (1957): 78-88.
——. "The First Period of Plautine Revival." *Latomus* 19 (1960): 230-252.
——. "Naevius and the Metelli." *Historia* 9 (1960): 414-439.
——. "Review of Marconi, *La Cronologia di Livio Andronico.*" *Gnomon* 43 (1971): 680-687.
Mazzarino, S. *Il pensiero storico classico.* Bari, 1968.
McDonald, A.H. "Rome and the Italian Confederation (200-186 B.C.)." *JRS* 34 (1944): 11-33.
——. "The Roman Conquest of Cisalpine Gaul (201-191 B.C.)." *Antichthon* 8 (1974): 44-53.
McDonnell, M. "Divorce Initiated by Women in Rome." *AJAH* 8 (1983): 54-80.
——. "Ambitus and Plautus' Amphitruo, 65-81." *AJP* 107 (1986): 564-576.
McShane, R.B. *The Foreign Policy of the Attalids of Pergamum.* Urbana, 1964.
Méautis, G. "Aspects religieux de l' «affaire» des Bacchanales." *REA* 42 (1940): 476-485.
Mele, A. "Il pitagorismo e le popolazioni anelleniche d'Italia." *AION* 3 (1981): 61-96.
Mello, M. *Mens Bona.* Naples, 1968.
Mette, H.J. "Die römische Tragödie und die neufunde zur griechischen Tragödie." *Lustrum* 9 (1964): 5-211.
Meyer, R.D. *Literarische Fiktion und historischer Gehalt in Ciceros De Oratore.* Stuttgart, 1970.

Michel, A. *Rhétorique et philosophie chez Cicéron.* Paris, 1960.
Millar, F. and Segal, E. *Caesar Augustus: Seven Aspects.* Oxford, 1984.
Moevs, M.T.M. "Le Muse di Ambracia." *Bolletino d'Arte* 66 (1981): 1-58.
Momigliano, A. "Review of L. Robinson, *Freedom of Speech in the Roman Republic.*" *JRS* 32 (1942): 119-124.
——. "Review of J. Perret, *Les origines de la légende troyenne de Rome.*" *JRS* 35 (1945): 99-104.
——. "Atene nel III secolo a.C. e la scoperta di Roma nelle storie di Timeo di Tauromenio." *RivStorItal* 11 (1959): 529-556.
——. *Terzo contributo alla storia degli studi classici e del mondo antico.* Rome, 1966.
——. "How to Reconcile Greeks and Trojans." In *Settimo contributo alla storia degli studi classici e del mondo antico.* Rome, 1984: 437-462.
Mommsen, T. *Römische Forschungen.* Berlin, 1879.
——. *Römisches Staatsrecht.*³ Leipzig, 1887-1888.
——. *Römisches Strafrecht.* Leipzig, 1899.
More, J.H. "Cornelius Surus: Bureaucrat and Poet." *Grazer Beiträge* 3 (1975): 241-262.
Moritz, L.A. *Grain-Mills and Flour in Classical Antiquity.* Oxford, 1958.
Münzer, F. *Römische Adelsparteien und Adelsfamilien.* Stuttgart, 1920.
Musso, O. "Sulla datazione del 'Truculentus' di Plauto." *StudItalFilCl* 41 (1969): 135-138.
Naudet, J. "Essai de classification chronologique des comédies de Plaute." *JSav* (1838): 328ff., 406ff.
Niese, B. *Geschichte der griechischen und makedonischen Staaten seit der Schlacht bei Chaeronea.* Gotha, 1883-1903.
Nilsson, M.P. *The Dionysiac Mysteries of the Hellenistic and Roman Age.* Lund, 1957.
North, J.A. "Conservatism and Change in Roman Religion." *PBSR* 31 (1976): 1-12.
——. "Religious Toleration in Republican Rome." *PCPS* 25 (1979): 85-103.
Ogilvie, R.M. *A Commentary on Livy, Books 1-5.* Oxford, 1965.
Orth, W. *Königlicher Machtanspruch und städtische Freiheit.* Munich, 1977.
Pailler, J.M. "Bolsena, 1970. La maison aux peintures, les niveaux inférieures et le complexe souterrain." *MEFRA* 83 (1971): 384-402.
——. "'Raptos a diis homines dici...' (Tite-Live, XXXIX, 13): les Bacchanales et la possession par les nymphes." *Mélanges Heurgon* (1976) II: 731-741.
——. "La spirale de l'interpretation: les Bacchanales." *Annales ESC* 37 (1982): 929-952.
——. "Les pots cassés des Bacchanales." *MEFRA* 95 (1983): 7-39.
——. "Caton et les Bacchanales: séduction et tenacité d'un mirage historique." *PBSR* 54 (1986): 29-39.
Palmer, R.E.A. *Roman Religion and Roman Empire.* Philadelphia, 1974.
Parke, H.W. and Wormell, D.E.W. *The Delphic Oracle.* Oxford, 1956.
Pascal, C. "Lo Scipio di Ennio." *Athenaeum* 3 (1915): 369-395.
Perna, R. *L'originalità di Plauto.* Bari, 1955.
Perret, J. *Les origines de la légende troyenne de Rome (281-31).* Paris, 1942.
Peruzzi, E. *Origini di Roma.* Bologna, 1973.
Petersmann, H. *T. Maccius Plautus: Stichus.* Heidelberg, 1973.
Phillips, E.D. "Odysseus in Italy." *JHS* 73 (1953): 53-67.
Pichon, R. "L'affaire des rhetores latini." *REA* 6 (1904): 37-41.
Pighi, J.B. *De Ludis Saecularibus populi romani quiritium.* Amsterdam, 1965.
Piper, D. "Latins and the Roman Citizenship in the Roman Colonies: Livy, 34.42.5-6; Revisited." *Historia* 36 (1987): 36-50.
Pomeroy, S. *Goddesses, Whores, Wives, and Slaves.* New York, 1975.
Porte, D. "Claudia Quinta et le problème de la lavatio Cybèle en 204 av. J.-C." *Klio* 66 (1984): 93-103.
Poucet, J. *Les origines de Rome: tradition et histoire.* Brussels, 1985.
Préaux, J. "Caton et l'ars poetica." *Latomus* 25 (1966): 710-725.
Primmer, A. *Handlungsgliederung in Nea und Palliata: Dis Exapaton und Bacchides.* Vienna, 1984.

Prowse, K.R. "Numa and the Pythagoreans: A Curious Incident." *Greece and Rome* 11 (1964): 36-42.
Questa, C. *T. Maccius Plautus: Bacchides.* Florence, 1975.
Quinn, K. "The Poet and his Audience in the Augustan Age." *ANRW*, II.30.1 (1982): 75-180.
Radke, G. "Vergils Cumaeum Carmen." *Gymnasium* 66 (1959): 217-246.
Rawson, E. "Lucius Crassus and Cicero." *PCPS* 17 (1971): 79-88.
———. "The First Latin Annalists." *Latomus* 35 (1976): 689-717.
———. *Intellectual Life in the Late Roman Republic.* Baltimore, 1985.
———. "Theatrical Life in Republican Rome and Italy." *PBSR* 53 (1985): 97-113.
Reinach, S. "Une ordalie par le poison a Rome et l'affaire des Bacchanales." *RevArch* 11 (1908): 236-253.
Rich, J.W. "Roman Aims in the First Macedonian War." *PCPS* 30 (1984): 126-180.
Richardson, J.S. "The Triumph, the Praetors and the Senate in the Early Second Century B.C." *JRS* 65 (1975): 50-63.
Richter, W. "Staat, Gesellschaft und Dichtung in Rom in 3. und 2. Jahrhundert v. Chr." *Gymnasium* 69 (1962): 286-310.
Riess, E. "Notes on Plautus." *CQ* 35 (1941): 150-162.
Rilinger, R. *Der Einfluss des Wahlleiters bei den römischen Konsulwahlen von 366 bis 50 v. Chr.* Munich, 1976.
Ritschl, F. *Parerga Plautina et Terentiana.* Leipzig, 1845.
Rizzo, F.P. *Studi ellenistico-romani.* Palermo, 1974.
Robinson, L.A. *Freedom of Speech in the Roman Republic.* Baltimore, 1940.
Roesch, P. "Le culte d'Asclepios à Rome." In G. Sabbah, *Médicins et Médecine dans l'anti-quité.* Saint-Etienne, 1982: 171-179.
Ronconi, A. "Saggio per un commento al proemio degli annali di Ennio." In *Poesia Latina in Frammenti.* Genoa, 1974: 13-28.
Rosen, K. "Die falschen Numabücher." *Chiron* 15 (1985): 65-90.
Rostagni, A. *La letteratura di Roma repubblicana ed augustea.* Bologna, 1939.
———. *Suetonio de poetis e biografi minori.* Turin, 1944.
Rousselle, R.J. *The Roman Persecution of the Bacchic Cult, 186-180 B.C.* Diss., Binghamton, N.Y., 1982.
———. "Liber-Dionysus in Early Roman Drama." *CJ* 82 (1987): 193-198.
Roux, G. "La terrasse d'Attale I à Delphes." *BCH* 76 (1952): 141-196.
Rowell, H.T. "The 'Campanian' Origin of C. Naevius and its Literary Attestation." *MAAR* 19 (1949): 17-34.
Rudolph, H. *Stadt und Staat im römischen Italien.* Leipzig, 1935.
Ruebel, J.S. "Cato, Ennius, and Sardinia." *LCM* 2 (1977): 155-157.
Saller, R.P. *Personal Patronage under the Early Empire.* Cambridge, 1982.
———. "Martial on Patronage and Literature." *CQ* 33 (1983): 246-257.
Salmon, E.T. *Roman Colonization under the Republic.* London, 1969.
———. *The Making of Roman Italy.* London, 1982.
Sauerwein, I. *Die Leges Sumptuariae als römische Massnahme gegen den Sittenverfall.* Hamburg, 1970.
Schaaf, L. "Die Todesjahre des Naevius und des Plautus in der antiken Überlieferung." *RhM* 122 (1979): 24-33.
Schilling, R. *La religion romaine de Vénus.* Paris, 1954.
Schmidt, E. *Kultübertragungen.* Giessen, 1909.
Schmidt, P.L. "Die Anfänge der institutionellen Rhetorik in Rom." In E. Lefèvre, *Monumentum Chiloniense. Festschrift für Erich Burck.* Amsterdam, 1975: 183-216.
Schmitt, H.H. *Untersuchungen zur Geschichte Antiochos, des Grossen und seiner Zeit.* Wiesbaden, 1964.
Scholz, U.W. "Der 'Scipio' des Ennius." *Hermes* 112 (1984): 183-199.
Schur, W. *Scipio Africanus und die Begründung der römischen Weltherrschaft.* Leipzig, 1927.
Schutter, K.H.E. *Quibus annis comoediae plautinae primum actae sint quaesitur.* Groningen, 1952.

Scullard, H.H. *Scipio Africanus: Soldier and Politician.* London, 1970.
——. *Roman Politics, 220-150 B.C.*[2] Oxford, 1973.
Sedgwick, W.D. "The Dating of Plautus' Plays." *CQ* 24 (1930): 102-105.
——. "Plautine Chronology." *AJP* 70 (1949): 376-383.
Segal, E. *Roman Laughter.* Cambridge, Mass., 1968.
——. "The Purpose of the Trinummus." *AJP* 95 (1974): 252-264.
——. "Scholarship on Plautus 1965-1976." *CW* 74 (1980-1981): 353-433.
Shatzman, I. "The Roman General's Authority over Booty." *Historia* 21 (1972): 177-205.
Sheets, G.A. "The Dialect Gloss, Hellenistic Poetics and Livius Andronicus." *AJP* 102 (1981): 58-78.
Shipp, G.B. "Greek in Plautus." *WS* 66 (1953): 105-112.
——. "Plautine Terms for Greek and Roman Things." *Glotta* 34 (1955): 139-152.
Siber, H. "Analogie, Amtsrecht und Rückwirkung im Strafrecht des römischen Freistaates." *AbhLeipz* 43.3 (1936): 1-77.
Sihler, E.G. "The Collegium Poetarum at Rome." *AJP* 26 (1905): 1-21.
Simon, E. "Apollo in Rom." *JDAI* 93 (1978): 202-227.
Skutsch, O. "Review of E. Marmorale, *Naevius poeta.*" *CR* 65 (1951): 174-177.
——. *Studia Enniana.* London, 1968.
——. *The Annals of Quintus Ennius.* Oxford, 1985.
Slater, N.W. *Plautus in Performance: The Theater of the Mind.* Princeton, 1985.
——. "The Dates of Plautus' *Curculio* and *Trinummus* Reconsidered." *AJP* 108 (1987): 264-269.
Smith, R.E. "The Law of Libel at Rome." *CQ* 45 (1951): 169-179.
——. "Latins and the Roman Citizenship in Roman Colonies: Livy, 34,42,5-6." *JRS* 44 (1954): 18-20.
Solmsen, F. "Aeneas Founded Rome with Odysseus." *HSCP* 90 (1986): 93-110.
Sordi, M. "Il confine del Tauro e dell' Halys e il sacrificio in Ilio." In M. Sordi, *Politica e religione nel primo scontro tra Roma e l'Oriente.* Milan, 1982: 136-149.
Spranger, P.P. *Historische Untersuchungen zu den Sklavenfiguren des Plautus und Terenz.*[2] Stuttgart, 1984.
Stewart, Z. "The God Nocturnus in Plautus' Amphitruo." *JRS* 50 (1960): 37-43.
Stockert, W. "Die Anspielungen auf die Bacchanalien in der Aulularia (406-414) und anderen Plautuskomödien." In R. Hanslik, et al., *Antidosis: Festschrift für W. Kraus.* Vienna, 1972: 398-416.
Strachan-Davidson, J.L. *Problems of the Roman Criminal Law.* Oxford, 1912.
Strasburger, H. *Zur Sage von der Gründung Roms.* Heidelberg, 1968.
Suerbaum, W. *Untersuchungen zur Selbstdarstellung älterer römischer Dichter.* Hildesheim, 1968.
——. "Discussion on Badian, Ennius and his Friends." *Entretiens Fondation Hardt* 17 (1972): 200.
Tamm, B. "Le temple des Muses à Rome." *Opuscula Romana* 21 (1961): 157-167.
Tarditi, G. "La questione dei baccanali a Roma nel 186 a.C." *PP* 37 (1954): 265-287.
Taylor, L.R. "The Opportunities for Dramatic Performances in the Time of Plautus and Terence." *TAPA* 68 (1937): 284-304.
Thomas, G. "Magna Mater and Attis." *ANRW* II. 17.3 (1984): 1499-1535.
Tierney, J.J. "The Senatus Consultum De Bacchanalibus." *Proceedings of the Royal Irish Academy* 51 (1947): 89-117.
Till, R. "Die Anerkennung literarischen Schaffens in Rom." *Neue Jahrbücher* 115 (1940): 161-174.
Toohey, P. "Politics, Prejudice, and Trojan Genealogies: Varro, Hyginus, and Horace." *Arethusa* 17 (1984): 5-28.
Toynbee, A.J. *Hannibal's Legacy.* Oxford, 1965.
Turcan, R. "Religion et politique dans l'affaire des Bacchanales." *Revue de l'histoire des religions* 181 (1972): 3-28.
Vahlen, J. *Ennianae Poesis Reliquiae.* Leipzig, 1928.

Vermaseren, M.J. *Cybele and Attis*. London, 1977.

Virgilio, B. *Il tempio stato di Pessinunte fra Pergamo e Roma nel II-I secolo a.C*. Pisa, 1981.

Vitucci, G. "Pitagorismo e legislazione 'Numaica'." *Problemi attuali di scienca e di cultura, AccadLinc* 473 (1976): 153-162.

Vogt, J. "Vorläufer des Optimus Princeps." *Hermes* 68 (1933): 84-92.

Voisin, J.-L. "Tite-Live, Capoue et les Bacchanales." *MEFRA* 96 (1984): 601-653.

Wagner, W. *De Plauti Aulularia*. Bonn, 1874.

Walbank, F.W. *Philip V of Macedon*. Cambridge, 1940.

——. *A Historical Commentary on Polybius*. I. Oxford, 1957; II. Oxford, 1967; III. Oxford, 1979.

——. "Political Morality and the Friends of Scipio." *JRS* 55 (1965): 1-16.

——. "The Scipionic Legend." *PCPS* 13 (1967): 54-69.

Waltzing, J.-P. *Étude historique sur les corporations professionelles chez les Romains*. Louvain, 1895-1900.

Warde Fowler, W. *The Religious Experience of the Roman People*. London, 1911.

Warnecke, B. "Ad Naevium et Bacchylidem." *Philologus* 71 (1912): 567-568.

Waszink, J.H. "Camena." *ClMed* 17 (1956): 139-148.

——. "Tradition and Personal Achievement in Early Latin Literature." *Mnemosyne* 13 (1960): 16-33.

——. "Zum Anfangsstadium der römischen Literatur." *ANRW* I.2 (1972): 869-927.

Watson, A. *Roman Private Law around 200 B.C*. Edinburgh, 1971.

Weber, E. "Die trojanische Abstammung der Römer als politisches Argument." *WS* 85 (1972): 213-225.

Weinstock, S. "Review of K. Latte, *Römische Religionsgeschichte*." *JRS* 51 (1961): 206-215.

Welles, C.B. *Royal Correspondence in the Hellenistic World*. London, 1934.

West, A.F. "On a Patriotic Passage in the Miles Gloriosus of Plautus." *AJP* 8 (1887): 15-33.

Westaway, K.M. *The Original Element in Plautus*. Cambridge, 1917.

White, P. "*Amicitia* and the Profession of Poetry in Early Imperial Rome." *JRS* 68 (1978): 74-92.

Will, E. *Histoire politique du monde hellénistique*. Nancy, 1967.

Willems, P. *Le sénat de la république romaine*. Louvain, 1883.

Williams, G. "Some Problems in the Construction of Plautus' Pseudolus." *Hermes* 84 (1956): 424-455.

——. "Phases in Political Patronage of Literature in Rome." In B.K. Gold, *Literary and Artistic Patronage in Ancient Rome*. Austin, 1982: 3-27.

——. "The Genesis of Poetry in Rome." In E.J. Kenney and W.V. Clausen, *The Cambridge History of Classical Literature, II: Latin Literature*. Cambridge, 1982: 53-59.

Wiseman, T.P. *Clio's Cosmetics: Three Studies in Greco-Roman Literature*. Leicester, 1979.

——. "Cybele, Virgil and Augustus." In T. Woodman and D. West, *Poetry and Politics in the Age of Augustus*. Cambridge, 1984: 117-128.

Wissowa, G. "Naevius und die Meteller." *Genethliakon für C. Robert* (1910): 51-63.

——. *Religion und Kultus der Römer*². Munich, 1912.

Wright, J. "Naevius, Tarentilla Fr. I (72-74 R³)." *RhM* 115 (1972): 239-242.

——. *Dancing in Chains: The Stylistic Unity of the Comoedia Palliata*. Rome, 1974.

Zehnacker, H. "Tragédie prétexte et spectacle romain." In *Théâtre et spectacles dans l'antiquité*. Actes du Colloque de Strasbourg, 1981: 31-48.

Zorzetti, N. *La Pretesta e il teatro latino arcaico*. Naples, 1980.

INDEX

Acarnania, 13

Accius, L. (dramatist), 80-82, 83n, 89, 103n

Achaea, 66

Achilles, 12

Acilius, C. (senator), 176

Acilius Glabrio, M'. (cos. 191), 69, 70, 134, 136, 139n, 140

Aebutia (aunt of P. Aebutius), 35

Aebutius, P. (*eques*), 35, 36, 46, 59, 62, 64, 65

Aegina, 29, 30

Aelius, C. (trib. mil. 178), 121n

Aelius, T. (trib. mil. 178), 121n

Aelius Paetus, Sex. (cos. 198), 120

Aelius Stilo, L. (*grammaticus*), 184

Aemilius Lepidus, M. (cos. 187), 117, 119n, 120

Aemilius Paullus, L. (cos. 182), 173

Aemilius Regillus, L. (pr. 190), 119n

Aemilius Scaurus, M. (cos. 115), 182, 183

Aeneas, 11-12, 13n, 14, 15-16, 18, 20, 85. *See also* Trojan Legend

Aesculapius, 8, 39

Aetolia: conflict with Acarnania, 13; in First Macedonian War, 27-28, 29; and Attalus I, 29-30; defeated by Rome, 65, 66, 69; and Fulvius Nobilior, 69, 113-114; Ennius in, 113, 115n

Africa, 2, 21, 22-25, 26, 28

Alba, 12

Alcaeus (Epicurean philosopher), 177

Alcibiades (Athenian general), 161

Alexander the Great, 11n

Ambracia, 70, 89n, 114, 132, 138n

Amicitia: Rome and Seleucus, 13-14, 20; Rome and Pergamum, 19, 29, 150; in Peace of Phoenice, 32; in Peace of Apamea, 66; and patronage, 79, 112-113, 120; and booty, 139

Anti-Hellenism: in suppression of Bacchants, 56-57, 76-77; and Cato, 56-57, 175-176; as posture by Romans, 72-73, 76-77, 168, 170, 171, 174, 177-178, 186, 189, 191-192; as restraint upon individuals, 77, 78; as criticism of Scipio Africanus, 101; associated with Plautus, 128, 152-156; in the burning of "Numa's books", 166, 168-170, 174, 190; and sumptuary laws, 171, 174, 178; and expulsion of intellectuals,

173-174, 177-178, 190; and Marius, 181; and censorial edict of 92, 186; and L. Crassus, 189. *See also* Hellenism

Antiochus III (king of Syria): at war with Rome, 15, 20, 56, 69, 70, 71, 132, 133, 149; relations with Attalus I, 16n, 17n, 30; settlement with Rome, 66, 70; exactions from, 70, 135

Antiqui commentarii, 81, 105

Antonius, M. (cos. 99), 182, 184, 188

Antonius Gnipho, M. (rhetor), 191

Apollo, 8n, 10, 30, 39

Appuleius Saturninus, L. (trib. 103), 183n, 185, 186

Apulia, 36, 43n, 58, 60, 154

Aquileia, 67

Aricia, 59

Ariminum, 67

Aristoxenus of Tarentum (writer), 160, 161

Arpinum, 45, 68

Arretium, 67

Athena, 15, 19n

Athens, 154, 156, 174-176

Atilius Caiatinus, A. (cos. 258), 25n

Atiniis, Maras (Pompeian aedile), 59n

Atinius, C. (Bacchant leader), 59

Atinius, M. (Bacchant leader), 59

Atintania, 28

Attalus I (king of Pergamum), 6, 15, 17, 19, 29-32, 150

Aurelius Opilius (rhetor), 184

Aventine hill: shrine of Liber, 39; as base for plebeian dissent, 47, 48n, 58; and Bacchanalia, 51n, 57; portent on, 85; site of dramatic guild, 87, 88, 89, 105-106, 128; home of Ennius, 107, 111, 119

Bacchanalian cult: alleged excesses of, 34, 35, 50-51, 60, 62, 63, 64, 65, 151; rites of, 34, 39, 48-49, 50-54, 63, 75, 96n, 151-152; repression of, 35-39, 40, 42-43, 46, 60, 73-74, 76, 151-152; in Livy's account, 35-36, 46, 51-54, 58-59, 61-65, 76; in the Tiriolo inscription, 36-38, 43, 45, 54-55, 62, 74n, 76; as "*coniuratio*", 44, 47-48, 56-57, 58-59, 64, 73, 77-78; organization of, 54-55; members of, 58-61, 76

Bacchus, 34, 39, 50, 54n, 63, 75n